Glencoe Marketing Series

RETAILING

MERCHANDISE
CUSTOMERS

DECA CONNECTION

In partnership with
BusinessWeek

Priscilla R. McCalla

McGraw Hill **Glencoe**

New York, New York   Columbus, Ohio   Chicago, Illinois   Peoria, Illinois   Woodland Hills, California

About the Author

PRISCILLA R. McCALLA has extensive experience in marketing education as the Professional and Program Development Director of DECA (Distributive Education Clubs of America), an association of students that is dedicated to co-curricular education of students with interests in marketing, management, and entrepreneurship. She has also served as a contributing writer for Glencoe's *Marketing Essentials*. With a background in retail marketing education and fashion marketing education, Priscilla R. McCalla brings her perspective and marketing expertise to Glencoe's first edition of *Retailing*.

Glencoe

The **McGraw·Hill** Companies

Printed in the United States of America.

Send all inquiries to:
Glencoe/McGraw-Hill
21600 Oxnard Street, Suite 500
Woodland Hills, CA 91367

ISBN 0-07-861400-7 (Student Edition)
ISBN 0-07-861402-3 (Teacher Annotated Edition)

1 2 3 4 5 6 7 8 9   079   09 08 07 06 05 04

Advisory Board

Glencoe/McGraw-Hill's advisory board of marketing educators provides up-to-date research to address the needs of today's workplace. The board brings its expertise and experience to establish the foundation for this innovative, real-world, marketing education program. Glencoe/McGraw-Hill would like to acknowledge the following companies and individuals for their support and commitment to this project:

Exploring the World of Retailing

As part of the Glencoe Marketing Series, this first edition of *Retailing* focuses on the real-world business perspective by using examples from the retail business world to illustrate retailing features, concepts, and activities. Information on featured companies, organizations, their products, and services is included for educational purposes only, and does not represent or imply endorsement of the Glencoe marketing program. The following are some of the companies represented in the feature *Hot Property* and throughout the text:

Table of Contents

Table of Contents

Table of Contents

Table of Contents

Table of Contents

Welcome to *Retailing*

Welcome to *Retailing*—part of the Glencoe Marketing Series. Get ready to learn about one of the most exciting—and competitive—businesses in the world. Retailing is a subject that you can relate to and make your own. After all, retailing is all around us. We find signs of it everywhere—not just in malls and shopping centers, but on street corners, television and radio, in catalogs, and on the Internet.

Understanding the Unit

The units introduce you to the retail industry, retailing strategies, store operations, and retailing careers. Each unit opens with a preview and concludes with application activities featuring a reading activity from *BusinessWeek* magazine, as well as a retail-marketing simulation. The 16 chapters in *Retailing* are divided into four units:

UNIT 1: The Retail Business

UNIT 2: Retail Business Strategy

UNIT 3: The Retail Store

UNIT 4: Exploring Careers in Retailing

Previewing the Unit

Each unit opener spread focuses on the content of the upcoming unit.

The unit opener photo illustrates a concept relevant to the upcoming unit. Ask yourself, "How does the photo relate to the content of the unit?"

Unit Overview

The *Unit Overview* provides a brief road map of the unit chapters.

In This Unit...

The titles of the unit chapters are listed on the left-hand side of the unit opener spread. Think about what you can learn in each chapter. A quotation helps you focus on what is to come.

Unit Lab Preview

The *Unit Lab Preview* prepares you for *The Virtuality Store,* the unit's culminating real-world simulation and hands-on activity.

The Marketing Wheel

This visual representation of the National Marketing Education Standards highlights the two main parts of marketing—the foundations and the functions. The functions of marketing relate to how marketing is applied in the retail business world: Distribution, Financing, Marketing-Information Management, Pricing, Product/Service Management, Promotion, and Selling. The functions or foundations addressed in each unit are listed on this page.

Closing the Unit

UNIT 1 ACTIVITIES

BusinessWeek News

THE E-BIZ SURPRISE

Since mid-2000, when the stock market slump began turning dot-coms into dot-goners, the popular perception of the Internet has spiraled ever downward. By last year, Internet bankers and analysts, those one-time masters of the business universe, were targets of government investigations. A book titled *dot.con*, deriding the Net as "the greatest story ever sold," became a bestseller. The bold and transforming vision of the Net had dissolved into a digital dud.

To the surprise of many, the Net is actually delivering on many of its supposedly discredited promises. It's now apparent the Internet is connecting far-flung people and businesses more tightly than ever. It is helping companies slash costs. It is speeding the pace of innovation and jacking up productivity. Says Andrew S. Grove, chairman of Intel Corp., "Everything we ever said about the Internet is happening."

Even Internet companies themselves—poster children for business excess during the boom—are finally turning the corner. Of the publicly held Net companies that survived the shakeout, some 40 percent were profitable in the fourth quarter of 2002. Meanwhile, online advertising is staging a comeback, boosting fortunes.

How the heck did all this happen? As it turns out, many consumers and businesses never mistook the over-inflated Internet stocks for the underlying value of the Internet. They kept

going online. Says Margaret C. Whitman, chief executive of eBay, Inc., "More consumers are coming online every day."

Still, in the eight years since the Web went commercial, it already has shaken up many industries. Music fans sharing 35 billion song files annually are battering the recording industry. Dot-coms, such as Expedia Inc., now the top leisure-travel agency, online or off—helped shutter 13 percent of traditional travel-agency locations last year.

Further out, bold new projects will unfold, providing a glimpse of the next generation

of e-business. The range is every bit as vast as the Internet itself. It features gobs of wireless systems for tracking inventory, reading electric meters, and connecting with customers. Many will find themselves plunked, Oz-like, into new markets and businesses. The journey, after all, is just beginning.

By Timothy J. Mullaney, with Heather Green in New York, Michael Arndt in Chicago, and Robert D. Hof and Linda Himelstein in San Mateo, Calif.

Excerpted by permission. May 12, 2003. Copyright 2000-2003, by The McGraw-Hill Companies, Inc. All rights reserved.

CREATIVE JOURNAL

In your journal, write your responses:

CRITICAL THINKING
1. What are some reasons that some dot-com compan[ies] survived the dot-com shakeup?

APPLICATION
2. Which types of businesses do you think are best s[uited to] doing business on the Web? If you were going to [start a] business, which business would you choose that [would be able] to use the Internet successfully?

Go to **businessweek.com** for current *BusinessWe[ek]*

BusinessWeek NEWS

A reading and writing exercise entitled *BusinessWeek News* concludes each unit. A relevant excerpt from a real *BusinessWeek* article caps the unit content.

UNIT LAB

The Virtuality Store

At the end of each unit, the unit lab simulation *The Virtuality Store* will take you on an exciting journey through the world of retailing.

UNIT LAB

UNIT 1 ACTIVITIES

The Virtuality Store

You've just entered the real world of retailing. The Virtuality Store offers the latest and most popular consumer goods and services. Acting as the owner, manager, or employee of this store, you will have the opportunity to work on different projects to promote the success of your business.

Turn On the Electric Channel—Add a Web Site

SITUATION You and a silent partner have owned and operated a small electronics store called **Giga Gear** for one year. You started small, catering to tweens, teens, and Gen-Xers by offering the latest Game Boys, Palm Pilots, computer games, XBox, and a small selection of music CDs. You were smart to locate near a high school, but during summer break, sales drop off. However, you've read that CDs, videos, and computer software are the best selling items on the Internet. Not only that, most of your customer base—teens under 18—will total 77 million on the Web by the year 2005. You've thought about expanding into cyberspace, but some companies have flopped. Still, there is potential for your business.

ASSIGNMENT Complete these tasks:
- Plan your basic e-tail store with one or two unique features to attract your customers.
- Estimate your start-up costs including design, shipping, maintenance, and storage.
- Create a final report.

TOOLS AND RESOURCES To complete the assignment, you will need to:
- Conduct research at the library, on the Internet, or by phone.
- Ask other retail stores about experiences with Web sites.
- Have word-processing, spreadsheet, and presentation software.

RESEARCH Do your research:
- Find out the most important characteristics of a retail Web site.
- Go to other similar Web sites and identify and assess their features.
- Get cost estimates for designing and implementing basic Web sites with purchasing features.

REPORT Prepare a written report using the following tools:
- *Word-processing program:* Prepare a written report with a site map outline and list of features, as well as a market overview and customer analysis.
- *Spreadsheet program:* Prepare a chart comparing other competitor Web sites with yours. Prepare a budget chart with your estimates.
- *Presentation program:* Prepare a ten-slide visual presentation with key points, some visuals, and text.

PRESENTATION AND EVALUATION You will present your report to your silent partner and to the bank that may finance your plan. You will be evaluated on the basis of:
- Knowledge of the e-tail Web-site business.
- Continuity of presentation
- Voice quality
- Eye contact

PORTFOLIO
Add this report to your career portfolio.

Understanding the Chapter

Each unit of *Retailing* includes three to five chapters. Each chapter focuses on one specific area of retailing, such as non-store retailing, site management, or promotion and advertising.

Previewing the Chapter

The chapter opener resources are designed to capture your interest and set a purpose for reading.

Chapter Opener Photo

The chapter opener photo focuses on the chapter topic. You might ask yourself, "How does this photo relate to the chapter title?"

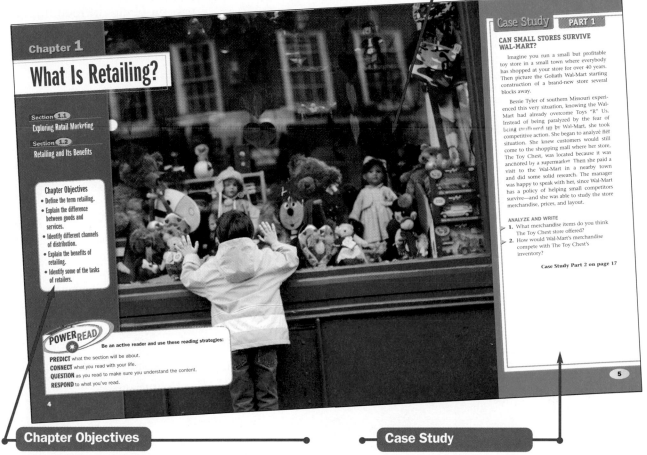

Chapter Objectives

The objectives help you identify exactly what you are expected to know upon completion of the chapter.

Using the Sections

Each chapter of *Retailing* is divided into two sections: by using the activities and resources in each section, you can maximize learning.

AS YOU READ . . .

You Will Learn lists the knowledge you can expect to learn.

Why It's Important explains how the chapter concepts relate to your world.

Key Terms list major terms presented in each section.

Case Study

Each chapter opens with the Case Study, Part 1, that presents a real-world retailing situation. Critical-thinking questions help focus content. Part 2 continues within the chapter.

Photographs and Figures

Photographs, illustrations, charts, and graphs reinforce content. Captions with questions guide you.

Quick Check

The section-ending *Quick Check* helps you to review and respond to what you have read.

Understanding the Features

Special features in each chapter are designed to interest and promote your understanding of chapter content. Features incorporate activities, such as critical-thinking questions, to help you integrate what you have learned.

World Market presents interesting stories of retailing in action around the world.

Hot Property

Hot Property profiles successful or creative retail businesses, both large and small. Two critical-thinking questions focus on chapter topics.

Profiles in Marketing

Profiles in Marketing provides insight through personal interviews of successful or noteworthy individuals working in retailing careers. A chapter-related, critical-thinking question follows the feature. The "Career Data" column gives the education, skills, outlook, and career-path information for this career.

THE Dot Com SHOP

The Dot.Com Shop links chapter content to the expanding world of e-commerce and e-tailing.

Selling Point

Selling Point presents brief, memorable facts to illustrate retailing issues and trends.

ETHICAL PRACTICES

Ethical Practices links chapter content to current ethical issues in marketing, as well as legal, community-service, and character-education issues and practices.

Math Check

Math Check provides a math problem related to chapter discussions.

TECH NOTES

Technology is today's number-one marketing trend. *Tech Notes* highlights the wide range of technological applications enhancing retailing today. An exercise directs you to the book's Web site at **marketingseries.glencoe.com**.

Worksheets and Portfolio Works

At the end of each chapter's text, before the review section, special write-on worksheet pages provide review and skill-building activities related to chapter content.

Chapter Worksheets

Two one-page worksheets give you the opportunity to complete an activity or exercise and apply the chapter content in a variety of interesting formats.

Portfolio Works

The *Portfolio Works* worksheet at the end of each chapter guides you through the development of an employability portfolio. The portfolio is developed throughout the course. You can assess, reflect, and plan for your career. Record what you have learned and how you would demonstrate those necessary values, skills, personal qualities, and knowledge. These activities provide the foundation for a career development portfolio. Save these pages for a prospective employer to demonstrate your combination of retailing knowledge and workplace skills needed to succeed in a retail career.

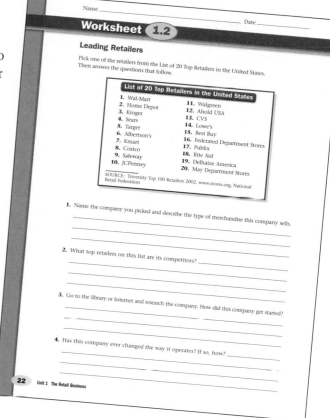

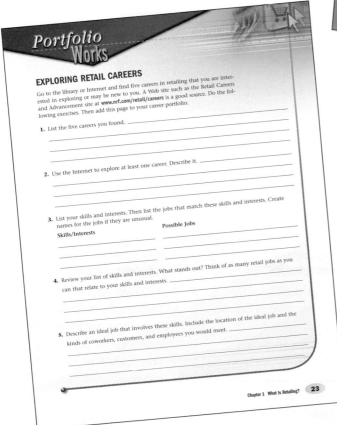

You can also include in your portfolio documents that demonstrate your marketing competencies, employability skills, career goals, service and leadership activities, as well as employment letters, a résumé, and a job application form.

Building an employability portfolio helps you relate what you learn in school to the skills you will need to succeed on the job. When you have completed the project, you will have a visual résumé to use in your job search.

Understanding Assessments

At the end of each chapter, *Chapter Review and Activities* presents a chapter summary with key terms, recall and critical-thinking questions, and a variety of activities targeting academic and workplace skills.

Chapter Summary

The *Chapter Summary* is a bulleted list of the main points developed within each section, related to the chapter objectives. The key terms are listed with page references alongside the summary points.

Cross-Curriculum Skills

These skill-building exercises are divided into two categories: work-based learning and school-based learning. *Work-Based Learning* activities are hands-on projects that help you develop identified Foundation Skills and Workplace Competencies. *School-Based Learning* activities ask you to apply academic skills, such as math, science, and literacy skills, to real-life scenarios related to retailing.

Chapter 1 — Review and Activities

CHAPTER SUMMARY

Section 1.1 Exploring Retail Marketing

retailing (p. 7)
products (p. 7)
goods (p. 7)
services (p. 7)
retail customer (p. 7)

- Retailing is the selling of products, or goods and services, to the customer.
- Goods are items that are made, manufactured, or grown which people want to buy and use. Services are things that make us feel better or enhance our lives in some way.

Section 1.2 Retailing and Its Benefits

manufacturer (p. 12)
channel of distribution (p. 12)
direct channel (p. 12)
indirect channel (p. 13)
wholesaler (p. 12)
producer channel (p. 13)

- A channel of distribution is the path a product takes from where it is made to the consumer. A direct channel of distribution is one in which the product path leads directly from the manufacturer to the consumer. An indirect channel of distribution is one in which the product path follows more than one step, moving from the manufacturer to the wholesaler, to the retailers, and then to the consumer. A producer channel of distribution is a type of indirect channel of distribution in which the manufacturer also owns its retail stores.
- Retailing benefits customers by offering competitive pricing and a wide variety of products. It benefits the community by providing employment opportunities and supporting school and philanthropic efforts. It benefits the economy because the retail industry is one of the largest employers in the country, and retail sales contribute to our nation's economic growth.
- Retailer tasks include buying merchandise or products, determining selling prices, storing, advertising, promoting, displaying, selling, and servicing merchandise, providing customer service, managing risk, and hiring and managing employees. These tasks translate into a wide variety of retail jobs and career paths, including those in stores and behind the scenes.

CHECKING CONCEPTS

1. **Define** retailing.
2. **Describe** the difference between goods and services.
3. **Name** the channels of distribution.
4. **Explain** three benefits of retailing.
5. **List** three tasks of retailers.
6. **Identify** two ways retailers use computers.
7. **Describe** the difference between a manufacturer and a wholesaler.

Critical Thinking

8. **Explain** how retailing has become global.

Chapter 1 — Review and Activities

CROSS-CURRICULUM SKILLS

Work-Based Learning

Basic Skills—Writing
9. Write a letter to your favorite retailer and explain why you buy its product.

Interpersonal Skills—Teaching Others
10. Using key terms from this chapter, create your own word puzzle, such as a crossword puzzle. Trade your puzzle with that of another student and solve each other's puzzles.

School-Based Learning

Math
11. Abdul bought five T-shirts ($9 each) and two pairs of jeans ($22 each) from Old Navy. What is the total cost of the T-shirts and jeans? (You do not need to calculate tax.)

Science
12. Many clothes are made from synthetic, or manufactured fibers, such as acrylic, nylon, and rayon. Using an encyclopedia, find out more about these fibers.

DECA CONNECTION

Role Play: Hardware Store Employee

SITUATION You are to assume the role of an employee of a locally owned hardware store. You are leaving your job to attend college where you will major in marketing. Your career goal is to own a retail store someday. You have been asked by the hardware store's owner to help train a new employee (judge). This is the new employee's (judge's) first job. During the course of training, the new employee (judge) asks why you plan to own a store.

ACTIVITY Explain to the new employee (judge) the many and varied duties of a retail business owner.

EVALUATION You will be evaluated on how well you meet the following performance indicators:
- Explain employment opportunities in marketing.
- Describe types of business activities.
- Explain marketing and its importance in a global economy.
- Explain the concept of management.
- Explain the nature and scope of purchasing.

INTERNET ACTIVITY

Use the Internet to access the National Retail Federation's Web site and click on "About NRF" to answer the following questions:
- How many U.S. retail establishments does the NRF represent?
- How many U.S. workers does it represent?
- How many retail associations does the NRF represent?

➡ For a link to the NRF to answer these questions, go to **marketingseries.glencoe.com**.

marketingseries.glencoe.com

Checking Concepts

Seven review questions help you check your understanding of the text by defining terms, describing processes, and explaining concepts. The last exercise asks you to use your critical-thinking skills.

DECA Connection

In every chapter-review section, the *DECA Connection* offers specially created, DECA-approved role-play activities. These activities provide opportunities to practice for DECA's participating events that relate to retailing, and are based on a real DECA role-play situation.

Internet Activity

In every chapter-review section, the *Internet Activity* provides a Web-based research activity. Resources for each exercise can be found through the book's Web site **marketingseries.glencoe.com**.

The DECA Connection

DECA is an association of marketing students that sponsors skill-building events. It is a co-curricular club with chapters in more than 6,000 high schools. The membership includes representation from all 50 states, four U.S. territories, the District of Columbia, and two Canadian provinces. All DECA activities further student development in one or more of the following areas: leadership development, social intelligence, vocational understanding, and civic consciousness. Through individual and group DECA activities with the marketing education instructional program, students develop skills to become future leaders in the areas of marketing and management.

DECA Builds Leadership Skills

The structure of a DECA chapter encourages leadership development for student members. Each chapter elects officers who, with the membership, choose an annual program of work. Committee chairpersons may organize and execute the activities in the program. Local activities encourage every member to act responsibly as a leader or member of a group. Chapter activities focus on the advantages of participating in a free enterprise system, marketing research, and an individual's civic responsibility.

National DECA provides opportunities for local chapter officers and members to receive additional training. Annual Regional Conferences are held in the fall each year. In the spring, students may attend the Leadership Development Academy at the Career Development Conference (CDC). During the summer, students can attend a State Officer Leadership Institute. The skills and leadership qualities gained are shared with all members of the chapter. The recognition received by individuals and teams within a DECA chapter serve as a showcase of the marketing program to your local school and community.

The following is a listing of the individual DECA competitive event areas:

- Apparel and Accessories Marketing Series
- Business Services Marketing Series
- Food Marketing Series
- Full Service Restaurant Management Series

- Marketing Management Series
- Quick Service Restaurant Management Series
- Retail Merchandising Series
- Vehicles and Petroleum Marketing Series

The *Retailing* Web Site

The *Retailing* Web site draws on the vast resources of the Internet to expand your exploration of career topics.

The student site includes the following:

- Chapter Objectives
- Interactive Practice Tests for each chapter with automatic scoring
- Math exercises and help with solving *Math Check* exercises
- E-flashcard games
- Web links for doing feature exercises from *Tech Notes, The Dot.Com Shop,* and *Internet Activities*
- DECA Competitive Events practice
- National Skills Standards
- RRA test preparation information
- Disability Support Links

At the *Career Clusters* Web site, you can explore career options with print and .pdf resources as well as links to job-search tips, external career planning sites, and educational resources.

Reading Strategies

How can you get the most from your reading? Effective readers are active readers. Become actively involved with the text. Think of your textbook as a tool to help you learn more about the world around you. It is a form of nonfiction writing—it describes real-life ideas, people, events, and places. Use the reading strategies in the *Power Read* box at the beginning of each chapter along with strategies in the margins to help you read actively.

 Make educated guesses about what the section is about by combining clues in the text with what you already know. Predicting helps you anticipate questions and stay alert to new information.

Ask yourself:

- What does this section heading mean?
- What is this section about?
- How does this section tie in with what I have read so far?
- Why is this information important in understanding the subject?

 Draw parallels between what you are reading and the events and circumstances in your own life.

Ask yourself:

- What do I know about the topic?
- How do my experiences compare to the information in the text?
- How could I apply this information in my own life?
- Why is this information important in understanding the subject?

 Ask yourself questions to help you clarify meaning as you read.

Ask yourself:

- Do I understand what I've read so far?
- What is this section about?
- What does this mean?
- Why is this information important in understanding the subject?

RESPOND React to what you are reading. Form opinions and make judgments about the section while you are reading—not just after you've finished.

Ask yourself:

- Does this information make sense?
- What can I learn from this section?
- How can I use this information to start planning for my future?
- Why is this information important in understanding the subject?

More Reading Strategies
Use this menu for more reading strategies to get the most from your reading.

BEFORE YOU READ ...

SET A PURPOSE
- Why are you reading the textbook?
- How does the subject relate to your life?
- How might you be able to use what you learn in your own life?

PREVIEW
- Read the chapter title to preview the topic.
- Read the subtitles to see what you will learn about the topic.
- Skim the photos, charts, graphs, or maps. How do they support the topic?
- Look for key terms that are boldfaced. How are they defined?

DRAW FROM YOUR BACKGROUND
- What have you read or heard concerning new information on the topic?
- How is the new information different from what you already know?
- How will the information that you already know help you understand the new information?

AS YOU READ ...

PREDICT
- Predict events or outcomes by using clues and information that you already know.
- Change your predictions as you read and gather new information.

CONNECT
- Think about people, places, and events in your own life. Are there any similarities with those in your textbook?
- Can you relate the textbook information to other areas of your life?

QUESTION
- What is the main idea?
- How do the photos, charts, graphs, and maps support the main idea?

VISUALIZE
- Pay careful attention to details and descriptions.
- Create graphic organizers to show relationships that you find in the information.

NOTICE COMPARE AND CONTRAST SENTENCES
- Look for clue words and phrases that signal comparison, such as *similarly, just as, both, in common, also,* and *too.*
- Look for clue words and phrases that signal contrast, such as *on the other hand, in contrast to, however, different, instead of, rather than, but,* and *unlike.*

NOTICE CAUSE-AND-EFFECT SENTENCES
- Look for clue words and phrases, such as *because, as a result, therefore, that is why, since, so, for this reason,* and *consequently.*

NOTICE CHRONOLOGICAL SENTENCES
- Look for clue words and phrases, such as *after, before, first, next, last, during, finally, earlier, later, since,* and *then.*

AFTER YOU READ ...

SUMMARIZE
- Describe the main idea and how the details support it.
- Use your own words to explain what you have read.

ASSESS
- What was the main idea?
- Did the text clearly support the main idea?

- Did you learn anything new from the material?
- Can you use this new information in other school subjects or at home?
- What other sources could you use to find more information about the topic?

UNIT 1

THE RETAIL BUSINESS

> "A computer is not—and will never be—a substitute for getting out in your stores and learning what's going on."
>
> —Sam Walton
> Founder of Wal-Mart

2

UNIT OVERVIEW

Retailing is one of the most profitable businesses in the world. The largest corporation is a retail business—Wal-Mart. Retailing continues to grow rapidly in the United States and globally with new opportunities.

We will begin by focusing on the nature of retailing in Chapter 1, discovering the factors that set it apart from other types of marketing businesses. Chapter 2 will explore the great variety of retail businesses that you may choose to enter. Chapter 3 examines traditional store-based businesses, or "brick and mortar" stores, which have existed for centuries. In Chapter 4, you will discover the expanding world of the cyber marketplace and other types of non-traditional retail businesses that thrive without actual stores.

■ UNIT LAB Preview
The Virtuality Store

Think about all the retail, or e-tail, Web sites you've seen on the Internet. Do you ever go to the actual stores represented by the Web sites? Some retail Web sites are more popular than others. Why?

These functions are highlighted in this unit:
- Promotion
- Selling
- Product/Service Management
- Pricing

Chapter 1

What Is Retailing?

Chapter Objectives

- Define the term retailing.
- Explain the difference between goods and services.
- Identify different channels of distribution.
- Explain the benefits of retailing.
- Identify some of the tasks of retailers.

Be an active reader and use these reading strategies:

PREDICT what the section will be about.

CONNECT what you read with your life.

QUESTION as you read to make sure you understand the content.

RESPOND to what you've read.

CAN SMALL STORES SURVIVE WAL-MART?

Imagine you run a small but profitable toy store in a small town where everybody has shopped at your store for over 40 years. Then picture the Goliath Wal-Mart starting construction of a brand-new store several blocks away.

Bessie Tyler of southern Missouri experienced this very situation, knowing the Wal-Mart had already overcome Toys "R" Us. Instead of being paralyzed by the fear of being swallowed up by Wal-Mart, she took competitive action. She began to analyze her situation. She knew customers would still come to the shopping mall where her store, The Toy Chest, was located because it was anchored by a supermarket. Then she paid a visit to the Wal-Mart in a nearby town and did some solid research. The manager was happy to speak with her, since Wal-Mart has a policy of helping small competitors survive—and she was able to study the store merchandise, prices, and layout.

ANALYZE AND WRITE
1. What merchandise items do you think The Toy Chest store offered?
2. How would Wal-Mart's merchandise compete with The Toy Chest's inventory?

Case Study Part 2 on page 17

Exploring Retail Marketing

AS YOU READ ...

YOU WILL LEARN
- To define the term retailing.
- To explain the difference between goods and services.

WHY IT'S IMPORTANT

Retailing is all around us and is one of the most profitable industries in the world.

KEY TERMS
- retailing
- products
- goods
- services
- retail customer

PREDICT

What do retailers sell?

Retailing Is Everywhere

When you think about retailing, you probably think of a shopping mall and the stores in the mall. You probably also think about making purchases from a salesperson and carrying those purchases home with you. You might also think of making purchases by catalog or through a Web site. That is retailing, too.

As we look at retailing, we will examine the many types of retailers and the places where they do business. Business is not always conducted in a store. Retailing is all around us—in some places that might surprise you.

The Beginnings

From earliest times, people have spent their days providing for their most basic needs—food, shelter, and clothing. As time progressed and those basic needs were met, people wanted more goods and services than they were able to provide for themselves. Retailers emerged to make those goods and services available.

The earliest form of retailing was trading, or the swapping of goods and services. Farmer A might produce more grain than one family could use, and Farmer B might have a bumper crop of apples. The farmers would then trade their grain for apples, thereby providing both families with added variety in their diets. Money was introduced to make trading more convenient. Archaeologists have found evidence of marketplaces in excavations of ancient Greek and Roman sites, along with goods that were bought and sold, such as olive oil, fabrics, jewelry, and furniture.

Past to the Present

Later, during medieval times and the Renaissance (1200s–1600s), trade between countries grew. For example, Marco Polo and his brother Maffeo Polo of Italy visited the Far East and returned with silk fabrics and spices that were highly prized. The result of increased trade was a greater selection of goods available to more people.

As retail customers, people continued to want a greater variety of goods, prompting the growth of trade. Columbus traveled to America searching for a shorter trading route to the Far East. That trade with America brought enormous wealth to European nations and led to the settlement of the American continents.

In the 19th century, the desire for goods and services led to the development of catalog retailers, and then Internet retailers in the 20th century. More retailing innovations await us in the 21st century.

What Is Retailing?

Retailing is the selling of products to the customer. **Products** include goods and services that have monetary value. **Goods** are tangible items that are made, manufactured, or grown that people want to buy and use. An automobile is an example of a manufactured item. It is made by people or robots, then assembled and shipped to the auto dealer where customers purchase it.

Services are things that people do for us that make us feel better or enhance our lives in some way. Services are often intangible; that is, we cannot hold a service in our hands. An example of a service is auto repair. The dealer employs mechanics to check the systems of our cars and make sure that they work properly. The car will then safely take us where we want to go. You pay for the service that provides you with peace of mind about your safety and protects the car, which is a very large investment.

Many retailers fall between two categories—goods retailers and service retailers. For instance, a hairdresser or barber is primarily offering a service for sale. He or she will cut and style your hair but will also sell products. Most hairdressers or barbers carry a line of shampoos and conditioners and other hair-care products, such as hairbrushes or hair dryers and curling irons. So, the hairdresser or barber is selling both a service and goods.

The **retail customer** is the purchaser of the goods and services from retailers. Retail customers purchase goods and services for their own use or the use of their families. It is important to remember that the products are not resold. The customer or consumer uses the goods and services.

Retailers Offer Variety

Retailing makes a vast variety of goods and services available to consumers. If you want to buy a pair of shoes, you do not think about whether they are available. You think about what type of shoe, what color, and what style you want. You know that shoes are available when you want to buy them.

Here is an example of some of the steps you would have to take to make a wool sweater if retailers did not make sweaters available for you to purchase:

1. You would have to raise sheep.
2. When their fleece was ready, you would shear or shave the fleece, or wool.
3. Then you would clean the wool.
4. Next, you would spin the wool into yarn and dye it your desired color.
5. Finally, you would knit the yarn into your sweater.

Most would agree that this is a pretty exhausting process. You would probably not have many sweaters!

retailing the selling of products to the customer

products goods and services that have monetary value

goods tangible items that are made, manufactured, or grown

services intangible things that people do for us that make us feel better or enhance our lives

retail customer purchaser of goods and services from retailers

THE Dot Com SHOP

Peddling Merchandise
Operating an e-tail business on an electronic channel—the Web—can be costly, due to design, delivery, returns, and operating expenses. Though many larger dot-com companies crashed in the 1990s, small stores such as Harris Cyclery of West Newton, Massachusetts, actually increased sales using a basic Web site. Today a third of Harris's bicycle business rides in on the Web to get hard-to-find parts and personal service.

➡ Describe an e-business's home page to your class after viewing one through **marketingseries.glencoe.com**.

Compare the sweater-making process with going to your local mall to purchase a sweater. You can select from a variety of fibers, from cashmere to acrylic and everything in between. You are also able to select from a multitude of colors ranging from basic colors to this year's latest fashion colors. There are many styles to choose from, long sleeve, short sleeve, crew neck, or turtleneck. You get the picture. The selection is great. Retailers offer us such a variety of options that you might purchase more than one sweater if you had the money to do so.

We take for granted the selection and choice of merchandise available to us. Think about the different stores at your local mall that offer sweaters for sale. You can probably think of several without any effort. You can select from department stores or specialty stores. Department stores have sweaters in several departments, and specialty stores have them, too. You have only to go from store to store to discover the exact item you want. Those choices of retailers can become even greater when we add catalog and Internet retailers to the possibilities, which open up stores to the world.

Retailing Is Global

People all over the world engage in some type of retailing. Advances in communications and the Internet have made retailing even more of a global activity than ever before.

The global nature of retailing is expanding. Large companies have retail outlets in other countries. For example, McDonald's® has restaurants in Europe, Japan, and China, as well as in most other parts of the world. JCPenney has stores in Mexico as well as in the United States. You can buy a Coke or Pepsi in London, England, or in Seoul, South Korea.

Many companies based in foreign countries have outlets in the United States. For instance, Benetton and Burberry are European retailers with outlets in this country. Benetton is an Italian company that has stores in many large malls throughout the United States, including

Birth of the Department Store

Frenchman Aristide Boucicaut was not afraid of taking chances in 1852. Unfortunately, his fabric-store partner was not so adventurous, stating, "I prefer to leave you to continue your experiments alone." Boucicaut did continue and built the Bon Marché in Paris—the first department store. He originated the concept of grouping specialty shops under one roof, increasing volume, and lowering markup. No more bargaining—prices were fixed. Boucicaut transformed retailing as profits increased ten times in eight years. His "experiment" was tested in America by 1862 when Alexander Turney Stewart opened the first U.S. department store, the A.T. Stewart store, in New York City.

What concepts did Boucicaut originate?

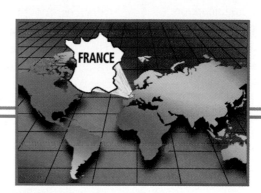

those in Washington, D.C., New York City, Denver, Chicago, Dallas, and Los Angeles. Burberry is an upscale British retail company. It was originally known for rainwear and outerwear with its signature tan and red plaid linings. The company has recently expanded its merchandise offerings to include shoes, handbags, shirts, golf shirts, and other clothing and accessory items. Burberry has stores in the United States in cities such as New York City and Washington, D.C.

Retailers allow goods from across the globe to be regularly accessible to us. We routinely purchase items made or assembled in other countries. We buy shoes made in Spain and Italy; clothing made in Sri Lanka, China, and Mexico; electronics made in Japan and South Korea. The list goes on and on. You probably own things from all around the world.

Many domestic and international retailers offer customers several ways to shop. A retailer often has a store where you can make purchases. However, the company may also publish catalogs for your convenience, and it may have a virtual store on its Web site. You may notice that retailers may make some items available only on their Web sites or in their catalogs. They want to encourage you to shop with them in several different ways to increase the chances that you will buy from them.

Internet Retailers

Internet retailers sell their goods and services through the Internet. Their "click-and-mortar" businesses are similar to catalog retailers in the way that they purchase and warehouse, or store, their merchandise. Internet retailers will place photos and descriptions of their products on their Web sites. Customers browse the Web sites and make purchases right there. Amazon.com is a well-known example of an Internet retailer.

The Internet has added to the ease of at-home shopping. It also enables us to shop from any location in the world if we have access to a computer. The possibilities of Internet shopping are endless, and the choices are infinite.

In addition, many international Web sites will provide a currency exchange service to let you know how much you are spending in U.S. dollars if you are not familiar with the local currency.

Catalog Retailers

Catalog retailers sell their products through the mail or other delivery services. A typical catalog retailer will purchase goods and store them in a warehouse. Many catalog retailers do not have actual stores. Horchow is an example of a catalog retailer that specializes in upscale merchandise but does not operate a retail store. The retailer will create a catalog that lists photographs and descriptions of merchandise for sale. The descriptions give as much information about the merchandise as possible. The catalogs are then mailed to a list of prospective customers. Customers can call a toll-free telephone number to make their purchases.

Catalogs have also contributed to the growth of global retailing. Years ago catalogs served people who lived in isolated areas, far from retail stores in the cities. The success of the first mail-order catalog from Sears came from filling the needs of these people. Today catalogs are designed for ease of shopping. They appeal to customers who choose to spend their free time in ways other than shopping in stores. Catalogs enable us to shop from any location on earth at any time of the day or night.

Retailing Is High Tech

Retailing is high tech. Not only do retailers take advantage of the Internet to increase their customer base and ease purchasing for their customers, but they also use technology in other ways.

LET YOUR FINGERS DO THE SHOPPING Today shoppers are not limited by location or transportation. Catalogs allow purchases by phone, mail, and e-mail. *Do catalog retailers need stores to operate?*

Retailing Video

Some large retailers make use of video technology to train their employees. For instance, a large company might have a television broadcasting facility at its headquarters. A satellite feed is used to broadcast training information or other company information to their employees nationwide or worldwide.

Retailing Computers

Most retailers, large or small, use computers to keep track of inventory and to track orders. They use computerized cash registers to complete sales transactions and send that sales data, or information, directly to their office computers. Some retailers will set up computerized reordering based on the sales data fed into their registers.

Computers also make it possible for retailers to gather important data about their customers and their demographics. Retailers can track customer buying habits then use that information to make better informed buying decisions for the store. If a store carries more products that customers want, the results are better sales, happier customers, and higher profits for the retailer.

Most areas of retailing require some type of computer knowledge. Sales associates must use scanners and computerized cash registers. Computer use increases as you go up the company ladder. Today retailers need to use the most up-to-date information and sales figures to make their best and most informed decisions.

Retailers Are Everywhere

From the time you awake in the morning to the time you go to sleep at night, you have made contact with goods and services made available through retailing. The bed where you sleep was purchased from some type of retail establishment. Your toothbrush, clothing, and breakfast food were all purchased somewhere. The transportation you use to get to and from school, as well as your schoolbooks and supplies, all came from some type of retailer. After school, the CDs you play, the television you watch, and the computer you use to complete your homework were all retail purchases.

TECH NOTES

Kiosks Catch On

The need for less floor space and fewer employees makes kiosks the choice of many retailers. About 80 percent of major retailers plan to include kiosks in their stores.

An in-store kiosk is a space that contains a computer terminal connected to the store's offices or Internet. Customers and salespeople can view inventory, check availability, place orders, scan bar codes, and check prices. Stores such as Home Depot even provide job applications at Career Center kiosks. Though some kiosk experiments have failed, others have become total cybermalls, such as the one at Kowloon Station in Hong Kong.

➡ Write a paragraph about cybermalls after researching information through **marketingseries.glencoe.com.**

QUESTION

How have retailers been able to expand global business?

Quick Check ✓

RESPOND to what you've read by answering these questions.

1. Define retailing. _____

_____

2. What is the difference between goods and services? _____

_____

3. Name some types of retailers. _____

_____

Retailing and Its Benefits

AS YOU READ ...

YOU WILL LEARN

- To identify different channels of distribution.
- To explain the benefits of retailing.
- To identify some of the tasks of retailers.

WHY IT'S IMPORTANT

Knowing what retailers do and how retailing benefits customers will give you an understanding of how retailing affects the world.

KEY TERMS

- manufacturer
- channel of distribution
- direct channel
- indirect channel
- wholesaler
- producer channel

PREDICT

Name some of the advantages that retailers offer.

manufacturer business that makes or produces a good for sale

channel of distribution path merchandise takes from where it is made to the final consumer

direct channel path that leads directly from manufacturer to consumer

Nature of Retailing

Retailing makes our lives better and offers us convenience, variety, and a world from which to make our choices. Many characteristics of retailing are shared by all retailers. Other characteristics are unique to a particular type of retailer.

The most important characteristic that all retailers share is the desire to make their products available to their customers when the customer wants them and where they want them. How retailers achieve that depends upon the type of retailer and their customers' demands.

Channels of Distribution

It is fundamental that we understand how products get from the manufacturer to the retailer. The **manufacturer** is the business that makes or produces the goods for sale. Goods move through channels of distribution. As illustrated in **Figure 1.1**, a **channel of distribution** is the path a product takes from where it is made to the final consumer.

Channels of distribution can be further broken down into direct and indirect channels of distribution. A **direct channel** of distribution is one in which the path leads directly from the manufacturer to the final consumer. An example of this is the Avon Company. Avon manufactures its own cosmetics and then sells them directly to the customer through a network of salespersons who call directly on the customers.

An **indirect channel** of distribution is one in which the path follows more than one step. The item moves from the manufacturer to a wholesaler, then to the retailer, and finally, to the consumer. A **wholesaler** buys large quantities of merchandise and then resells it in smaller quantities to retailers, who in turn sell it to the customer. The path of flowers at your local florist is an example of an indirect channel of distribution. First, large flower growers grow flowers. The grower then sells them to flower wholesalers, who in turn sell them to the florist where you purchase them. For example:

1. A flower grower produces 500 dozen tulip bulbs.

2. A wholesaler purchases 250 dozen of the tulip bulbs.

3. Your local florist does not need 250 dozen tulip bulbs.

4. The wholesaler allows the local florist to buy 20 dozen.

5. You, the customer, purchase a single dozen of the tulip bulbs.

A third type channel of distribution is a variation of an indirect channel of distribution. It is a **producer channel** of distribution. In this type of channel, the manufacturer also owns its retail stores, so the good goes from manufacturer to retail store to consumer. An example of this type channel of distribution is Levi Strauss. This company manufactures its products and then sells them in its own stores to the final customer.

There are some companies, such as Costco and Sam's Warehouse, that act as both wholesalers and retailers. Both of these companies sell to businesses, thereby acting as wholesalers. They also sell to individual customers, thus acting as retailers.

indirect channel path that follows more than one step

wholesaler one who buys large quantities of a product and then resells it in smaller quantities to retailers

producer channel manufacturer also owns its retail stores; product goes from manufacturer to retail store to customer

Benefits of Retailing

You probably already know that retailing is a very large industry. In fact, the U.S. Department of Labor, Bureau of Labor Statistics, lists the retail industry as the second-largest industry nationally, in both the number of stores, or outlets, and in the number of employees. Retailing offers goods and services that we all want and need. Retailers provide benefits beyond simply providing goods and services. We will now look closely at some additional benefits provided by retailers and at who gains from those benefits. We know that retailing benefits its customers, but retailing also benefits the community as well as local and national economies.

Figure 1.1

Channels of Distribution

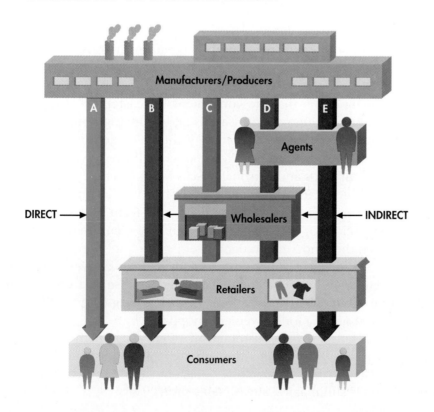

DIRECT

INDIRECT

Manufacturers/Producers

Agents

Wholesalers

Retailers

Consumers

PATHS TO THE CONSUMER
There are many "roads," or paths, that lead to a product's final destination—the consumer. *Grocery stores make their own brands of products sometimes. What type of channel is used for those items?*

Figure 1.2

Channel Advantage

BENEFITING CUSTOMERS
Retailers are always looking for ways to benefit their customers. Using different retail channels is good business. *What other advantages does Internet shopping provide?*

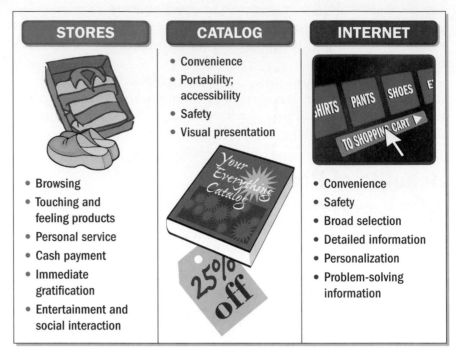

STORES

- Browsing
- Touching and feeling products
- Personal service
- Cash payment
- Immediate gratification
- Entertainment and social interaction

CATALOG

- Convenience
- Portability; accessibility
- Safety
- Visual presentation

Your Everything Catalog

25% off

INTERNET

SHIRTS PANTS SHOES E'

TO SHOPPING CART ▶

- Convenience
- Safety
- Broad selection
- Detailed information
- Personalization
- Problem-solving information

Math Check

GOODS AND SERVICES

Calculate a retail purchase: You just bought a new bicycle for $250 plus 8 percent sales tax. Assembly costs $35. What is your total bill?

➡️For tips on finding the solution, go to **marketingseries.glencoe.com**.

Benefits to Customers

We have already said that retailers benefit their customers by having goods and services available where and when those customers want them. **Figure 1.2** lists some of the ways retailers use different types of retailing, or channels, to benefit customers. Retailers provide other benefits to their customers. Retailers are able to purchase from a variety of sources. This provides customers a greater selection of products than they would have if they had to depend on their own resources to find those products.

Retailers make shopping easier for their customers. Retailers offer store shopping hours that are convenient for customers. They offer extended hours during holiday seasons and shopping hours after the normal workday, or when customers want to or are able to shop. Retailers also offer customer services. Some of those services include accepting credit cards and personal checks for payment, and assembly of merchandise. For instance, your bicycle shop will assemble the new bicycle you purchase there. Repairs are another form of customer service. The bicycle shop will also change your bike's flat tire if necessary or straighten the fender if you dent it.

Retailers also make shopping easier by having convenient locations. There are retailers selling similar merchandise at a downtown location, a suburban mall, or a local strip shopping center. Different types of locations are for convenient shopping.

Finally, retailers benefit customers by offering competitive pricing. There is a great deal of competition among retailers for your shopping dollars. Retailers compete for those dollars by keeping prices as low as possible while still making a reasonable profit.

Benefits to the Community

Retailers also benefit the local community. They provide a source of employment for teenagers and adults. Many local retailers hire high school students who are enrolled in marketing classes. The retailer not only provides a job, but also provides valuable training. In addition, they support community activities, such as school and philanthropic efforts. For instance, Joe, the owner of Joe's Pizza, will buy an ad in the high school football program and probably in the yearbook, too. The students, faculty, and their families are his customers. Joe wants to let them know he supports their efforts, as well as to keep his business name and logo in their minds. Retailers will also sponsor Little League teams, the Special Olympics, and other worthwhile organizations. Many national retailers with local outlets support national philanthropic efforts. Bloomingdale's department store supports a nationwide effort to find a cure for colon cancer. A local dentist might support community beautification efforts by allowing his or her staff to plant flowers or collect litter on public land during office hours. These are only a few of the ways that retailers support the local community.

CONNECT

Find a local retailer who sponsors some type of community service. You may be able to volunteer.

Benefits to the Economy

In addition, the sales generated by retailers support employment in the community. That means that the employees have the money to

Hot Property

Old Navy and the Fleet

Old Navy

Old Navy first set sail in 1994 as part of the Gap, Inc. fleet of companies. Gap was founded in 1969 by Donald and Doris Fisher in San Francisco, California, with a single store. It is now one of the top retailers in the world with about 4,200 stores, including Gap, Banana Republic, and Old Navy in six countries. Answering customer needs for hip but affordable clothing, the first three Old Navy stores opened in northern California. The chain expanded rapidly and earned $1 billion in its first three years. Old Navy then entered international waters in 1991, launching 12 stores in Canada.

INNOVATIVE MARKETING

From its beginnings, innovative marketing and quirky promotions have kept Gap, Inc. and Old Navy afloat. The name "Gap" was a humorous reference to "The Generation Gap" of the 1960s when the differences between people under 30 and over 30 became a popular issue. Today Old Navy's marketing strategies, such as employees wearing headsets, have continued to create waves. TV ad campaigns such as "The Denim Game" ranked high on the Top 20 "Brand Recall" list (viewers remembered store name), surpassing the majority of Super Bowl advertisements. Old Navy's campy commercials have featured an odd collection of pop culture personalities, such as Barbara Eden, Eartha Kitt, and Morgan Fairchild, as well as TV personality Molly Sims. By targeting cost-conscious customers, unique marketing and promotions help Old Navy continue to cruise the high seas.

1. Identify Old Navy's type of retail business.
2. Who do you think is the typical customer at Old Navy stores?

spend on eating at restaurants, going to the movies, getting medical care, and shopping at other retail establishments. The same is true for benefiting the national economy. Local retailers purchase products from national companies. Your local grocer might purchase Green Giant frozen vegetables for his or her store. Green Giant is a national company, and its sales contribute to the health of the nation's economy. Retailing is very important to the national economy. The retail industry is one of the largest employers in the country.

NEEDS AND WANTS During difficult economic times, when jobs are hard to find and the stock market is not doing well, people will still satisfy their needs and wants. They will continue to buy food and clothing, though they might select less expensive items. During less prosperous times, families will continue to buy groceries every week, but they might buy beans and hot dogs instead of the steak and asparagus that they might purchase during more prosperous times.

The same is true for clothing purchases. If you want a new sweater for school, you might choose the acrylic one that you can wash in your washing machine at home and save on dry-cleaning bills. However, during times of economic growth and prosperity, you might buy a pure wool sweater that has to be dry cleaned, even if it is a luxury!

SALES AND THE ECONOMY Multiply those buying decisions by the nation's population, and you will begin to understand how retail sales reflect the nation's economic condition. Economists use the monthly report of all retail sales to see if sales are up or down from the previous month and to assess the nation's economic health. These sales figures are particularly important during the holiday selling season, because the holiday season is usually the busiest and most profitable time for retailers.

QUESTION

What do you think is the greatest benefit offered by retailers?

What Retailers Do

With so many retail businesses in operation, retailers perform a variety of job tasks. Those tasks are necessary for the smooth and efficient functioning of their stores. In a small retail operation, the owner or manager might perform all these jobs. Larger retailers will probably have specially trained employees to perform various combinations of these tasks. Some of the tasks are the following:

Buying Merchandise

The retailer must determine what merchandise will be purchased, when, and in what quantities. Buying too many of a particular item will result in a loss of funds available to purchase other items. Failure to purchase enough items can result in a loss of sales. This is an area that requires both product knowledge and an awareness of customer likes and dislikes.

Determining Selling Price

Once the merchandise is purchased, the retailer must then determine a selling price that is fair to the customer, but the price must allow the retailer to make a profit. After all, that is why they are in business.

Most retailers use a predetermined formula for determining selling price based on the cost price of the product.

Storing Goods Purchased

Retailers purchase goods in sufficient quantities so they are available when the customers want them. This often means storing at least part of them from a particular order. Suppose a sporting goods retailer purchases six dozen footballs. There would be very little need to have all six dozen on the selling floor at one time. The retailer would probably decide to keep six or eight of them on the selling floor and store the remainder in the back room or some other type storage facility.

Advertising and Promoting Products

Retailers must advertise and promote the products that they offer. This is essential so customers will be aware of the goods and services offered. It is also important to let regular customers know what products are new, while also attracting new customers. Retailers are continually trying to expand their customer base. Advertising and promotion are important tools in building and expanding a customer base.

Displaying Merchandise

Merchandise must not only be displayed in a neat and attractive manner, they must also be shown at their absolute best. Customers want to see what is available. It is important to show merchandise to their best advantage to appeal to the customer. The retailer wants the customer to want them.

Selling Goods or Services

While all the retailers' tasks are important, this is probably the most important task. If the goods or services available do not sell, the retailer will not stay in business very long. Selling products requires knowledge of them, and friendly sales associates who enjoy helping customers make good buying decisions.

Servicing Products

Once goods are purchased by the customer, many retailers then must handle maintenance of those goods. Appliance retailers may offer repair services; many offer service contracts that allow for preventative maintenance. That helps to keep the appliance in tip-top working condition, which means a happy, satisfied customer.

Case Study PART 2

CAN SMALL STORES SURVIVE WAL-MART?

Continued from Part 1 on page 5

After analyzing her small toy store in comparison to Wal-Mart, Bessie Tyler decided that her store had a fighting chance, but she would need to make some changes. She stopped carrying the items that Wal-Mart sold for less with better selection—such as bicycles and sporting goods. She concluded that she needed to specialize to survive, so she focused on a wide variety of board games, educational toys, and unique dolls and doll clothes—things that Wal-Mart couldn't provide. Today Bessie Tyler's toy store is raking in higher profits than ever—all because she carefully analyzed her possibilities and looked at the retail picture from a different angle.

ANALYZE AND WRITE

1. What changes allowed Bessie Tyler to keep her customers, even though they also shopped at Wal-Mart?

2. Do you think her attitude and strategies would help other small retailers survive large competitors? Why?

Providing Customer Services

The retailer must also determine what customer services will be offered. Will they take credit cards? Offer delivery service? What about offering alterations? The list goes on. The retailer must determine the services that the customer wants and will use as well as which of those services to offer.

Risk Management

Risk management includes many things. One of the biggest risks involves the purchasing of goods and services. Will the products sell? Sales are vital to the continuation of any business. The retailer must also consider several risks that can be covered by insurance. Some of those include the risk to the store building from storms, fire, or other catastrophes. Retailers must also think of customer and employee liability. Accidents happen to the most diligent people, and that possibility must be considered. There is also the issue of theft, from customer shoplifting as well as employee pilferage. There are other risks, and there are many factors a retailer must consider.

Hiring and Managing Employees

The retailer must find and hire reliable, friendly, and honest employees. Once an employee is hired, he or she must be trained in the methods of that particular retailer. This task also includes payroll functions and benefits management.

MARKETING SERIES *Online*

Remember to check out this book's Web site for career information and more great resources at **marketingseries.glencoe.com**.

Career Areas of Retailing

Our discussion of retailing would not be complete without taking a look at some of the career options offered by the retail industry. Jobs in the retailing industry range from entry level to chief executive officer. The National Retail Federation Foundation classifies retail jobs and careers into the following broad categories.

- **Marketing and Advertising** Marketing and advertising jobs involve persuading or convincing people to buy the goods or services that the retailer has to sell. This area includes advertising, promotion, publicity, and visual merchandising. Job titles in this area include marketing director, graphic designer, and visual merchandiser.

- **Store Operations** This area includes the physical site operations of the store, such as the heat and air conditioning, carpeting, paint, and interior and exterior appearance of the building. Job titles in this area include operations manager and building contracts manager.

- **Loss Prevention** Loss prevention includes the prevention of shoplifting and employee pilferage. Shoplifting is the theft of merchandise by customers or persons not employed by the retailer. Employee pilferage is the theft of merchandise or money by store employees. Job titles include loss prevention manager and store detective.

A PERSONAL INVESTMENT

Jim Vaughn
Store Owner
Whalebone Surf Shop

What does your job entail?

"I am a small retailer. My job entails everything. I design the T-shirts; I do the advertising; I design the TV ads, the radio ads, and the newspaper ads. My wife has been helping out tremendously with that. Speaking as a small retailer for 30 years, I also clean the bathrooms and wait on the customers. We do it all—from A to Z. I've been working seven days a week for over 25 years—90 hours a week for six months of the year."

What skills are most important?

"A sense of humor and imagination. You have to have a sense of humor to deal with people, or you'll turn away customers."

What kind of training did you have?

"I received on-the-job training, beginning 30 years ago. My original background had nothing to do with retail. My college courses weren't directly related to retail—but I wanted to have a surf shop."

What is your key to success?

"It used to be, 'I'll be leaving and going on a surf trip soon.' That was my carrot, but the reality is trying to get the bills paid. When the day is done, I really do enjoy what I do. If you've got to work, you might as well go with a spring in your step."

Why are attitude, a sense of humor, and conversational skills so important in a retail career?

Career Data: Store Owner

Education and Training
Degrees in business, marketing, and associated fields; on-the-job training

Skills and Abilities
Communication skills, financial skills, creativity, organizational skills, versatility

Career Outlook Average growth through 2010, but leisure-based businesses are cyclical by nature

Career Path A typical career path can begin at the sales associate level and move to management. With a business plan and financing, an entrepreneur can open a store. Small-store owners can consider opening additional locations, creating a franchise, or licensing the name and business plan to other entrepreneurs.

- **Store Management** This employment area deals with day-to-day operations of the retailer, such as managing employees, opening the doors on time, and having cash in the registers. Job titles include store manager, assistant store manager, and department sales manager.

- **Finance** The financial area includes tracking and paying invoices, calculating merchandise discounts, and balancing daily sales receipts. Some jobs in this area are chief financial officer, controller, internal auditor, and accounts payable clerk.

- **Human Resources** Job responsibilities include interviewing, hiring, training personnel, and managing employee benefits. Typical jobs include personnel manager, compensation and benefits manager, and human resources director.

■ **IT and E-Commerce** This category includes Internet marketing, Web-site design and maintenance, information management, and data processing. Typical jobs in this area include e-commerce director, Web-site designer, and e-merchandise manager.

■ **Sales** Jobs in this area involve the direct selling of the retailer's products to the customer. The National Retail Federation Foundation also includes jobs related to receiving and checking in products before they reach the sales floor. Jobs include sales associate, cashier, store receiver, and stock helper.

■ **Distribution, Logistics, and Supply-Chain Management** This employment area includes warehousing functions and getting merchandise to the retail store when they are needed. Some jobs in this area are head of distribution and logistics, distribution center manager, and traffic manager.

■ **Merchandise Planning and Buying** This area includes the planning of product selections, buying products, and pricing the goods for sale. Typical jobs in this area are general merchandise manager, divisional merchandise manager, merchandise buyer, assistant buyer, and merchandise planner.

■ **Entrepreneurship** This category involves owning and operating your own business. An entrepreneur would be a business owner of either an independent or franchise business.

The retail industry offers many exciting and lucrative positions. Those positions offer career opportunities, not just jobs. You can understand why the retail industry is the nation's second largest employer by looking at the number of job titles.

Quick Check ✓

RESPOND to what you've read by answering these questions.

1. What is the most important characteristic that all retailers share? _____

_____

_____

2. What are three benefits of retailing? _____

_____

_____

3. Describe at least three tasks that retailers perform. _____

_____

_____

_____

Name _____ Date _____

Worksheet 1.1

Your Favorite Retailer

Check your local newspaper ads and pick out one that advertises your favorite retail store. Then answer these questions:

1. What kind of merchandise does this store sell? _____

_____

_____

_____

2. Why do you like this store? Explain. _____

_____

_____

_____

3. How long has this store been in business? _____

_____

_____

_____

4. What similar stores compete with your favorite store? _____

_____

_____

_____

_____

5. What advantages do the competition stores have over your favorite store?

_____

_____

_____

_____

6. What advantages does your favorite store have over the competition stores?

_____

_____

_____

_____

Worksheet (1.2)

Leading Retailers

Pick one of the retailers from the List of 20 Top Retailers in the United States. Then answer the questions that follow.

List of 20 Top Retailers in the United States

1. Wal-Mart
2. Home Depot
3. Kroger
4. Sears
5. Target
6. Albertson's
7. Kmart
8. Costco
9. Safeway
10. JCPenney
11. Walgreen
12. Ahold USA
13. CVS
14. Lowe's
15. Best Buy
16. Federated Department Stores
17. Publix
18. Rite Aid
19. Delhaize America
20. May Department Stores

SOURCE: Triversity Top 100 Retailers 2002, www.stores.org, National Retail Federation

1. Name the company you picked and describe the type of merchandise this company sells.

   _____

   _____

   _____

2. What top retailers on this list are its competitors? _____

   _____

   _____

   _____

3. Go to the library or Internet and research the company. How did this company get started?

   _____

   _____

   _____

4. Has this company ever changed the way it operates? If so, how? _____

   _____

   _____

   _____

Portfolio Works

EXPLORING RETAIL CAREERS

Go to the library or Internet and find five careers in retailing that you are interested in exploring or may be new to you. A Web site such as the Retail Careers and Advancement site at **www.nrf.com/retail/careers** is a good source. Do the following exercises. Then add this page to your career portfolio.

1. List the five careers you found. _____

_____

_____

_____

2. Use the Internet to explore at least one career. Describe it. _____

_____

_____

_____

3. List your skills and interests. Then list the jobs that match these skills and interests. Create names for the jobs if they are unusual.

Skills/Interests   **Possible Jobs**

_____   _____

_____   _____

_____   _____

4. Review your list of skills and interests. What stands out? Think of as many retail jobs as you can that relate to your skills and interests. _____

_____

_____

_____

5. Describe an ideal job that involves these skills. Include the location of the ideal job and the kinds of coworkers, customers, and employees you would meet. _____

_____

_____

_____

CHAPTER SUMMARY

Section 1.1 Exploring Retail Marketing

retailing (p. 7)
products (p. 7)
goods (p. 7)
services (p. 7)
retail customer (p. 7)

- Retailing is the selling of products, or goods and services, to the customer.

- Goods are items that are made, manufactured, or grown which people want to buy and use. Services are things that make us feel better or enhance our lives in some way.

Section 1.2 Retailing and Its Benefits

manufacturer (p. 12)
channel of distribution
     (p. 12)
direct channel (p. 12)
indirect channel (p. 13)
wholesaler (p. 12)
producer channel (p. 13)

- A channel of distribution is the path a product takes from where it is made to the consumer. A direct channel of distribution is one in which the product path leads directly from the manufacturer to the consumer. An indirect channel of distribution is one in which the product path follows more than one step, moving from the manufacturer to the wholesaler, to the retailers, and then to the consumer. A producer channel of distribution is a type of indirect channel of distribution in which the manufacturer also owns its retail stores.

- Retailing benefits customers by offering competitive pricing and a wide variety of products. It benefits the community by providing employment opportunities and supporting school and philanthropic efforts. It benefits the economy because the retail industry is one of the largest employers in the country, and retail sales contribute to our nation's economic growth.

- Retailer tasks include buying merchandise or products, determining selling prices, storing, advertising, promoting, displaying, selling, and servicing merchandise, providing customer service, managing risk, and hiring and managing employees. These tasks translate into a wide variety of retail jobs and career paths, including those in stores and behind the scenes.

CHECKING CONCEPTS

1. **Define** retailing.
2. **Describe** the difference between goods and services.
3. **Name** the channels of distribution.
4. **Explain** three benefits of retailing.
5. **List** three tasks of retailers.
6. **Identify** two ways retailers use computers.
7. **Describe** the difference between a manufacturer and a wholesaler.

Critical Thinking
8. **Explain** how retailing has become global.

CROSS-CURRICULUM SKILLS

Work-Based Learning

Basic Skills—Writing

9. Write a letter to your favorite retailer and explain why you buy its product.

Interpersonal Skills—Teaching Others

10. Using key terms from this chapter, create your own word puzzle, such as a crossword puzzle. Trade your puzzle with that of another student and solve each other's puzzles.

School-Based Learning

Math

11. Abdul bought five T-shirts ($9 each) and two pairs of jeans ($22 each) from Old Navy. What is the total cost of the T-shirts and jeans? (You do not need to calculate tax.)

Science

12. Many clothes are made from synthetic, or manufactured fibers, such as acrylic, nylon, and rayon. Using an encyclopedia, find out more about these fibers.

 CONNECTION

Role Play: Hardware Store Employee

SITUATION You are to assume the role of an employee of a locally owned hardware store. You are leaving your job to attend college where you will major in marketing. Your career goal is to own a retail store someday. You have been asked by the hardware store's owner to help train a new employee (judge). This is the new employee's (judge's) first job. During the course of training, the new employee (judge) asks why you plan to own a store.

ACTIVITY Explain to the new employee (judge) the many and varied duties of a retail business owner.

EVALUATION You will be evaluated on how well you meet the following performance indicators:

- Explain employment opportunities in marketing.
- Describe types of business activities.
- Explain marketing and its importance in a global economy.
- Explain the concept of management.
- Explain the nature and scope of purchasing.

 INTERNET ACTIVITY

Use the Internet to access the National Retail Federation's Web site and click on "About NRF" to answer the following questions:

- How many U.S. retail establishments does the NRF represent?
- How many U.S. workers does it represent?
- How many retail associations does the NRF represent?

➡ For a link to the NRF to answer these questions, go to **marketingseries.glencoe.com**.

Chapter 2

Types of Retail Businesses

Chapter Objectives

- Explain the NAICS categories for the retail industry.
- Name the types of business organization.
- Identify the types of retail business ownership.
- Describe how competition affects retail evolution.

POWER READ

Be an active reader and use these reading strategies:

PREDICT what the section will be about.

CONNECT what you read with your life.

QUESTION as you read to make sure you understand the content.

RESPOND to what you've read.

A "DURABLE" REPUTATION

Retail Business can be any type or size. Privately owned comic book stores are small retail businesses. Some stores begin as one type of retailer and develop into other, bigger retail businesses. For years, L.L. Bean was mainly a catalog retailer. Then the company expanded.

The Maine-based retailer L.L. Bean sells sporting goods and outdoor clothing, such as khakis and cozy sweaters. Even with a 91-year history, it wasn't until 2001 that the company opened its first store outside of Maine. It has always relied on quality and a loyal following to stay in business and keep customers "happy campers." With years of catalog retailing experience, L.L. Bean went online with its Web site in the 1990s. Innovative policies such as accepting returns without question, even on items purchased years before, and realistic size guidelines for customers made L.L. Bean's catalog and Web site successes and caused further store expansion—all the way to Asia. However, in the mid to late 1990s, the Asian financial crisis hit, and L.L.Bean had to lay off 350 workers—the first major layoff in its history. So the company regrouped and opened more U.S. stores and targeted its catalog customers. But, in the meantime, similar stores such as Lands' End, Eddie Bauer, J.Crew, and Gap emphasized style over traditional durability, and L.L. Bean's sales stopped growing.

ANALYZE AND WRITE

1. Name other competing stores that belong to the same category as L.L. Bean. How do they differ from L.L. Bean?
2. Identify some reasons for L.L. Bean's slow growth in the 1990s to the present.

Case Study Part 2 on page 41

Types of Retailers

AS YOU READ . . .

YOU WILL LEARN

- To explain the NAICS categories for the retail industry.

WHY IT'S IMPORTANT

The NAICS classification system helps to illustrate the scope of the retail industry.

KEY TERMS

- NAICS
- sales associates
- merchandise variety
- merchandise assortment

NAICS North American Industry Classification System, a system used to categorize industries in North America, developed by the United States, Canada, and Mexico

PREDICT

Preview the headings in this section and identify the main topics.

Using Categories

As discussed in Chapter 1, retailers make goods and services available to their customers. This section will focus on the types of retailers according to types of merchandise they sell, and their types of stores. Section 2.2 will examine the different types of ownership of retail stores.

Retailers are as diverse as the goods and services that people need and want. Retailers are categorized, or sorted, so we can better understand the scope of the retail industry and all the parts that make up the whole industry. There are several ways to do that sorting. One way to sort retailers is by the type of products that a particular retailer offers.

NAICS Codes

The North American Industry Classification System (**NAICS**) is a system used to categorize industries on the North American continent. The governments of the United States, Canada, and Mexico worked together to develop this system of classification for mutual benefit. The use of the NAICS allows these nations to compare business statistics by industry. Each country compares the statistics for its own country with other countries. Each industry and classification is clearly defined by the system.

The Retail Industry

The retail industry has a separate classification. The NAICS uses 12 categories and code numbers for the retail industry. The 12 categories classify retailers by the types of products they sell. In addition, this system classifies types of retail stores. There is one exception—the last category classifies non-store retailers. You can see the retail classification names and code numbers in **Figure 2.1.** Most of a retailer's competition comes from the other retail businesses within its classification.

In the last two decades, a greater diversity of retailers has developed. Retailers carry similar merchandise in a greater variety of types of stores. For example, new specialists include musical instrument, pet supply, and other types of stores. The Internet has enabled new forms of retailers, such as automobile sellers with merchandise and services at fixed prices. This variety of forms of retail increases competition and helps consumers satisfy their needs for merchandise.

Figure 2.1

NAICS Retail Industry Categories

Code	Category	Approximate Number of Stores
441	Motor Vehicle and Parts Dealers	123,000
442	Furniture and Home Furnishings Stores	64,000
443	Electronics and Appliance Stores	44,000
444	Building Material and Garden Equipment and Supplies Dealers	93,000
445	Food and Beverage Stores	149,000
446	Health and Personal Care Stores	83,000
447	Gasoline Stations	127,000
448	Clothing and Clothing Accessories Stores	157,000
451	Sporting Goods, Hobby, Book, and Music Stores	69,000
452	General Merchandise Stores	37,000
453	Miscellaneous Store Retailers	130,000
454	Non-store Retailers	45,000

Source: U.S. Census Bureau 2002

ASSORTED RETAILERS The wide variety of retailers and retail stores illustrates why the retail industry is one of the greatest sources of revenue for the United States. *In which category would you place video-game stores?*

Retail Categories and Types of Stores

Studying the NAICS retail categories allows you to see the enormous scope of the retail industry and consider the wide variety of retail establishments. As each category is discussed and the types of stores are listed and described, think of examples of those retail stores found in your community.

Motor Vehicle and Parts Dealers

Retailers in this category sell motor vehicles from a fixed location, such as a showroom or open lot where the vehicles are on display. This category includes new and used car dealers; recreational vehicles dealers; and motorcycle, boat, aircraft, golf-cart, snowmobile, and utility-trailer dealers. Auto dealerships, such as those that sell Ford, Chevrolet, Toyota, or Honda automobiles, are retail stores. Their prices are usually flexible, and buyers may be able to bargain with sales associates for extra features and lower sale prices, but the dealers usually make profits. As mentioned before, some automobile sellers offer their goods, or cars, at fixed prices—a practice that is fairly new. For example, Saturn automobiles sell at fixed prices. Automotive parts, accessory, and tire stores such as NAPA Auto Parts stores and Just Tires stores are also classified in this NAICS category.

Furniture and Home Furnishings Stores

This category includes new furniture and home furnishings sold from retail stores. Other stores in this category include mattress and bed stores such as Mattress Discounters. Other types of furniture stores in this category include office furnishings stores such as Office Outfitters. Home furnishings stores sell floor coverings, window treatments, and other home furnishings such as lamps and kitchenware. Floor coverings include rugs and carpets, vinyl floor coverings, and floor tile. This category includes stores that sell floor coverings and install them.

Window treatments include curtains, drapes, blinds, and shades. Stores such as the Blind Spot and Windows Unlimited specialize in providing window treatments. Besides window treatment stores, some of the many other stores in this category are bath shops such as Bed Bath & Beyond, and kitchenware stores such as Lechters. Custom picture-frame stores and linens stores also belong in this category.

Electronics and Appliance Stores

Stores in this category sell electronics and appliances. A very large subgroup includes appliance, television, and electronic stores. Those stores sell household appliances such as stoves and refrigerators, and electronic products such as televisions and computers. Retailers might also sell repair services. This category includes household appliance stores, including ones that sell sewing machines and vacuum cleaners. Computer centers sell computers, computer software, and related products such as cables and surge protectors. These stores may also offer servicing and repair services for appliances or equipment they sell.

Camera and photographic supplies stores sell those products and may also include camera repair service and film processing. Ritz Camera Centers are good examples of stores that sell cameras and provide camera repair and film development services. Stores that sell cell phones, telephones, video cameras, pagers, and stereos also fit into this profitable category.

Building Material and Garden Equipment and Supplies Dealers

These retailers sell building material and garden equipment from their stores. Think about all the types of stores that sell products dealing with the construction of a home or office building. Those stores include lumber yards, hardware stores, paint and wallpaper stores, cabinet stores, window and door stores, lighting-fixtures stores, ceiling fan stores, fencing stores, garage door stores, plumbing supply stores, wood-floor stores, and window stores. Top retail corporations such as Home Depot and Lowe's also fit into this category. Retail businesses operate all over the world.

The lawn and garden equipment and supplies subcategory includes outdoor power equipment stores and nursery, garden centers, and farm-supply stores. Franks Nursery is an example of a nationwide garden center in this category. Stores such as Home Depot and Lowe's have garden centers within their stores. Many smaller, local, and independently owned nurseries also fit in this retail category.

Food and Beverage Stores

These stores sell food and beverages and have special equipment (freezers, refrigerated display cases, refrigerators) for displaying the food and beverages. This category is a large one and includes grocery stores and supermarket chains such as Kroger, and delicatessens and convenience stores such as 7-Eleven.

In the last 15 years or more, consumers have changed their purchasing habits. People used to shop at traditional supermarkets. Now food retailers include discount stores and warehouse clubs, such as Wal-Mart—the largest food retailer in the world. The third largest is France's Carrefour, which is a *hypermarket*, slightly smaller than a *supercenter* like Wal-Mart. This category also includes a large variety of specialty food retailers that includes fish markets, bakeries, and wine and liquor stores.

Supermarkets and convenience store retailers face increasing competition from other types of retailers. The large discount stores and warehouse clubs are growing rapidly. Stores such as Wal-Mart, Target, and Kmart have spearheaded this trend. Moreover, other retailers, such as drugstore chains, now offer basic grocery items such as milk and bread that have been available at convenience stores.

Health and Personal Care Stores

Stores that sell health and personal care products include pharmacies and drugstores, such as CVS; beauty supply stores, such as Sally Beauty Supply; optical stores such as LensCrafters; and health-food and supplements stores such as General Nutrition Centers.

Gasoline Stations

Stores in this group sell retail automotive fuels and automotive oils. These two products can be sold in combination at a convenience store. ExxonMobil is an example of a company with gasoline stations located nationwide. Gasoline stations have specialized equipment to store and dispense the fuels. This category includes gasoline stations with or without convenience stores, marine service stations, and truck stops.

Clothing and Clothing Accessories Stores

Typical stores in this group sell men's, women's, or children's clothing. This large category also includes retailers that specialize in bridal wear, Western wear, or fur clothing stores. Stores that sell uniforms for work or school also belong in this category.

Clothing accessories stores also sell products that include hats, costume jewelry, and belts. Other stores in this category sell luggage and leather goods, such as Wilsons Leather Stores.

Sporting Goods, Hobby, Book, and Music Stores

This category is inclusive of a variety of recreational retailers. Sporting goods stores retail new sporting goods, such as bicycles, camping gear, exercise and fitness equipment, and specialty sports footwear. Other types of stores in this category include exercise equipment stores such as fitness resource stores and pro shops at country clubs.

CONNECT
Do you have a bakery in your neighborhood? Does it sell more than baked goods?

Selling Point !
► BIG SALES
Women purchase $70 billion in apparel and accessories each year. 53 percent of those purchases are made at department stores.

Hobby, toy, and game stores sell new toys, games, and hobby and craft supplies. Stores include craft supply stores, game stores, hobby shops, magic supply stores, and toy stores.

Sewing, needlework, and piece goods stores sell sewing supplies, fabrics, patterns, yarns and other needlework accessories. Jo-Ann Fabrics is an example of a national fabric store.

Musical instrument and supplies stores sell new musical instruments, sheet music, and related supplies. This category includes stores that specialize in selling only pianos.

Book, periodical, and music stores sell new books and magazines, newspapers, and prerecorded audio and video media. This category also includes religious bookstores, newsstands, prerecorded compact-disc music stores, video stores, and record stores. Barnes & Noble bookstores and Tower Records are two well-known examples of stores from this category.

SELLING MUSIC A hundred years ago, customers went to their favorite music store to buy sheet music and a piano to play it. Now music stores carry everything from CDs to electric guitars. *Why do you think music stores are categorized with sporting goods, book, and hobby stores?*

General-Merchandise Retailers

Stores in this category sell a wide range of products with no single merchandise line being most prominent. Some types of general merchandisers include:

- Discount stores

- Specialty stores (e.g., drugstores)

- Category specialists

- Department stores

Department stores have separate departments for various merchandise items, such as apparel, jewelry, home furnishings, and linens. Each department has separate cash registers and sales associates.

Some other general-merchandise retailers include catalog showrooms, dollar stores, and general stores.

DISCOUNT STORES Discount department stores sell a wide variety of general merchandise but at reduced prices. They have centralized customer checkout areas, usually in the front of the store.

Warehouse clubs and supercenters usually sell general lines of new merchandise, such as clothing, appliances, and furniture, also at reduced prices. These stores also sell groceries. The sale of groceries distinguishes warehouse clubs from discount department stores.

Miscellaneous Store Retailers

Retailers in the miscellaneous store category include those that sell new products that do not fall into any of the other categories. They sell products with unique characteristics. Some retailers in this group include:

- Florists

- Used-merchandise stores (used products, antiques, secondhand goods, consignment stores, flea markets, rare book stores, and thrift stores; not including autos)

- Pet stores

- Office supplies and stationery stores

- Gift, novelty, and souvenir shops (retail gifts, novelty merchandise, souvenirs, greeting cards, seasonal and holiday decorations, and curios)

- Art galleries

- Auction houses

- Candle shops

- Closet-organizer stores

Humane Retailing

"Take one pet and call me in the morning," reads the title of a magazine article. This advice may be close to the truth. Recent studies suggest that taking care of an animal helps people live healthier, happier, and longer lives. That's good news for the almost 60 percent of American households that count one or more pets as part of the family.

As a leading retailer specializing in pet supplies, PETCO understood the special bond between humans and animals decades ago. In 1965, it opened its doors to all kinds of pets and their owners. Believing that animals deserve the same standard of treatment as people, they dedicate their 635 stores nationwide to "quality animal care."

SELECTION AND SERVICE

Each store offers one-stop shopping and a selection of over ten thousand items, ranging from the practical to the fun. Premium foods and pet carriers are mixed in with colorful bandannas for the pooch, action figures that swim with the fishes, and berry-treat sticks that only a rodent could love. In addition, many stores offer special services, including pet photography, low-cost vaccinations, obedience classes, and head-to-tail grooming for your favorite cat or dog.

Retail profits aside, PETCO established the PETCO Foundation in 1999, which has raised over $13 million for the betterment of companion animals everywhere. The PETCO Foundation is committed to the "4 Rs": Reduce, Rescue, Rehabilitate, and Rejoice. Following PETCO's example, all types of retail businesses can blend business with service to the community.

1. What type of retail business is PETCO, and what characteristics do you think make it special?
2. If you were preparing for a retailing job that sells specialized products, what would you want to learn?

QUESTION

Do sales associates need to know about products they sell? Why or why not?

sales associates retail employees who sell merchandise and products to customers

Non-Store Retailers

Retailers in this category sell their merchandise and products from areas other than a fixed location. These retailers might use infomercials, paper and electronic catalogs, door-to-door sales, in-home demonstrations, portable stalls, or vending machines. Some of these retailers may also operate traditional stores. For example, JCPenney sells merchandise from its store and its catalog, the most popular catalog in the United States.

Electronic shopping includes e-tailers who sell all types of merchandise using the Internet. Chapter 4 will explore more about non-store retailers.

Retail Sales Associates

All the types of retailers have **sales associates** who sell their merchandise and products to their customers. Retail sales associates receive both general sales training to know the basics of selling and special product training in order to be effective at their jobs.

In addition, sales associates must have detailed knowledge specific to the products they sell. For instance, a new car sales associate must have product knowledge that is specialized and specific to the particular brand of automobile being sold.

Variety of Merchandise

It is important to realize that most retailers carry merchandise that falls into more than one of the categories listed. Retailers put together merchandise variety and assortments that their customers want to buy.

Stores such as Victoria's Secret sell a combination of women's apparel, hosiery, and bath and fragrance products. The product or merchandise lines that a retailer carries are known as the **merchandise variety**. Another example involves a clothing retailer. You would expect a clothing store to carry jackets, pants, shirts, blouses, and tops. All of those lines are the merchandise variety.

Retailers also have merchandise in an assortment. A **merchandise assortment** is the number of items within each merchandise line. Look again at the clothing retailer and the shirts/blouses/tops category. Within that merchandise category, the retailer might have woven shirts, knit shirts, and sweaters. Those shirt or blouse styles represent the retailer's merchandise assortment. The same is true for the different types of retailers and the categories of merchandise they carry for sale.

merchandise variety the product or merchandise lines that a retailer carries

merchandise assortment the number of items within a merchandise line

Quick Check

RESPOND to what you've read by answering these questions.

1. Why is the NAICS important? _____

_____

_____

_____

_____

2. How many NAICS categories are there for the retail industry? _____

_____

_____

_____

_____

_____

3. How are store and non-store retailers alike? How are they different? _____

_____

_____

_____

_____

_____

Types of Retail Ownership

AS YOU READ ...

YOU WILL LEARN

- To name types of business organizations.
- To identify types of retail business ownership.
- To describe how competition affects retail evolution.

WHY IT'S IMPORTANT

Business organization is basic to understanding the retail industry. Knowing the types of ownership helps you understand how stores are organized.

KEY TERMS

- single proprietorship
- partnership
- corporation
- independent store
- entrepreneur
- chain stores
- franchisee
- franchisor
- franchise

PREDICT

Choose one key term and explain what you think it means.

single proprietorship a business that is owned by one person

partnership an agreement between two or more persons to go into business together

Who Owns the Store?

As you begin to look at the types of retail business ownership, think about some of the places of business where you shop regularly. Some of them probably include clothing stores, music stores, restaurants, movie theaters, and so on. You know that retailers are part of our daily lives. Now consider who owns those retail businesses.

Some businesses are probably owned by local merchants, others by large national chains, and still others by international business conglomerates. The types of business ownership vary from the very small, one-owner business to the huge corporation with thousands of stockholders as owners. There are also other types of retail business ownership that you may not recognize. How about a franchise business or a cooperative?

Business Organization

Retail businesses fall into one of three types of organizations. There are advantages and disadvantages to each type:

- Single proprietorship
- Partnership
- Corporation

Single Proprietorship

A **single proprietorship** is a business that is owned by one person. That person is the one who originates the idea for the business and obtains the financing for the business. That person also determines the business location and product and service offerings, and also makes all the other decisions involved with business ownership. If the business is successful, the owner keeps all the profits. That person also assumes the risks of the business operation. If the business loses money or fails, the single proprietor is the one responsible for the financial loss.

Partnership

A **partnership** is an agreement between two or more persons to go into business together. The partners each provide funds to start the business. The partners jointly share the advantages and risks of business ownership. Before entering any partnership, the participants should carefully review the tasks, responsibilities, and expectations of each of the partners. It is important for the partners to agree upon their duties

World Market

Mongolian Specialty

Everything old is new again—at least to people visiting Mongolia who discover the country's portable housing. Tents called *gers* (Mongolian for *house*) have been the traditional Mongolian dwelling for thousands of years. Designed to be packed up and reassembled quickly by nomadic herdsmen moving from pasture to pasture, gers are easily transported. Circular in structure, their latticework walls and cone-shaped roofs are covered with one or more layers of felt lashed down by rope. An opening on top of the roof allows for light and air flow. A wooden or flap door that's colorfully decorated with painted birds, flowers, and trees is the only way in.

Gers have also become an unusual new venture. Travelers fortunate enough to have stayed in one usually want to take the experience home. Spacious, weatherproof, and fun, they use the remarkable ger for camping, meditation, and as a spare room. For a few thousand dollars, tourists purchase a handcrafted souvenir that lasts a lifetime

What type of business organization in Mongolia would most likely sell gers? Explain why.

and responsibilities in advance. Like a single proprietorship, the partners assume personal responsibility for the business's risks.

Corporation

A **corporation** is a more complex form of business organization. A corporation charter is granted by the state in which the business will be established. The corporation sells stock to investors who become the owners of the corporation. Those investors are called *shareholders*. A corporation is more expensive to start, but corporations do offer the advantage of limited liability. If the business should fail, the owners are liable for losses only up to the amount of stock they have purchased.

Types of Stores and Ownership

If you are thinking of starting a business of your own, or you want to invest in a business, there are many options to study and many decisions to make. One decision concerns the type of ownership that would be best for your particular retail business. There are many different kinds of stores and several types of business ownership that are common today.

Independent Stores

An **independent store** is owned privately. The business has one location, and the owner has no agreements with merchandise groups or franchises. The owner is usually a local businessperson closely involved in the daily operation of the business, which includes daily contact with customers.

corporation a form of business for which a charter is granted by the state in which the business will be established. The corporation sells stock to investors who become the owners of the corporation.

independent store a store that is owned privately, having one location

Math Check

TOY STORY

Rita just opened her own toy store. Her start-up costs were $25,020. Her rent and monthly expenses for the first year will be $30,000. How much will she need to make per month in the first year to cover these costs?

➡ For tips to find the solution, go to **marketingseries.glencoe.com.**

entrepreneur person who takes the risk of opening a new business, often acting as the manager and operator of the business

chain stores stores that have at least two locations and are owned by one company or person

CONNECT

What other stores besides chain stores offer discounts?

DISADVANTAGES OF INDEPENDENCE A disadvantage of independently owned stores is that retail prices charged in these stores tend to be higher than those in large discount stores. Independent retailers do not have the advantage of purchasing in large quantities that would allow them to take advantage of discounted prices for large quantities. Examples of independent retailers are all around your community. Some independent retailers might include small clothing retailers, barbers or hairdressers, or shoe-store owners. The term *locally owned* generally refers to an independent retailer.

ADVANTAGES OF INDEPENDENCE There are definite advantages to this type of ownership as well. For retailers, those advantages include close contact with the business's customers that allows personal insights into the customer's needs and wants. Another advantage is that independent retailers are able to respond quickly to changes in the business climate or to customer desires.

Independent stores are often where entrepreneurs begin their careers. An **entrepreneur** is a person who has the vision and knowledge to start a new business. This owner takes the risk of opening a new business. The entrepreneur will often act as the manager as well as operator of the business.

Chain Stores

Chain stores have at least two locations, and most have numerous locations. Chain-store locations can be local, regional, national, or international. These types of stores are owned by one company or person. That owner makes the company policy decisions, including purchasing decisions. In many situations, the chain-store owner is located some distance from the local store.

ADVANTAGES AND DISADVANTAGES OF CHAINS Chain stores have the advantage of being able to purchase in quantity, which enables them to offer lower prices. Chain stores also offer a variety of customer services, and they hire people locally.

However, because of central ownership, chain stores may not be able to respond as quickly to changing local business conditions. The chain-store decision makers also do not have the advantage of frequent contact with local customers. So, they are not always in tune with customer needs and wants. JCPenney is an example of an international chain store; Steinmart is a national retail chain. You can probably name several regional and local retail chains in your area.

Store Groups

Store groups are usually owned by large companies or corporations. The best way to explain this type of business ownership is by example: Sears, Roebuck and Company owns the Sears retail chain; Sears also owns Lands' End and Allstate Insurance. All of these companies operate independently of one another. They do not share common management or decision making like a retail chain. Each is operated as an independent unit with its own management structures, but all stores are owned by one corporation or company.

Profiles in Marketing

THE WELL-DRESSED SHOP

Christine McNamara
Manager
The Dress Shop

What does your job entail?
"I'm the manager and co-buyer for the store, so I do buying, hiring, display work, inventory, scheduling, and attend business association meetings. I do payroll, waiting on customers— I pretty much do everything. At the beginning and end of the season, I work an average of about 50 hours a week. The beginning of fall and spring are always the heavy times."

What do you like most about your job?
"The art part of it, the visual displays—it's one of my biggest strengths. It's a nice balance with dealing with the customers."

What are your most important skills?
"Communication with people. In retail that's key. You have to be outgoing."

What kind of training did you have?
"My training was all one-on-one with the store owner. I started out as a sales associate. She slowly brought me into more aspects of what she did."

What advice would you give to students?
"The biggest problem that we have is when we hire kids who are used to shopping in the mall where no one talks to you— they don't know how to speak properly. Take English courses and speak with people."

What is your key to success?
"It's knowing the customer. We're smaller stores—and you have to work with clients one-on-one in order to get them to stay."

Why do you think verbal skills are so important in a small, independent chain store?

Career Data:
Retail Clothing Store Manager

Education and Training
Degrees in design and marketing

Skills and Abilities
Communication skills; people skills; creativity, versatility, and patience

Career Outlook Slower than average growth or no change through 2010

Career Path A typical career path can begin at the sales associate or trainee level. Sales force members can be promoted to management, human resources, accounting, or any number of back-office positions.

Manufacturer Retail Stores

Just as the title implies, these retail stores are owned by a manufacturer. The manufacturer might own the store in the mall to sell its products. Consider the Liz Claiborne stores. They sell Liz Claiborne products exclusively. The products might be available elsewhere, but the manufacturer is also selling its own products as a retailer. These stores can also be located at *factory outlet malls*. The stores are known as *factory stores*. They perform the same functions as other manufacturer-owned stores because they sell their own products.

► NATURAL RETAIL People join co-ops to get good prices as well as specialized merchandise. *What is another advantage of belonging to a co-op?*

franchisee person or persons who pay a fee to a company to operate a business under the franchisor's trade name

franchisor a business that leases its trade name and operating system to another person, or franchisee

franchise agreement or contract between the franchisor and franchisee to sell a company's goods or services at a designated location

TECH NOTES

A Franchise for the Birds

Wild Birds Unlimited, a chain of bird-feeding supply stores with more than 300 stores throughout the United States and Canada, offers potential franchise owners a wealth of information through its Web site. Interested parties can request information through an online form, view lists of franchisee support services, and start-up expenses in pop-up windows—and fill out a downloadable application form in Microsoft® Word. A clickable map shows locations of existing stores.

➡ Name two support services offered by this franchisor and see other franchise opportunities through **marketingseries.glencoe.com.**

Franchise Businesses

The franchise system allows a business (the franchisor) to lease its trade name or business system to another business entity (the franchisee). The **franchisee** pays a fee to the **franchisor** when the business is started and pays royalties, or a percentage of profits, after the business is started. An agreement between the franchisor and franchisee states the exact terms of the business operation. The International Franchise Association (IFA) notes that the actual **franchise** is the agreement or contract between the franchisor and franchisee to sell a company's products or services at a designated location. However, the term franchise has become the common name for a business operating under this system.

You probably recognize fast-food franchises, such as McDonald's, Burger King, and Hardee's. Other examples of franchise businesses cover the scope of retail operations, such as maid services and photo processors.

BENEFITS OR DRAWBACKS? Franchising offers many benefits as well as some drawbacks. A franchisee has the immediate benefit of name recognition of the franchisor's brand. The franchisee also receives support and advice from the franchisor. Also, the initial fee to start a franchise business is smaller than the investment needed to start an independent business.

A drawback is that the franchisee is locked into the franchisor's business system. Also, the franchisor must rely on royalty payments and has little control over the particular business operation.

Cooperatives

Cooperatives (also known as co-ops) are stores that are owned by a group of people who sell products only to the people who belong to the cooperative. People interested in a cooperative buy stock in the business and become eligible to participate in the cooperative. Their stock ownership allows them to take part in the management of the cooperative and have buying privileges. Many cooperatives are formed to buy food products.

 marketingseries.glencoe.com

Voluntary Chain Stores

A voluntary chain consists of a group of retail stores that carry similar products. The stores form an association in order to purchase products at better prices than they would pay individually. Each store retains its independence and ownership.

The Independent Grocers Association (IGA) is one example of a voluntary chain. The members of IGA are able to purchase in large quantities, or volume, and pass the savings on to their customers.

Lease Department

Lease departments are usually part of a larger retail operation. A small business makes an agreement with a larger one to rent space within the larger store. The small business may carry expensive items or specialized services that the larger retailer is unable to offer. Some lease departments include beauty salons, fur salons, or fine jewelry departments. This arrangement benefits both retailers.

Lease Dealerships

This type of business ownership occurs when a retail company owns the building and land where a business is located. The land-owning company leases the building and land to a dealer who will run the business. The agreement is that the dealer will purchase products from the company. The dealer agreement also states that the business will

Case Study — PART 2

MORE THAN A "DURABLE" REPUTATION
Continued from Part 1 on page 27

"They had a wonderful niche for a long time, but it's been eclipsed. It's still associated with terrific quality, but not much style." This was one retail analyst's reaction to L.L. Bean's second round of layoffs. With a tough economy, high health-care costs, and competition, this stable company had to make adjustments, such as layoffs and offers of free shipping. By May 2003, L.L. Bean wasn't the only outdoors retailer with growing pains. Competitor Eddie Bauer became a possible retailer for sale. L.L. Bean began to consider buying Bauer's 469 stores—a bold move for a company that took over 80 years to expand outside of the quaint state of Maine.

ANALYZE AND WRITE

1. Do you think L.L. Bean's problems were caused by company mistakes? Why?
2. Explain what L.L. Bean has done to "evolve" and stay in business.

Figure 2.2

Competition and Evolution

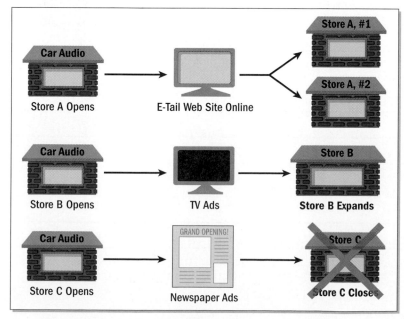

Store A Opens → E-Tail Web Site Online → Store A, #1 / Store A, #2

Store B Opens → TV Ads → Store B Expands

Store C Opens → Newspaper Ads (GRAND OPENING!) → Store C Closes

SURVIVAL OF THE RETAILER
Retailers have always needed to reinvent themselves to stay in business. Many new methods have developed because of competition. *Besides using a Web site, what other methods can retailers use to increase sales?*

MARKETING SERIES *Online*

Remember to check out this book's Web site for retail information and more great resources at **marketingseries.glencoe.com.**

be operated according to the company's business guidelines. For example, many gasoline service stations are owned by oil companies that lease stations to dealers.

Retail Evolution

Just as no rock band or movie is number one on the charts forever, no retailer is the top leader forever. Retailers make every effort to stay on top, but competition is fierce among similar types of retail businesses. This constant competition for the leadership position causes retail evolution. (See **Figure 2.2** on page 41.)

When competitors introduce innovative ideas for doing business, another business owner will quickly follow if the idea is a good one and is adaptable to the business. Retailers are constantly reinventing themselves and how they do business. In this way, retailing is in a constant state of evolution. Retailers are constantly reinventing themselves and how they do business. In this way, retailing is in a constant state of evolution.

Many retailers are using the Internet to increase sales and broaden their customer base. Those same retailers are also using Internet sites, such as eBay, to help them sell merchandise overstocks or past-season merchandise. When a retail store orders or buys more merchandise than it can sell, there are overstocks. In the past, overstocks were discarded at the store, donated to charity, or sold to a jobber. Today, by using the Internet, even a small retailer is able to efficiently sell that merchandise to customers. This is only one example of how retailing is evolving because of technological advances. We can only guess at the changes to come.

QUESTION

What causes retail evolution?

Quick Check ✓

RESPOND to what you've read by answering these questions.

1. What are the three types of business organization? _____

_____

_____

_____

2. What is a franchise? _____

_____

_____

_____

3. How is an independent store different from chain stores? _____

_____

_____

_____

Worksheet 2.1

Your Neighborhood Retailer

Read a copy of your local newspaper and complete this exercise.

Types of Stores

1. List the names of retail stores advertised in the main section of the newspaper. Then identify the type of store for each one, using the NAICS categories.

Name of Store	Category of Store
_____	_____
_____	_____
_____	_____
_____	_____
_____	_____
_____	_____
_____	_____
_____	_____
_____	_____

Types of Ownership

2. Which stores are independent? _____

_____

_____

3. Which stores are chain stores? _____

_____

_____

4. Which stores are franchises (if known)? _____

_____

_____

5. Which type of store is most numerous? _____

_____

_____

Worksheet 2.2

Buying Habits

1. For one week, keep a record of where you shop, what you buy, and how you spend. Ask a friend or family member to do the same.

	Store	**Items Purchased**	**Price**
Monday	_____	_____	_____
	_____	_____	_____
Tuesday	_____	_____	_____
	_____	_____	_____
Wednesday	_____	_____	_____
	_____	_____	_____
Thursday	_____	_____	_____
	_____	_____	_____
Friday	_____	_____	_____
	_____	_____	_____
Saturday	_____	_____	_____
	_____	_____	_____
Sunday	_____	_____	_____
	_____	_____	_____

2. Write a short paragraph. Describe or compare and contrast your buying habits with those of your friend or family member.

_____

_____

_____

_____

_____

_____

_____

_____

_____

_____

_____

Portfolio Works

EXPLORING RETAIL BUSINESSES

Recall experiences you have had as a shopper. Answer these questions to help you determine the type of retail business you might like to explore further. Add this page to your career portfolio.

1. Where is your favorite place to shop? _____

   _____

2. What type of business ownership is it? _____

   _____

3. Does its type of ownership affect your shopping experience? If so, how? If not, why not?

   _____

   _____

   _____

   _____

4. What is your least favorite place to shop? _____

   _____

5. What type of business ownership is it? _____

   _____

6. Does its type of ownership affect your shopping experience? If so, how? If not, why not?

   _____

   _____

   _____

   _____

7. Do you think your shopping experiences could influence your choice of the type of retail business where you would like to work? Why or why not? _____

   _____

   _____

   _____

CHAPTER SUMMARY

Section 2.1 Types of Retailers

NAICS (p. 28)
sales associates (p. 34)
merchandise variety
(p. 35)
merchandise assortment
(p. 35)

- The North American Industry Classification System (NAICS) is a system used to categorize industries on the North American continent. The NAICS classification system uses 12 categories and code numbers for the retail industry. The 12 categories classify retailers by the types of products they sell.

Section 2.2 Types of Retail Ownership

single proprietorship
(p. 36)
partnership (p. 36)
corporation (p. 37)
independent store
(p. 37)
entrepreneur (p. 38)
chain stores (p. 38)
franchisee (p. 40)
franchisor (p. 40)
franchise (p. 40)

- Businesses, including retail, are usually organized as single proprietorships, partnerships, or corporations. A single proprietorship is a business owned by one person, and a partnership is business owned by two or more people. A corporation is based on a corporation charter granted by the state in which the business will be established. The corporation sells stock to investors who become the owners of the corporation.

- Types of retail business ownership include independent stores, chain stores, group stores, manufacturer retail stores, franchise businesses, cooperatives, voluntary chain stores, lease departments, and lease dealerships. An entrepreneur is a person who has the vision and knowledge to start a new business, often an independent store.

- Competition affects retail evolution as retailers seek new ways to compete and attract customers to stay in business.

CHECKING CONCEPTS

1. **Explain** what NAICS means.
2. **Identify** who uses the NAICS and explain what it does.
3. **Name** three of the categories identified by the NAICS.
4. **Define** single proprietorship and partnership.
5. **Compare** the three types of business organization.
6. **Define** entrepreneur.
7. **Explain** the terms franchise, franchisee, and franchisor.

Critical Thinking

8. **Name and describe** two types of retail business ownership other than franchise ownership.

CROSS-CURRICULUM SKILLS

Work-Based Learning

Basic Skills—Writing

9. Imagine you own a retail business and you need only one employee to help you. Consider the qualities you would look for in a worker, and write a classified ad to find that employee.

Interpersonal Skills—Teaching Others

10. Create a chart that explains the three basic types of business organization. Share your chart with another student.

School-Based Learning

Social Studies

11. Draw a map of a nearby shopping area. Name streets and identify the types of retail businesses based on the NAICS classification system (furniture stores are blue; clothing stores are red).

Language Arts

12. Write a radio script to advertise a business in your area and read it to your class. Use information from a newspaper ad.

 **CONNECTION**

Role Play: Toy Store Employee

SITUATION You are to assume the role of an employee of a successful toy store. Your store currently has one location in a suburban area of a mid-sized town. The store's owner (judge) is thinking of expanding to a second store and taking a partner to help with the expansion expenses. The store's owner (judge) knows that you are studying marketing and retailing in high school and has asked you to present a report about the advantages and disadvantages of the proposed business expansion and business partnership.

(ACTIVITY) Present your report to the store's owner (judge) during an informal meeting.

EVALUATION You will be evaluated on how well you meet the following performance indicators:

- Explain the types of business ownership.
- Describe the nature of legally binding contracts.
- Analyze critical banking relationships.
- Use proper grammar and vocabulary.
- Make oral presentations.

 **INTERNET ACTIVITY**

Use the Internet to access the Mrs. Fields Famous Brands Web site and click on Brand and Franchising Information.

- Explain how Mrs. Fields Famous Brands offers corporate support.
- Name two training sessions available to franchisees.

➡️For a link to Mrs. Fields Famous Brands to do this exercise, go to **marketingseries.glencoe.com**.

Chapter 3

Store-Based Retailing

Chapter Objectives

- Identify the types of store-based retailers.
- Explain the importance of service retailers.
- Identify the types of service retailers.

POWER READ

Be an active reader and use these reading strategies:

PREDICT what the section will be about.

CONNECT what you read with your life.

QUESTION as you read to make sure you understand the content.

RESPOND to what you've read.

THE ORIGINAL COFFEE BEAN SPROUTS

In 1963, coffee was referred to as mud, Joe, and even dishwater. Far from exotic, canned coffees like Maxwell House® and Yuban® warmed the cups of millions of office workers and homemakers—and cost about 25 cents a cup at the local diner. But Mona and Herbert Hyman longed for the taste of something richer than "the richest kind." So, the specialty coffee shop Coffee Bean & Tea Leaf® was born in Los Angeles. A loyal following sought its comfortable atmosphere, roasted whole bean coffees from around the world, and enjoyed the first Ice Blended® coffee drinks. These offerings were innovative in the 60s and 70s, and they caught on as the company expanded in a few states.

It wasn't long before competitors woke up to the coffee fad and started brewing for business. Then Starbucks burst on the scene in the 1980s, expanding tremendously in the 1990s. As the world consumed Starbucks, the company took first place among coffee cafés. However, Coffee Bean held on with a modest customer base until a new chapter in its business life began.

ANALYZE AND WRITE

1. What kind of store is Coffee Bean & Tea Leaf?
2. What disadvantages do you think stores like Coffee Bean & Tea Leaf had when Starbucks opened for business?

Case Study Part 2 on page 61

Types of Store-Based Retailers

AS YOU READ ...

YOU WILL LEARN

- To identify the types of store-based retailers

WHY IT'S IMPORTANT

Becoming familiar with the types of store-based retailers allows you to know which retailer will best satisfy a shopping need.

KEY TERMS

- store-based retailer
- general-merchandise retailer
- department store
- junior department store
- specialty store
- discount department store
- variety store
- off-price retailer
- outlet store
- warehouse club
- food retailer
- supermarket
- convenience store
- supercenter

PREDICT

What different kinds of retailers can you name?

store-based retailer a retailer who operates and conducts business from a fixed location

general-merchandise retailer a retailer who sells a large variety of merchandise

Shopping for Retailers

In Chapter 2, you learned about the NAICS categories of retailers, which are determined by the types of merchandise and products that retailers have for sale. This chapter focuses on the types of stores where retailers sell their merchandise

Just as retailers sell merchandise and products from more than one NAICS category, you can purchase the same product from several types of retail stores. If you need new tennis balls, you can find them at your local sporting-goods store. You might also find tennis balls at a department store, a warehouse-club store, or a discount store. Where you end up purchasing your tennis balls will depend on certain factors. If price is your main concern, you will probably decide to buy at a large discount store. If convenience and service are more important to you, then the local sporting-goods store might be the place where you decide to make your purchase because you may receive more personalized service. Different kinds of store-based retailers serve particular customers' needs and wants.

What Are Store-Based Retailers?

A **store-based retailer** operates and conducts business from a fixed location. A store-based retailer opens its doors to walk-in customer traffic. Store-based retailers display merchandise for customers to inspect and purchase. Many stores have beautiful and useful things beckoning so you will enter the store, touch the merchandise, and buy a little of that magic to take home. Retail-store owners hope that you will find their merchandise enticing, so they make every effort to make their stores and merchandise as appealing as possible.

Store-based retailers are still the most prevalent form of retailing. There are many types of store-based retailers. Each of the different types of store-based retailers has distinguishing characteristics. In addition, general-merchandise retailers who operate from fixed locations are not grouped with food retailers.

General-Merchandise Retailers

A **general-merchandise retailer** sells a large variety of merchandise. These retailers also offer different kinds of customer services. The customer service offerings will depend on the type of retailer. We will look at some of the customer services as we discuss each type of store-based retailer.

Department Stores

A **department store** separates various merchandise lines into different departments, or sections. For example, televisions and radios might be in one department, hair products and cosmetics in another, and shoes in yet another. The departments have sales associates assigned to work in the specific departments, which have cash registers and checkout stations. Shopping in a department store can be like shopping in a series of smaller specialty stores under one roof. Department stores sell a variety of merchandise: clothing, furnishings, and accessories. They also sell furniture, housewares, small and/or large appliances, and linens.

Department stores originated in the main shopping areas of large cities. Department stores are usually large establishments that employ many people. They also offer a variety of customer services. It is convenient for customers to use the gift-wrap service or to have appliance purchases delivered directly to their homes. Many department stores also offer personalized services such as alterations, bridal registries, baby-gift registries, and personal shoppers.

BRANCH STORES The popularity and prosperity of a store might lead to the opening of a branch store. A branch store generally sells much the same merchandise as the main, or parent store, only on a smaller scale. Branch-store merchandise is usually tailored to the needs of the customers in the branch store's shopping area. For example, a branch store located in an area with a large population of families with young children will likely carry a large selection of children's clothing and related merchandise.

TWIG STORES Another offshoot of a department store is called a twig store. Like branch stores, twig stores are owned and operated by department stores. As the name implies, twig stores are smaller than branch stores. Twig stores usually sell a limited line of merchandise. An example of a twig store could be one located in the same downtown shopping area as the parent store. The twig store might also be located in an area of office buildings. A twig store might sell career clothing and related accessory items. Some of the accessory merchandise might include business shoes, scarves, and jewelry. Twig stores allow department stores to compete with smaller specialty stores.

CHARACTERISTICS OF COMPETITION Department stores offer a wide selection of merchandise. They also offer the convenience of being able to take care of many shopping needs with one stop. Since every convenience has its price, department-store prices can be somewhat higher than those of other types of retailers. This is because the department-store retailer must pay the salaries of a large staff, finance a large merchandise inventory, and pay the expenses of the services offered by the store. Customers may not appreciate the department store's expenses if they affect their shopping budgets. Therefore, smaller stores and other types of retailers are able to survive and compete against the advantages offered by large department stores—especially if the smaller specialty stores offer good prices and service. Customer loyalty also can give small stores an advantage over large stores that do not offer personalized service.

department store a retailer who separates merchandise into different departments, or sections

Selling Point

MALL STALL
At least 300 older malls (those with one or two anchor stores) have closed since the mid-1990s.

CONNECT
Have you ever purchased an expensive item such as a stereo or computer? Did you research and compare prices and places beforehand?

junior department store a smaller version of a department store that does not carry as many merchandise lines

specialty store a store that sells a limited type of merchandise

Department stores face competition, not only from other department stores but also from the specialty retailers who sell the same or similar merchandise. Department stores have to be creative to meet such fierce competition. Strategies may include having sales, designating a section of the store for lower pricing, including restaurants, and creating designer-specific departments within stores to compete with specialty boutiques.

Macy's is an example of a large department store. In fact, Macy's in New York City claims to be the biggest store in the world! It is also one of the oldest retail establishments.

Junior Department Stores

A **junior department store** also sells more than one line of merchandise. Like their bigger counterparts, junior department stores separate merchandise into departments. Each one has its own sales associates, cash registers, and checkout stands. Unlike a regular department store, however, junior department stores do not carry *all* merchandise lines. Instead, they specialize in just a few. Junior department stores often sell clothing, as well as linens and a limited line of home furnishings. They usually do not carry appliances or furniture.

Junior department stores offer most of the same services as a department store. Junior department stores can specialize in higher-priced merchandise or more moderately priced merchandise, depending on the particular store. Like department stores, junior department store prices are generally somewhat higher than those of other retailers. The reasons are similar: Both kinds of department stores have large staffs to pay and customer services to finance.

Malls usually have at least one or two anchor stores, which are large retail stores that draw customers to the mall. The anchor store will generally be either a department store or a junior department store. Neiman-Marcus and Saks Fifth Avenue are examples of high-end junior department stores.

Specialty Stores

A **specialty store** sells a limited type of merchandise. Many of the small retailers you visit at the mall are specialty retailers: Cartier sells jewelry; Barnes & Noble sells books; and Williams-Sonoma sells kitchenware. A number of specialty retailers sell clothing. Foot Locker is a specialty retailer that offers athletic shoes and some athletic clothing. Many of these merchandise items fall into the clothing and accessories category. Many shoppers prefer the environment of a smaller store that offers a wider variety of one type of merchandise.

Specialty retail stores usually have one cash register and checkout station. They also offer customer services. They will likely be able to mail packages for you and wrap gifts. Specialty stores accept major credit cards and, in some cases, offer their own credit cards.

Apparel specialty stores have been affected by shifts in trends such as older customers buying fewer clothes than do teenagers. Also, casual dress in the workplace has affected apparel sales and the specialty stores that carry more traditional apparel.

Category Specialty Stores

Category specialty stores carry a complete assortment of merchandise at discounted prices. Their offerings can dominate a category and, therefore, draw customers away from department stores by charging lower prices. Circuit City and Toys "R" Us are examples of category specialists.

Discount Department Stores

A **discount department store** sells its merchandise at low prices. This kind of store sells from separate departments. However, individual departments usually do not have sales associates assigned to them to aid customers. Discount department stores are usually self-service and have a centralized checkout area. The checkout area might have several cash registers staffed by cashiers.

Discount retailers are able to sell their merchandise at lower prices, in part because they buy goods in large volumes and, in part, because they do not have to support a large staff. Discount retailers are not as concerned with the ambiance of their shopping environment.

Target is a good example of a discount department store. At Target, you can buy electronics, cameras, clothing, and pet food. Target stores are well-lit and clean, and their merchandise is clearly and openly presented in wide aisles. Target even has scanners in several locations in the store so that customers can check the price of any item. If you are not able to find an item that you need, red phones placed around the store will put you in touch with a sales associate who will help you.

Math Check

THE BEST CHOICE

Hideo would like to buy a new stereo. He sees two ads for stereos in the newspaper. The warehouse store has the model he wants for $115.99. The department store has the same model at $139.00, but all stereos are 20 percent off this week. Which store should he go to for the best deal?

➡ For tips on finding out the solution, go to **marketingseries.glencoe.com**.

discount department store
a department store that sells merchandise at low prices

◀ **IF YOU CAN DREAM IT, BUY IT** Specialty stores concentrate on selling one thing. *What kinds of specialty stores can you name? Can you think of one you might like to see?*

BOOK-STORE SMARTS

Rich Fahle
Director of Creative Services
Borders Group, Inc.

What does your job entail?

"We are the group at Borders that is responsible for creation of all materials, whether it is an ad, an in-store magazine, e-mails sent out to customers, our signs in the store, our billboards, or our catalogs. I also oversee the group that does all the writing and copywriting for ads, signs, and collateral materials. You name it—from brochures to newsletters. We're always super-busy here. I'm always having to find new ways to use my staff effectively. It's a constant challenge to juggle and prioritize the workload without losing sight of the fact that everything we do connects to the customers."

What are your most important skills?

"The ability to communicate and the ability to translate. The role of my entire team is to never lose touch with the customer—and the customer's way of communicating."

What kind of training did you have?

"I came up through the ranks here. I've worked for a number of other companies. I also came up through the journalism ranks as a writer."

What is your key to success?

"Maintaining a high energy level and having a genuine enthusiasm for the work that I do, but also for what I sell. Books, music, and movies are very important to me personally, and I feel a real connection to what I sell."

How is it beneficial to personally use and enjoy the products you sell?

**Career Data:
Director of
Creative Services
for Retail Store**

Education and Training
Degrees in marketing, journalism, and creative arts

Skills and Abilities Language skills, people skills, organizational skills

Career Outlook Faster than average growth through 2010

Career Path A typical career can begin at the sales-floor level and work up. A strong marketing background and/or degree can possibly bypass sales work.

Variety Stores

variety store a small retail outlet that sells a variety of low-priced merchandise

A **variety store** is a retail outlet that sells different kinds of merchandise. These stores usually sell low-priced items including cosmetics, small housewares, souvenirs, postcards, and stationery. These stores are not as common as they once were.

Off-Price Stores

off-price retailer a retailer who buys merchandise directly from the manufacturer and sells it at low prices

This type of store sells merchandise at prices lower that those at department or specialty stores. An **off-price retailer** buys merchandise directly from the manufacturer. They buy end-of-season items, overproduced items, and items returned from other retailers. Ross Stores, Inc., are a well-known off-price retailer. They sell clothing, shoes, and housewares. You will probably see different merchandise each time you visit an off-price retailer. Off-price retailers do not offer other services such as gift wrapping or package delivery.

Outlet Stores

An **outlet store** is usually owned by the manufacturer of the merchandise being sold or a well-known retailer. Outlet stores, also called *factory stores*, sell merchandise that has been produced in too great a quantity, has not been purchased by, or has been returned by other retailers. Examples of the kind of merchandise found at outlet stores include prior-season merchandise, discontinued lines, manufacturer seconds, and slightly irregular items. Prices are lower at outlet stores, but you do not always get the latest styles or the best selection. You do get brand-name merchandise at lower prices. See **Figure 3.1** for a summary of general-merchandise retailers' characteristics.

QUESTION

Are variety stores as plentiful as department stores?

outlet store a manufacturer-owned store, also called a factory store, that sells overproduced or returned merchandise at low prices

---

Figure 3.1

Characteristics of General-Merchandise Retailers

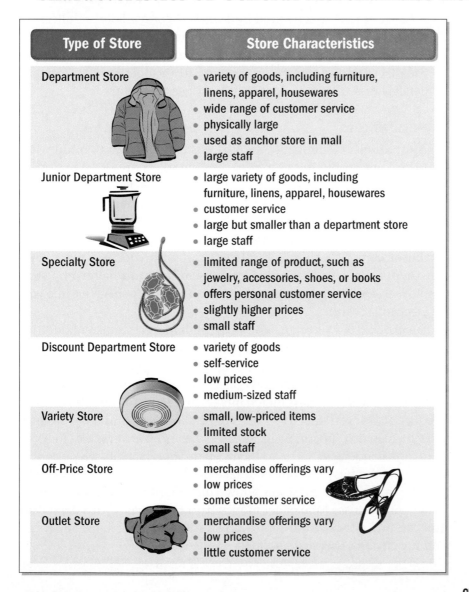

Type of Store	Store Characteristics
Department Store	• variety of goods, including furniture, linens, apparel, housewares • wide range of customer service • physically large • used as anchor store in mall • large staff
Junior Department Store	• large variety of goods, including furniture, linens, apparel, housewares • customer service • large but smaller than a department store • large staff
Specialty Store	• limited range of product, such as jewelry, accessories, shoes, or books • offers personal customer service • slightly higher prices • small staff
Discount Department Store	• variety of goods • self-service • low prices • medium-sized staff
Variety Store	• small, low-priced items • limited stock • small staff
Off-Price Store	• merchandise offerings vary • low prices • some customer service
Outlet Store	• merchandise offerings vary • low prices • little customer service

THE CONSUMER'S CHOICES
There are several places you can go to find goods to purchase. All of these retail establishments have different characteristics. *Why might a business offer more than one type of retailing establishment where customers can go to purchase the same goods?*

warehouse club a large store that offers volume discount prices and minimal variety, presentation, and service

food retailer a retailer who sells food and related goods

supermarket a self-service department store that sells mostly food and other retail merchandise

Warehouse and Wholesale Clubs

A **warehouse club**, or wholesale club, is a very large store that offers volume discount retailing, less variety, and minimal presentation and service. The stores often cover thousands of square feet. You may have to pay a membership fee to join the warehouse club. This type of retailer buys and sells in bulk, or large quantities. They sell electronics, household goods, books, clothing, and food items.

Merchandise selections at warehouse clubs are often inconsistent. If you fail to purchase something you like on one visit, the odds are that the next time you visit, that item probably will no longer be available. A warehouse club does not have a large investment in its building and its decoration, and it does not employ a large staff. For the most part, these clubs are self-service. You walk through the store and help yourself. You then pay at a centralized checkout station and package your own purchases. Warehouse clubs do accept credit cards, but do not usually offer other customer services. This scaled-back merchandising allows these stores to offer goods at lower prices.

Food Retailers

A **food retailer** sells food and related goods. Food retailers are specialized retailers. However, because they are such a large segment of the retail industry, they have a separate category. Think about all the places you can buy food, ranging from supermarkets and convenience stores to drugstores and warehouse clubs.

Supermarkets

A **supermarket** is probably the first place that comes to mind when you think about buying groceries. Supermarkets are the department stores of food retailing. Your local supermarket has departments for different kinds of food. The bakery has its own department, as do the deli, dairy, and produce sections.

Supermarkets have centralized cash registers and are self-service establishments. You go in and fill your cart with your purchases, then put them on the conveyor belt to be scanned and bagged by store employees. Some supermarkets may even have a self-checkout line with an electronic scanner.

Supermarkets will often offer other retail merchandise in addition to traditional grocery items. They have floral departments and pharmacy departments, and offer greeting cards, postage stamps, and magazines. In the past supermarkets carried fewer personal-care products since drugstores and mass merchants earned most of the sales of those products. However, since 1999, sales of personal bath and body products have increased at supermarkets, because they offer lower prices for these items and convenient access to them. Many supermarkets sell precooked meal items for busy customers to take home. Supermarkets take major credit cards, and many stores allow you to write checks for amounts over your purchase total or get money back if you pay with a debit card. You can buy gift certificates or special order unusual items. Supermarkets are customer-service providers, too.

Convenience Stores

A **convenience store** is a retail outlet that sells snack food items such as candy as well as staples like bread. They might also sell household items like light bulbs. It's not unusual for these stores to be open for extended hours, up to 24 hours a day, seven days a week. Many convenience stores, such as 7-11, also offer ready-to-eat foods, such as hot coffee and doughnuts. These stores are usually operated in conjunction with gasoline stations.

Convenience stores are very popular in foreign countries such as Japan and other countries in Asia and Latin America, where people might prefer to buy food in smaller quantities due to limited storage space.

Supercenters

A **supercenter** is a combination of a large discount department store and a discount supermarket. There is a growing trend for supercenters to also sell gasoline. All the departments are housed in the same building and operated by the same company. For instance, a Super Wal-Mart will not only have items you find at a basic Wal-Mart discount department store, but it will also sell food items. Supercenters are housed in large buildings and stock many products. Like a supermarket, a supercenter will separate goods into different departments. However, supercenters will stock some of their grocery items in large sizes or in multiple purchase units. Supercenters provide their customers with the convenience of shopping for discount department store items, such as clothing or appliances, while buying their groceries at the same place. **Figure 3.2** lists some different characteristics of food retailers that operate conventional supermarkets, supercenters, warehouse clubs, and convenience stores.

convenience store a small retail outlet that sells convenience foods as well as staples and household items at higher prices

supercenter a combination of a large discount department store and a discount supermarket

---

Figure 3.2

Characteristics of Food Retailers

NEED AND CONVENIENCE Even though food is a basic necessity, different kinds of food retailers compete for customer business by providing different services, prices, and varieties of products. *Which of these places might you go to in order to purchase food for a large party?*

	Conventional Supermarket	Supercenter	Warehouse Club	Convenience Store
Percentage food	70–90%	30–40%	60%	90%
Size (000 sq. ft.)	20–50	150–220	100–150	2–3
Variety	Average	Broad	Broad	Narrow
Assortment	Average	Deep	Shallow	Shallow
Number of checkout lines	6–10	20–30	10–15	1–2
Prices	Average	Low	Low	High

WAREHOUSE CLUBS AND FOOD Just as supercenters offer discount merchandise as well as food, most warehouse clubs dedicate about half their sales area to food items. You will find canned goods, frozen foods, beverages, and produce available for purchase. The food items are packaged in larger quantities than you would purchase at your local supermarket. If you want to buy olives at your local supermarket, you can purchase an individual can. At the warehouse club, those same olives will be available as a package of four cans. The same is true for other food items. However, you are usually able to purchase sodas by the case and bread by the individual loaf. Costco is an example of a warehouse-club retailer.

A Variety of Stores

As you review the many types of store-based retailers, you will notice that you can purchase some of the same items at any of these stores. The athletic shoes you need for your daily walk are available at any of the stores discussed above. A particular brand may not be available at all the stores, and prices will vary somewhat. However, you will find those shoes at a department store, junior department store, discount specialty store, department store, and even a warehouse-club store. The choice is yours. One thing you can be sure of is that all the stores will be competing for your business.

Quick Check

RESPOND to what you've read by answering these questions.

1. Describe two ways in which a department store differs from a specialty store. _____

_____

_____

_____

2. How is an off-price store different from an outlet store? _____

_____

_____

_____

_____

_____

3. List the four types of food retailers discussed in this section. _____

_____

_____

_____

_____

marketingseries.glencoe.com

Service Retailers

Service and Retailing

A **service retailer** is a retailer who sells something that is intangible or does not last very long. Services are not dependent on something that you can touch, look at, or store to use later. They are used almost as soon as they are provided, and they often depend on a specific learned skill.

Service retailers operate their core businesses from a fixed location just as merchandise retailers do. Like other retailers, service retailers are always tweaking their service offerings. Service retailers have close contact with their customers, or clients. They are always seeking to anticipate their customers' service needs. They have no actual goods to package, so service retailers strive to make their services appealing and attractive to their customers.

Types of Service Retailers

Service retailing includes financial services, personal services, entertainment services, lodging, and repair. Service retailing is a growing segment of the retail industry with its own classifications.

Financial Services

A **financial-services retailer** provides personal services that relate to money or other financial matters. Banks are probably the first financial services provider that comes to mind. They offer extended hours, drive-through banking, and ATMs (automated teller machines) that are accessible 24 hours a day. Any given bank will have an ATM at each branch and at several more locations such as supermarkets. Banks also offer safety deposit boxes, loan offerings, and credit cards.

Other examples of financial-services retailers are credit unions, accounting firms, tax-preparation firms, insurance companies, and stock-brokerage firms. Those companies are retailing-specific services that enhance your financial well-being and make your life easier by saving you time and giving you expert assistance.

Hospitality and Lodging Services

Hospitality and lodging services provide more than just a bed in which to sleep when you are away from home. Hotels, motels, and inns are all different kinds of establishments that provide you with a place to live for one or several days. They also offer services that improve your stay. Many otherwise no-frills motels will still offer rooms with cable TV or kitchenette.

AS YOU READ . . .

YOU WILL LEARN

- To explain the importance of service retailers.
- To identify the types of service retailers.

WHY IT'S IMPORTANT

Service retailing is a growing segment of retailing and provides valuable enhancements to our lives.

KEY TERMS

- service retailer
- financial-services retailer
- hospitality and lodging services
- maintenance and repair-service retailer
- personal services
- recreation and tourism services
- rental services

PREDICT

Name some jobs people your age or younger might have in service retailing.

service retailer a retailer who sells something that is intangible or does not last very long

financial-services retailer a retailer who provides personal financial services

hospitality and lodging services retail services that provide you with a place to live in comfort for one or several days

Hotels and inns offer even more, providing breakfast, dry cleaning, and other conveniences. Many hotels offer guests a gift shop where they can buy snacks, postcards, and toiletries. Most hotels also provide a concierge who is able to suggest local attractions and restaurants.

Campgrounds are another popular place to stay. Many people love to camp, and every year millions of people flock to camp sites throughout the country. While enjoying the out-of-doors, campers are able to rent space at camp sites throughout the country. The simplest camp sites provide just a place to pitch tents. Fancier camp sites have showers, grills, hookups for recreational vehicles (RVs), and other facilities. Camp sites are often on government land, such as national and state parks, but some are on private property.

Maintenance and Repair Services

maintenance and repair-service retailer a retailer who provides services that require special training and/or special equipment

A **maintenance and repair-service retailer** provides services that require special training, special equipment, or both. One maintenance service might be a housecleaning service. The housecleaning company hires the cleaners, trains them, provides the cleaning materials, and provides transportation to the client's home. Clients can make regular appointments to have their service done on a specific day of the week or by appointment. The service provides the additional advantage of having its employees bonded, which keeps the customer free of worry about theft. Other cleaning services might include rug and upholstery cleaners.

Lawn care, landscape maintenance, and pool-service companies are other businesses that provide specialized services for your home or business.

REPAIR SERVICES Repair services require special tools and training. Many repair businesses are small, independent retailers. A watch or jewelry repair specialist has different skills than those of a carpenter who completes repairs to your deck, but both are repair-service providers.

Appliance-repair services are offered at retail stores that sell appliances. Repair technicians often receive special training from the

SHOPPING FOR INTERESTS
People who teach or lead you in a physical activity are providing a specialized service that includes their time, knowledge, and expertise. *What other hobbies or interests can you think of that might require the service of classes or other lessons?*

appliance manufacturer. These technicians are then often called "certified technicians." Customers then have the comfort of knowing that their repairs are performed by someone who is a qualified professional. Other appliance-repair retailers receive general training and are able to repair most brands of appliances. The customer ha the choice of specialized-brand repairs or general-repair providers.

AUTOMOBILE REPAIR Most automobile dealers provide repair services for the automobiles they sell. Auto manufacturers have formal training programs for mechanics to become certified to repair their particular models. For example, General Motors has specialized training programs that certify auto technicians to work on their Oldsmobile automobiles. Completion of the training course allows the mechanic to become a repair specialist. There are also many independent auto-repair shops. Some provide repair service for all types of automobiles, while others might specialize. Again, the customers have the choice of which repair service will best satisfy their needs.

Personal Services

Personal services are services you use to enhance physical or emotional well-being. These services require specialized training. Examples of businesses or individuals who perform personal services include:

- physicians
- opticians
- barbers
- nail technicians
- dance teachers
- dentists
- hairstylists
- massage therapists
- personal photographers
- music teachers

Sewing and clothing alterations are yet another personal service. Embroidery shops are very popular personal-service retailers. The use of specialized equipment allows an embroiderer to quickly personalize clothing and household items. Many companies employ embroiderers to sew their company name or logo on employee shirts or tote bags.

Recreation and Tourism Services

Businesses in the **recreation and tourism services** industry provide leisure activities for their customers. Recreation services might include sports and similar activities that people participate in for fun. Bowling alleys and amusement parks such as Six Flags are some recreation businesses.

Case Study PART 2

THE ORIGINAL COFFEE BEAN SPROUTS

Continued from Part 1 on page 49

Doing steady but modest business in 1995, the Hymans sold some franchises for Coffee Bean & Tea Leaf to the Sassoon brothers, who opened shops in Singapore. The brothers then bought the company and expanded in ten countries.

Though Starbucks has more stores, Coffee Bean focuses on its advantages as it competes for second place. It franchises and owns stores. By contrast, Starbucks does not offer franchises. Franchises allow awareness of local customers, promoting community involvement. Iced drinks, which originated at Coffee Bean & Tea Leaf, account for half the revenue of coffee shops. It has a growing, younger customer base because younger people prefer Coffee Bean's lighter roast. The world drinks 400 billion cups of coffee daily. Thus, Coffee Bean stays in business—even when Starbucks and other coffee shops locate across the street or even next door. Melvin Elias of Coffee Bean & Tea Leaf says that "clustering" of shops in the same area on "coffee rows" proves there is room to grow in this market.

ANALYZE AND WRITE

1. What strategies and advantages have benefited Coffee Bean & Tea Leaf?
2. Could Coffee Bean & Tea Leaf operate as anything other than a store-based retail business? Why or why not?

personal services services you use to enhance physical or emotional well-being

recreation and tourism services a category of the retailing industry that provides leisure activities

Shopping Goes Under

Going down under doesn't always mean traveling to Australia. In Montréal, Canada's largest city, it means a trip to the Underground, a bustling social and commercial complex beneath the city's streets. In a region famous for icy winters and eight-foot snowdrifts, the climate-controlled environment—and more than 1,700 retail venues—provide year-round entertainment. Visitors can shop at trendy boutiques, find the perfect souvenir, catch a movie, or people-watch at one of the many public squares. Nearby cafés entice the tired. Small markets, spacious food courts, and restaurants of every kind feed the hungry.

Around half a million people pass through the city beneath the city each day. Connected by almost 20 miles of walkways, the Underground claims the largest protected pedestrian network in the world. Some say you could wander *and shop* here for days.

Name three benefits of having a retail business in Montréal's Underground.

Movie theaters, live theaters, and concert halls all provide services for recreational enjoyment. A hobby or craft shop can provide the lessons and equipment you need to begin or continue a hobby to enhance your free time.

A travel agent is a tourism services provider. He or she can help you determine a vacation destination, book an airline or rail ticket, secure a hotel room, rent a car, and purchase tickets for sightseeing attractions at your destination. Tour companies, too, provide sightseeing opportunities and transportation.

Rental Services

You've probably rented movies on videotape or DVD. You may have rented a costume or a tuxedo for a special occasion or a limo to go to a dance—or a truck to move. You may even have rented a place to live. **Rental services** provide a way to use hard goods that will have one-time or limited use without having to purchase anything.

Some companies, such as car rental companies, only rent one thing. However, there are rental companies that specialize in general rentals. Those companies rent everything from dishes to power tools. Those services are very convenient if you have a small job to do and you don't wish to purchase what you need. For a reasonable fee, you can rent the equipment for a day or a week. The rental sales associates will even demonstrate how to use the equipment you are renting. Business rental companies will rent office equipment and furniture to fulfill a temporary need. Real estate rentals include homes to rent, apartments, office buildings, and vacation properties. Real estate professionals can use their databanks to find just the right property.

CONNECT

What kind of service retailer might you or your family use once a month? What about once a year?

rental services services that provide a way to use goods without having to purchase anything

Restaurants and Food Services

The area of food service is large and diverse. Think about the different types of restaurants open for business. You might select a fine dining restaurant for a special occasion. You might eat at a casual family restaurant like Chili's for a meal with friends. On the way home from school, you may have a quick bite to eat inside or from the drive-through at a fast-food restaurant such as Taco Bell.

Think about some other places where you can buy prepared food. Convenience stores have coffee and other items available 24 hours a day. More and more supermarkets feature a sandwich counter or a prepared-food section. You can purchase a meal to take home that only has to be heated before eating. The supermarket will also heat the meal for you, if you want. Your school cafeteria is also a type of food-service retailer.

Caterers are also considered food-service retailers. Caterers will deliver freshly prepared meals with all the trimmings to your home, party location, or office. Hotels also provide food service with room service, restaurants, and catering service for parties held in the hotel.

There are a great many choices in the area of food service. You can eat out, you can order food delivered to your home, or you can go out and bring food home. You can choose from an extensive variety of restaurants that serve foods from all over the world. You make choices about food-service retailers almost every day.

QUESTION

Why would a movie theater be an example of service retailing?

Hot Property

Wendy's Old Fashioned Hamburgers®

If you're hungry, where can you go for something fast but good? Hint: You can't find it on the Internet—but you can go into one of 6,000 Wendy's Old Fashioned Hamburgers Restaurants. Treat yourself to a Biggie® Fry, creamy Frosty™, or to one of their trademark, square-shaped burgers with the toppings of your choice. "Quality is our best recipe," boasts the menu, which offers a variety of great-tasting items to satisfy hungry customers.

OPENING THE STORE

As a young boy, Wendy's founder, Dave Thomas, dreamed of owning his own restaurant where families could have fun and enjoy a good meal. In November 1969, at age 35, his dream came true. The first Wendy's Old Fashioned Hamburgers— named for his freckle-faced daughter—opened in Columbus, Ohio. The restaurant, with the homey atmosphere and fresh food, was an immediate

success. A decade later, there were a thousand new openings. To keep customers happy, salads and chicken were introduced for the health minded: a 99-cents selection for the cost conscious, the Classic quarter- and half-pounder for the really hungry, and longer operating hours for the late-nighters. It paid off. Today, with over $66 billion in sales, Wendy's is one of the largest and most famous fast-food enterprises.

Although Thomas passed away in 2002, his commitment to the best—food, service, and people—is still the company standard. Dave's way™ means doing the job right. "You can't clean a floor," he summed up, "with a dirty mop bucket."

1. If you were producing a Wendy's advertisement, what feature of the business would you spotlight first? Why?
2. How do you think Wendy's differs from other fast-food operations?

NOTE: The Wendy's name, design, and logo are registered trademarks of Oldemark, LLC, and are licensed to Wendy's International, Inc.

Security Services

Security-services retailers protect your home, person, and property. They fall into two groups: home security services and personal security services. Home-security services include burglar alarms and home security systems. Home-security systems can be installed while a home is being constructed or into an existing home. Another security service is personal-safety training. Many businesses that offer personal-safety or self-defense training. Security services are found in both big cities and small towns.

Transportation Services

Transportation-services retailers are in the business of moving people or products from one place to another. Transportation companies include airlines, trains, and bus companies. All these companies compete with one another to provide their services to the traveling public. American Airlines and United Airlines might offer competing fares for your next trip to Chicago. On the East Coast, local and national airlines might compete with train service to take you from New York City to Washington, D.C.

Other transportation services include taxis, limousines, and shuttle services. Another area of transportation services is that of moving products from place to place. Air freight, rail, and trucking companies all provide these transportation services.

Service retailers are found in every aspect of our lives. Just like the store-based retailers who sell you products, services retailers are competitive and continually seeking new and better ways to provide for their customers' needs and wants.

Quick Check

RESPOND to what you've read by answering these questions.

1. Name the nine categories of service retailers. _____

_____

_____

_____

2. What are three types of restaurant and food-service retailers? _____

_____

_____

_____

3. How are service retailers like product retailers? _____

_____

_____

_____

Worksheet 3.1

Food Shopping and Variety

Go to four different local stores and complete the following exercise.

A. Choose a Product

Choose a popular food product that comes in a standard amount, such as soda, water, milk, or pasta. Write down up to four brands you find in each store.

Product: _____

Store #1 Brands

_____

_____

_____

_____

Store #2 Brands

_____

_____

_____

_____

Store #3 Brands

_____

_____

_____

_____

Store #4 Brands

_____

_____

_____

_____

B. Compare and Contrast

1. Which store carried the most variety? _____

_____

_____

2. Which store had the item at the least expensive price? _____

_____

_____

_____

3. In which store would you buy this product? _____

_____

_____

_____

Worksheet 3.2

Create a Service Business

Think about a service business you might like to operate. Answer the following questions.

1. What is the service you wish to provide? _____

_____

_____

_____

2. What kinds of customers will your business serve? _____

_____

_____

_____

3. How many employees do you think you should have for your business? _____

_____

_____

_____

4. What method of payment would you prefer from the customers? _____

_____

_____

_____

5. What additional customer services will you offer? _____

_____

_____

_____

6. Write down any potential problems your business idea might have. _____

_____

_____

_____

Portfolio Works

EXPLORING SERVICE RETAILERS

Consider the service retailers discussed in this chapter and identify three careers
that provide a service that interests you. Do the following exercises. Then add this
page to your career portfolio.

1. List the three service careers you chose. _____

_____

_____

_____

2. Use the Internet to explore at least one service career. Describe it. _____

_____

_____

_____

_____

3. List your skills and interests. Then list the service jobs that match these skills and interests.

Skills/Interests   **Possible Jobs**

_____   _____

_____   _____

_____   _____

4. Review your list of skills and interests. What stands out? Think of as many service jobs as you can
that relate to your skills and interests. _____

_____

_____

_____

5. Describe an ideal service job that involves these skills. Include the location of the ideal job and
kinds of coworkers, customers, and employees you would meet. _____

_____

_____

_____

CHAPTER SUMMARY

Section 3.1 Types of Store-Based Retailers

store-based retailer
(p. 50)
general-merchandise
retailer (p. 50)
department store (p. 51)
junior department store
(p. 52)
specialty store (p. 52)
discount department store
(p. 53)

variety store (p. 54)
off-price retailer (p. 54)
outlet store (p. 55)
warehouse club (p. 56)
food retailer (p. 56)
supermarket (p. 56)
convenience store (p. 57)
supercenter (p. 57)

- Store-based retailers include general-merchandise retailers and food retailers. General-merchandise retailers sell a variety of merchandise and services. They include department stores, specialty stores, variety stores, off-price retailers, and outlet stores. Food retailers are specialized retailers, but they are a large segment of the retail industry. They include supermarkets and convenience stores.

Section 3.2 Service Retailers

service retailer (p. 59)
financial-services retailer
(p. 59)
hospitality and lodging
services (p. 59)
maintenance and
repair-service retailer
(p. 60)

personal services (p. 61)
recreation and tourism
services (p. 61)
rental services (p. 62)

- Service retailers operate their businesses from a fixed location and sell things that are intangible. They anticipate their customers' service needs and provide for them.

- Examples of service retailers include financial-services retailers, hospitality and lodging services, maintenance and repair services, personal services, recreation and tourism services, rental services, restaurants and food services, security services, and transportation services.

CHECKING CONCEPTS

1. **Define** store-based retailers.
2. **Describe** what general-merchandise retailers sell.
3. **Name** four examples of general-merchandise retailers.
4. **Identify** three maintenance and repair-service retailers.
5. **Compare** supercenters and warehouse clubs.
6. **Describe** service retailers.
7. **Explain** what the hospitality and lodging industry provides.

Critical Thinking

8. **Explain** why food retailers are categorized separately.

CROSS-CURRICULUM SKILLS

Work-Based Learning

Basic Skills—Reading

9. Use a classified telephone directory to find six different types of store-based retailers. Write the names, addresses, and phone numbers of each business and identify the types of retailers.

Interpersonal Skills—Teaching Others

10. Have students work in pairs to create a poster that describes one of the store-based retailers presented in this chapter.

School-Based Learning

Math

11. One outlet store sells jeans for $45 but offers a buy-one-get-one-free deal. A discount store offers the same jeans for $23 a pair. Which store sells for less?

Family and Consumer Science

12. Using advertising circulars from two different grocery stores, make a chart that compares the prices of six different products. Which store would you choose? Why?

Role Play: Department-Store Employee

SITUATION You are to assume the role of an experienced employee of a large department store. During the course of a conversation with a friend (judge), the topic of retail prices arises. Your friend (judge) asks why prices at department stores are higher than those at discount department stores.

ACTIVITY Explain to your friend (judge) the differences in organization and services provided by department stores and discount department stores.

EVALUATION You will be evaluated on how well you meet the following performance indicators:

- Describe the concept of price.
- Identify factors affecting a business's profit.
- Determine factors affecting business risk.
- Explain the nature of overhead/operating costs.
- Address people properly.

INTERNET ACTIVITY

Use the Internet to find the Old Navy Web site and answer the following questions:

- What type of retailer is Old Navy?
- What is the address of the Old Navy located closest to you?
- Choose one item you might buy at Old Navy and find out its price.

➡For a link to Old Navy to do this activity, go to **marketingseries.glencoe.com**.

Chapter 4

E-Tailing and Non-Store Retailing

Chapter Objectives

- Explain multichannel retailing.
- Explain e-tailing.
- Identify elements to include on a retail Web site.
- Identify the types of non-store retailers.

Be an active reader and use these reading strategies:

PREDICT what the section will be about.

CONNECT what you read with your life.

QUESTION as you read to make sure you understand the content.

RESPOND to what you've read.

dELiA*s—FROM MAILBOX TO MALL

A successful Internet business can sometimes begin as a mail-order catalog business.

The combination of trendy but functional clothing for teenage girls, realistic models, and clever catalog text made the mail-order retailer dELiA*s an instant hit. Thousands of customers began placing orders by phone and by mail. One year after the first catalog was mailed in the fall of 1994, sales reached $5 million. By 1997, sales for the spunky business rocketed to $100 million. Filled with optimism, chairperson/CEO Stephen Kahn exclaimed, "We are going to own this generation," as dELiA*s market expanded to include children's clothing and apparel for guys. Unfortunately, the New York-based corporation's magic seemed to run out as the new products failed to have the same success as the teen girls' market. Making matters worse, dELiA*s competition from copycat catalogs ate into business—and postage costs reduced profits. By 2000, dELiA*s was selling off the unprofitable parts of its business and looking for new ways to succeed.

ANALYZE AND WRITE

1. What advantages might a mail-order catalog have over a brick-and-mortar retail store?
2. Identify possible reasons that dELiA*s business may have weakened after expansion.

Case Study Part 2 on page 79

Channels and E-Tailing

AS YOU READ ...

YOU WILL LEARN

- To explain multichannel retailing.
- To explain e-tailing.
- To identify elements to include on retail Web site.

WHY IT'S IMPORTANT

Multichannel retailing is growing in use and popularity. It allows retailers more opportunities to come into contact with customers. E-tailing is an increasingly important way of doing business.

KEY TERMS

- multichannel retailing
- e-tailing

PREDICT

After quickly scanning this section, name some features on a retail Web site.

multichannel retailing the use of more than one method for reaching customers

Beyond the Store

This chapter will discuss multichannel retailing, e-tailing, and non-store retailing. Those are exciting aspects of the retail industry and ones that are growing in use and popularity with customers worldwide.

Multichannel Retailing

We have already said that retailers are always looking for new and better ways to serve their customers. Retailers also search for ways to attract new customers. One method retailers use to attract new customers is multichannel retailing. **Multichannel retailing** is the use of more than one method for reaching customers. The most common method to reach customers is through the retail store. Additional methods, or channels, for reaching customers include printed catalogs and Web sites. Multichannel retailing is becoming a more common practice and more important to the field of retailing.

J.Crew and Williams-Sonoma are examples of multichannel retailers. Both have retail stores in malls across the nation. Both companies mail printed catalogs to their customers. Both have Web sites where customers can browse and buy day or night. All three channels are important and work with one another.

Channel Advantages

Each channel offers its own advantages. The *retail store*, as a channel, offers customers the opportunity to touch and try the merchandise. Customers can pay for their purchases with a variety of payment options, including cash.

Printed catalogs are convenient. Catalog customers do not have to leave home to shop. Customers can shop at any time during the day or night. There are no store hours to worry about. Catalogs are portable: A customer can shop while riding on the bus to work or on a plane at 30,000 feet in the air.

A *Web site* offers the convenience of shopping at home or wherever there is Internet access. It also offers 24/7 shopping and ordering. By using a Web site, a retailer can reach customers throughout the world.

It is easy to see that using a multiple approach to attract customers is a smart way of doing business—one that offers maximum exposure to new or established customers. Multichannel retailing is a growing trend among retailers of all types.

What Is E-Tailing?

E-tailing is a relatively new concept in the retail industry. The e-tailing segment of retailing is growing and changing with advances in technology. Like retailing, e-tailing is the selling of goods or services to the customer. Unlike retailing, e-tailing takes place electronically in cyberspace—on the Internet. We can then define **e-tailing** as the selling of goods or services to the customer by means of the Internet.

E-tailing involves the selling of products or services from a business to a customer. E-tailing is a part of e-commerce. So that can also include the selling of goods or services from business-to-business, business-to-customer, or customer-to-customer.

E-tailers can have other channels for getting their goods and services to their customers. The e-tailer can have a brick-and-mortar store and might also publish a catalog. An e-tailer can also sell merchandise only from a Web site.

e-tailing the selling of goods or services to the customer by means of the Internet

Why E-Tail?

The decision-making process to become an e-tailer is similar to the decision-making process for any traditional retailer. The retailer must consider all the factors involved in this type of business channel. There are several questions a retailer must answer:

- Will a Web site increase my business?
- How much will the Web site cost to develop?
- How much will the site cost to maintain?
- What information should be included on the business Web site?
- What should the site look like?
- What is required to maintain the Web site?
- How much staff time will be required to maintain the Web site?

The answers to all of these questions must be determined and carefully considered before embarking on the creation of an electronic channel for a retail business.

Another main question to answer is: Why should a retailer begin a new business channel? There are several reasons to create an e-tailing channel for a business. One reason is that an electronic business channel will probably increase the store's customer base. More customers mean more sales, and more sales mean more profit. Another reason is that customers believe that a Web site, or electronic channel, indicates that the store is current or up-to-date. If a retailer does not have a Web site, the business may look behind the times. That perception may affect business if customers feel that the retailer is not as current as it could be.

People of all ages use the Internet. Younger people are an obvious market because of their familiarity with computer technology. Older people may use the Internet when they realize it is a safe and convenient way to shop without leaving home. People of in-between ages use the Internet for all of these reasons and more.

TECH NOTES

Robots Go Shopping

A shopping robot or "bot" is an automated price-comparison tool that allows consumers to find the best deals offered by online retailers. Some bots specialize in finding certain types of products, such as books or cars or prescription drugs, while others cover a wider range of merchandise.

➡How do bots help online retailers? Find the answer to this question after researching information about bots through **marketingseries.glencoe.com**.

BUILDING AN E-TAIL GIANT

Jeff Bezos
Founder and CEO
Amazon.com

In 1994, Jeff Bezos and his wife were on a cross-country trip when they had an idea: to start an electronic bookstore that customers could browse on the Internet. A few years later, Amazon.com became one of the most visited sites on the Web. *Time* magazine named Bezos Person of the Year and said that he "helped build the foundation of our future." Today Amazon carries products in every retail category imaginable.

What kind of training did he have?
Bezos graduated from Princeton in 1986 with a degree in electrical engineering and computer science. He landed at Bankers Trust Company in 1988 and became the firm's youngest vice president.

What is the key to his success?
Amazon and Bezos have created innovations in Internet retailing and marketing. Customers get purchase recommendations based on items they have previously viewed online. The company developed a connection between its online presence and the real world. Customers can order products online and pick them up at stores. Amazon now also fills orders for the online versions of Target and Toys "R" Us.

What does he most like about his job?
"I have the dream job," Bezos told *BusinessWeek* in July of 2002. "There's more innovation ahead of us than behind us. We're not in the Kitty Hawk stage anymore. Maybe we just built the DC-3. The DC-9 isn't even on the drawing board. Nobody has invented the jet engine. There is so much innovation to come. I'm having fun."

Do you think that the future will bring more innovation? Why?

**Career Data:
CEO/Company
Owner**

Education and Training
Bachelor's or master's degree in accounting, economics, finance, business, or company area of interest

Skills and Abilities
Analytical, communication, computer, decision-making, problem-solving, and long-range planning skills

Career Outlook As fast as average growth through 2010

Career Path General
Managers may advance to top executive positions, such as executive vice president or chief executive officer, in their firms, or they may take corresponding positions in other firms.

How does a retailer enter the world of e-tailing? The answer sounds simple and easy to accomplish. The retailer creates a Web site, but before doing so, the retailer must answer those important questions listed earlier. The answers must make business and financial sense. Once the decision is made, a businessperson should answer a few more practical questions before he or she becomes an e-tailer.

Creating a Web Site

The retailer must determine who will design the Web site. A good Web-site designer must be strong in both technical and visual design. There are technical issues involved in creating a Web site so that it will operate efficiently. There are also the design issues. The design should reflect the existing business in a positive way. For a Web-only business, the Web-site design should project a positive image for the business.

In-House or Professional Design

Is it feasible to design the Web site in-house? In other words, should the retailer take on the challenge of designing the Web site within the company? Should a professional Web-site designer be hired instead? The retailer should determine if he or she has the technical knowledge necessary to create a functional Web site. Then the retailer should determine if he or she has the design experience necessary to make the site attractive and inviting as well. If the retailer decides to hire a professional Web-site designer, then the retailer must find one who combines technical and creative talents to create an effective Web site.

Web-Site Address

Once the decision is made to create a Web site, then the retailer must register a Web-site address. The Web address should be one that is as similar to the store's name as possible so customers can find it on the Web. If a professional designer is hired, the designer should register the Web address for the retailer as soon as possible.

Information on the Web Site

Serious consideration should be given to the type of information that is going to appear on the Web site. An effective Web site will give basic information about the store: the store's name, address, phone and fax numbers, hours of operation, directions to get to the store, and an e-mail contact address.

ONLINE CATALOGS In addition to basic information, retailers may want to include an online catalog. A catalog will enable customers to buy from the Web site. If a catalog section is included, then credit-card information must also be provided. Customers will need to know what cards the retailer accepts for payment. The retailer may also consider using a preapproved credit-card or payment system such as PayPal.

OTHER WEB-SITE FEATURES Many retailers also include a "What's New" or a new products section. Other sections that might appear are an "About Us" section that gives a site map, a brief history of the business, and a section for customer comments. Providing customer comments that endorse the company and its products give new customers confidence about the store and shopping there. It's also a good idea to include a section for customers to sign up for e-mail notification of new products, sales, or other promotions. This is an easy way to get the business's name known to customers.

CONNECT

What are two types of payment methods that online retailers use?

LINKS ONLINE FEATURE A retailer can also include a "links" section. *Links* (hyperlinks) are onscreen connections to other Web sites you can get to with one click of a mouse button. Those Web-site links can connect to suppliers and other resources that the store's customers will find helpful and informative. For instance, a retailer who sells fishing equipment in a resort community might include a link to the state's Wildlife and Fisheries Web site, a link to a supplier's Web site about antique fishing lures, or even a link to a Web site that provides information about local weather and water conditions.

The Web Site's Image

What image should the Web site project? When considering the design of a Web site, a retailer with an existing store should have a site that resembles the store and its ambience, or atmosphere. Using the same color scheme and the same style of signage found in the store will give the Web site the store's image. Doing so will create a unified image between the store and the Web site.

If the e-tailer plans to do business from the Web site only, and not open a store, then the design of the Web site should be approached as if the e-tailer were designing an actual store. In other words, give serious consideration to factors like background colors, illustrations, photographs, and fonts. The look of the Web site should be unified and consistent throughout.

The Online Catalog

Selling company products and services from the Web site is a way to increase the business's customer base and attract new customers. The store's online catalog should clearly illustrate the products with color photographs and clear descriptions. This is the best place to provide a lot of product information. It is important to remember that Web

⮞ **VISUAL APPEAL Located in cyberspace, a store's Web site should remind its customers of its actual store on Main Street U.S.A.** *Why do you think a good Web-site design is so important?*

customers cannot touch, smell, or taste the merchandise. They appreciate online information. Providing as much information as possible will help make up for the lack of touch or taste. Customers will read as much or as little as they wish. Online catalogs should also be user-friendly and easy for customers to navigate. By providing links to different departments or categories of items, customers can shop as if they were in a physical store. Again, it is important that the online catalog reflect the image of the brick-and-mortar store.

Filling Online Orders

After attracting customers to a Web site with its great visual appeal, an e-tailer must decide how online orders will be filled. Someone on the store staff must be assigned to check the Web site at regular and frequent intervals for newly placed orders. Depending on the size of the store and Web site "hits," or number of customer visits, this could mean daily or even every hour. The merchandise for those orders has to be pulled from stock, packaged, invoiced, and shipped to the customer. This takes employee power. The staff must be available to work without compromising help to the customers in the retail store. Online orders deserve the same customer attention and prompt service as in-store customers.

Shipping Online Orders

Once a customer order is pulled from stock, the order must be packaged and shipped. When planning the budget for the Web site, an e-tailer must figure the cost of both packaging and shipping to be able to charge customers the appropriate fees.

- **Packaging** is important because it is the first thing the customer sees of a purchase. The packaging should be done carefully and neatly. Packaging is a good way to let customers know they are valued and that the merchandise is valued by the retailer. If the customer's purchase is fragile, then extra precautions must be taken to ensure the safe arrival of the purchase.

- **Shipping** methods should be determined from pre-determined options or simply stated in the online catalog. Customer orders should always be shipped promptly. When a shipment goes out, it is a good idea to notify the customer via e-mail. E-tailers need to fill online orders promptly and ship them just as promptly to get repeat business. It is equally important to notify customers of any delays in filling or shipping their order.

Online Customer Service

What types of customer services will the business offer from the Web site? Will the e-tail store offer to gift wrap purchases or offer express shipments? The e-tailer should post Web-site customer services policies on the Web site.

THE Dot Com SHOP

Navigating the E-Marketplace

How would you narrow down your search if you wanted to purchase something online? eBay is an Internet auction site that allows users to set up their own personal "stores" within one framework—just like a retail mall. Stores can be browsed or sorted by name, category, or type of merchandise—and all items are searchable. eBay users are really able to shop from many different places at once without having to leave the main site.

➡ Do an activity that guides you through setting up and browsing your personal online store through **marketingseries.glencoe.com**.

QUESTION

How quickly should an order be filled online?

Maintaining the Web Site

A retailer should pay close attention to the maintenance of the business's Web site. Retailers want customers to visit their stores often. They also want customers to visit their Web sites often. The smart e-tailer gives the same attention to the appearance of the site as to the appearance of the brick-and-mortar store. If customers see the same, unchanging Web site week after week, they may be disinterested in revisiting the site. They will think they have seen it all. New products should be prominently featured, and the Web site should be updated regularly. This will encourage online customers to visit the site more often. Customers will find more advantages than disadvantages to e-tailing, as outlined in **Figure 4.1**.

This raises the question of who will maintain the Web site. Is the retailer able to do so? An employee? A professional Web-site designer? The store's budget should include the cost of Web-site maintenance. If a professional Web-site designer provides maintenance, then that fee is figured into the store's budget as well. If an employee provides the Web-site maintenance, then that employee's hourly wages are also part of the Web-site budget. This way, the e-tailer can maintain an accurate accounting of the cost of the Web site.

Figure 4.1

E-Tail Advantages and Disadvantages

TO E-TAIL OR NOT? The number-one concern that customers have about buying online is safety. A store's Web site must stress the security of the site before customers will feel comfortable buying online. *What can online retailers do to reassure customers?*

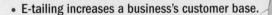
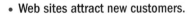

Advantages

- E-tailing increases a business's customer base.
- Web sites attract new customers.
- Customers can shop from their homes.
- A business's online store is never closed.
- Customers can shop 24/7, regardless of weather, traffic jams, or distance from the retail store.
- A well-designed, easy-to-use, and frequently updated Web site is a valuable channel for any business.

Disadvantages

- Customers are reluctant to release personal information on a Web site.
- Customers are concerned about the security of their credit-card accounts.
- Transactions may be interrupted on the Internet.
- Customers are unable to examine merchandise or try on clothing.

---

 marketingseries.glencoe.com

Whether a retailer decides to sell products or services from a Web site, the retailer's Web site should enhance the image of the existing store and its products and services.

Online Malls

Online malls consist of a group of similar e-tailers that form one large Web site. Each Web-site owner pays a fee, based on individual sales, to the online-mall operator. Online malls allow ease of shopping for customers. They provide access to a variety of products without having to go to numerous individual Web sites. For instance, Tias is an online antiques mall. Tias brings together the products of hundreds of antiques dealers nationwide. If you are interested in antique radios, you would go to that section of the Tias Web site and view all the antique radios available, regardless of the dealer to which they belong. As you view the radios that interest you, you can link to the particular dealer's Web site to make your purchase. The benefit to the customer is ease of shopping by viewing many choices at one time. The individual antique dealer benefits from greater exposure to more customers.

E-Tail's Future

With the tremendous growth of e-commerce and e-tailing in just a few years, consumers can expect to see more innovations in shopping and alternative ways of retailing in the 21st century.

Case Study PART 2

dELiA*s—FROM MAILBOX TO MALL

Continued from Part 1 on page 71

After selling the unprofitable parts of its business, dELiA*s decided to set its sights on becoming a multichannel retailer. It introduced a Web site with fashion and entertainment news, community rooms, online ordering, and catalog-request applications. It also opened brick-and-mortar retail stores, hiring former Limited chief Andrea Weiss as president in 2001. dELiA*s used its mail-order experience to determine where its customers live; what brands and styles have succeeded; and how to order and distribute merchandise. The current plan is to translate the style of the popular catalogs into a three-dimensional store. dELiA*s hopes to grow into a brick-and-mortar space without damaging its successful relationship with customers of the original catalog business.

ANALYZE AND WRITE

1. What information about its customers did dELiA*s obtain through mail-order experience?
2. How would having a successful catalog business help a company open stores?

Quick Check

RESPOND to what you've read by answering these questions.

1. Define e-tailing. _____

_____

_____

2. What are two factors that should be considered when determining who will design a store's Web site? _____

_____

3. What is an online mall? _____

_____

_____

Non-Store Retailing

AS YOU READ ...

YOU WILL LEARN

• To identify the types of non-store retailers.

WHY IT'S IMPORTANT

Retail business opportunitites have expanded beyond the walls of brick-and-mortar stores.

KEY TERMS

• non-store retailing
• direct selling
• vending machine
• catalog retailer
• direct mail
• telephone selling
• infomercial
• TV shopping channels
• street vendors

What Is Non-Store Retailing?

We have examined e-tailing, and we know that it is one type of non-store retailing. There are other types of retailing that do not operate out of a traditional store building. **Non-store retailing** is any form of retailing that takes place in areas other than fixed-location stores. Different forms of non-store retailing have advantages and disadvantages. Some types of non-store retailing include:

▪ In-home sales

▪ Vending machines

▪ Catalogs

▪ Internet sales

The U.S. Census Bureau groups these retailers into eight categories as listed in **Figure 4.2**. You will probably recognize examples of non-store retailing in your local community.

Direct Selling

Direct selling is a method of retailing in which a company representative or sales person comes to your home to sell the company's products or services. Direct-sales retailers go to the customer. In-home, party-plan retailers are also included in this type of retailing. Successful in-home sales companies sell products and services that range from home repairs to cosmetics. Such companies include Avon and Mary Kay.

Figure 4.2

Types of Non-Store Retailers

MANY WAYS TO SELL
Technology in the 20th century opened up many new avenues for retailers to reach customers. *Name the types of retailing that originated in the 20th century.*

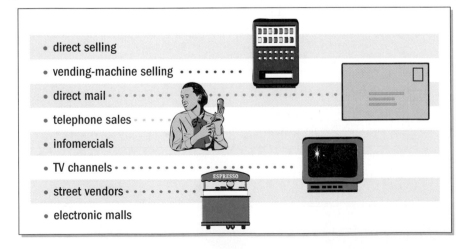

• direct selling
• vending-machine selling
• direct mail
• telephone sales
• infomercials
• TV channels
• street vendors
• electronic malls

World Market

The Well-Traveled Tulip

In the mid-1500s, Turkey introduced the tulip to Europe. The word *tulip* is from a word meaning "turban." The delicate flower became so popular in the Netherlands that it turned into a craze called tulipomania. Tulips became a Dutch national symbol. More than four centuries and almost 2,000 species later, the craze continues today. Everywhere you look in the Netherlands, you see flowers. Indoor and outdoor gardens along the canals display brilliant shades of color. Flower parades, festivals, and markets galore entice garden lovers.

Although most of us are unable to shop first-hand in Holland, cyberspace offers a convenient alternative. You can access the country's online flower shops and find full-color "catalogs" of bulbs for almost every season. Many of the sites also provide "tulip gurus," tips-and-tricks advisors—and even bulb encyclopedias. Although costs may be higher than in the United States, they still do not rival those of the 1630s. At the height of tulip mania centuries ago, for example, one rare bulb sold for more than 20 times a Dutchman's annual salary.

Discuss the advantages of operating an online store.

ROUTE SELLING Route selling is a form of direct selling. A sales associate of a company calls on customers to present and sell the company's products. The sales associate is assigned a regular route and a schedule of times to call on customers. The customer views the products, makes selections, and pays for the products. The route salesperson usually has the company's products available for immediate delivery. The company may provide a printed catalog or online ordering options.

Schwan's is a company that uses route selling as a channel for selling its products. Schwan's sells ice cream and other frozen food products. Schwan's provides a color catalog of all its products to facilitate ordering. A Schwan's customer can order directly from the sales associate by phone appointment. The customer also has the option of placing an order online. The products are delivered by the route sales associate at an agreed upon time. This is a convenient way to buy frozen foods—the food is delivered to your door when you want them. There are many other companies that offer route sales. Route selling is convenient because the shopping comes to you. On the other hand, you have to be home to receive the products.

CONSULTANT SELLING Another type of direct selling is consultant selling, which involves a specially trained consultant. The consultant brings sample products to the customer's home. The consultant discusses and advises the customer. Interior decorators often make consultant calls on customers. Consultant calls allow customers to view sample products in the environment in which they will be used. Consultant sellers may sell products like drapes, floor coverings, and upholstery.

non-store retailing a form of retailing that takes place in areas other than fixed-location stores

direct selling a method of retailing in which a company representative or sales person calls at a customer's home to sell the company's products or services

PREDICT
Name some different ways retailers can sell merchandise besides through a store.

CONNECT
Have you bought merchandise from an in-home consultant?

Math Check

HOME EARNINGS

Yolanda hosted a party for a company that sells decorative candles at home parties. She received a 30 percent discount on all candles as compensation. She bought holiday gifts totaling $362. What amount did she have to pay including 8 percent sales tax?

➡ For tips to find the solution, go to **marketingseries.glencoe.com.**

vending machine a machine that sells merchandise by inserting coins or bills into the machine, pressing a button, and receiving the item being purchased

catalog retailer vendor who sells merchandise through printed or electronic catalogs

HOME-PARTY SELLING Home-party selling happens when a customer invites friends for a party to view products for sale. A sales associate, as a direct seller of the participating company, is present to talk about the company's products, demonstrate them, and take orders from the guests. The host is usually rewarded for sponsoring the party by receiving company products as a gift or products at reduced prices. Sometimes the host is allowed to purchase specially produced merchandise available only to party hosts. This merchandise is available as an incentive for people to host more parties. Tupperware is one well-known example of a company that employs home-party selling.

Vending-Machine Selling

You probably know what vending machines are. To use a **vending machine**, insert coins or bills into the machine, press a button, and receive the item from inside the machine. Vending machines allow a retailer to do business without a sales associate. Vending machines can be located in businesses owned by other people besides the vending-machine owner.

Vending machines sell a wide variety of products from sodas and snacks to newspapers and laundry detergent. Vending machines are convenient and easy to use. Disadvantages of vending machines include breakdowns or running out of products. In either of these cases, the vending machine is out of business until a service representative repairs or refills it.

Catalog Selling

A **catalog retailer** sells merchandise through printed or electronic catalogs. This category includes retailers who use a combination of Internet and mail-order sales. Horchow publishes beautiful color catalogs and mails them to customers' homes. Horchow customers can also visit Horchow.com to view a wide selection of products online. Horchow has no traditional fixed-location store. They sell only from their printed or electronic catalogs.

 marketingseries.glencoe.com

The Great Outdoors Online

The U.S. Outdoor Store, headquartered in Portland, Oregon, has been selling outdoor wares of every description from its retail stores for over 50 years. However, in 1996, this great outdoors store went global when it opened its click-and-mortar doors to international cyberspace.

MERCHANDISE VARIETY

Search the e-tail store by category, keyword, or any one of 200 brand names and find merchandise at your fingertips for "all your snow, water, and land-sport needs." Hikers, campers, skiers, rafters, or simply the sports minded will find high-quality gear and outerwear from stainless-steel cooking utensils and woven beanies in assorted colors to mummy-shaped, goose-down sleeping bags. If it's books that you want, there are a variety of how-to publications, maps, and trail guides to point you in the right direction—and even a collection of spooky campfire stories. The cautious might also want to read *The Ultimate Guide to Wilderness Navigation*, a must for any emergency situation.

THE CUSTOMER IS ALWAYS SERVED

If you don't know the difference between *ascend*, *belay*, and *rappel*, or if you think a *crash pad* is a place to sleep, then talk to a customer rep, just a phone call or e-mail away. In fact, this outdoor online store advises customers to speak with the "people who actually do the sports." One outdoorsman makes a good point when discussing the merits of finding just the right boots to take care of your feet: "Treat them like kings," he says, "because without them, your face would be in the dirt."

1. What do you think are some advantages of shopping online for outdoor equipment?
2. Given a choice, would you rather shop online or visit the store in person? Why?

You can purchase almost anything you need or want from catalogs. Catalogs are convenient and easy to use. You can catalog shop anytime of the day or night, regardless of weather conditions. Many catalog retailers provide free shipping for returns. There is even a Web site for catalogs that lists a huge variety of printed catalogs that customers can request.

Direct-Mail Selling

Direct mail is mail that is delivered to your home. Direct mail is used to sell many different types of merchandise. Direct mail can consist of coupons, flyers describing merchandise or services, letters, or newspaper materials.

Telephone Selling

Telephone selling is a method of retailing in which a company representative telephones your home and makes a sales presentation for a product or service. Telephone sales are used for many types of products and services. You can hire someone to sweep your home's chimney, buy life insurance or a trip just by answering your phone. However, many people find telephone sales by telemarketers annoying and poorly timed, as well as time-consuming. In 2003, a law was enacted forbidding telemarketers from calling anyone listed on a "no call" list.

Selling Point !

EXPANDING CATALOGS
By 2010, 12 percent of all retail sales will occur through catalogs.

direct mail mail delivered to your home to sell merchandise

telephone selling a method of retailing in which a company representative phones a customer's home and makes a sales presentation

Do you think an infomercial influences you more than a regular commercial when you buy a product? Why?

infomercial a long TV commercial advertising merchandise that can be bought by mail order, telephone, online, or in a store

TV shopping channels channels that feature hosts who sell merchandise by describing merchandise as shown on the television screen

street vendors vendors who make their products available from sidewalk locations

Infomercial Selling

An **infomercial** is a long TV commercial advertising merchandise that can be bought by mail order, telephone, online, or even in a store. The sponsoring company purchases time from a television station. The ads usually run late at night when rates are lowest. Infomercials can last from 15 minutes to an hour. The infomercial provides product information and product demonstrations. Infomercials might also feature a celebrity spokesperson. Customers must wait for delivery of their purchases and pay shipping charges.

TV Shopping Channels

There are several television shopping channels, such as QVC and HSN (Home Shopping Network). They offer a variety of merchandise. **TV shopping channels** feature hosts who describe the merchandise shown on the television screen. Items are shown for a pre-determined amount of time. Customers are invited to phone their orders in and pay with credit cards. Purchases are delivered directly to the customer's home. Most television shopping channels operate 24 hours a day.

Street Vendors

Street vendors make their products available from sidewalk locations that might vary from day to day. Street vendors usually sell items for cash that are small and easily portable. Items such as watches, T-shirts, and snack foods are sold by street vendors. These vendors generally do not accept returns and offer no customer services.

Electronic Auctions

Electronic auctions provide sites for customer-to-customer or business-to-customer sales. Electronic auctions use the Internet and sell either new or used products. eBay is a well-known example and is one of the many non-store retailers doing business.

Quick Check

RESPOND to what you've read by answering these questions.

1. What is non-store retailing? _____

_____

_____

2. What are three types of direct selling? _____

_____

_____

3. What are three advantages of vending-machine selling? _____

_____

_____

Worksheet 4.1

Web-Site Plans

1. List five basic features of a good retail Web site.

   _____

   _____

   _____

   _____

   _____

   _____

   _____

   _____

   _____

2. Name three additional Web-site features that are helpful and explain why.

   _____

   _____

   _____

   _____

   _____

   _____

   _____

   _____

   _____

   _____

3. List four e-tail businesses that can benefit from a Web site and think of a name for each one.

   Type of Business   **Name**

   _____   _____

   _____   _____

   _____   _____

   _____   _____

Worksheet 4.2

Multichannel Strategy

1. Name six retail stores located in your area.

   _____

   _____

   _____

   _____

   _____

   _____

2. Which stores have Web sites? _____

   _____

   _____

   _____

   _____

3. Which stores operate e-tail stores? _____

   _____

   _____

   _____

   _____

4. Which stores send catalogs in the mail? _____

   _____

   _____

   _____

   _____

5. Name the stores that have all three channels. _____

   _____

   _____

   _____

   _____

Portfolio Works

THE *OCCUPATIONAL OUTLOOK HANDBOOK* ONLINE

Use the Internet to access the *Occupational Outlook Handbook* at **www.bls.gov/oco/**. Read the information on the home page to find out more about the OOH and use the link to "Tomorrow's Jobs" to identify two occupations you could explore. Then do the following exercises. Add this page to your career portfolio.

1. Describe the purpose of the *OOH* and how you can use it. _____

_____

_____

_____

_____

2. List the two occupations you found at the link "Tomorrow's Jobs." _____

_____

_____

3. Explain why you found those two occupations interesting. _____

_____

_____

_____

_____

4. What skills are needed? How could you acquire those skills? _____

_____

_____

_____

_____

5. Describe how one of those jobs could fit into your future. _____

_____

_____

_____

_____

CHAPTER SUMMARY

Section 4.1 Channels and E-tailing

multichannel retailing
(p. 72)

e-tailing (p. 73)

- Multichannel retailing is the use of more than one method for reaching customers. Those channels include retail stores, printed catalogs, and the Internet. Multichannel retailing allows businesses to serve their customers in new and better ways, which helps to increase sales.

- When businesses sell their products to the customer through the Internet, they are selling through e-tailing. E-tailing allows businesses to increase its customer base and increase sales. However, credit-card security must be stressed.

- An effective retail Web site will have basic information about the business, as well as an online catalog and a new products section. Some other helpful features include links to associated Web sites and a site map.

Section 4.2 Non-Store Retailing

non-store retailing (p. 81)

direct selling (p. 81)

vending machine (p. 82)

catalog retailer (p. 82)

direct mail (p. 83)

telephone selling (p. 83)

infomercial (p. 84)

TV shopping channels
(p. 84)

street vendors (p. 84)

- Non-store retailing is any form of retailing that takes place in areas other than a fixed store location. Types of non-store retailers include direct selling, vending machine selling, catalog selling, direct mail, telephone selling, infomercials, TV shopping channels, and street vendors.

CHECKING CONCEPTS

1. **Define** multichannel retailing.
2. **Name** three methods of direct selling.
3. **Explain** e-tailing.
4. **Identify** the elements of an effective retail Web site.
5. **Explain** one advantage and one disadvantage of e-tailing.
6. **Define** non-store retailing.
7. **Identify** the different types of non-store retailers.

Critical Thinking

8. **Explain** why businesses use multichannel retailing.

CROSS-CURRICULUM SKILLS

Work-Based Learning

Technology—Selecting Technology

9. If you were beginning a business selling jewelry, explain why you would or would not choose e-tailing to sell your products.

Interpersonal Skills—Working With Diversity

10. If your e-tail product line sells especially well in a country other than your own, what might you try to learn about that country? Why?

School-Based Learning

Arts

11. Develop a home page for an e-tail business of your choice. Create a poster by writing the text and drawing and coloring the elements to show how your home page would appear.

History

12. The Internet was developed in the 1960s. Use an encyclopedia to find out who developed the Internet and why.

 **CONNECTION**

Role Play: Retail Shop Employee

SITUATION You are to assume the role of employee of a small needlepoint shop in Honolulu, Hawaii. The store sells hand-painted canvases of beautiful tropical flowers. Local artists paint the canvases. The price for these canvases range between $50 and $100. The canvas with yarns can cost $250 each. The store's customers are residents of Honolulu and tourists. The store's owner (judge) would like to increase sales. The store's owner (judge) has asked you what it would entail to create a Web site for the store, complete with an online catalog.

ACTIVITY You are to make your recommendations about the proposed Web site to the store's owner (judge).

EVALUATION You will be evaluated on how well you meet the following performance indicators:

- Identify ways that technology impacts business.
- Create and post a basic Web page.
- Describe current business trends.
- Handle customer inquiries.
- Make oral presentations.

 **INTERNET ACTIVITY**

Amazon.com is one of the most widely recognized e-tailers today. Use the Internet to answer the following questions:

- Name three products sold at Amazon.com.
- Describe one feature at the Amazon.com homepage.
- Does the Amazon.com home page appeal to you? Why or why not?

➡️ Find a link to Amazon.com to do these exercises through **marketingseries.glencoe.com**.

BusinessWeek News

THE E-BIZ SURPRISE

Since mid-2000, when the stock market slump began turning dot-coms into dot-goners, the popular perception of the Internet has spiraled ever downward. By last year, Internet bankers and analysts, those one-time masters of the business universe, were targets of government investigations. A book titled *dot.con*, deriding the Net as "the greatest story ever sold," became a bestseller. The bold and transforming vision of the Net had dissolved into a digital dud.

To the surprise of many, the Net is actually delivering on many of its supposedly discredited promises. It's now apparent the Internet is connecting far-flung people and businesses more tightly than ever. It is helping companies slash costs. It is speeding the pace of innovation and jacking up productivity. Says Andrew S. Grove, chairman of Intel Corp., "Everything we ever said about the Internet is happening."

Even Internet companies themselves—poster children for business excess during the boom—are finally turning the corner. Of the publicly held Net companies that survived the shakeout, some 40 percent were profitable in the fourth quarter of 2002. Meanwhile, online advertising is staging a comeback, boosting fortunes.

How the heck did all this happen? As it turns out, many consumers and businesses never mistook the over-inflated Internet stocks for the underlying value of the Internet. They kept going online. Says Margaret C. Whitman, chief executive of eBay, Inc., "More consumers are coming online every day."

Still, in the eight years since the Web went commercial, it already has shaken up many industries. Music fans sharing 35 billion song files annually are battering the recording industry. Dot-coms, such as Expedia Inc., now the top leisure-travel agency, online or off—helped shutter 13 percent of traditional travel-agency locations last year.

Further out, bold new projects will unfold, providing a glimpse of the next generation of e-business. The range is every bit as vast as the Internet itself. It features gobs of wireless systems for tracking inventory, reading electric meters, and connecting with customers. Many will find themselves plunked, Oz-like, into new markets and businesses. The journey, after all, is just beginning.

By Timothy J. Mullaney, with Heather Green in New York, Michael Arndt in Chicago, and Robert D. Hof and Linda Himelstein in San Mateo, Calif.

CREATIVE JOURNAL

In your journal, write your responses:

CRITICAL THINKING

1. What are some reasons that some dot-com companies have survived the dot-com shakeup?

APPLICATION

2. Which types of businesses do you think are best suited for doing business on the Web? If you were going to start a business, which business would you choose that could be able to use the Internet successfully?

 Go to **businessweek.com** for current *BusinessWeek* Online articles.

UNIT LAB

The Virtuality Store

You've just entered the real world of retailing. The Virtuality Store offers the latest and most popular consumer goods and services. Acting as the owner, manager, or employee of this store, you will have the opportunity to work on different projects to promote the success of your business.

Turn On the Electric Channel—Add a Web Site

SITUATION You and a silent partner have owned and operated a small electronics store called **Giga Gear** for one year. You started small, catering to tweens, teens, and Gen-Xers by offering the latest Game Boys, Palm Pilots, computer games, XBox, and a small selection of music CDs. You were smart to locate near a high school, but during summer break, sales drop off. However, you've read that CDs, videos, and computer software are the best selling items on the Internet. Not only that, most of your customer base—teens under 18—will total 77 million on the Web by the year 2005. You've thought about expanding into cyberspace, but some companies have flopped. Still, there is potential for your business.

ASSIGNMENT Complete these tasks:
- Plan your basic e-tail store with one or two unique features to attract your customers.
- Estimate your start-up costs including design, shipping, maintenance, and storage.
- Create a final report.

TOOLS AND RESOURCES To complete the assignment, you will need to:
- Conduct research at the library, on the Internet, or by phone.
- Ask other retail stores about experiences with Web sites.
- Have word-processing, spreadsheet, and presentation software.

RESEARCH Do your research:
- Find out the most important characteristics of a retail Web site.
- Go to other similar Web sites and identify and assess their features.
- Get cost estimates for designing and implementing basic Web sites with purchasing features.

REPORT Prepare a written report using the following tools, if available:
- *Word-processing program*: Prepare a written report with a site map outline and list of features, as well as a market overview and customer analysis.
- *Spreadsheet program*: Prepare a chart comparing other competitor Web sites with yours. Prepare a budget chart with your estimates.
- *Presentation program*: Prepare a ten-slide visual presentation with key points, some visuals, and text.

PRESENTATION AND EVALUATION You will present your report to your silent partner and to the bank that may finance your plan. You will be evaluated on the basis of:
- Knowledge of the e-tail Web-site business.
- Continuity of presentation
- Voice quality
- Eye contact

> **PORTFOLIO**
> Add this report to your career portfolio.

UNIT 2

RETAIL BUSINESS STRATEGY

> "You have to recognize when the right place and the right time fuse and take advantage of that opportunity. There are plenty of opportunities out there."
>
> —Ellen Metcalf
> Motivational Writer

UNIT OVERVIEW

Retail stores come in all shapes, sizes, and locations. In this unit we will look at the components necessary for the operation of a retail store. Retailers must make decisions about their stores and their customers. Those decisions make up a retailer's strategy. This unit will discuss retail-strategy decisions and why they are so important.

Chapter 5 focuses on the retail mix, including target-market information. The merchandise-assortment decisions and inventory strategies that retailers consider are examined in Chapter 6. When market strategy and merchandise-planning decisions are made, retailers focus on buying and pricing merchandise, as discussed in Chapter 7. In Chapter 8, you will discover how retailers select locations and sites for their stores.

UNIT LAB Preview
The Virtuality Store

Think about all the retail stores where you shop regularly. How do retailers choose store locations?

These functions are highlighted in this unit:
- Marketing-Information Management
- Product/Service Management
- Financing
- Selling
- Pricing

Chapter 5

Retail Market Strategy

Chapter Objectives

- Explain target markets.
- Discuss market segmentation.
- Explain competitive advantage.
- Describe the types of retail business expenses.
- Explain the importance of business credit.
- Explain types of retail business risks.

POWER READ

Be an active reader and use these reading strategies:

PREDICT what the section will be about.
CONNECT what you read with your life.
QUESTION as you read to make sure you understand the content.
RESPOND to what you've read.

94

MAGAZINE MART

Sometimes a retail store may have had its beginnings as a different business.

Sharika began in the 1990s as an independent online journal featuring African-American poetry, stories, and community and national news. The magazine also highlighted art and history. Then, an e-tail mail-order store developed in association with the e-zine, selling T-shirts, books, jewelry, and related products. Imported wood-carved sculptures, fabrics, paintings, and other unusual items caused the e-tail business to take off. Soon the retail business needed more space. So when a suitable brick-and-mortar store location became available, publisher Aleta Carter obtained a small business loan and leased the space. However, operating a retail store proved to be quite different than creating an online journal. Different laws applied, and handling of purchasing, pricing, inventory, and accounting was not easy for the new retailer. Lack of a planned retail mix and uncontrolled growth threatened to slow down the brisk sales.

ANALYZE AND WRITE

1. What sorts of products might a store such as *Sharika* carry?
2. What challenges did the new retail store face?

Case Study Part 2 on page 105

Retail Strategy

AS YOU READ...

YOU WILL LEARN

- To explain target markets.
- To discuss market segmentation.
- To explain competitive advantage.

WHY IT'S IMPORTANT

Retailers must determine to which customer groups their merchandise and services appeal.

KEY TERMS

- retail mix
- target market
- target-market profile
- market segmentation
- demographics
- psychographics
- geographics
- product mix
- services mix
- competitive advantage

PREDICT

Do you think you are a part of a target market?

retail mix the combination of decisions retailers make to create and operate a store

target market the specific group of people on whom a retailer focuses merchandising and service decisions

target-market profile a description of the target market customers

Retailing, Products, and the Customer

In this chapter, you will learn how retailers determine which customer groups they want to target when planning merchandise and service offerings for their store. You will also find out how retailers determine which products and services to offer. Then you will learn about some of the financial decisions that retailers have to make before opening for business and during every day a store is open for business.

What Is Retail Strategy?

Successful retailers leave little to chance. They plan and make many critical decisions before a store opens for business. The term **retail mix** describes the combination of decisions retailers make to create and operate a retail store. Those decisions involve what kinds of merchandise and services to be offered, the prices to charge, the store location, advertising, displays, sales associates, and other factors that will make them competitive in their market. Retailers target specific customer groups to be the primary focus of their merchandising and promotional efforts.

Target Market

Retailers know that they cannot sell all things to all people. They know they must target their merchandise and service decisions to specific groups of potential customers. When retailers begin the decision-making process, they must first determine who their target market will be. A **target market** is the specific group of people on whom a retailer focuses merchandise and service-offering decisions. Defining a target-market is naming the potential customer. The target-market decision is the most important decision. It affects all the other decisions that come after it. A poorly defined target market will result in inconsistent decisions and poor sales. Retail competition is fierce. Retailers must make merchandise and service decisions that meet the wants and needs of their target market.

Retailers gather as much information as possible about their target market. One way that a retailer can identify characteristics of the target market is to create a target-market profile. The **target-market profile** is a description of the target-market customers. This profile provides information about potential customers that impacts almost all decisions. Retailers spend a lot of money and effort compiling and studying target-market information. Retailers are constantly updating that information in order to stay ahead of their customers' wants and needs.

Good Taste in Retailing

I scream, you scream, we all scream for *gelato*? Italians do, especially in the summer. As the temperature climbs, locals and tourists make their way to the nearest café, kiosk, or pushcart to cool off with a gelato. Italian for "frozen," gelato has a long history. Although recipes differ from region to region, gelato is a low-fat blend of milk and natural ingredients churned to perfection.

From *Gelato di Cioccolata* (chocolate) to *Vaniglia* (vanilla), the Italian ice cream gets rave reviews for intense flavor and creamy texture. It's "like baby food for the angels," gushes one fan. Pure flavorings and fresh fruits—strawberries, peaches, blackberries, lemons, sour cherries—are the best advertisement. One well-known street vendor adds a little suspense to the mix as his marketing strategy. Every afternoon at exactly one o'clock, he unveils his glass display of gelato and reveals the flavors of the day.

If you were marketing gelato in the United States, who would be your target market? Why?

Market Segmentation

Market segmentation is a way of analyzing a market by specific characteristics in order to create a target market. Customer characteristics include the categories of demographics, psychographics, geographics, and product benefits. Those broad categories include information areas, or segments, that provide specific information about customers.

By compiling demographic, psychographic, geographic, and product benefits information, retailers can apply the information when making decisions.

DEMOGRAPHICS Demographics are statistics that describe a population in terms of personal characteristics such as age, gender, income, occupation, education, and ethnic background information.

Imagine the differences in merchandise and services that a retailer would offer to a teenage target market or a target market of older professionals. Income levels tell a retailer how much money customers have to spend. *Discretionary income* is the money customers have left after providing for their basic needs in life—needs such as shelter and food. The amount of discretionary income tells a retailer about how much money customers are likely to spend. A retailer would not sell much high-cost luxury merchandise to customers with low discretionary incomes. Occupational information helps to define likely customer interest in certain products or services. Ethnic group information also helps to define and refine customer interest information.

market segmentation a way of analyzing a market by specific characteristics in order to create a target market

demographics statistics that describe a population in terms of personal characteristics

psychographics studies of consumer lifestyles as reflected in attitudes, interests, and opinions

Selling Point !

→ **CALL ME ISABELLE**
One company has created a segmentation tool called *Cohorts*. It classifies groups of customers with similar characteristics under easily identified personal names such as *Isabelle* or *Ryan*.

geographics information about where customers live

product mix the types of merchandise that a retailer offers for sale

CONNECT

Why might knowing the weather patterns in your town help retailers come up with their product mix?

PSYCHOGRAPHICS Psychographics are studies of consumer lifestyles as reflected in attitudes, interests, and opinions. This information includes ways customers spend their leisure time. Do customers play tennis or do they work on home improvement projects? The answers to those questions create psychographic information.

GEOGRAPHICS Geographics provide information about where customers live. Do customers live in a cool or warm climate? Do customers live in urban, suburban, or rural areas? In what part of town do they live? Geographic information provides the answers. If a retailer is planning to open a children's clothing store, geographic information will be very helpful. Knowing which areas of town have families with children will make a difference in chosing a location.

PRODUCT BENEFITS Marketers study consumers' behaviors, needs, and wants regarding specific products. A company will make different types of vitamins for different age groups with different needs.

Product Mix

Product mix refers to the types of merchandise that a retailer offers for sale. Target-market information applied to product selection will reflect the needs and wants of the customers. That will result in merchandise and product selections that are most likely to satisfy the customer's needs and wants. **Figure 5.1.** gives an example of a product mix.

Figure 5.1

Product Mix

A DAY AT THE BEACH
Different retailers depend on different factors to determine what kinds of products they should offer. *Why might this store have this kind of product mix? What other products might it offer at different times of the year?*

CARIDAD SPORTING GOODS STORE
Miami Beach, Florida

MIXING IT UP **Different stores will offer more or fewer items in their retail mix.** *What kind of a store might have a limited assortment of merchandise in its retail mix?*

Most retail stores carry a variety of merchandise. A clothing store might stock dressy, business, and casual clothing, plus shoes and accessory items. The specific items within each classification are selected to appeal to the store's target market. For example, the target market for one clothing store might be a 25- to 50-year-old professional woman. That store might stock a greater selection of business-type clothing and accessories than a clothing store whose target market is working mothers with young children. The second store might offer a greater selection of casual clothing in easy-to-care-for fabrics.

Services Mix

Target-market information also contributes to the decisions made about the **services mix**, or the number and kinds of services offered by a retail establishment. Customers of most retail establishments expect certain services as a matter of course. Services such as parking, accepting credit cards and checks, and accepting purchase returns are basic services. Other services will depend on the retailer, the type of merchandise and the target-market expectations. Services such as alterations at a clothing store or merchandise delivery and repairs from an appliance store might be good additions to basic services.

Goods and Services Mix

The goods and services mix is the combination of goods and services that are unique to a particular retail establishment. Those combinations are based on information derived from the target-market customer profile. Retailers tailor those offerings to their customers. The combinations might change from time to time as retailers adjust to changing customer wants and needs.

services mix the number and kinds of services offered by a retail establishment

Who's on My Site?

How can online retailers find out who their target markets are when they never see them? Services such as Media Metrix conduct both online and offline research to find out and predict the behavior of online consumers. They combine demographics with user statistics to determine which sites are used by certain types of people and why. With this information, retailers can tailor their sites to appeal to their customers.

➡ For an activity that helps you find out more about specific Internet market segments, go to **marketingseries.glencoe.com**.

competitive advantage an
intangible factor that makes
one retail store more desirable
to customers than its
competitors

QUESTION

What are three factors
that give a retail business
competitive edge?

**KEEPING YOUR
CUSTOMERS HAPPY A
successful business will
keep the same customers
coming back again and
again.** *What kind of a store
might be more dependent
on individual customer
loyalty for financial
success?*

Competitive Advantage

Competitive advantage is that intangible factor that makes one retail establishment more desirable to customers than another. We live in an age of heavy retail competition. Customers are able to purchase the same or similar products at several locations. Competitive advantage can be the extra edge a retailer needs to make the difference between a successful operation and one that struggles to stay in business.

The factors that contribute to a competitive advantage are often difficult to pinpoint. One factor is customer service. Customer service is a major component in building a competitive advantage. Sayings such as "The customer is asking" and "The customer is always right" are based on the fact that customers enjoy special treatment. Making customers feel welcomed and feel valued is a big factor in building a competitive advantage. A friendly atmosphere in a store encourages customers to patronize a retail business.

Attention to detail is another important factor. Details such as impeccable store maintenance, well-presented merchandise, and careful packaging tell customers that not only are they are valuable to the store, but the merchandise is special and valuable, too. That makes customers feel good about their purchases.

Another factor that can give a competitive edge is stocking unusual merchandise or merchandise not found in other competing stores. Unusual merchandise cannot be copied easily by competitors.

Many other factors, such as learning regular customers' names and addressing them by name, that can also make a customer feel special, valued, and welcome. Finding out customer preferences and phoning or e-mailing them to notify them of an item may encourage them to stop in at the store. Customers may appreciate a follow-up phone call or e-mail that determines if the customer is happy with a purchase or if the customer has questions about its use. All of this adds up and helps to create a competitive advantage.

Customer loyalty is another factor in creating a competitive advantage. Customer loyalty means that customers will want to shop at a particular store when the customer wants or needs a product that the store carries. It is easy to understand the advantage that customer loyalty offers a business. Customer loyalty is another intangible that has to be reinforced daily and each time a customer visits the retail business.

MARKETING SERIES *Online*

Remember to check out this book's Web site for retail strategy information and more great resources at **marketingseries.glencoe.com**.

Quick Check ✓

RESPOND to what you've read by answering these questions.

1. Why is determining a target market important? _____

_____

_____

_____

_____

_____

2. What are the four major categories of market segmentation? _____

_____

_____

_____

_____

_____

3. Why is it important for a retailer to develop a competitive advantage? _____

_____

_____

_____

_____

_____

Financial Strategy

AS YOU READ ...

YOU WILL LEARN

- To describe the types of retail business expenses.
- To explain the importance of business credit.
- To explain types of retail business risks.

WHY IT'S IMPORTANT

All retail businesses incur expenses and have risks. It is necessary to know what they are and how to anticipate them to be profitable.

KEY TERMS

- operating expenses
- interest expenses
- cost of goods sold
- profit
- risk
- risk management

PREDICT

What are some business risks?

operating expenses everyday expenses such as rent, office supplies, telephone, salaries, and utilities

interest expenses expenses paid to finance loans a business obtains

cost of goods sold the price a retailer pays for the merchandise that is for sale

Retail Business Expenses

Some of the most important decisions retailers make, besides retail-strategy decisions, concern the finances of the business. It costs money to start a business and to keep a business operating. Retailers make financial decisions concerning merchandise purchases, operating expenses, employee salaries, and much more. You will now learn about some of those financial matters and how they affect a retail business.

Business Expenses

Every business generates expenses before it opens its doors. What kinds of expenses can retailers expect? How will those expenses be paid? Those are questions that retailers must answer. There are three major categories of business expenses: operating expenses, interest expenses, and cost of goods sold.

OPERATING EXPENSES Operating expenses occur each day in the course of doing business. **Operating expenses** are everyday expenses such as rent, office supplies, telephone, Internet access, salaries, and utilities. Operating expenses do not include the cost of the merchandise that the business has for sale.

INTEREST EXPENSES **Interest expenses** are the expenses a retailer pays to finance any loans the business obtains. A retail business can have loans to cover the costs of store fixtures, equipment, merchandise purchases, or the store building.

COST OF GOODS SOLD The **cost of goods sold** is what the retailer pays for the merchandise that is for sale. The cost of goods sold includes the cost of the merchandise as well as any shipping costs for getting the merchandise to the place where it will be sold.

Retail Loans

Most business expenses are paid for by money made through the operation of the business. In other words, revenue from selling merchandise or services covers most business expenses. However, most businesses, at one time or another, have to borrow money. There are various ways for retailers to borrow money.

Most retailers have good relationships with their banks. Banks can help retailers by assisting them with loans to support their businesses. Bank loans can be either long-term loans or short-term loans. Long-term loans are repaid over long periods of time, usually at least five years and up to 30 years, in some cases. Retailers use long-term loans for major purchases like a buying a store building, remodeling an existing building, or obtaining store fixtures or equipment. Short-term loans are usually repaid over 30 days, 60 days, or 90 days.

Short-term loans can help a retailer through times, such as holiday seasons, when merchandise has to be purchased in quantities larger than usual. Short-term loans are also useful for unplanned expenses such as unexpected repairs.

Profiles in Marketing

A LITTLE KNOWLEDGE GOES...

Gregg Ambach
Vice President of Marketing
Analytics, Knowledge Networks

What does your job entail?
"I work with packaged-goods manufacturers, people who are selling merchandise in grocery stores and drugstores. I do statistical analysis of sales data, as well as anything from trying to create forecast models of sales to prediction models. We try to explain what marketing methods are doing for the business. We ask, 'What are you getting for your advertising investment? What are you getting when you print a coupon?' My workload ebbs and flows like anything, but 40 to 50 hours a week is pretty normal."

What skills are most important?
"I'd say being able to translate statistical analyses into a format and language that the typical business consumer can understand. There are lots of people that can do statistics, but they can't explain them to a business audience that's probably not well versed in statistics."

What kind of training did you have?
"I have a master's degree in statistics, and I started in this industry as an intern while I was in graduate school. I've been doing this ever since."

What is your key to success?
"I try to get exposure to as many different things as I can. I try to learn from everybody. I've had a lot of bosses and clients, and I've learned something from every one of them."

Why are good communication skills particularly important for explaining numbers and statistics?

Career Data: Market Researcher

Education and Training
Degrees in statistics, marketing, general business, or language and communication

Skills and Abilities Strong math and analytical skills; good communication abilities

Career Outlook Faster than the average growth through 2010

Career Path Degrees in statistics and marketing are important starting points.

Nutrition in a Cup

Jamba Juice

Jama—it's a West African word meaning "to celebrate". Blending *jama* with fresh juice creates Jamba Juice®, the leader in freshly blended-to-order fruit smoothies. These tasty concoctions of fruit and nonfat yogurt or sorbet are packed with vitamins, minerals, and fiber. Sprinkle in Jamba Boosts, made from combinations of ingredients such as ginseng, ginkgo, or other natural supplements, and you have nutrition in a cup.

Kirk Perron, a serious cyclist and fitness buff, first hit on the business idea in 1990. After vigorous workouts, he would reward himself with a smoothie. Realizing that others might enjoy the same experience, Perron opened his first store in San Luis Obispo, California. Other stores followed, and today millions of patrons are lining up to order smoothies, a variety of juices, and "good-for-you snacks" in over 370 stores across America.

TASTE-TESTED STRATEGY

Perron's philosophy is simple—rely on word of mouth and the best ingredients available. The company philosophy is also simple, reflecting a set of core values: *F.I.B.E.R.*, or Fun, Integrity, Balance, Empowerment, and Respect. At Jamba Juice, no detail is too small, including straws that are actually tested for their "suckability factor." The real test, however, is in the tasting.

Not long ago, one smoothie enthusiast took a "straw poll" to find some of the country's best smoothies. The ratings—1 to 4 straws—were based on factors such as taste and nutrition. Jamba Juice was a 4-straw winner, praised for its "clear fruit flavors" and "lovely consistency."

1. What one marketing strategy has contributed to Jamba Juice's success? Why?
2. Why do you think most Jamba Juice customers buy smoothies—for flavor or nutrition? Explain.

Math Check

RETAIL CULTURE

Alita makes salsa to sell at Peruvian Culture Night at her school. She buys the salsa ingredients for $25.09, and two boxes of containers for $3.29 each. She sells each container of salsa for $3.75. She sells 23 salsa containers. How much profit has she made?

➡ For tips on finding the solution, go to **marketingseries.glencoe.com.**

Business Credit

Credit is important for retailers. Retailers often use credit when making purchases for their businesses. Retailers can purchase merchandise, fixtures, and supplies on credit. Business credit works like consumer credit. The retailer makes a purchase from a supplier. The supplier agrees to wait 30 days or 60 days for payment of the purchase. The use of this type of business credit is often referred to as trade credit.

Many credit-card companies now issue business credit cards in a business's name. Those credit cards can be used like other credit cards to make purchases for the business. It is very important for a retailer to maintain good credit. Just like consumers, retailers must pay their bills as agreed. It is also important for a retail business not to amass a large amount of outstanding credit obligations. Before a credit-card company will give you or a retail business a credit card, the company considers several factors to be sure that you are worth the risk. These factors are the "Five Cs of Credit:"

- Capacity—ability to pay
- Character—reliability
- Credit history—amount of past debt and record of repayment
- Capital—assets owned after debt
- Collateral—property or valuables owned for security

Retail Store Profit

Retailers, like all business people, are in business to make a profit. **Profit** is the money left after expenses are deducted from sales. It can be expressed as a formula: sales−expenses=profit.

Profit is the retailer's reward for running an efficient and effective business. Making a profit is the test of a retailer's ability to make good decisions about all aspects of the business. Businesses must make a profit or they will not stay in business.

Retail Business Risk Management

All businesses must deal with different types of risks. A **risk** is a situation or occurrence that can lead to financial loss for a business.

Dealing with these business risks in a retail setting is called risk management. **Risk management** involves handling business risks in a way that minimizes negative impact on the business while being legal and ethical. It is important for a retailer to be able to recognize sources of possible risks for a business. A retailer can take the necessary steps to eliminate business risks where possible when he or she is able to recognize and identify these risks. It is not possible to eliminate all business risks, so retailers must be able to minimize the impact of those risks on the business.

Types of Business Risks

Business risks fall into three categories:

- Economic risks

- Natural risks

- Human risks

These risks can result in loss of revenue or inventory. **Figure 5.2** on page 106 displays different ways to account for inventory loss.

ECONOMIC RISKS Economic risks result from a downturn, or negative shift, in the nation's economy. During times of economic downturn, retailers must be alert to changes in customer behavior and adjust inventory and expenses accordingly.

Economic risks can also occur when certain types of merchandise or products become obsolete. Retailers must remain current with trends in their industry and with customer buying habits to guard against having their inventory filled with products customers no longer want. The fashion business and technology business are particularly vulnerable to this type of risk because these kinds of products change and evolve so quickly.

Case Study — PART 2

MAGAZINE MART
Continued from Part 1 on page 95

The store *Sharika* had to re-evaluate its retail mix to keep up with its unexpected sales. Steps to improve the store's operation included the installation of a point-of-sale inventory system, hiring a bookkeeper, and employing people with retail experience. As a result, the store became more stable and more successful. After analyzing its target market, strategies for the store's growth included: opening an art gallery on the same block; improving the e-tail store so that it could spotlight new items also carried in the brick-and-mortar store; and developing a community through Internet chat rooms and bulletin boards. The marketing program also included establishing relationships with local schools and charity groups, sponsoring food drives, and children's book readings. Retail growth attracted new e-zine readers, while the magazine promoted the store's image.

ANALYZE AND WRITE

1. What were some solutions to the store's problems?
2. Can you think of some potential risks for this store?

profit the money left after expenses are deducted from sales

risk a situation or occurrence that can lead to financial loss for a business

risk management handling business risks in a way that minimizes negative impact on the business

Figure 5.2

Sources of Inventory Shortages

WHERE DID THAT BAG GO?
Employee-theft incidents outnumber shoplifting incidents. *Why might employee theft result in greater financial loss than shoplifting?*

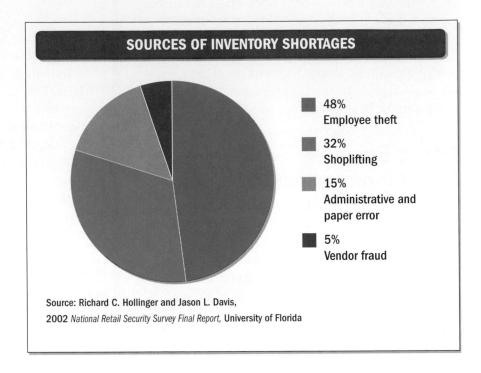

SOURCES OF INVENTORY SHORTAGES

- **48%** Employee theft
- **32%** Shoplifting
- **15%** Administrative and paper error
- **5%** Vendor fraud

Source: Richard C. Hollinger and Jason L. Davis,

2002 *National Retail Security Survey Final Report,* **University of Florida**

CONNECT

Imagine that your home town has been hit by a natural disaster. What impact do you think it would have on local businesses?

NATURAL RISKS The most common natural risks result from natural occurrences such as:

- Hurricanes

- Floods

- Tornadoes

- Earthquakes

- Fires

Retailers are able to protect against natural disasters by buying insurance to protect their buildings, equipment, fixtures, and inventory. Certain kinds of insurance against natural disasters can be very costly. For instance, flood insurance is very expensive in most areas. If an area is identified as a flood zone by the government, property owners may be required to have flood insurance.

Other natural risks that insurance may cover may sometimes be caused by people, but they are considered to be natural risks. Examples include riots, civil unrest, oil or chemical spills, arson, and terrorism and war. Some risks, such as acts of war and any type of civil unrest, may not be covered by typical insurance policies. All of these risks can destroy property and cause businesses to be shut down temporarily or permanently.

HUMAN RISKS People cause *human risks*. Human risks occur in the areas of security and safety. *Security risks* are things like burglary, which can happen if someone breaks into a store and steals or damages merchandise, fixtures, or equipment. Security risks also include theft. Theft falls into two categories:

- Internal theft

- External theft

Internal theft This is also known as employee theft or *employee pilferage*. Dishonest employees can cost a business a great deal of money. In retailing, employee theft can include both the theft of merchandise itself and the theft of cash from the register. Employee theft is often difficult to detect and can go on for a long time before being detected. Retailers should carefully interview potential employees before hiring them. The retailer should also phone employers and check references. While taking these measures will not guarantee the honesty of new hires, they can help screen out some dishonest job applicants.

External theft External theft, or *shoplifting*, is another area for large potential losses. Shoplifting can take the form of customers stealing merchandise. Another form of shoplifting occurs when customers switch price tags. For example, a dishonest customer will switch the price tag of an inexpensive item with one of greater value. The customer then purchases the item at the lower price, and the retailer loses the difference.

Protection Retailers can protect themselves against theft by educating their employees. Training employees to look for suspicious behavior in both customers and other employees is a good strategy. A retailer can also look carefully at the store to make sure there are no blind spots that would allow a thief to be unwatched. Many retailers install mirrors, two-way mirrors, and sensor systems to merchandise. Those items can be costly, but are often worth the cost since they also serve as *deterrents*, or things that prevent shoplifting from occurring. Retailers should always prosecute shoplifters. This, too, will serve as a deterrent.

Retailers also need to be vigilant about dealing with vendors. It is important for a retailer to carefully check incoming merchandise against the merchandise invoice to ensure that all items billed to the retailer have actually been received by the store. While everyone makes mistakes, there are some dishonest vendors, too. Either way, shortages cost the retailer money.

Safety Risks *Safety risks* affect employees and customers. Accidents can happen to either group. Retailers must be diligent in providing a safe environment in which to work or shop. Employee safety training provides instruction about safety procedures and accident prevention. Retail companies that sell perishable products must train their employees in the proper handling and storage of those products. Retail companies that sell potentially harmful products, such as paint or glass products, should also provide employee training for the proper handling of those items.

ETHICAL PRACTICES

Giving Back

Many large-scale retail companies are celebrating their good fortune by giving back to their communities. Every year, employees of the outdoor merchandiser Timberland are able to spend 40 paid hours of their time participating in community service. Nearly 95 percent of Timberland employees take advantage of this program, benefiting over 200 community organizations. Since the program began in 1992, over 200,000 hours of service have been logged worldwide, improving communities in 21 different countries.

QUESTION

Who commits internal theft?

TECH NOTES

An E-Book for Auditors

Audits provide retailers with information about the performance of their businesses. Though audits are often conducted by consultants from outside firms, they can also be done by a manager or business owner using forms and checklists. In 1991, the Small Business Administration (SBA) published "Audit Checklist for Growing Businesses." As a convenience to small business owners, many SBA publications can be read online or downloaded free of charge.

➡️Write a review after reading "Audit Checklist for Growing Businesses" through **marketingseries.glencoe.com**.

Proper store maintenance is another way a retailer can ensure a safe environment. A clean, well organized, and clutter-free store has fewer places for accidents to happen. Retailers must also make sure that the store exterior is safe and free of hazards that might cause a fall or other accidents. In cold climates, store owners and employees must be sure to clear walkways by shoveling snow and clearing ice off the sidewalks. Besides showing concern for customer and employee safety, proper maintenance can prevent costly lawsuits.

If an accident or emergency takes place, it is important that employees have been trained in accident-handling procedures. In cases of serious accidents, employees must be trained on what to do while waiting for paramedics to arrive. Retailers can help protect their businesses from accident claims by buying liability insurance, or insurance that will protect them from any damages that might result because of an accident.

Good Business Management

Creating and running a business involves making many decisions. Retailers make choices about the retail mix and the kinds of financial and product risks they are willing to take in order to be competitive in their market. Businesses must strive to balance the financial needs of the business with the needs and wants of retail customers in order to stay in business and prosper.

Quick Check

RESPOND to what you've read by answering these questions.

1. What are three types of retail business expenses? _____

_____

_____

_____

2. Name two types of loans a retailer might use. _____

_____

_____

_____

3. What are the three categories of business risks? _____

_____

_____

_____

Worksheet 5.1

Market Segmentation

The following is an example of a simple consumer survey questions. This information is used by retailers to determine what kind of products to market to you. Mark which category each question falls into: *demographics*, *psychographics*, *geographics*, and *product benefits*.

	Demographic	Psychographic	Geographic	Product Benefits
1. What is your gender?	_____	_____	_____	_____
2. What is your age?	_____	_____	_____	_____
3. What is your occupation?	_____	_____	_____	_____
4. What is your monthly income?	_____	_____	_____	_____
5. What level of education have you attained?	_____	_____	_____	_____
6. Have you ever purchased anything over the Internet?	_____	_____	_____	_____
7. What are your hobbies?	_____	_____	_____	_____
8. In what kind of activities do you participate?	_____	_____	_____	_____
9. What is your zip code?	_____	_____	_____	_____
10. What kinds of magazines do you read?	_____	_____	_____	_____
11. How many movies do you see per month?	_____	_____	_____	_____

Worksheet 5.2

Spice Up Your Market

Read the scenario below and answer the questions that follow.

You make great guacamole. Whenever you bring it to school, parties, or family gatherings, people ask you for the recipe or tell you that you should sell it. You decide to figure out a way to sell your guacamole at a local farmers' market that takes place once a week.

1. Name some business expenses you might have. _____

   _____

   _____

   _____

2. Guacamole is your core product. What are some other products that you might want to

   add to your product mix? _____

   _____

   _____

   _____

3. What kind of prices will you charge? _____

   _____

   _____

   _____

4. Will you have any special advertising, packaging, or display? _____

   _____

   _____

   _____

5. Who is your target market? _____

   _____

   _____

   _____

6. How many employees will you have? _____

   _____

   _____

   _____

Portfolio Works

EXPLORING JOBS THROUGH THE INTERNET

Many businesses, including retail businesses, post job openings at their Web site. Access the Web site of an interesting retail business that posts job openings and do the following exercises. One good resource is the Retail Companies Web page on the NRF Foundation's Retail Careers and Advancement Web site at **www.nrf.com/RetailCareers**. Add this page to your career portfolio.

1. List three jobs that you found. _____

   _____

   _____

   _____

   _____

2. Choose one that interests you and explain why you find it interesting.

   _____

   _____

   _____

   _____

   _____

3. What qualifications are required? Are they qualifications you have or could have? What would you need to do to become qualified? _____

   _____

   _____

   _____

   _____

   _____

4. Discuss whether you would enjoy this career opportunity and explain why or why not.

   _____

   _____

   _____

   _____

CHAPTER SUMMARY

Section 5.1 Retail Strategy

retail mix (p. 96)
target market (p. 96)
target-market profile
    (p. 96)
market segmentation
    (p. 97)
demographics (p. 97)
psychographics (p. 97)
geographics (p. 98)
product mix (p. 98)
services mix (p. 99)
competitive advantage
    (p. 100)

- A target market is the specific group of people to whom a retailer tailors its merchandising and service-offering decisions. Target-market information helps retailers determine their product mix (type of merchandise for sale) and services mix (number and kinds of services offered). Retailers use target-market profiles to identify characteristics of their target market.

- These customer characteristics are used for market segmentation and include demographics, psychographics, and geographics.

- To have a competitive advantage, businesses may offer special customer services, careful packaging, and unusual merchandise; and learn customers' names and preferences, and develop customer loyalty.

Section 5.2 Financial Strategy

operating expenses
    (p. 102)
interest expenses
    (p. 102)
cost of goods sold
    (p. 102)
profit (p. 105)
risk (p. 105)
risk management
    (p. 105)

- There are three categories of retail business expenses: operating expenses, interest expenses, and the cost of goods sold. Cost of goods sold is what the retailer pays for merchandise to be sold by the store. Profit is the money left after expenses are deducted from sales, or sales−expenses=profit.

- Business credit, also called trade credit, allows retailers to purchase merchandise, fixtures, and supplies now and pay later.

- Risk is a situation or occurrence that can lead to financial loss for a business. Dealing with business risk is called risk management, and it falls into three categories: economic, natural, and human.

CHECKING CONCEPTS

1. **Explain** target markets.
2. **Name** four categories used when describing a business's market segmentation.
3. **Discuss** how retailers determine their product mix and their services mix.
4. **Define** competitive advantage.
5. **Describe** the three categories of retail business expenses.
6. **Explain** the importance of business credit.
7. **Define** profit using a mathematical equation.

Critical Thinking

8. **Name** the three types of business risks. Explain why one risk is more common than the other risks.

CROSS-CURRICULUM SKILLS

Work-Based Learning

Information—Acquiring and Evaluating Information

9. Survey 15 people to find out where they like to shop for music, clothes, and food. Make a chart of your findings.

Thinking Skills—Seeing Things in the Mind's Eye

10. Imagine that you open a bakery in your community. Develop a target-market profile for your business.

School-Based Learning

Language Arts

11. Interview a local business owner. Ask, "How does knowing your target market help you make business decisions?" Write a summary.

Math

12. During March, Terrific Toys had operating expenses of $10,000, interest expenses of $2,000, and cost of goods sold of $14,000. To make a $5,000 profit, how much do sales need to be?

Role Play: Store Employee

SITUATION You are to assume the role of an experienced employee of a successful kitchenware store. The store sells high-end cookware and gourmet food items. It is located in a small shopping center located in an affluent suburb. The local population consists of professional, two-income couples and singles. The store's owner has asked you to orient a new employee (judge) by providing information about the store. During the training, the employee (judge) asks you why the store always has what customers want.

ACTIVITY You must explain to the new employee (judge) about target markets, product mix, and customer service.

EVALUATION You will be evaluated on how well you meet the following performance indicators:

- Select target market.
- Explain the concept of product mix.
- Orient new employees.
- Describe factors used by marketers to position products/businesses.
- Explain the nature of positive customer/client relations.

INTERNET ACTIVITY

Use the Internet to access the National Association for Retail Marketing Services (NARMS).

- Explain whom NARMS represents.
- Describe one feature of the Web site.

➡️For a link to NARMS to answer these questions, go to **marketingseries.glencoe.com**.

Chapter 6

Merchandise Planning

Section 6.1
Merchandise Assortment

Section 6.2
Receiving Goods and Inventory

Chapter Objectives

- Explain merchandise plans.
- Describe the components of a merchandise plan.
- Define merchandise life cycles.
- Explain the receiving process.
- Explain the concept of inventory control.
- Describe inventory systems.
- Explain stock turnover.

POWER READ

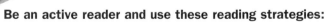

Be an active reader and use these reading strategies:

PREDICT what the section will be about.

CONNECT what you read with your life.

QUESTION as you read to make sure you understand the content.

RESPOND to what you've read.

URBAN RENEWAL

Many retailers develop a reputation for quality merchandise that meets their specific market needs. Home Depot takes pride in its reputation for selling products and services aimed at do-it-yourself consumers. Targeting merchandise to the right market at the right time is just as important for other types of stores, as Urban Outfitters discovered.

Urban Outfitters started out as a small store near the University of Pennsylvania in 1970. Since then its unique mix of used, ethnic, retro, and urban clothing for men and women has helped it expand into a popular chain with over 50 stores in North America, three stores in Europe, and an online store. Offering an eclectic assortment of merchandise, the business gained fans by constantly updating and changing its inventory and being in touch with the changing tastes of its young customers. However, trends can be difficult to predict. For example, when the Philadelphia-based retailer began carrying slick, high-tech fashions, the store found that its merchandise was not moving, and sales were declining. Urban Outfitters suffered another blow when it opened more stores in smaller college towns. The expansion backfired because most students in these college towns return home for the holidays—the most important selling season for a retailer.

ANALYZE AND WRITE

1. Why might it be risky to change inventory?
2. Do you think the store's business would have improved if management had closely watched its inventory? Why?

Case Study Part 2 on page 125

Merchandise Assortment

YOU WILL LEARN

- To explain merchandise plans.
- To describe the components of merchandise plans.
- To define merchandise life cycles.

WHY IT'S IMPORTANT

Merchandise plans enable retailers to make better decisions about merchandise needed to meet sales goals for their businesses.

KEY TERMS

- merchandise plan
- merchandise life cycle
- staple merchandise
- fashion merchandise
- seasonal merchandise
- convenience merchandise
- basic stock list
- model stock list
- never-out list

PREDICT

What do you think a retailer must consider when planning merchandise for a store?

merchandise plan a basic budgeting tool that assists the retailer or buyer in meeting departmental or classification goals

Merchandising Decisions

Before a retailer actually buys any merchandise for a store, he or she must make decisions and plans to make the buying process more efficient. Good planning can help a retailer reach goals, ensuring success for the business. Once a retailer has made decisions about the target market for a business, then decisions can be made about the merchandise that will be carried in a store. A retailer must make these decisions before purchasing any merchandise for the store. There are a number of merchandise choices available to retailers. By studying target market information, a retailer can narrow the choices.

One of the most challenging tasks for a retailer is providing the right merchandise at the right prices—and at the right time. How does a retailer do this? Let's look at some of the decisions about merchandise assortments a retailer must make and tools that will help make those decisions. Section 6.2 of this chapter will examine some of the ways to keep track of merchandise once it arrives at the store and becomes part of the business's inventory.

The Merchandise Plan

Merchandise planning is a method that retailers use to make intelligent decisions before they purchase merchandise for their stores. Depending on the size of the store, merchandise planning is done for the entire store, each department within the store, and then each classification of merchandise within a department. Retailers of all sizes benefit from merchandise planning.

Merchandise planning can be a valuable tool to help prevent retailers from *over-buying* (buying too much of one type of merchandise) as well as *under-buying*. Good merchandise planning also prevents having too much merchandise arrive at the wrong time as well as having too little merchandise to meet customer demand in a particular season.

The **merchandise plan** is a basic budgeting tool that assists the retailer or buyer in meeting department or classification goals. A merchandise plan often uses figures from the previous year to create the plan for the current year. The plan often often includes important information such as planned sales, planned stock, planned reductions, and planned purchases.

A retailer can make merchandise plans for a specific department or for a classification of merchandise. A *merchandise classification* is a group of similar items. Creating merchandise plans by classification will give a retailer more specific information. In a clothing store, classifications can include sweaters, shirts, or trousers. In a sporting-goods store, a classification might be tennis rackets. In a small store, all brands of tennis rackets stocked might be placed in one classification. In a larger store, one major brand might be its own classification. For example, Wilson® tennis rackets might be one classification with several racket styles.

Components of a Merchandise Plan

Most merchandise plans begin with a sales goal for the time period being planned, which is usually six months (see **Figure 6.1**). The next step involves using figures based on sales from the previous year that are broken down by month into their four components:

- **Planned Sales** *Planned sales* are expressed in dollar figures and reflect the sales needed to meet the goal for a particular month.

- **Planned Stock** *Planned stock* is the dollar amount of merchandise that a store needs in order to meet the planned sales goal.

- **Planned Reductions** *Planned reductions* are the dollar amounts of any decrease in the selling price of merchandise. That figure includes markdowns, adjustments, and loss from shoplifting or pilferage.

- **Planned Purchases** *Planned purchases* are the dollar amounts of needed merchandise to meet planned sales goals.

TECH NOTES

Merchandising Software

Retailers use computer software in various ways to develop and use merchandise plans. Some of the tasks that merchandising software performs include preparing forecasts, building assortments, allocating merchandise, and managing categories. Many types of merchandising software can be used online, while other types can be installed directly onto your computer.

➡Review a list of merchandising software and compare the features of each through **marketingseries.glencoe.com**.

Figure 6.1

Six-Month Merchandise Plan

REACHING FOR THE GOAL Many retailers plan on increasing sales by 10 percent over their last year's earnings. Expected reductions are estimated at 5 percent, but may actually be more or less. *What are the total planned purchases for this plan?*

SIX-MONTH MERCHANDISE PLAN								

Fall Season 20____   Department Electronics   No. 83

		August	Sept	Oct	Nov	Dec	Jan 20____	Total
	Last year	82,000	96,000	90,000	100,000	94,000	80,000	
Sales	Plan	90,200	105,600	99,000	110,000	103,400	88,000	
	Actual							
Retail Stock	Last year	328,000	336,000	297,000	360,000	291,400	224,000	
BOM (Beginning	Plan	360,800	369,600	326,700	396,000	320,540	246,400	
of month)	Actual							
	Last year	12,300	14,400	13,500	15,000	14,100	12,000	
Retail Reductions	Plan	11,685	13,680	12,825	14,250	13,395	11,400	
	Actual							
	Last year	N/A	N/A	N/A	N/A	N/A	N/A	
Retail Purchases	Plan	110,685	76,380	181,125	200,530	176,580	135,540	
	Actual							

IN SEARCH OF "NEXT"
Some market researchers target youth groups to keep in touch with the latest trends and fads. Peer-group researchers work all over the world gathering information. *Do you think researchers can help define the merchandise life cycle of a product? Why?*

merchandise life cycle
customer-acceptance levels and buying levels of an item of merchandise

ETHICAL PRACTICES

Kinder Cosmetics

Animal testing in the cosmetics industry has been practiced for many years, but many customers believe it is unethical, and some sales have declined. In June 2002, the European Parliament officially banned the sale of animal-tested cosmetics throughout Europe. This regulation also prohibits any animal testing in the European Union. An estimated 38,000 animals will be spared annually due to the ban.

Merchandise Life Cycles

After creating a merchandise plan, the retailer must consider some other factors that will assist with merchandise assortment planning. First, it is important to understand the concept of merchandise life cycles. The term **merchandise life cycle** refers to customer acceptance levels and buying levels of an item of merchandise, or product. There are four stages in this cycle:

- Introduction

- Growth

- Acceptance

- Decline

Introduction

During this phase of the life cycle, when the product is first introduced, there are few sales made. A limited group of customers, or target group, is buying the product. Customer acceptance cannot be determined yet. The product is available at relatively few locations. A retailer who is considering buying merchandise at this stage of the cycle will want to purchase only small quantities and watch those items carefully to judge customer acceptance.

Growth

The growth phase of the life cycle occurs when customer acceptance of the product begins to grow. Sales increase, and the product is available in more locations. A retailer who buys the product at this stage of the cycle can feel comfortable buying larger quantities.

Acceptance

This stage occurs when there is the greatest customer acceptance of the product. The product is available at many locations and is a consistent seller. At this stage a retailer who buys the product should carefully watch the quantities purchased and also look for early signs of declining sales.

Decline

During the decline stage of the merchandise life cycle, customers are becoming tired of the product. Retailers begin to see sales fall off. If retailers continue to buy the product at this stage, they may need to mark it down.

Merchandise Assortment Planning Tools

Retailers are always looking for ways to improve and refine their purchasing. They study their sales and inventories to find the areas they can improve—and to make certain they have the merchandise to satisfy their customer's needs. One tool or method involves categorizing

CONNECT

Think of a product that is in the decline stage. Does it cost less now than when it was introduced?

Profiles in Marketing

HOME IMPROVEMENT

Rich Victor
General Manager and
Mechanical Engineer
Moody Tools, Inc.

What does your job entail?
"Because our company is small, my job entails a lot. We decide which product lines to focus on, with a view toward the markets we want to approach. What are the growth markets that need small tools? Those are the kinds of things we think about in terms of our product lines. I also oversee all the purchasing, scheduling, and manufacturing. I'd say I'm working about 55–60 hours a week, fairly consistently."

What are your most important skills?
"Being able to visualize and multitask, and to see how everything fits together."

What kind of training did you have?
"I have a bachelor's degree in mechanical engineering. I've worked in quality control disciplines, design engineering, manufacturing supervision, sales, and marketing—I've done a little bit of everything."

What is your key to success?
"I've got a lot of experience and have done a variety of things. That experience lets you view things differently and adjust to changes—which usually come from outside. Big changes don't usually come from inside the company. You try to do your absolute best at everything."

Do you think Moody Tools considers the merchandise life cycle of its products when deciding which tools to make? Why?

Career Data: Product Planner

Education and Training
Associate's or bachelor's degrees in marketing, engineering, and/or business

Skills and Abilities
Knowledge of the specific product and market, language and people skills, ability to multitask, organizational skills

Career Outlook As fast as average growth through 2010

Career Path A typical career path can begin anywhere within an organization, from the frontline sales staff to entry-level management.

QUESTION

Does fashion merchandise sell well year after year? Why?

staple merchandise
merchandise that sells well over a long period of time

fashion merchandise
merchandise that sells well for several seasons but not as long as staple merchandise

seasonal merchandise
merchandise that sells well at certain times of the year

convenience merchandise
merchandise that is purchased by customers without much planning or thought

---

types of merchandise. Many retailers have learned that certain merchandise sells continuously, season after season. Other merchandise sells only at certain times of the year—or by season. Let's look at some of the types of merchandise that retailers stock in their stores.

Types of Merchandise

In-depth knowledge of the types of merchandise that the store carries helps a retailer when planning merchandise purchases. Merchandise can be categorized into four types: staple merchandise, fashion merchandise, seasonal merchandise, and convenience merchandise.

STAPLE MERCHANDISE **Staple merchandise** sells well over a long period of time. For example, in a clothing store, T-shirts are a staple of the summer season, but T-shirts also sell well season after season. There are even certain colors that are popular every year, such as white, black, red, and navy. The popularity of other colors varies from year to year, depending on the year's current fashion colors.

FASHION MERCHANDISE **Fashion merchandise** sells well for several seasons, but not year after year as does staple merchandise. For example, a women's clothing retailer might find that pleated skirts are popular for several seasons. However, after those several seasons, customers begin to lose interest in that style, and another skirt style becomes the big seller.

SEASONAL MERCHANDISE **Seasonal merchandise** sells well at certain times, or seasons, of the year. The most obvious example is holiday decorations. Halloween decorations usually do well in September and October of any year, but they quickly lose popularity and sales after Halloween.

CONVENIENCE MERCHANDISE **Convenience merchandise** is merchandise that customers buy without much planning or thought. Drugstore customers will buy headache remedies when they are in the store. They may not think very much about the purchase and probably won't make a special trip to buy unless they are ill.

Stock Lists

Another tool that retailers use to help plan their purchases is stock lists. No retailer wants to lose a sale. Therefore, many retailers employ stock lists to assist planning and maintenance of their inventories. There are three types of stock lists used by retailers: basic stock list, model stock list, and never-out list.

BASIC STOCK LIST A **basic stock list** is used for items that a store should always keep in stock. A basic stock list is used for staple merchandise. For example, the list for a sporting-goods store might include tennis balls, golf balls, footballs, and soccer balls. The basic stock list is illustrated in **Figure 6.2**. This list also indicates the quantity of the item that a retailer should order when reordering merchandise. Daily monitoring of items on the basic stock list will result in a consistent supply of those items and no lost sales.

Figure 6.2

Basic Stock List Form

ALWAYS AVAILABLE This basic form helps retailers keep their best-selling staple items in stock. *Why should a retailer keep a stock of basic merchandise?*

							Jan Sales		Feb Sales		Mar Sales	
BASIC STOCK LIST FORM												
Stock	**Description**	**Size**	**Packing Units**	**Cost**	**Retail**	**Min. Stock**	**This Year**	**Last Year**	**This Year**	**Last Year**	**This Year**	**Last Year**
202	Reebok Shoes Women's Classic	7	10			2						
203	Reebok Shoes Women's Classic	6	10			1						
204	Nike Shoes Men's Air Jordan	11	10			2						
205	Nike Shoes Men's Air Jordan	10	10			3						

MODEL STOCK LIST The **model stock list** is used for fashion merchandise. Since fashion merchandise is more apt to change than staple merchandise, the model stock list is shorter and does not list style numbers. The model stock list for a girls' department would include fancy dresses, but would not list style numbers because the styles change.

NEVER-OUT LIST The **never-out list** is used for the most popular merchandise in a store. This list changes often. Items are added to or dropped from the list as their popularity increases or decreases.

Using All Resources

By using tools such as stock lists and merchandise plans, and understanding merchandise life cycles and types of merchandise, retailers can make the best decisions about assortments and purchases.

basic stock list list used for items a store should always have in stock

model stock list list used for fashion merchandise

never-out list list used for the most popular merchandise that should always be in stock

Quick Check ✓

RESPOND to what you've read by answering these questions.

1. What are the four components of a merchandise plan? _____

_____

2. Identify the four stages of the merchandise life cycle. _____

_____

3. Name the three types of stock lists. _____

_____

Receiving Goods and Inventory

AS YOU READ ...

YOU WILL LEARN

- To explain the receiving process.
- To explain the concept of inventory control.
- To describe inventory systems.
- To explain stock turnover.

WHY IT'S IMPORTANT

Receiving merchandise properly ensures that the right merchandise and quantities are in stock. Inventory control ensures proper merchandise levels to help a retail business reach its sales goals.

KEY TERMS

- purchase order
- invoice
- inventory
- inventory control
- stock turnover

PREDICT

Name some tasks you think retailers must do when receiving merchandise to prepare it to sell.

purchase order order form that lists the style numbers of the merchandise being purchased, the amount, the delivery date, and terms of purchase

invoice a bill for merchandise

Receiving Merchandise

After a retailer orders merchandise, the merchandise arrives at the store and becomes part of the store's inventory. Inventory is a key factor in the success of a retail business. This inventory must be received, checked in, marked, and handled properly. Those steps are very important to ensure that the merchandise will reach the sales floor in a timely manner and in perfect condition.

The receiving process is a series of steps to deal with incoming merchandise. Proper procedures for receiving merchandise will help ensure that the merchandise ordered is what was received and that the proper quantities have been received. Merchandise purchased for a retail business travels from the vendor, or supplier, to the store, then to the selling area—and from there to the customer. It is important that the flow of merchandise be a smooth and efficient process.

Receiving Area

Most retail businesses have a designated area for receiving and checking in new merchandise arrivals. A large store might have a special building designed to receive new merchandise. A small retail business might use a part of the store's backroom. It doesn't matter where the receiving takes place, as long as the merchandise is properly received. The receiving space is used to perform the receiving process:

- Receive the merchandise.

- Check in the merchandise.

- Mark the merchandise with the selling price.

- Move the merchandise to the selling area of the store to be seen by customers.

Checking-In Merchandise

When retailers purchase merchandise, the purchase is recorded on a purchase order. A **purchase order** is an order form that lists the style numbers of the merchandise being purchased, the amount purchased, the desired delivery date, and possibly the terms of purchase. A copy of the purchase order should be available in the receiving area when the merchandise arrives.

When the vendor prepares the merchandise for shipment, the vendor sends an invoice to the retailer who has ordered the merchandise. An **invoice** is a bill for the merchandise. An invoice has much the same

World Market

South-American Assortment

The famous Ver-o-Peso Market of Belem, Brazil, offers one of the Southern Hemisphere's most exotic shopping experiences. *Vero-o-peso* means "see the weight." This phrase dates back to the time when merchants checked in at a weigh station to weigh merchandise for sale. Located at the mouth of the Amazon River, the open-air market stretches out along the water in a mix of plazas and rambling structures.

Each morning, fishmongers, produce merchants, and peddlers arrive in small boats to prepare an assortment of the region's products for sale. Customers can choose from a variety of fruits and vegetables, fish from the Amazon basin, medicinal herbs, ornamental plants, and fragrant roots to refresh the home. Some stalls display items that may seem unusual to Western tourists, but are familiar to local residents—medical remedies such as crocodile teeth and dried snakes, used to treat health and spiritual conditions. Other stalls might offer amulets, locally made pieces of jewelry or textiles, or bottles filled with potions, oils, and lotions. At Ver-o-Peso, tourists can enjoy learning about Brazilian culture by visiting the market as well as by dining on the local cuisine.

What kind of receiving areas do you think the market stores have?

information as the purchase order. The invoice will list the style numbers of the merchandise, the quantities purchased, the shipping date, and the terms of purchase. When the merchandise arrives at the store, the retailer should match the invoice with the copy of the purchase order. A quick comparison of the two documents should be made. This is done to check that the style numbers and quantities are the same on both the purchase order and the invoice. If the two documents agree, then the merchandise is ready to be checked in.

TYPES OF CHECKING IN The purpose of *checking in* merchandise is to verify that the arriving merchandise is what was ordered and that the merchandise is in good condition. In large retail businesses, specific employees receive and check in merchandise. A small retailer will assign that task to an employee or do the checking in personally. Types of checking-in include:

- Quantity check

- Indirect check

- Quality check

Checking in begins with counting the arriving merchandise by style number. The quantities are then checked against the invoice. This method of checking merchandise is called the *quantity check*. The other two methods of checking in merchandise are the *indirect check* and the *quality check*. The indirect method records the style numbers and quantities, which are later compared to the invoice. The quality check ensures that the merchandise is properly made—and that the merchandise has the same quality as the samples shown to the store's buyer. The buyer usually conducts a quality check.

Marking Merchandise

After new merchandise is received and checked in, it is ready to be marked with its selling price. The selling price is marked on a price ticket. Many retailers use Universal Product Codes (UPC). The UPC codes are recorded on vertical bars that contain information about the merchandise and its price.

Computer scanners that also record sales information can read the UPC codes. Many vendors preticket their merchandise with UPC codes and prices. If a retailer does not use UPC codes, then price tickets must contain information such as style numbers and color codes, and any other information the retailer finds necessary. Price ticket information helps a retailer keep track of which merchandise is selling.

Merchandise Handling

The last and very important step in the receiving process is to move merchandise to the store's selling area. For a large company, this might mean transporting merchandise by truck from a warehouse to the store where it will be sold. For a small retailer, this could mean a trip of a few yards into the next room. It is important for new merchandise to reach the selling area promptly. If merchandise is not in the selling area, it cannot be sold. Remember, selling merchandise is the main goal of a retail business.

FUTURE PRICING
Technology pays in saved time and accuracy for retailers who use digital ticketing devices. *If a retail store's style includes hand-marked price tags, what information should be included on the tag?*

Inventory

Inventory refers to the merchandise that retailers have for sale. That includes merchandise in the selling area; merchandise that has been purchased and is stored for future selling; and merchandise waiting to be returned to the vendor, such as damaged merchandise. Merchandise inventory is a retailer's most important asset, representing close to a third of the total assets for a merchandise store such as Wal-Mart. However, other retailers, such as beauty salons, hotels, and household repair providers, who offer more services, carry very little or no merchandise in their inventories and assess their positions by analyzing factors other than inventory. If a merchandise retailer manages inventory effectively, the store will be successful. Inventory is important because it represents the merchandise available for sale.

Retailers must keep enough inventory on hand to meet customer demand. However, too much merchandise can tie up money that could be spent on new merchandise or used for other business expenses. Retailers do not want to keep more inventory on hand than necessary. Storage space is nonproductive space and is often limited. Retailers also may have to pay tax on inventory they have. Therefore, it is important for inventory levels to be efficiently managed and controlled.

Inventory Control Systems

Retailers of all sizes can make use of technological advances to make their inventory management more efficient. Computer terminals are able to send sales information directly to suppliers, who also use technology to make their shipping more efficient. Retailers can use various methods to control inventory.

Inventory control means managing inventory levels to make sure a store has enough merchandise to meet sales goals without having too much inventory on hand. Inventory control also means accounting for the items in the inventory, merchandise in the selling area, and merchandise that is stored.

- Inventory control can ensure proper merchandise levels to help a retail business reach its sales goals.

- Inventory control helps to balance stock so there is never too much merchandise or too little merchandise for a given period of time.

- Stock turnover information can help retailers compare the efficiency of their business with that of competitors.

Retailers can use either a physical inventory system, a perpetual inventory system, or a combination of both systems.

Case Study — PART 2

URBAN RENEWAL
Continued from Part 1 on page 115

To regain its market and lost customers, Urban Outfitters went back to offering arty, retro styles. It also began opening stores in malls. Although experience with stand-alone shops has helped the store move into suburbia with a proven formula, the new mall locations provide new challenges. For example, it's less expensive to lease and redecorate a mall space than renovate an old industrial location, but the company must now work with landlords and abide by mall rules. Urban Outfitters must operate during mall hours and find ways to benefit from mall promotions and patrons.

The costs and risks will be worthwhile if the store can fill a niche left open by more traditional clothing retailers.

ANALYZE AND WRITE
1. What merchandise-planning decision did Urban Outfitters make to regain sales?
2. How might inventory vary in their mall stores versus the stand-alone stores?

inventory merchandise retailers have for sale

inventory control managing inventory levels to ensure enough merchandise to meet sales goals without having too much inventory on hand

Hot Property

Educational Assortments

Discovery Channel TV viewers who love cable television's Discovery Channel will also be fans of the Discovery Channel Stores. Located in 36 states and Puerto Rico, the chain of about 160 stores is actually a retail spin-off from TV channels that focus on education—Discovery, TLC, Animal Planet, The Travel Channel, Discovery Kids, and Discovery Health. Shows such as *Unsolved History*, *The Crocodile Hunter*, *Discovery Quest*, and *Great Chefs* are only a few examples of the series that make this family of networks a leader in real-world entertainment.

RETAIL ENTERTAINMENT

Combining media and marketing, each store features a unique assortment of more than 2,000 items that reflect programming to help you to "Explore your world and entertain your brain." The Discovery Channel Stores are geared toward children of all ages, as well as their parents.

Customers are encouraged to play with the toys and games *before* they buy. Amateur astronomers will want to try out the telescopes. Nature enthusiasts can browse the rock samples and collection of rubber reptiles. Those who like the water may want to examine the remote underwater Cyber Shark. There are videos of your favorite programs and how-to books that will teach anyone how to make beaded bracelets or put together a working snow machine from a simple household battery.

Before the Discovery Channel, one 20th century critic said, "I find television very educational. The minute somebody turns it on, I go to the library and read a good book." Today he might want to go to the Discovery Channel Store instead.

1. Describe some inventory systems that could be used in a Discovery Channel Store.
2. How would you arrange a large number of items in the Discovery Channel Store—by age, theme, or channel? Explain.

Physical Inventory System

When using physical inventory systems, retailers take a *visual inventory* and physically count the merchandise in their inventories. Counting the merchandise can take place at regular times during the year or annually.

Many retailers take counts of part of their inventory on a rotation basis at regular intervals, such as daily or weekly. By counting portions of the inventory regularly, the entire inventory can be calculated during a given time period. This method of counting inventory is called *tickler control*.

An *annual inventory* counts all the merchandise in a retailer's inventory. During the annual inventory, employees count each item of merchandise by working in teams of two people. One employee counts the merchandise, while the other employee records the count on inventory sheets. After the annual inventory is completed, the value of the merchandise in the inventory is calculated. The retailer reports that amount to the Internal Revenue Service (IRS) for tax purposes and uses it for business financial documents.

CONNECT

How is counting inventory for a store similar to keeping track of a checkbook balance?

Perpetual Inventory System

When using a *perpetual inventory system*, retailers keep track of merchandise that is received and sold on a daily basis. Perpetual inventories can make use of point-of-sale register terminals or by manual means. Point-of-sale terminals use a scanner to record sales information. Each day the retailer is able to review sales information to monitor items that are selling well and those that are not.

The manual system of perpetual inventory is more time-consuming and less accurate than the computer system. An employee makes manual entries into an inventory record log. Recorded information includes merchandise that is sold and merchandise that is received into the inventory.

Many retailers use a combination of both the physical and perpetual inventory control systems—using the best of both methods. The perpetual inventory system provides the daily inventory information a retailer needs, and the physical inventory system provides an accurate annual count of the inventory. Retailers can also cross-check the information from the physical inventory and the perpetual inventory to correct figures, if necessary.

Stock Turnover

Checking stock turnover is another way to assess retail-inventory management. **Stock turnover** is the number of times the average inventory is sold during a time period, which is usually a year. A high stock-turnover rate means that the stock is selling quickly. A low stock-turnover rate means that the stock is selling more slowly. Retailers use stock-turnover rates to compare their business to their competition's business. Stock-turnover rates can be figured for an entire store or for one department or classification within the store.

Stock-turnover rates are calculated in units of merchandise or in dollars. These formulas calculate stock turnover:

$$\text{Stock turnover in } \textbf{units} = \frac{\text{Number of units sold}}{\text{Average number of units of stock on hand}}$$

$$\text{Stock turnover in } \textbf{dollars} = \frac{\text{Dollar sales of merchandise}}{\text{Average dollar value of merchandise on hand}}$$

The best stock-turnover rates vary depending on the type of store. Fine jewelry stores usually have lower stock-turnover rates than those of convenience stores.

Retailers like to have a high stock-turnover rate. That means that business is operating efficiently. A high rate provides the advantage of high sales volume, along with the ability to purchase new merchandise without spending more than the budget allows. Employees like a high rate because it means that they are busy. However, retailers must avoid a stock-turnover rate that is *too* high. An extremely high rate can mean there is not enough merchandise available to meet the planned sales goals, or that certain merchandise is out of stock, resulting in back orders.

Math Check

TURNING IT OVER

Thahn's watch store just celebrated one year in business. Thahn wants to know the stock-turnover rate for six months to check his progress. Over 12 months, his sales totaled $156,000. His average inventory on hand totaled $68,000. What was the rate?

➡ For tips on finding the solution, go to **marketingseries.glencoe.com.**

stock turnover the number of times the average inventory is sold during a time period, usually a year

QUESTION

What does a very high stock-turnover rate mean for a business?

Using Inventory Methods

Receiving and controlling merchandise properly ensures that the right merchandise and quantities are in stock. By understanding and applying the resources and tools that are available, such as inventory control systems and merchandise handling, retailers can reach sales goals.

Quick Check ✓

RESPOND to what you've read by answering these questions.

1. What are the four steps in the merchandise receiving process? _____

_____

_____

_____

_____

_____

2. What are two types of inventory control methods? _____

_____

_____

_____

_____

_____

_____

3. Why is stock turnover important? _____

_____

_____

_____

_____

_____

_____

_____

_____

Worksheet 6.1

Taking Inventory

You work after school in the office and school supply department of a drugstore. You've just counted merchandise in stock. Fill in the form below and calculate the total retail value of the inventory.

School Store _____

INVENTORY FORM

Date _____ 20 ___   Counted by _____

Page Number _____   Checked by _____

Description of Merchandise	Units on Hand	Unit Price		Total Retail Value	
backpacks	15	$29	.99		
spiral notebooks	30	4	.79		
notebook paper	38	3	.59		
erasers	60		.29		
pencils	100		.25		
medium-point pens	45		.89		
fine-point pens	51		.89		
printer paper (250 ct.)	10	6	.49		
ink cartridges	10	22	.95		
posterboard (white)	15		.59		
posterboard (colored)	10		.79		
protractors	5	2	.19		
rulers (6")	6		.39		
rulers (12")	12		.79		
pocket calendars	15	4	.95		
Total Retail Value					

Worksheet 6.2

Merchandise Planning Crossword

Complete the crossword puzzle using key terms from the chapter.

ACROSS

1. merchandise that sells well at certain times of the year
3. merchandise that sells well over a long period of time
4. form that lists the style numbers of the merchandise being purchased, the amount, the delivery date, and terms of the purchase
6. merchandise that sells well for several seasons but not as long as staple merchandise
7. bill for merchandise
11. merchandise that retailers have for sale

DOWN

2. list used for fashion merchandise
5. a basic budgeting tool used to assist the retailer or buyer to meet departmental or classification goals
8. list used for the most popular merchandise that should always be in stock
9. merchandise that is purchased by customers without much planning or thought on their part
10. list used for items a store should always have in stock
12. the number of times the average inventory is sold during a time period, usually a year

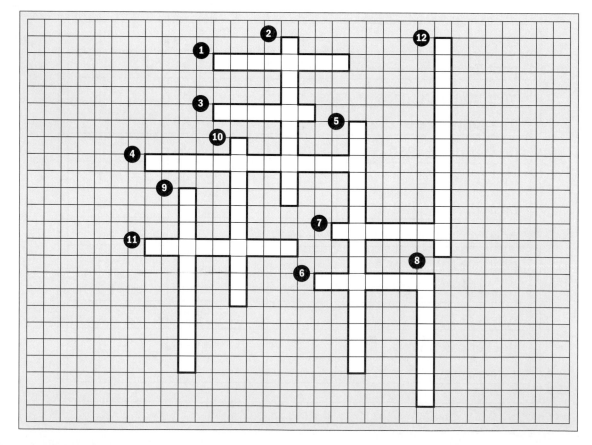

Portfolio Works

EXPLORING CAREERS IN RESOURCE MANAGEMENT

Trade organizations may list career and networking opportunities through their Web sites. Use the Internet to access a retail trade organization of your choice. Do the following exercise. Then add this page to your career portfolio.

1. What is the name and URL of the trade organization you found? _____

_____

_____

_____

2. What steps do you need to take to access career information? _____

_____

_____

_____

3. What jobs are currently available? _____

_____

_____

_____

4. Choose a job to research further and tell what you learned. _____

_____

_____

_____

5. What qualifications are necessary? _____

_____

_____

_____

6. Would you be interested in pursuing this type of career further? Why?

_____

_____

_____

CHAPTER SUMMARY

Section 6.1 Merchandise Assortment

merchandise plan (p. 116)
merchandise life cycle
    (p. 118)
staple merchandise
    (p. 120)
fashion merchandise
    (p. 120)
seasonal merchandise
    (p. 120)
convenience merchandise
    (p. 120)
basic stock list (p. 121)
model stock list (p. 121)
never-out list (p. 121)

- The merchandise plan is a basic budgeting tool that is used to assist the retailer or buyer in meeting departmental or classification goals. It often uses figures from the previous year upon which to base plans for the current year.

- The components of a merchandise plan include planned sales, planned stock, planned reductions, and planned purchases.

- Merchandise life cycle refers to the customer acceptance and buying levels of an item of merchandise. There are four stages: introduction, growth, general acceptance, and decline.

Section 6.2 Receiving Goods and Inventory

purchase order (p. 122)
invoice (p. 122)
inventory (p. 125)
inventory control
    (p. 125)
stock turnover (p. 127)

- Most retail businesses have a designated area for receiving and checking in new merchandise. This process includes comparing the purchase order to the invoice. The merchandise is then marked with its selling price and moved to the area of the store where it will be sold.

- Inventory control means managing inventory levels to ensure that enough merchandise is available to meet sales goals without having too much inventory on hand.

- Retailers can use a perpetual inventory control system, a physical inventory system, or a combination of both.

- Stock turnover refers to the number of times the average inventory is sold during a time period, which is usually a year.

CHECKING CONCEPTS

1. **Define** merchandise plan.
2. **Explain** the merchandise life cycle.
3. **Name** the four types of merchandise.
4. **Compare** the three types of stock lists.
5. **Explain** the merchandise receiving process.
6. **Define** inventory control.
7. **Describe** the two types of inventory control systems.

Critical Thinking

8. **Explain** why retailers want a stock-turnover rate that is not too high.

CROSS-CURRICULUM SKILLS

Work-Based Learning

Information—Organizing and Maintaining Information

9. Good Art sells the work of local artisans. The owner of this store usually has about 100 pieces in stock for sale. Do you think she should use a perpetual or a physical inventory control system? Explain your answer.

Technology—Selecting Technology

10. Do you think the owner of Good Art should invest in a point-of-sale register? Why or why not?

School-Based Learning

Math

11. Last year's sales were $76,000. If your merchandise plan called for a 10 percent increase in this year's sales, what figure would you write in your plan?

Arts

12. Think of a specific type of retail business and draw a diagram to illustrate how the receiving process might work at that business. Include a floor plan of the receiving area and show where the different activities would take place.

 **CONNECTION**

Role Play: Assistant Manager

SITUATION You are to assume the role of assistant manager of a family owned grocery store. You are training a new employee (judge) on your store's receiving process for both canned goods and frozen products. The new employee (judge) asks why you spend so much time on the receiving process.

ACTIVITY You are to explain to the new employee (judge) the steps of the receiving process and the importance of each.

EVALUATION You will be evaluated on how well you meet the following performance indicators:

- Explain the receiving process.
- Explain storing considerations.
- Explain the employee's role in expense control.
- Explain types of business risk.
- Orient new employees.

 **INTERNET ACTIVITY**

Use the Internet to access the APICS Web site and click on About APICS.

- What is APICS and when was it founded?
- Describe what it does today.

➡ For a link to APICS to do this exercise, go to **marketingseries.glencoe.com.**

 marketingseries.glencoe.com

Buying and Pricing Merchandise

Chapter Objectives

- Explain the role of the buyer.
- Determine what to buy.
- Determine quantities to buy.
- Discuss the importance of when to buy.
- Explain factors affecting pricing decisions.
- Define markup and markdown.

POWER READ

Be an active reader and use these reading strategies:

PREDICT what the section will be about.

CONNECT what you read with your life.

QUESTION as you read to make sure you understand the content.

RESPOND to what you've read.

ENDLESS WINTER

When a retailer is a good buyer, savings are passed on to the customer. For example, many florists buy flowers in bulk at wholesale markets every morning before dawn so they can sell fresh flowers at good prices. In fact, wholesale buying is common among many retailers. But when a store such as Sport Chalet experiences huge growth, how are prices kept in line with added expenses from expansion?

Sport Chalet got its start when Norbert Olberz bought a small sporting-goods store for $4,000 in 1959. While living in a house behind the store, Olberz and his family ordered high-quality goods, offered expert advice to customers, and made smart decisions to expand the business. When the 1960 Winter Olympics boosted the popularity of snow skiing, Sport Chalet was one of the first shops to offer rental services. Olberz was also one of the earliest suppliers for scuba divers, mountain climbers, and backpackers.

In the mid-1970s, the shop moved its non-alpine sports goods to a 30,000-square-foot location across the street from its original store where a ramp was installed so skiers could practice ski maneuvers, such as schussing down the mountains. Since then, Sport Chalet has established more than 40 stores across southern California and Nevada as well as a successful online store. With such growth, how did the store keep its identity? How did it adjust to the larger-scale buying and selling?

ANALYZE AND WRITE

1. What merchandise did Olberz buy to grow his sporting-goods business?
2. What buying challenge did growth present to this chain of stores?

Case Study Part 2 on page 147

Buying Merchandise

AS YOU READ ...

YOU WILL LEARN

- To explain the buyer's role.
- How to determine what to buy.
- How to determine quantities to buy.
- To discuss the importance of when to buy.

WHY IT'S IMPORTANT

Understanding the role that buying plays is important for understanding the retail business. Buying the right merchandise to satisfy customer needs is one of the most important decisions in the retail mix.

KEY TERMS

- open-to-buy
- want slip
- vendor
- dating terms
- shipping terms
- FOB
- centralized buying
- quantity discounts
- decentralized buying

PREDICT

 Why do you think deciding how much to buy is an important decision?

Buying, Selling, and Pricing

Once retailers have made decisions about market strategy, merchandise planning, and retailing, they can then make decisions about purchasing and pricing merchandise. In this chapter you will learn about buying merchandise. You will also examine merchandise pricing and how retail selling prices are determined.

The Buyer's Job

Having the right amount of merchandise is one of the most important factors for any retail business. If there is too much merchandise, customers may not purchase it. However, having too little merchandise offers customers limited choices and might result in out-of-stock situations.

Understanding *when to buy* results in having the merchandise in the store at the time customers want it. Buy merchandise too early, and customers are not ready to buy it. Buy it too late, and the customers have already bought from the competition.

Who does the buying for a retail business? It depends upon the business. Large retailers employ buyers whose job is to purchase merchandise for the business. Smaller retail businesses might be a one-person operation. That store's owner often manages the business and purchases the merchandise that the business will sell. Regardless of the size of the business, the job of the buyer has basic characteristics:

1. The buyer determines the amount of money available to make purchases for a given time period.
2. The buyer determines the merchandise the store's customers want and will purchase.
3. The buyer then determines the best vendor or supplier for each item to be bought for the store.
4. The buyer negotiates the best terms and discounts possible for those items bought from each vendor.
5. The buyer determines the best time for the merchandise purchases to arrive at the store.

That's a big job! The buyer's job requires accurate knowledge of the business's target-market customers and an outstanding sense of what customers want to buy, often before the customers themselves know. We will now look more closely at each of the five characteristics of the buyer's job.

1001 Magic Carpets

A hand-loomed Turkish carpet is a work of art resulting from long months of labor and thousands of years of tradition. Richly colored and intricately designed, a Turkish carpet served as a bride's dowry, a handsome pad for guests, and a covering to keep out the cold. By the 14th century, these carpets had become prized possessions of European nobility. They've been popular ever since.

Buyers often travel directly to Turkey to find the best bargains. Beautiful flat weaves, embroidered silks, and intricately knotted wool rugs stock the shops and stalls scattered throughout major cities. Finding the rugs is easy, but buying can be the challenge. Hard-sell tactics by vendors are common—but are softened by offerings of mint or sweet-apple tea. Bargaining is expected as a time-honored dance between seller and client. Experienced buyers suggest offering half of the rug's price, then settling at about 70 percent of that. Buyers advise not to feel obligated to buy, even if the "shop attendant has unrolled 40 carpets for you."

When is bargaining for retail merchandise expected in the United States?

Determining Available Money

The amount of money a buyer is able to spend for new purchases is determined by the merchandise plan, explained in Chapter 6. Remember that the merchandise plan can be created for an entire department, or for one classification of merchandise for which the buyer is responsible.

Open-to-buy is a term that refers to the amount of money that is available to purchase merchandise after other merchandise purchases have been subtracted. The merchandise expenses include items received and ordered for the time period being considered. Open-to-buy is figured for a specific time period, such as a buying season or for a month in that season.

For example, if a toy store has planned purchases for the month of May totaling $1,500, has already received merchandise that equals $300, *and* has placed orders for merchandise that equal $400, the open-to-buy figure for the month of May would be $800. Open-to-buy is a useful tool that buyers use to manage their purchasing budget for new or unexpected purchases.

Open-to-buy is calculated according to this formula:

$$\text{Planned Purchases} - (\text{Merchandise Received} + \text{Merchandise Ordered}) = \text{Open-to-Buy}$$

$$\$1,500 - (300 + 400) = 800$$

open-to-buy amount of money available to purchase merchandise after other purchases have been subtracted

Math Check

OPEN-TO-BUY

Ayesha is running a beach shop. In June, her planned purchases total $3,300. She's ordered merchandise that costs $1,400 and received a shipment of goggles worth $300. What is her open-to-buy figure?

➡ For tips on finding the solution, go to **marketingseries.glencoe.com**.

Have you ever made a special request to a store? Was the store able to fulfill it? If not, how did you feel about that store?

Determining What Customers Want

A buyer must make decisions about which merchandise is right for the store's customers. The buyer can use many tools to help with these purchasing decisions.

TARGET-MARKET INFORMATION A buyer uses target-market information to determine general information about the business's customers. That information must be translated into merchandise preferences or, in other words, merchandise that customers will buy.

SALES RECORDS Sales records are the records of customers' past purchases. For example, sales records can determine if customers of a women's clothing store will be more likely to purchase skirts or pants with suits.

CUSTOMER PREFERENCES Customer preferences are items that customers like more than others, such as chocolate ice cream over vanilla. Both the sales associates who help customers and buyers can spend time in the selling area talking with customers to learn about their preferences.

CUSTOMER REQUESTS Customers can request merchandise items that are not available. Sales associates can record requests on want slips, or they can verbally inform the buyer. See **Figure 7.1** for an example of a want slip. A **want slip** is a form used to inform a buyer of a specific request from a customer for merchandise that the store or department does not have in stock or does not carry. Customer requests are usually specific. For example, a customer might ask for a certain shoe style by a certain manufacturer. This request might be satisfied by a special order. However, if several customers request the same item, the requests might indicate a trend in customer demand. If that is so, then the buyer might want to add that item to the regular merchandise offerings.

want slip a form used to inform a buyer of a specific request from a customer for merchandise that the store or department does not have in stock or does not carry

MAKING DECISIONS Just as consumers decide what to buy, buyers pay attention to customers and decide what to sell. *What are some ways a small retail store could best determine the needs of its customers? What about a large retail store?*

Figure 7.1

Want Slip

WANT SLIP

Item requested _____ Brand name _____

Size _____ Style _____ Quantity _____

Item description _____

_____

Your name _____

Adress _____
      Street   City   State   ZIP code

Telephone (____) _____

EMPLOYEE: PLEASE FORWARD IMMEDIATELY TO YOUR SUPERVISOR

Employee Signature _____

Store No. _____ Dept. No. _____ Date _____

WHAT YOU WANT IS WHAT YOU GET *Many retail salespeople will fill out want slips for their customers and give them to their buyer. Why would a want slip help a buyer figure out what to purchase?*

SHOPPING THE COMPETITION A buyer will often *shop the competition,* or visit other stores that are in competition with the one that employs the buyer. A visit to the competition entails looking carefully at the merchandise that is for sale in the competing store or department. Things to look for include the variety of styles in a particular category of merchandise and the quantities of merchandise in a merchandise category. A buyer will also try to find out if the competition has merchandise categories that are not carried by the buyer's store. If they do, then the buyer should determine the reason and whether that missing category is something that should be added to the merchandise assortment. Shopping the competition is a good way for a buyer to assess how his or her store's merchandise compares to that of the competition.

These buying tools can help a buyer make decisions about what customers want and what merchandise to buy. A good buyer will combine all those resources with an educated sense about the merchandise.

Vendor Selection

Once the buyer determines which merchandise needs to be purchased and how much money can be spent, the next step is to determine the best vendor for each item. A **vendor** is a company from which a buyer purchases merchandise. Buyers of fashion merchandise will look at the various current styles before making a decision about which ones to buy. The buyer of fashion merchandise might look at merchandise from several vendors before buying.

When a buyer has an established relationship with a vendor, there is a certain comfort level for both of them. The buyer knows the vendor is reliable and will be able to fill the orders as agreed. The buyer also knows that the quality of the merchandise will be acceptable to the store and its customers.

vendor company from which a buyer purchases merchandise

Boutique for the Unique

You know that shopping bots may find the best prices for merchandise on the Web—but the customer must act as a store buyer to determine the quality and unique style of an item. For people looking for cutting-edge gadgets and equipment, e-tailers such as Technoscout.com do both and offer their pick of custom-searched merchandise. Weekly e-mails alert customers to the latest items from atomic watches to 3D TV converters.

➡ Find and describe three unique items that are priced right for a specialty electronics store through **marketingseries.glencoe.com**.

 marketingseries.glencoe.com

Once a buyer commits to order merchandise, it is important for that merchandise to arrive on time and in the quantities and quality specified. When selecting a new vendor, a buyer must ask some important questions. Will the vendor be able to produce and deliver the merchandise as promised? Is a vendor's merchandise of the same quality to which the store's customers are accustomed? If the merchandise quality is lower than customer expectations, the customers will not buy the merchandise. If the quality is higher than customers expect, then the higher price for the higher quality will probably discourage sales.

Negotiating Terms and Discounts

The buyer negotiates the best terms and discounts possible for merchandise bought from each vendor. The buyer's objective is to make a profit for the business. In order to do this, the buyer must obtain the best terms for each purchase.

Buying terms deal with dating and shipping. **Dating terms** deal with the date when the bill for merchandise has to be paid to the vendor. The usual dating terms are *2/10, net 30*. This means that if the buyer or store pays the bill within ten days of the invoice date, the store can deduct two percent for paying the vendor early. If the retailer does not take advantage of the dating discount, then the entire invoice amount is due within 30 days of the billing date. Two percent may not sound like a big discount, but the totals for several purchases can add up to a considerable amount of money. Taking advantage of dating discounts reduces the cost of the merchandise purchased by the buyer.

dating terms terms that deal with the date when the bill for merchandise has to be paid

shipping terms terms that deal with how the merchandise will get from manufacturer to the store, who pays for shipping, and when ownership changes hands

Shipping terms refer to how merchandise will get from the manufacturer to the store; who pays for the shipping (manufacturer or buyer); and when ownership of the merchandise changes hands. Negotiating shipping terms is one of the major transactions buyers have to perform. Shipping terms are important for three reasons: First, shipping charges can be very costly, and they can add to the cost of the merchandise if the store has to pay shipping. On the other hand, paying shipping costs

Figure 7.2

Common Shipping Terms

GETTING FROM POINT A TO POINT B Different types of shipping terms give the vendor and the store different responsibilities. *Which of these shipping terms might be best suited to moving expensive merchandise?*

TERMS	RETAILER AND VENDOR CONDITIONS
FOB origin, freight collect	The store pays the shipping charges and owns the merchandise while it is in transit.
FOB origin, collect	The vendor pays the shipping charges, and the store owns the merchandise while it is in transit.
FOB destination, freight collect	The store pays the shipping charges, and the vendor owns the merchandise while it is in transit.
FOB destination, freight prepaid	The vendor pays the shipping charges and owns the merchandise while it is in transit.

Hot Property

Designer Affordable

TARGET   Target was launched in 1962, as a spin-off of a Minneapolis-based department store. Today, with more than 1,000 stores across the U.S., Target boasts, "No matter where you live or where you go, there's bound to be a Target nearby." Even if there isn't, one may be coming soon—as new stores are opening at the rate of 80 to 100 per year. Target was originally built for shoppers who wanted to buy less expensive goods without waiting in long lines. Although affordable and quick, with enough checkout counters for every few customers, Target is not your average discount store.

DISCOUNT VARIETY, DESIGNER STYLE

Take a turn down any brightly lighted aisle, and you'll find hundreds of items for every season—from colorful picnic ware for summertime fun to school wear for students of any age. However, mixed in with the everyday are designer names that would attract even the most sophisticated customer. "Guests," as Target customers are called, can find bedroom décor by Todd Oldham, who created product lines for MTV and Nickelodeon. Designer Isaac Mizrahi creates women's sportswear and accessories. Architect and industrial designer Michael Graves lends his world-renowned artistic touch to housewares. Target's own line makes up 40 percent of all its merchandise. To keep up with what's hip, Target regularly scouts the latest styles in the U.S. and Europe. The goal, says Target's vice president of merchandising, is to give people choices and to find the "unexpected, the wow."

1. What would be the best shipping terms for a store like Target that buys a lot of merchandise?
2. Target's motto is "Expect more. Pay less." What does "expect more" mean to you regarding what customers want?

---

will decrease the profit the vendor makes on the sale. Second, whoever owns the merchandise while it is in transit, or traveling to the store, must pay insurance to cover loss or damage of the shipment. Third, whoever owns the merchandise while in transit must file any claims for loss or damage by the shipping company. Most shipping terms are FOB. **FOB** means *free on board*, or the ownership of the merchandise in transit determines if freight charges are free. **Figure 7.2** explains different kinds of FOB charges between the vendor and the store.

Timing Merchandise Deliveries

The buyer determines the best time for merchandise purchases to arrive at the store. Timing is crucial. The buyer doesn't just order merchandise and wait for delivery. The timing of merchandise deliveries is an important decision, and merchandise deliveries must be timed for the moment when the customer is ready to buy—or sales will be lost.

Merchandise that arrives after customers want it is a problem. Customers may have already purchased the items at other retailers. This costs the store money as well as customer goodwill and confidence.

FOB free on board, or the ownership of merchandise in transit determines if freight charges are free.

QUESTION
Why would it be a problem if a vendor delivered merchandise earlier than arranged?

Types of Buying

You have read about the various aspects of the buyer's job and the buying process. Many of these tasks are the same for large retail businesses and for small ones. Large retail chains often use centralized buying. **Centralized buying** is a type of buying in which all buying for the chain is completed from one location. The buyer for one department will buy merchandise for that department in all the stores of the chain. This type of buying gives the buyer control over the merchandise for the entire chain and facilitates the same consistent image from store to store in the chain. Centralized buying also allows a buyer to take advantage of quantity discounts. **Quantity discounts** are offered for large or bulk purchases.

The other approach to buying that chain stores use is decentralized buying. **Decentralized buying** means that buying decisions are made at the local store level. Buyers do not use this method of buying as often as centralized buying.

centralized buying a type of buying in which all buying for a chain is completed from one location

quantity discounts discounts offered for large purchases

decentralized buying buying decisions made at the local store level

Store Buying Policies

Most stores have policies that dictate the types of merchandise that buyers can purchase for customers. Many store policies dictate brands that can be purchased or price points for selling merchandise. For instance, a gift store's buying policy might dictate that candles be sold for between $5 and $30. That would mean that the buyer could not bring in candles that would have to be sold at $40. Other policies concern store image. Products that do not promote a store's image might be prohibited.

Buyers must be knowledgeable about a variety of policies and procedures in order to provide their stores and customers with the right merchandise at the right time—and in a way that satisfies the needs of retailers, vendors, and customers alike.

Quick Check ✓

RESPOND to what you've read by answering these questions.

1. What are the five characteristics of the buyer's job? _____

_____

_____

2. Why is it important to take advantage of dating discounts? _____

_____

_____

3. What factors do buyers consider when negotiating shipping terms? _____

_____

_____

Pricing Merchandise

Name That Price

You've just learned about some of the important tasks involved in buying for a store. Once the buyer has purchased the merchandise, that merchandise must be given a selling price. The **price** of merchandise or services is the amount of money a retailer asks a customer to pay for that merchandise or service offered. The selling price of an item is very important. The selling price of merchandise or services must be balanced between the price that customers will pay and the price that makes a profit for the retailer.

Factors Affecting Selling Price

If the selling price of an item is too high, customers will not buy it—and if it is too low, customers will not see any value in the merchandise and will not buy it. In addition, the price of an item must allow the retailer to make a profit. To make a profit, the selling price must include:

- The cost of the merchandise itself

- The expenses of getting the merchandise to the store

- A share of the retailer's overhead expenses

- A return on investment

Markup is the term used to express the difference between the cost price of merchandise or services and the selling price of the merchandise or services. There are three major factors that affect the selling price of merchandise or services:

- Competition

- Supply and demand

- Customer acceptance

Competition

Competition among retailers is fierce. Retailers must consider the prices their competitors are charging for the same or similar merchandise or services. A retailer can charge prices that are either the same as the competition, below the prices charged by the competition, or above the prices charged by the competition.

AS YOU READ ...

YOU WILL LEARN

- To explain factors affecting pricing decisions.

- To define markup and markdown.

WHY IT'S IMPORTANT

Pricing decisions play a key role in a retailer's profit. Pricing decisions also affect customers' shopping decisions. Decisions about markup and markdown also affect a retailer's profit.

KEY TERMS

- price
- markup
- return on investment
- market share
- markdown

PREDICT

Why do you think stores might have competing sales?

price amount of money a retailer asks a customer to pay for merchandise or a service

markup the difference between the cost price of merchandise or services and the selling price

When a retailer is charging prices that are the *same* as the prices of the competition, those prices are *meeting the competition*. When pricing merchandise or services the same as those of the competitor, a retailer must rely on factors other than price to encourage customers to by at the business. These factors might include customer loyalty or a convenient location.

If a retailer decides to ask a price that is somewhat *higher* than that of the competition, then customers must see an extra value in shopping where the price is somewhat higher. The extra value might be a convenient location or extra services provided by the retailer.

When a retailer decides to ask prices that are lower than the prices charged by the competition, then the retailer is planning on selling the merchandise or service in greater quantities than the competition can sell. The retailer is relying on many customers to buy and take advantage of the lower price.

Supply and Demand

The law of supply and demand states that if the supply is limited, prices are higher. If the supply is plentiful, prices are lower. *Demand* for merchandise or a service is the quantity that customers will buy. There is also seasonal demand to consider. For example, holiday decorations will sell at a higher price before the holiday than after the holiday. *Supply* refers to the quantity of merchandise or a service that is available for customers to buy. If supplies are limited, customers are willing to pay more. For instance, customers will pay more for fresh peaches during an off-season period than they will when the crops are just harvested and there are plenty of fresh peaches readily available.

Customer Acceptance

Customer acceptance means how the customer will accept the prices that a retailer is asking for merchandise or services. It is important for retailers and buyers to know their target market well enough to predict and judge

➤ **CALCULATING PRICE** The tools that retailers use to calculate price and discounts have advanced over the years, but the factors that influence them have not changed much. *What are some factors that affect pricing decisions?*

the level of customer acceptance. Will the target-market customers be willing to pay more for more services or convenience? Are the target-market customers sensitive to price and unwilling to pay for convenience? The answers to these questions will affect a retailer's pricing decisions.

Other Factors

When retailers determine the selling price of merchandise or services, they are concerned first with making a profit on that particular item. Retailers must make a profit to be able to finance both their current business needs and any future changes, purchases, or expansions. In addition to profit, there are other factors that retailers consider when setting their prices. Those factors are:

- Return on investment

- Market share

Return on Investment

Return on investment is a percentage figure used to express the return (or profit) on the cost of merchandise or services plus the expenses necessary to sell the merchandise or service. For example, a dry cleaner might charge $5.00 to dry-clean a suit. Assume that the expenses (equipment use, chemicals, employee salaries, rent, etc.) to clean the suit are $3.80. You subtract the $3.80 expenses from the $5.00 price. That leaves $1.20. You the divide the $1.20 by $3.80 to get the return on investment to dry-clean the suit. The return on investment for cleaning the suit is 30 percent.

$$\$5.00 - \$3.80 = \$1.20 \div \$4 = .30 \text{ or } 30 \text{ percent}$$

Market Share

Market share is one retailer's part of the total sales of merchandise and services by all retailers in the selling area. When retailers attempt to increase their market share, they might lower their prices to increase sales. Retailers use market share as a guide to tell them how well their business is doing compared to the competition. Market share can be figured on a single product, classification of merchandise, or for the business as a whole.

Competition Pricing

You have learned how retailers use price as a method of meeting or challenging their competition. Retailers will price the same or similar merchandise or services at the same, or slightly higher, or slightly lower prices than their competition. Remember that when a retailer uses competition pricing, there must be other factors that will draw customers to that retailers' business. Competition pricing is so often used that retailers should not depend on this strategy alone. Customer loyalty and outstanding customer service can also make a huge difference in a retailer's success.

TECH NOTES

Bundling Online

Online retailers have caught on to the practice of *price bundling*. For example, Amazon.com may pair one book with another book on a similar subject and offer both titles at a discount. Bundles available through Dell.com include various combinations of computer hardware, software, and related products. Price bundling benefits retailers by boosting sales. It also benefits consumers, who believe that they're getting more for their money.

➡ Find and list specific examples of price bundling by visiting the online retailers through **marketingseries.glencoe.com**.

return on investment percentage figure representing the return (or profit) on the cost of merchandise or services plus the expenses necessary to sell them

market share one retailer's part of total sales of merchandise and services in the retailer's selling area

CONNECT

Have you ever stopped buying a certain product when its price was increased? What was the product?

RIDING THE WAVES

Debbie Harvey
Director of Merchandise Buying
Ron Jon Surf Shop

What does your job entail?

"I buy clothing and merchandise for Ron Jon Surf Shop in Coco Beach, Florida. The store is open 24 hours a day, 365 days a year, so there is a lot of turnover in merchandise, including board-sports equipment, diving apparatus, apparel, and accessories. They also have stores in Ft. Lauderdale, Florida, Orange, California, and Long Beach Island, New Jersey. The biggest challenges of buying are ordering the right amount of merchandise, dealing with vendors, and keeping all the merchandise selling well at the same time. I prepare for a lot of retail activity for Ron Jon Miami in July, and I attend the Surf Expo in September. We have to stay ahead of the market by predicting trends at least nine months before merchandise is received in the stores."

What skills are most important?

"I would say that you need to be able to organize and coordinate goods. You also need to be able to recognize quality and trends. Working well with people is important because you do a lot of negotiating."

What is your key to success?

"The key to buying is staying on top of things. Watch fashion trends and read trade publications like *Women's Wear Daily*—and pay attention to teen magazines and surf magazines—and watch MTV. Fashion trends usually start on the West Coast and travel east. Popular trends are spreading a lot faster because of television and the Internet. The most important signal is what the customers are wearing."

What is the most important thing for buyer to keep in mind? Why?

Career Data: Merchandise Buyer

Education and Training High school courses in marketing, accounting, business, and consumer education; two-year and/or four-year college programs in business administration, marketing, or finance; in-store training

Skills and Abilities Organizational skills, attention to detail, computer skills, accuracy; ability to discern quality, recognize trends, work well with people, negotiate, manage budgets, make decisions

Career Outlook Slower than average growth through 2006

Career Path A typical career path begins at the sales associate or trainee level and proceeds through assistant to head buyer. Some individuals may advance to business manager and executive positions.

Markdown

A **markdown** is a reduction in the original selling price of merchandise or services. You will often see marked-down prices on sale items. While markdowns reduce the total profit of the merchandise that is marked down, they do serve a purpose for retailers. Retailers can use markdowns as a tool to help to attract new customers. Markdowns help sell merchandise that is not selling as well as expected. Retailers should plan for markdowns or price reductions as part of doing business when making their merchandise plans. The merchandise plan allows for price reductions under *planned reductions*.

There are two main reasons retailers reduce prices:

- To reduce inventory

- To generate additional sales

Markdowns can help reduce inventory by helping to sell items that are selling slowly. Markdowns can also be used to sell merchandise that has been bought in too large quantities. They can attract new customers looking for a bargain.

Timing Markdowns

When should a retailer use markdowns? Taking markdowns too late means that there will probably be a second markdown as well, which will dig deeper into the retailer's profit. The rule of thumb is that the first markdown is always the cheapest. That means that it is the one that costs the retailer the least profit. Some retailers use *merchandising optimization software* to help determine the best prices and time for markdowns. Retailers must watch merchandise carefully. As soon as it shows signs of not selling as expected, a retailer must take a markdown.

Selling Markdown Merchandise

When a retailer has marked-down merchandise that remains unsold, there are several methods for liquidating that leftover merchandise. By using one or more strategies, a retailer can recoup costs and even potential profits. Some strategies include:

1. Sell, or *job-out*, the remaining marked-down merchandise to another retailer. Stores such as T.J. Maxx and Ross carry some of this type of merchandise.

2. Consolidate the marked-down merchandise and sell it at another store under the same ownership.

Case Study · PART 2

ENDLESS WINTER
Continued from Part 1 on page 135

To maintain its identity and high level of service, Sport Chalet hires former Olympians, amateur athletes, and professionally certified experts, in addition to typical retail employees. To answer distribution challenges, Sport Chalet opened a 326,000-square-foot distribution center and implemented new software. Return on the investment for the software system came in less than two months. Olberz has also kept his personal stamp on the large business. In 1998, he distributed nearly 300,000 shares of Sport Chalet valued at $1.5 million to employees who had more than ten years on the job and managers with more than one year of experience to celebrate Sport Chalet's most profitable year. With such foresight and care, Sport Chalet has managed to turn profits despite an unsteady California economy and dry, warm winters.

ANALYZE AND WRITE

1. What kind of market share do you think is held by Sport Chalet?
2. What are some factors besides good prices that may have allowed customer acceptance of Sport Chalet's prices?

markdown reduction in the original selling price of merchandise or services

3. Use the Internet by placing the marked-down merchandise on an auction Web site such as eBay, or create a special clearance Web site for the store.

4. Donate the marked-down merchandise to charity and use the cost value as a tax deduction.

5. Carry over the marked-down merchandise to the next season.

By clearing unsold merchandise, the retailer can avoid having unwanted merchandise occupy the selling area of the store. Also, unsold, out-of-season merchandise can weaken a store's image and discourage business.

QUESTION

What is one reason to clear unsold merchandise?

Buying and Selling

Buying and selling merchandise is different for retailers than for customers. A buyer must research the market and balance factors such as price, vendors, customer requests, and markdown, in order to manage a store. Though many things contribute to the choice of products a retailer may offer, in the end, it is the customers' wants and needs that determine what is bought and sold.

Quick Check ✓

RESPOND to what you've read by answering these questions.

1. Name three factors that affect selling price. _____

_____

_____

_____

_____

_____

2. What are three factors that a retailer considers when setting prices? _____

_____

_____

_____

_____

_____

3. What are two reasons that a retailer takes markdowns? _____

_____

_____

_____

_____

Worksheet 7.1

A Buyer's Guide

Go to a store or a retail establishment and ask to speak with the person responsible for purchasing merchandise. Ask this person the following questions and fill out the worksheet below.

1. What kind of merchandise does your store sell? _____

_____

_____

_____

_____

2. When do you purchase inventory (example: daily, monthly, weekly)? _____

_____

_____

_____

_____

3. How do you decide what to buy for your store? _____

_____

_____

_____

_____

_____

4. How do you select vendors? _____

_____

_____

_____

_____

5. How often does inventory arrive at your store? _____

_____

_____

_____

_____

Worksheet 7.2

Understanding Markdown

Go to a store that is having a sale, or check out newspaper or Internet ads for a sale. Pick one ad and fill out the worksheet below.

1. What kind of merchandise is on sale? _____

   _____

   _____

   _____

2. Does the retailer list the reason for the sale? If so, what is it? _____

   _____

   _____

   _____

   _____

3. Pick one item. Does the retailer list the original price? If so, what is it? _____

   _____

   _____

   _____

   _____

   _____

4. Does the retailer give a percentage off, or just list a different price? _____

   _____

   _____

   _____

   _____

5. If the retailer gives you enough information to calculate the difference between the original price and the final markdown, calculate the difference.

   _____

   _____

   _____

   _____

   _____

Portfolio Works

EXPLORING COMPETITION

1. Imagine you are the owner of a small retail store. You need to assess your competition, so you compare the type, quality, and price of merchandise in your store to that of your competitor. List the type, quantity, and prices of your merchandise.

_____

_____

_____

_____

_____

_____

2. Visit a store in your community that would compete with your imaginary store, and then create a graphic organizer or chart on a separate sheet of paper that includes the information listed.

- Three merchandise categories (such as CDs, DVDs, and videos)

- Three to five pieces of merchandise within each category, such as the name of individual CDs

- Your retail price of each individual item

- Competitor's price of each individual item

- Your markup on each item

- Your markdown on any item

3. Study the information on your graphic organizer or chart and then write a sentence that describes why you think you can or cannot be competitive by carrying the merchandise in your store.

_____

_____

_____

_____

_____

Add this page to your career portfolio.

CHAPTER SUMMARY

Section 7.1 Buying Merchandise

open-to-buy (p. 137)
want slip (p. 138)
vendor (p. 140)
dating terms (p. 140)
shipping terms (p. 140)
FOB (p. 141)
centralized buying
    (p. 142)
quantity discounts
    (p. 142)
decentralized buying
    (p. 142)

- Understanding the role buying plays in the success of a retail business is key to understanding the retail business. Buying the right merchandise to satisfy customer needs is one of the most important decisions in the retail mix.

- Buyers must determine what to buy by using information from their customers and other factors.

- Buyers must look at their market and determine how much to buy.

- Buyers must determine when to buy, using the knowledge they have of their market.

Section 7.2 Pricing Merchandise

price (p. 143)
markup (p. 143)
return on investment
    (p. 145)
market share (p. 145)
markdown (p. 147)

- Pricing decisions play a key role in a retailer's profit. Pricing decisions also affect customers' shopping decisions. Factors affecting pricing decisions include competition, supply and demand, customer acceptance, return on investment, market share, and competition pricing.

- Decisions about markup and markdowns affect a retailer's profit. Markup is the difference between the cost price of merchandise or services and the selling price. A markdown is a reduction in the original selling price.

CHECKING CONCEPTS

1. **Explain** the buyer's job.
2. **Describe** how the buyer determines what to buy.
3. **Describe** how the buyer determines what quantities to buy.
4. **Describe** how the buyer determines when to buy.
5. **Explain** three major factors affecting pricing decisions.
6. **Explain** market share.
7. **Define** markup and markdown.

Critical Thinking

8. **Explain** how the consumer influences a buyer's purchasing decisions.

CROSS-CURRICULUM SKILLS

Work-Based Learning

Thinking Skills—Problem Solving

9. Choose a partner. One of you will act as the retail buyer; the other will act as the vendor. Negotiate terms for a purchase of 2,500 pairs of shoes for a department store chain. Write down the terms.

Interpersonal Skills—Teaching Others

10. Create a graphic organizer that explains the three major factors that affect the selling price of merchandise or services.

School-Based Learning

Computer Technology

11. Use the Internet to find a wholesale vendor of computer printer-ink cartridges and a retail vendor of computer printer-ink cartridges. Create a chart that shows the markup of three ink cartridges.

Math

12. You order 20 shirts from a manufacturer. The shipping charges are $10.95 per ten shirts. The terms are FOB destination, freight collect. How much do you pay if each shirt costs $23.50?

Role Play: Buyer

SITUATION You are to assume the role of buyer for the men's furnishings department of a family-owned department store. The store has one location in the downtown area of a medium-sized town. You have recently hired a new assistant buyer (judge).

(ACTIVITY) You must explain to the assistant buyer (judge) the importance of negotiating favorable shipping terms when buying new merchandise.

EVALUATION You will be evaluated on how well you meet the following performance indicators:

- Negotiate contracts with vendors.
- Explain factors affecting pricing decisions.
- Explain the nature of buyer reputation/vendor relationships.
- Explain the types of business risk.
- Orient new employees.

Use the Internet to find online retail stores such as Dell Computers.

- Identify five products or services that are markdowns.
- Share your lists through e-mails.
- Have one person compile a final list.

➡️For a link to Dell Computers to answer these questions, go to **marketingseries.glencoe.com**.

Chapter 8

Site Locations and Selection

Chapter Objectives

- Identify the types of retail locations.
- Explain the difference between a strip center and a mall.
- Define trade areas.
- Explain retail site-selection criteria.
- Explain the importance of traffic for a retail business.

Be an active reader and use these reading strategies:

PREDICT what the section will be about.

CONNECT what you read with your life.

QUESTION as you read to make sure you understand the content.

RESPOND to what you've read.

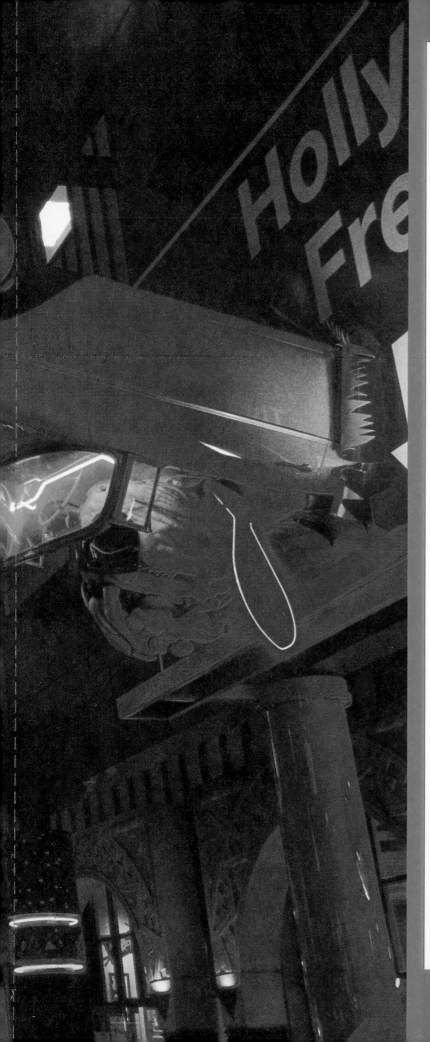

SUPERMARKET SAVVY

The Hard Rock Café is easily recognized by the car above its entrance. Sites for these famous restaurants are planned for and located in cities that attract hungry tourists as a regular target market. However, sometimes locations for food retailers must adapt to changing market needs, as Roger Chen learned.

Most ethnic food retailers are mom-and-pop operations, but the Tawa chain of supermarkets has gained national prominence. Roger Chen opened his first 99 Ranch Supermarket in Westminster, California's Little Saigon area, in 1984. Where else could one buy canned bamboo shoots, dried rice noodles, and live geoduck clams? By offering fresh and packaged foods to Chinese and Vietnamese immigrants, the full-service supermarket spread to other states, including Washington, Nevada, Hawaii, and Arizona.

However, as the chain grew, the Chinatowns in which the stores first thrived began to die out. Younger Asians and Asian Americans were moving to the suburbs—and many took their relatives with them. Second- and third-generation Asians in America were becoming *Pan-Asian*. That meant that as English became their primary language, these younger customers began to identify with all Asian cultures and food as well as with their own Chinese and Vietnamese cultures. The future success of Tawa markets would depend on how retailer Roger Chen responded to the changes in his target market.

ANALYZE AND WRITE

1. What site location changes do you think Tawa had to make?
2. How might population shifts affect retail business locations?

Case Study Part 2 on page 165

Retail Store Locations

AS YOU READ ...

YOU WILL LEARN

- To identify the types of retail locations.
- To explain the difference between a strip center and a mall.

WHY IT'S IMPORTANT

Understanding the different types of retail locations helps retailers place stores in the best locations for the types of merchandise they sell.

KEY TERMS

- shopping center
- strip center
- mall
- kiosk
- central business district
- freestanding location

PREDICT

Do you think a store has a greater chance of succeeding in a mall or in a storefront on "Main Street"?

shopping center a group of retail stores and service businesses operated as one business by one owner

The Importance of Location

Have you ever wondered how a retail store owner decides where to locate a new store? Should the retailer locate a store in a small shopping center or in a large shopping mall? Does the retailer look for nearby stores that carry similar merchandise offerings? Does the retailer look for the best rental prices? What guidelines does a retailer use when deciding where to locate a store? We will examine the factors that go into making that decision in this chapter. We will also look at the types of locations for retail stores. Choosing the location of a retail store is a serious decision. First, we will look at the types of locations a retailer might select for a business and the advantages that are offered by each type of retail location.

Types of Store Locations

There are many types of locations a retailer can choose. The location of a business is an important factor in the success of a business. The store location is also related to the store image and the types of merchandise and services the store offers. If a retailer locates a business too far away from the store's target market, the number of customers will be fewer than if the location were convenient for target customers.

A retailer must also determine what type of location is best for a particular type of store. There are many types of retail locations available, such as shopping centers, business districts, and freestanding locations. A retailer must carefully study a prospective location and consider all the location options. Once a retailer signs a lease or purchases a site, the commitment is long term. Each type of location has specific advantages.

Shopping Centers

Shopping centers are familiar places to most people. A **shopping center** is made up of a group of retail stores and service businesses. Shopping centers are built, owned, and managed by one person or business. The owner operates a shopping center as one business. Retailers rent space from the shopping-center owner or a management company. The retailer becomes a tenant of the shopping-center owner. There are two types of shopping centers:

- Strip centers

- Malls

LOCATION ADVISOR

T. J. Reid
Retail Consultant and Author
*What Mother Never Told Ya
About Retail*

What are the most important things to remember when choosing a location?

"The old phrase 'location, location, location' is still important. There are differences between an urban mall and a small store that is a destination shop. A retailer needs to ask, "Do I want to spend the money it takes to go into a mall? Do I want to follow the rules I have to abide by in a mall? Am I ready to be open seven days a week?'

"With a small store, you can hang balloons on the outside of the shop or choose not to open on Sunday or close at 3 P.M. You have to think long and hard about the type of atmosphere you want."

What are some common mistakes people make?

"A lot of people want to go where there's no competition. That's the worst thing you can possibly do, because people like to shop where they know they can find something. Having similar merchandise around you feeds you rather than deprives you. You don't want to be the only game in town.

"Some retailers don't estimate the demographics of the area. Too many people go into business without doing research about the median income of the customers in the area; how many children per family; the need for the product in that area; and how many cars pass by a store site every day.

"We may think that we're so creative and talented that whatever we do will work—without research. However, I've never seen a store that followed its statistics and demographics that didn't work. The tried and true works. So follow the rules, and your probability of success will be so much better."

Is having competition nearby an advantage or disadvantage for a store? Why?

Career Data: Location Finder/ Market Analyst

Education and Training
Associate's or bachelor's degrees in marketing, statistics, and/or business

Skills and Abilities
Knowledge of the specific product and market, language and people skills, ability to multitask, and organizational skills

Career Outlook Faster than average growth through 2010

Career Path A typical career path can begin anywhere within an organization, from the frontline sales staff to entry-level management.

Strip Centers

Strip centers are shopping centers located in neighborhoods all over the country. A **strip center** is a group of stores that features a parking lot in front and is not an enclosed shopping area. It houses retail businesses that are connected by walkways or sidewalks.

strip center a group of stores that features a parking lot in front and is not an enclosed shopping area.

What is the greatest advantage for a retailer to locate in a mall?

Strip shopping centers are convenient places to shop because they feature businesses that customers often visit. A typical neighborhood strip shopping center might have a grocery store, a drugstore, a fast-food or take-out restaurant, a music store, a dry cleaner, and a craft store. Strip shopping centers are convenient for another reason: Customers can run several errands in one stop. For example, a customer can drop off dry cleaning, buy a few groceries, pick up a prescription, and buy film for a camera in one trip. Rental rates at strip centers are usually less expensive than those at malls.

Malls

Most people in this country have been to a shopping mall at least once or even weekly. A **mall** is a shopping area that is usually enclosed and has customer parking near the mall building. Separate parking structures may also be situated near or attached to the mall structure. There are many types of stores in a mall. The owners of a mall usually plan for a variety of stores to offer customers a good selection of places to shop.

mall shopping area that is usually enclosed and has customer parking near the mall building

➤ **BIG NAMES, BIG BARGAINS** Name-brand and designer retailers often locate in outlet malls where they sell their merchandise at lower prices. Outlet stores often carry merchandise that may not be available in local retail malls. *What type of customer would most likely shop at an outlet?*

MALL ADVANTAGES One advantage of a mall is that customers can shop for the same merchandise at several stores. If you want a new pair of shoes, you are able to look for shoes at department stores and several specialty shoe stores and compare. Mall customers have the advantage of one-stop shopping. A mall owner might plan to have department stores as anchor stores and an assortment of specialty stores that sell complementary merchandise. The mall might also have a variety of restaurants and other service providers. Customers can complete as many shopping tasks in one stop as they can at a strip center. In fact, the variety of stores in a mall is a significant reason why customers want to shop there. Mall customers appreciate the wide variety of stores that provide a large selection of merchandise and services. The mix of stores at a particular mall will depend on the type of mall and its demographics.

Malls also offer the convenience of climate control. For customers, climate control means not having to carry an umbrella on a rainy day, and for the retailer, it can mean not having to shovel winter snow in front of the store.

TYPES OF MALLS There are different types of malls, such as:

- Regional malls

- Fashion malls

- Outlet malls

Different malls feature stores that appeal to specific customer groups. For example, an outlet mall will appeal to customers looking for brand names at reduced prices. A fashion mall might appeal to customers who want to shop at expensive stores carrying high-fashion merchandise.

KIOSKS Kiosks are another place to shop in many malls. A **kiosk** is a freestanding, small shopping space. Kiosks can vary in size, from about 40 to 500 square feet. Because of limited space, a kiosk usually carries only one type of merchandise. Kiosks sell items that range from bonsai plants and candles to hair accessories and cell phones. A kiosk offers a small retailer the opportunity to have a presence in a mall and benefit from the customer traffic that a mall provides. Since the rent for kiosk space is usually a lot lower than for a store location, a kiosk is sometimes a good choice for some types of retailers.

Business Districts

Retailers may also locate in a central business district, which is a different shopping environment than a strip center or mall. A **central business district** is an exterior shopping area that has developed without very much planning. The mix of stores is varied. There is little or no planning or organization for a variety of stores that offer a variety of merchandise and services. A downtown, main street shopping area is an example of a central business district location. Business districts also exist in suburban areas. A suburban town might also have a main street area that has a variety of stores that sell merchandise and services.

THE Dot Com SHOP

It's a Jungle Out There

Going to a music store can be inefficient; you may have to go to several locations to find what you want. At online retailer Amazon.com, you can browse through hundreds of thousands of new and used CDs in a matter of minutes. A brick-and-mortar store would have to be huge to offer this kind of variety and convenience. By offering music for sale online, Amazon.com keeps overhead costs low, their selection high—and their customers satisfied.

➡ For an activity that takes you to an online music store and shows you how to search by keyword, genre, or artist, go to **marketingseries.glencoe.com**.

kiosk a freestanding, small shopping space usually located in a mall

central business district an exterior shopping area that has developed without much planning

CONNECT

How large is your town or city? Does your town or city have more freestanding stores than malls?

Central business district shopping areas are usually located in downtown areas that have other types of businesses and office complexes. Much of the customer traffic comes from office workers in the area. Some customers drive into central business districts, while others make use of public transportation to shop there. Many cities have renovated and revitalized their older, sometimes historic downtown areas to promote retail business and improve their economies. Retail rental rates in a central business district will vary depending on the number of other businesses nearby and the popularity of the area.

Freestanding Locations

freestanding location a store that is not attached to other retail stores

A **freestanding location** is a store that is not attached to other retailers. As the name implies, the location stands alone. A warehouse club or hypermarket may need a large space that would be available in a freestanding location. Some advantages of this type of location include:

- Lower rent

- More parking

- Better visibility

- No direct competition

- Convenience

- Few restrictions on signs, hours, or merchandise

- Ability to expand

RECYCLED RETAIL
Redeveloped downtown areas have succeeded in revitalizing inner cities and attracting new residents. *Why might you shop in such a retail shopping area?*

Gems of the Sea

There are many stories about the origin of the black pearls found in the deep lagoons around Tahiti, the largest island of French Polynesia. One story says that the pearls were created when the god Oro descended from the sky on a rainbow, washing bits of color into the sea. These pearls grow within the pearl pocket, or reproductive organ, of the black-lipped oyster, and today they are cultivated in farms off the Tahitian shores.

Pearl farmers watch over and tend their crop of oysters. If the weather is too warm, the oysters are moved to a cooler place. If the weather is stormy, they are immersed more deeply in the sea. In about two years, gems form in a variety of colors, from black to pink to peacock green. When harvested and ready for market, pearl farmers sell the pearls to jewelers and retailers worldwide.

Island visitors find the pearls especially appealing. Besides being a beautiful souvenir of the island, these pearls are reasonably priced at the site where they originate. Global jewelry shop prices for the pearls vary: $100 for an average, small-sized pearl up to $10,000 for the highest quality. The pearling industry has benefited the local economy, generating jobs and encouraging workers to stay on the island that many people call paradise.

What type of store location would you choose for a jewelry store selling black pearls? Why?

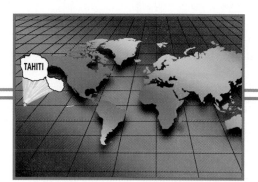

A retailer in a freestanding location must be able to attract customers without the benefit of other businesses to help generate customer traffic. For that reason, small retailers generally do not locate in freestanding locations. Megastore Target is a retailer that does use freestanding locations. Target, Costco, and Home Depot operate freestanding stores that are able to attract enough customer traffic without the help of other stores.

Business Climate

Before a retailer makes a final decision about a location for a store, there is another factor that should be considered: the business climate of the town or area. The retailer should determine if the business climate near the store would be a good one. A retailer must evaluate factors such as the demographics of the town or area—not only the current demographics but also the future demographic projections. What will the population of the town or area look like in five or ten years? Will the population composition remain fairly constant, or will it change and no longer fit the retailer's target market?

The retailer should also become familiar with the employment trends in the town or area. If employment rates are high, then there is a good possibility that consumers will be spending more money than if employment rates are low. Also, if a town or city is dependent on one or two industries, the retailer should find out if those industries are healthy and growing.

> **Selling Point** ❗
>
> → **BOOMING CLIMATE**
> The largest segments of America's 78 million baby boomers (born 1946–1965) are located in Falls Church, VA, suburban Washington, DC, Marin County, CA, suburban San Francisco, CA, and Putnam County, NY.

Acceptance

A retailer must consider if the town will accept a new retail business. Will the new store be welcomed? Or, will the town look upon business development as an undesirable situation? Another factor to consider is the availability of workers nearby. The retailer needs to know what the size of the available worker groups is in the town. How old are potential employees? What is the educational level of the workers? The answers to these questions must fit with the retailer's plan for locating and staffing the business.

Competition

A retailer must also consider competition when reviewing a town's or area's business climate. The retailer should find out how many other stores sell the same or similar merchandise or services in the town or area. Some competition is good, but if there are too many of the same type of store in one area, there may not be enough customers to support all of the stores.

Retailers should also evaluate the age of the competitive stores. Are the competitors' stores up-to-date with modern equipment and fixtures? Or, are the competitive stores showing signs of age with old or worn fixtures and equipment? The retailer should completely evaluate potential competition before determining a location. Considering business climate as well as all the different types of locations in an area will ensure a successful retail store location.

Quick Check ✓

RESPOND to what you've read by answering these questions.

1. What are the three broad categories of shopping locations? _____

_____

_____

_____

2. What are two differences between strip centers and malls? _____

_____

_____

_____

3. Why would a small retailer be unlikely to locate in a freestanding location? _____

_____

_____

_____

Store Site Selection

Elements of Site Selection

This section will examine business trade areas, as well as the other criteria that retailers use when selecting a specific site for a store. The section will also discuss how retailers decide to rent a location or buy a location.

Trade Area

Understanding a retail business's trade area is important when selecting a site for a store. The **trade area** is the geographic area from which the store draws most of its customers. This is the area where most of the sales occur. **Figure 8.1** illustrates a computer program that retailers use to identify and understand trade areas. The type of store, the merchandise or services offered, and the amount of competition in the area all have an effect on the size of a business's trade area. For example, a rug-cleaning service located in a populated suburban area of single-family homes may not have competition within 20 miles.

Figure 8.1

Trade Areas

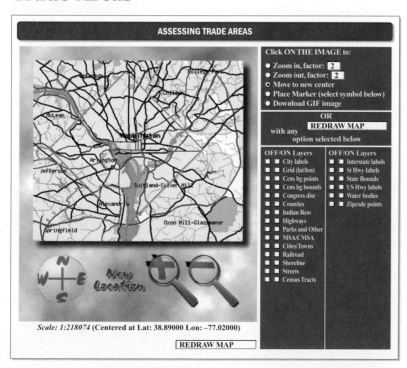

COMPETING WITH A TIGER
To get the big picture of a retailer's trade area, computer-generated maps, such as the TIGER map, can plot a surrounding trade area for a store. *Why is it important to know where customers live?*

Hot Property

Location, Location, Location

Each morning millions of people find their way to the nearest Starbucks to wake up with a "tall" or "grande" fresh brew. Fortunately, America's #1 coffee house is not hard to find. At least, that's how Howard Shultz, Starbucks' chairman and chief global strategist, planned it.

In 1971, Starbucks opened its first store in Seattle's historic Pike Place Market. Twelve years later, Shultz bought out the original owners. He had traveled to Milan, Italy, and was intrigued by the number of that city's espresso bars—one on almost every corner. Shultz thought: If in Italy, why not America? Create the Starbucks experience with quality hot and cold coffees, a bistro-like atmosphere, fresh fine pastries, and the customers will come.

Soon the Starbucks two-tailed siren logo popped up everywhere—along bustling city streets, down county roads, on neighborhood outskirts, and in hotels, bookstores, department stores, and airports. To pick these locations, Starbucks researchers use tallying methods and customer profiling to find the right spots— keeping their potential site maps top secret.

GLOBALIZATION OF COFFEE

In 1996, Starbucks opened internationally. The company now boasts locations in 27 countries, including one in China's Forbidden City, a tea drinker's territory. The passion for coffee has transcended culture and has created a language of its own—caffe latte, cappucino, espresso, and Frappuccino® iced blended beverage. With almost 6,300 locations and increasing sales ($3.3 billion in 2002), Starbucks is no fad. As one writer notes, "Starbucks isn't going anywhere—50 percent of the adult population drinks a cup or more of coffee every day."

1. What are two methods that Starbucks uses to help select store sites?
2. Describe what you think would be the ideal coffee-house location in your area.

PREDICT

What do you think is the most important thing to consider when choosing a store location?

trade area geographic area from which a store draws most of its customers and sales

traffic the number of people who pass a retail location during a given period of time

That rug-cleaning business has a trade area of 20 miles or more. Look again at that same 20-mile area, but this time focus on a children's clothing store. If there are two other children's clothing stores in that area, then the trade area becomes smaller, or about six or seven miles. For a coffee shop such as Starbucks, with multiple sites, the trade area might be only a few blocks.

Other Site-Selection Criteria

When selecting a specific site location, store retailers become involved in a commitment that can last for a long time. You already know that the trade area of a retail business is a major factor in the success or failure of that business. There are eight other criteria that retailers can use to evaluate a potential business site.

Traffic

The term **traffic** refers to the number of people who pass a retail location during a given period of time. The people can be in their cars or on foot. Many retailers will count traffic to aid in making a decision about a store site. Counting only people who are definitely potential customers of that store can give retailers a more useful traffic count. A retailer can have thousands of people pass by the business each day. However, if the people passing by are not potential customers, they won't be purchasing merchandise or services from the retailer. Retailers need customers to buy their merchandise or services.

Ease of Access

Ease of access refers to the ability of customers to get in and out of the store site easily. If a site is located directly off a busy highway, but it is difficult to get onto the highway from the site, then that site does not have ease of access. However, if a traffic light were placed at either end of the parking area, access to the site would be a lot easier. That would make the site more acceptable to potential customers.

Parking

Parking areas may not seem like a major consideration for store locations. However, if customers cannot park their cars, they probably will not want to shop at the store. The site under consideration should provide adequate parking nearby. Most customers will not park a great distance from the stores where they want to shop. Retailers should also consider the condition of the parking area. Is the parking area in good condition, or is it full of potholes?

The site should allow for good traffic flow as well. It should accommodate a significant number of cars each day but not to the point of congestion. A retailer can analyze the amount of traffic by examining the presence of employers in the area, schools, and so on. Traffic levels may vary by time of day as well. City and county resources or state highway departments also have traffic flow information which a retailer can use when planning and designing parking areas.

Lighting is an important consideration in a parking area. The parking area should be well lit at night so customers feel safe leaving and returning to their cars. Also, customers do not want to have their car doors nicked while they are shopping. The parking spaces should be well marked and roomy enough for customers to drive their cars in and out easily.

Visibility

It is important for a retail site—store or mall—to be visible to customers. **Visibility** is the ability of the site to be easily seen by customers. When customers have difficulty seeing a store, they may shop elsewhere.

Case Study | PART 2

SAVVY SUPERMARKETS
Continued from Part 1 on page 155

As Asians in America moved into the suburbs, so did the 99 Ranch Supermarkets. The supermarkets serve as anchor stores for outdoor malls with restaurants, bakeries, magazine stands, and jewelry stores. To accommodate the relocation of its target market, the Tawa food chain expanded, opening Welcome Supermarkets and 99 Ranch Markets in Milpitas, Fremont, Anaheim, San Gabriel, and other suburbs of San Francisco and Los Angeles. Tawa also diversified its shelves by stocking foods from Japan, Korea, Indonesia, and other Asian countries to represent the Pan-Asian tastes that second-generation immigrants developed. However, now an added benefit of locating in the suburbs is that non-Asians also go to the stores for the produce, which is often fresher and less expensive than in the mainstream supermarkets. These new customers are also seeking products with new flavors.

ANALYZE AND WRITE
1. How has Tawa markets adjusted store sites to population shifts?
2. What new target market has developed for Tawa? Why?

ease of access ability of customers to get in and out of a business site easily

visibility ability of the site to be easily seen by customers

Figure 8.2

Evaluating a Site

LOCATION RATINGS A checklist is one tool a retailer can use to help decide where to do business. *Which factor might be very important for a fast-food restaurant location?*

Rate each of the following criteria on a scale of 1 to 10, with 1 being excellent and 10 being poor.		
Pedestrian Traffic	Number of people	_____
	Type of people	_____
Vehicular Traffic	Number of vehicles	_____
	Type of vehicles	_____
	Traffic congestion	_____
Parking Facilities	Number and quality of parking spots	_____
	Distance to store	_____
	Availability of employee parking	_____
Transportation	Availability of mass transit	_____
	Access from major highways	_____
	Ease of deliveries	_____
Store Composition	Number and size of stores	_____
	Affinity	_____
	Retail balance	_____
Specific Site	Visibility	_____
	Placement in the location	_____
	Size and shape of the lot	_____
	Size and shape of the building	_____
	Condition and age of the lot and building	_____
Terms of Occupancy	Ownership or leasing terms	_____
	Operations and maintenance costs	_____
	Taxes	_____
	Zoning restrictions	_____
	Voluntary regulations	_____
Overall Rating	General location	_____
	Specific site	_____

CONNECT

Do you prefer to shop in a mall or in a less crowded location?

MARKETING SERIES *Online*

Remember to check out this book's Web site for career information and more great resources at **marketingseries.glencoe.com.**

It is also just as important for customers to be able to see how to enter and exit the parking area. If customers can see the store site, but they cannot tell how to get to it, they probably won't stop. They can shop elsewhere, and they will.

Competition

When choosing locations, a retailer must assess many factors, which can be noted on checklists, such as the checklist in **Figure 8.2**. One of those factors is competition in the nearby area. It is beneficial to have some competition nearby. Customers want to compare the quality and value of the merchandise or services offered for sale. If the nearest competition is too far away, customers will not have that opportunity and might decide to shop where they can make those comparisons.

When assessing the competition, a retailer should also consider the proximity of the location to the nearest mall or large shopping area. If a mall or shopping area is nearby, it might help draw customers to the site. If a mall or large shopping area is too far away, customers might think the site is too inconvenient and will bypass the store when shopping at the mall or large shopping area.

Zoning

Zoning laws restrict the types of businesses that can be located in an area. For instance, certain types of businesses cannot be located in residential areas, or neighborhoods with homes. Each town or city has its own zoning laws. It is important to check with the town or city government to find out the zoning laws for a business site. Sometimes zoning laws also limit the hours during which a business is able to operate. The types of signage, or signs, may also be restricted. For example, a bright neon sign or an oversized sign may be prohibited near a residential area.

Lease Terms

If the site under consideration is located in a shopping center or a mall, the retailer will probably have to lease the store. A **lease** is a rental agreement between a landlord and a renter for a property. Any lease should be reviewed carefully before signing. The terms, or conditions, of the lease should be clearly stated. There are many lease terms that require careful review before the retailer signs a lease agreement. Some lease terms include:

- Amount of the rent

- Services provided by the landlord

- Length of lease

- Lease renewal terms

TYPES OF LEASES There are two types of leases that retailers use when renting store space:

- Percentage

- Fixed-rate leases

The percentage lease is the most common form of lease. Under this type of lease arrangement, the rent is based on a percentage of the store's sales. The retailer will usually pay a maintenance fee as well. Malls usually use this type of lease, which is signed for a period of from five to ten years.

Under the terms of a fixed-rate lease the retailer pays a fixed rent per month. This type of lease is often used by community and neighborhood centers. Having a fixed amount to pay each month is an advantage for a retailer who wants stable expenses. There are a few variations on both types of leases; however, the retailer should completely understand the terms of any type of lease before signing one.

TECH NOTES

TIGER vs. GIS Software
Retailers can use geographic information systems (GIS) software to locate the best site for a new business. GIS software accesses data from a national digital map available through the U.S. Census Bureau. This map is known as TIGER (Topologically Integrated Geographic Encoding and Referencing). See **Figure 8.1** on page 163 for an example. The TIGER mapping engine can be used for free, and GIS software features are useful to retailers. The features might include population characteristics and locations of competing businesses.

➥Compare several types of GIS software to the TIGER maps through **marketingseries.glencoe.com**.

lease a rental agreement between a landlord and a renter for a property

QUESTION
Can any store be located in a residential area? Why?

Math Check

RENT OR BUY?

Tera is about to open a motorcycle shop. He must choose between a space for rent or a small building for sale. The rent is $1,200 per month, but he cannot make any improvements. The monthly payment for the building would be $800, but he must pay taxes and extra insurance at $300/month. What is the better monthly rate?

➥ For tips on finding the solution, go to **marketingseries.glencoe.com**.

Merchandise Sold

When considering a site, the retailer should once again review the target-market information of the business after collecting information about the potential site. Are the retailer's merchandise and services still compatible with the location? Reviewing the merchandise and services several times before acquiring a site can save costly errors. It may be necessary to make minor adjustments in the merchandise or services in order to make the site and business a compatible match. If the store location shows real potential of being a successful site, then any minor adjustments could be well worth the time and effort.

Securing a Business Site

Once a retailer has determined the best possible site for the business, how does that retailer secure, or obtain, the site for the business? The retailer may want to consider options for owning or leasing a site. A retailer can buy a building in which to locate the store. When a retailer owns property, the business is responsible for all repairs and upkeep. The other option is for the retailer to lease, or rent, business space. The results of the retailer's site search might lead the retailer to either lease an entire building for the business or to lease store space. If the retailer decides that the business would be best located in a strip shopping center or in a mall, then the retailer would have to lease space. Whatever the retailer decides is the best option, store location is very important to the success of a retail business.

Quick Check

RESPOND to what you've read by answering these questions.

1. What is a business's trade area? _____

_____

_____

2. What are nine site selection criteria? _____

_____

_____

_____

3. Why is competition important when selecting a business location? _____

_____

_____

_____

Name _____ Date _____

Worksheet 8.1

The Right Spot

You are planning on opening a retail store. Choose the type of store you will open. Then write the descriptions of ideal site-selection criteria for your store:

Type of Store _____

1. Trade area _____

_____

2. Traffic _____

_____

3. Ease of access _____

_____

_____

4. Parking _____

_____

_____

5. Visibility _____

_____

_____

6. Competition _____

_____

_____

7. Zoning _____

_____

_____

8. Lease terms _____

_____

_____

9. Merchandise and location _____

_____

_____

Worksheet 8.2

Location Analysis

1. Pick a popular chain store located in your town or city.

   Name of store: _____

2. Use the Internet or the phone book to find all the locations of this store in your area. In the box, sketch a simple map of your town and use stars to mark the locations of the chain store.

   [ ]

3. How many stores in the chain are in malls? _____

   _____

   _____

4. How many stores in the chain are in strip centers? _____

   _____

   _____

5. How many stores in the chain are freestanding stores? _____

   _____

   _____

6. Which type of store location is the most popular for this chain of stores? _____

   _____

   _____

CHOOSING A BUSINESS LOCATION

You are preparing to open a school supply store. Do the following exercise. Then add this page to your career portfolio.

1. Using a local map, choose at least three locations that are possible sites for your store. List them below.

_____

_____

_____

2. Go to the three sites and observe the traffic that passes by the locations. Describe the traffic for each location.

_____

_____

_____

_____

_____

_____

3. In the space below, draw a graphic organizer or chart that lists the advantages and disadvantages of each site.

CHAPTER SUMMARY

Section **8.1**   Retail Store Locations

shopping center (p. 156)
strip center (p. 157)
mall (p. 158)
kiosk (p. 159)
central business district
    (p. 159)
freestanding location
    (p. 160)

- Different retail locations include shopping centers, business districts, and freestanding locations. Understanding the types of retail locations helps retailers open certain stores in the best locations for the types of merchandise they sell.

- A trip center is usually not enclosed, but a mall is enclosed. Knowing how different shopping areas, such as strip centers and malls, are organized will help retailers select locations that are best suited for their stores.

Section **8.2**   Store Site Selection

trade area (p. 164)
traffic (p. 164)
ease of access (p. 165)
visibility (p. 165)
lease (p. 167)

- A trade area is the geographic area from which the store draws most of its customers. It is an important factor for the retailer when making merchandise and location decisions.

- Site-selection criteria may include trade area, traffic, ease of access, parking, visibility, competition, zoning, lease terms, and merchandise sold. These factors can help a retailer evaluate a potential business site that will contribute to a store's success.

- Traffic refers to the number of people who pass a retail location during a given period of time. Counting only the people who go by the location who are potential customers can help a retailer select a good location.

CHECKING CONCEPTS

1. **Describe** the types of retail locations.
2. **Explain** the difference between a strip center and a mall.
3. **Define** trade areas.
4. **Describe** retail site-selection criteria.
5. **Explain** the importance of traffic.
6. **List** at least two of four terms in a lease.
7. **Name** one factor that a retailer should review several times before deciding on a store site.

Critical Thinking

8. **Explain** why you think it would be important for a dry-cleaning shop to have ease of access.

CROSS-CURRICULUM SKILLS

Work-Based Learning

Information—Organizing and Maintaining Information

8. Design a spreadsheet for retail sites that lists their different criteria. Include shopping center, strip center, mall, kiosk, central business district, and freestanding location.

Interpersonal Skills—Participating as a Team Member

9. Working in groups of four, each group will interview a local retailer. Ask the following question and any others you think are relevant: What factors did you consider when choosing this site? Have a member of the group write a summary of your findings.

School-Based Learning

Writing

10. Draw on your personal experience as a shopper to write an essay about how location affects where you shop.

Social Studies

11. Use graph paper to create the floor plan of a shopping mall. Use different colored cutouts to represent different types of stores. Add a legend that identifies the different types of businesses.

Role Play: Family-Store Employee

SITUATION You are to assume the role of an employee for a family clothing store located in the downtown area of a small town. The store has been a success with the town residents and the residents of another small town ten miles away. The store's owner (judge) is considering expanding the business by opening another store in the nearby small town.

ACTIVITY The store's owner (judge) has asked for your recommendations regarding a site for the proposed new store.

EVALUATION You will be evaluated on how well you meet the following performance indicators:

- Explain factors to consider when selecting a store site.
- Assess trading area.
- Conduct location feasibility study.
- Present findings and recommendations.
- Address people properly.

Use the Internet to find and print out a map of your community.

- Mark at least two sites for a sporting goods store.
- Mark any competitors' shops.
- Draw a circle around the potential trade area for each site.
- Justify your choices.

➡️For a link to Internet maps to begin this exercise, go to **marketingseries.glencoe.com**.

BusinessWeek News

JUST HOW DEEP ARE THOSE TEEN POCKETS?

Youth-apparel chains are branching into ever-smaller niches. It's a typical summer day in the San Fernando Valley. Economic slowdown or not, the malls are swarming as teens with nothing but time on their hands and allowances in their pockets check out the scene. And, lately, no place has been packing them in more than Hollister Co. at the Westfield Shoppingtown Mall in Canoga Park, Calif. The new chain, an offshoot of Abercrombie & Fitch Co. that opened last year, is geared to the wanna-be surfer-and-skateboarder teens. "After they opened, everybody at school said: 'What a great store, you have to see it!'" gushes 15-year-old Vanessa White, who's picked up 15 shirts and ten pairs of pants there in the past four months.

Retailers across the country are betting big that there are plenty more buyers like Vanessa around. Nearly a dozen chains are launching new store concepts. Their target? Anyone from the 7- to 12-year-olds, known as tweens in the marketing world, to the teenagers and young adults they imitate.

Largely, though, it is a teen fad. Pembroke Pines (Fla.)-based Claire's Stores Inc., which operates 3,000 teen stores under four names, is testing a chain called Velvet Pixies that will cater to preteen girls with name-brand clothes like MUDD and Esprit. Abercrombie & Fitch's Hollister is going after a slightly younger group than its preppy parent

with lower prices—and City of Industry (Calif.)-based Hot Topic Inc., which draws the MTV crowd, has started Torrid to offer trendy fashions for large-size girls age 15 to 29.

Irresistible

Many retailers can't resist the fact that teenagers are the fastest-growing population group. Teenage Research Unlimited, a Northbrook (Ill.) market researcher, says that the number of teens will rise 7% by 2010, to 33.9 million, the largest teen market ever.

Today's specialty operators are casting smaller, more specialized nets. Stores are geared to particular teen styles and niches, or tighter age groupings. Hollister appeals to wanna-be surfers, for example. Abercrombie, for example, already has 275 units of what it believes can be a 400-store store.

By Robert Berner with Christopher Palmeri

CREATIVE JOURNAL

In your journal, write your responses.

CRITICAL THINKING

1. Why do you think some retailers are targeting sales to different groups of teens?

APPLICATION

2. If you were opening a clothing store for teens, what kind of clothing would you sell to what types of teens? Why? Name your store and describe the clothing.

 Go to **businessweek.com** for current *BusinessWeek* Online articles.

■ UNIT LAB

The Virtuality Store

You've just entered the real world of retailing. The Virtuality Store offers the latest and most popular consumer goods and services. Acting as the owner, manager, or employee of this store, you will have the opportunity to work on different projects to promote the success of your business.

Begin the Search—Find a Store Location

SITUATION You are the managing partner of a clothing store that has a target market of teenaged girls. Your partner provides the financing for the business and has input in major business decisions. The location of your store is a major business decision. You have been searching for a store location for months and have narrowed the choice to three possibilities. Each site has approximately 1,500 square feet of space. One location is in a strip shopping center located in a suburban area with a population of families with young children and some teens. The second location is near the campus of the local community college. The location is a small cottage-style house located in a shopping district of similarly situated businesses. The third location is a mall location near the food court and a department store that carries moderately priced merchandise.

ASSIGNMENT Complete these tasks:
- Determine the best location for your store, keeping location criteria in mind.
- Estimate the approximate monthly rent for each location.
- Make a report to your partner.

TOOLS AND RESOURCES To complete the assignment, you will need to:
- Have word-processing, spreadsheet, and presentation software.

RESEARCH Do your research:
- Research the demographics and psychographics of the population of each of the locations.

- Determine local rents for properties similar to the ones described.
- Determine the trade area of each location.

REPORT Prepare a written report using the following tools:
- *Word-processing program*: Prepare a written report listing the demographic and psychographic characteristics for the population of each location and a description of the trade area for each location.
- *Spreadsheet program*: Prepare a chart comparing the rents of the three locations. Prepare a chart to illustrate approximate trade areas for each of the proposed locations.
- *Presentation program*: Prepare a ten-slide visual presentation with key points, photos of each proposed location, a key descriptive text.

PRESENTATION AND EVALUATION You will present your report to your silent partner and the bank that may finance your plan. You will be evaluated on the basis of:
- Your knowledge of store-site selection criteria
- Continuity of presentation
- Voice quality
- Eye contact

■ **PORTFOLIO**

Add this report to your career portfolio.

UNIT 3
THE RETAIL STORE

❝The principle was right there—you couldn't miss it. The more you did for your customers, the more they did for us.**❞**

—Debbi Fields
Founder,
Mrs. Fields Cookies

UNIT OVERVIEW

There are many aspects to a retail store. In Unit 3, you will learn about all the work involved with conceiving, organizing, designing, and operating a retail store. Each chapter will look at a different element.

Chapter 9 focuses on how retailers create store image and promote sales through design and visual merchandising. Different methods of promotion and advertising are key strategies examined in Chapter 10, with emphasis on the promotional mix. In Chapter 11, you will learn about selling techniques, the steps of a sale, as well as customer needs. Chapter 12 focuses on the importance of good customer service. In Chapter 13, you will learn about the store manager's role managing staff and other operations.

■ UNIT LAB Preview

The Virtuality Store

A great deal of work goes into creating a unified visual merchandising concept for a store. Can you create a cohesive visual merchandising plan?

Functions of Marketing

- Marketing-Information Management
- Financing
- Selling
- Pricing
- Distribution
- Promotion
- Product/Service Management

Foundations
- Professional Development
- Economics
- Business, Management, Entrepreneurship
- Communication, Interpersonal Skills

Academic Concepts • Technology

These functions are highlighted in this unit:
- Marketing-Information Management
- Product/Service Management
- Promotion
- Selling

177

Chapter 9

Store Design and Visual Merchandising

Chapter Objectives

- Explain the importance of store image.
- Discuss the importance of store design.
- Explain the importance of store layout.
- Define visual merchandising.
- Explain the use of visual merchandising in retailing.
- Describe the styles of displays.

POWER READ

Be an active reader and use these reading strategies:

PREDICT what the section will be about.

CONNECT what you read with your life.

QUESTION as you read to make sure you understand the content.

RESPOND to what you've read.

A RETAIL "BYTE"

In the 1970s, Apple launched the personal computer revolution with the Apple II. In the 1980s, Apple reinvented the personal computer with the Macintosh. Apple had a small but loyal customer base. However, as PCs began to dominate the business world, Apple lost customers in the educational and creative markets. The Windows system gained customers, and it was clear that Apple needed to adapt to survive.

In 1997, Apple decided to sell products directly to customers for the first time through an online Apple Store. Within a week, it became the third largest online e-commerce site. In 1998, Apple expanded its market with a new design when the iMac came out in four colors, changing the way people look at computers. iMacs became fashionable home accessories, as well as office machines. So when Apple announced the opening of its own brick-and-mortar stores in 2001, customers had high expectations—and authorized dealers were concerned.

ANALYZE AND WRITE

1. What are some other companies that have used design to set themselves apart from competitors?
2. What kind of expectations do you think customers had for the Apple retail store?

Case Study Part 2 on page 191

Store Design

AS YOU READ ...

YOU WILL LEARN

- To explain the importance of store image.
- To discuss the importance of store design.
- To explain the importance of store layout.

WHY IT'S IMPORTANT

Store design and layout help create a retail store's image for customers and can affect the success of the business.

KEY TERMS

- store image
- fixtures
- store layout
- impulse purchases

PREDICT

Which of the key terms listed affect store image?

store image the personality of the store, made up of many parts that work together to create a store's image

Creating a Good Impression

This chapter will discuss the elements of store design, visual merchandising, and why they are important. Retailers use store design to help project the image of their businesses. Visual merchandising is also one of the most important tools that retailers use for creating store image and atmosphere. This chapter will also focus on store displays and their part in creating an effective visual-merchandising effort.

A store's design begins to influence customers before they enter the store. Good store design has a positive effect on customers. It functions to make customers want to explore the store. Good design also showcases the store's merchandise. A store's design should be created to project the store's image. Once we look at store design, we will also look at store layout. The way layout is used in a store is a factor in the sale of its merchandise or services and in how customers move through the store.

Store Image

What is store image? **Store image** can be described as the personality of the store. There are many elements that combine to create a store's image. All the elements are important. Some components of store image can include:

- Type of merchandise and services
- Quality of merchandise and services
- Sales associates
- Design and layout of the store
- Bags and packaging
- Colors of the store décor
- Store fixtures and equipment
- Lighting
- Music
- Scent

World Market

The Floating Market

Every day for more than a century, hundreds of people have made their way to a narrow canal between two rivers in southern Thailand. Many residents come to conduct business as usual. Tourists in water taxis also come to see this unusual sight. They've all come to *Damnoen Saduak,* Thailand's famous floating market. In the manner of their ancestors, the market's vendors skillfully maneuver small boats through the crowded waterway, selling and trading their wares. The region produces an abundance of fruits and vegetables—cabbages, papayas, onions, chilies, sprouts, and coconuts—which spill out of baskets lined end-to-end on boats of every description. Shoppers can also find snacks, souvenirs, and practical goods such as wide-brimmed hats and cooking gadgets.

Because of the crowds, locals tell newcomers to arrive early for a traditional Thai breakfast of fried peanuts and a spicy rice porridge called congee served with pickled vegetables and hot sauce.

The unusual atmosphere and unique appearance of the Saduak market are part of its appeal. Name some U.S. retail stores that use unusual or unique design to attract customers.

The overall effect of all factors creates the store's image. Store image, in turn, affects how customers feel about the store and how they react to the store's ambiance. The store image should serve to remind customers what is unique and special about the store.

Store Design

Store design is so important that many retailers hire professional store designers. Store designers are experts in customer traffic patterns and in knowing which types of merchandise sell best in particular locations within a store. However, where does the design of a store begin? It begins with the customer's first impression of the store. When a customer arrives at a store, his or her first impression starts with a store's exterior. That means that the exterior of the store is just as important as the interior for creating the good impression that the retailer wants to give customers.

Exterior Store Design

Think about the first three things a customer sees when viewing the store's exterior:

- Front windows

- Front door

- Store sign

CONNECT

The next time you go to a retail store, write down the first thing that you notice about the store. Does it relate to your image of the store?

EYE APPEAL Matching the store image to its target-market customers is one aspect of store design. *What type of customers might shop at this store?*

FRONT WINDOWS When a store is located in a shopping center, the first thing that customers see is the front window. The front windows are probably used to display merchandise. The merchandise in the windows should be arranged nicely in a pleasing pattern that is interesting for customers to view. The merchandise in the windows should attract customers and make them want to go into the store. The merchandise and display in the windows should also attract new customers to the store. In order to attract new or returning customers, the windows should be clean and well lit. The lighting should illuminate the merchandise at night so it can be seen. The lighting during the day is also important so that the merchandise looks its best.

FRONT DOOR The front door is also important. As with all other aspects of the exterior, the front door should project the same image as the rest of the store. Remember that as customers walk or drive by when the store is not open, they see the closed door and the windows and get impressions of the store. The color and style of the front door should complement the image that the store projects in other areas.

STORE SIGN The windows and door should work together with the store sign to present a cohesive image for the business. The store sign should be consistent with the other design elements of the store. A store sign should be recognizable and be designed with colors and fonts that are coordinated with the overall image of the store.

Interior Store Design

The interior of the store is where customers walk around to browse and buy the store merchandise. The interior space design should encourage customers to browse and feel comfortable. The interior design of a store should be consistent with the store image. The interior image of any store should be one that makes the store's target customers feel comfortable. For example, a clothing store with target customers who

are teenage girls will have a very different image than a store with target customers who are 25- to 50-year-old professional women. There are several aspects of the store interior to consider when planning the design.

SELLING SPACE The selling space is the most important of the interior spaces. The selling space is what customers see each time they visit the store. This area of the store includes the elements of the store's interior design, such as the colors of the walls and flooring, as well as the different types of fixtures that are used. **Fixtures** are permanent or moveable store furnishings that hold or display merchandise. Lighting is another important interior element that affects the selling space. Lighting is important for customers see the merchandise and to feature certain items of merchandise.

BEHIND THE SCENES There are also spaces behind the scenes, or out of the selling area, that customers do not see. Those spaces are important too. The behind-the-scenes spaces contribute to the efficient running of the store and must be considered when the retailer plans the overall design of the store. Depending on the size of the store, some or all of the behind-the-scenes areas can be combined in one area. Some of those spaces include:

- Receiving and marking area

- Merchandise storage area

- Supplies storage area

- Office area

- Mechanical necessities area for heating and air conditioning

Store Layout

All the elements of interior store design combine in the store layout. **Store layout** is the arrangement of the store's merchandise, fixtures, and equipment. The layout includes elements such as the placement of the cash register, wrap desk, fitting rooms, and the merchandise arrangement. The store's merchandise layout should present the store's merchandise to its best advantage and help sell that merchandise. An effective store layout encourages customers to move from one merchandise area to another and through as much of the store as possible. Retailers know that the longer customers stay in the store, the more likely they are to buy. **Figure 9.1** on page 184 illustrates four types of layouts: free-flow, spine, loop, and grid.

Retailers must determine which merchandise they will place in specific locations of the store layout. When retailers make merchandise-placement decisions, their goal is to maximize each square foot of the selling space. Retailers want the selling space to be as productive as possible.

fixtures permanent or moveable store furnishings that are used to hold or display merchandise

store layout the arrangement of the store's merchandise, fixtures, and equipment

QUESTION
What does a store's layout accomplish?

Figure 9.1

Store Layouts

CUSTOMER PATHS The way that traffic flows through a retail store can be determined by the floor plan, or layout, of the store and its merchandise. *Why do retailers want customers to move through as much of the store as possible?*

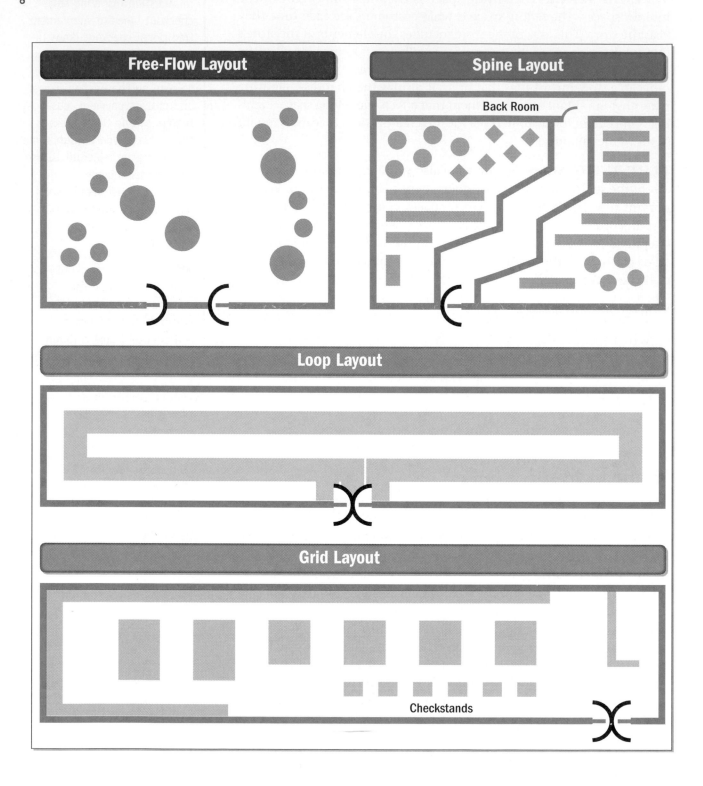

Free-Flow Layout

Spine Layout

Back Room

Loop Layout

Grid Layout

Checkstands

Best Merchandise

There are some principles that retailers can follow when determining merchandise placement. One principle is called *best merchandise forward*. To attract customers, the retailer places merchandise near the entrance of the store or department—or where it can be seen from the escalator. For example, a bookstore owner will place an arrangement of well-publicized bestsellers near the entrance of the store to inform customers that the book is available and to encourage them to come in and buy a copy.

Impulse Purchasing

Impulse-purchase items are placed where customers can see them and where they are easy to buy. **Impulse purchases** are items that are usually inexpensive and ones that customers might buy without much thought. For example, that same bookseller will place bookmarks, pocket calendars, and other book accessories near the register. Those items are easily added to a purchase without much thought on the part of the customer.

All Design Elements

Retailers use good placement and store layout as part of the overall store design that helps project the image of their businesses. Other design elements, such as displays, interior colors, lighting, and so on, are also important in contributing to visual merchandising—which is the focus of the next section. All these design elements can have a positive effect on customers and can contribute to the success of a business.

Math Check

IMPULSIVE BUDGET

Donovan went grocery shopping with $55. His total bill was $53.50, but he noticed a special on candy bars as he was checking out: three for $2.50. Did he have enough money to buy the candy too?

➡ For tips on finding the solution, go to **marketingseries.glencoe.com**.

impulse purchases items that are inexpensive and that customers buy without much thought

---

 Quick Check ✓

RESPOND to what you've read by answering these questions.

1. What are three elements of a store's exterior design? _____

_____

_____

_____

2. What is the most important interior space in a retail store? _____

_____

_____

_____

3. What are the goals of an effective store layout? _____

_____

_____

_____

Visual Merchandising

AS YOU READ ...

YOU WILL LEARN

- To define visual merchandising.
- To explain the use of visual merchandising in retailing.
- To describe the styles of displays.

WHY IT'S IMPORTANT

Visual merchandising ties the store image components together. Certain display styles are most effective for particular types of merchandise.

KEY TERMS

- visual merchandising
- display
- promotional display
- institutional display
- display props
- decorative display props
- functional display props

PREDICT

Pick one key term and define it before reading the section.

visual merchandising the integrated look of the entire store

display a presentation of merchandise to attract customers so they will examine the merchandise.

The Total Look

Visual merchandising is the integrated look of the entire store and is composed of all the visual aspects of a store. Good visual merchandising effectively uses all the components of store image that were discussed in the previous section. Visual merchandising is the store's appearance and the atmosphere it projects to everyone who enters.

Many people mistakenly think that visual merchandising is composed of only the displays in the store. While displays are very important to visual merchandising, they are only one component. Visual merchandising should always reflect the image that the retailer wants the store to project. Then it should work together with the design of the store to create one unified presentation.

Components of Visual Merchandising

The components of visual merchandising are the same ones that contribute to a store's image. As you have learned, the exterior components of the store include the sign, the front door, and the front windows. The store interior includes the selling space and any other spaces that customers might occupy, such as fitting rooms and restrooms. Within the selling space, the colors of the walls and the flooring, the lighting, the fixture types, the store layout, and the displays are all components of the interior visual merchandising. The exterior elements and interior elements of a store's visual merchandising should all integrate to present a cohesive visual presentation. A store's visual merchandising helps to create the atmosphere and personality of the store, which can attract and keep customers.

Display

We have all seen displays at stores in a local mall or shopping center. A **display** is a presentation of merchandise to attract customers so they will examine merchandise. Displays are the most important element of a store's interior visual merchandising. Retailers make use of displays for many purposes. However, there are two main purposes of any specific display:

- To help sell merchandise

- To reinforce the store's image by creating goodwill

Promotional Displays

Displays that are created to help sell merchandise are called promotional displays. A **promotional display** is designed to sell merchandise—either regularly priced merchandise or sale merchandise. Promotional displays can appear in the store's windows or various locations throughout the store. These displays can attract attention for the arrival of new spring fashions or for a best-selling book. A retailer might also use promotional displays to inform customers about an annual sale event.

Institutional Displays

Retailers can create institutional displays to help promote a local charitable event. An **institutional display** is also designed to generate goodwill for the store. Institutional displays also commemorate holidays. Lord & Taylor and Saks Fifth Avenue stores create incredible window displays each year in December. All of the windows in their New York City stores are decorated to tell stories. People from all over the country travel to New York City each year to walk by those windows. They are so popular that retailers set up designated areas to help with flow of the crowds. Those two stores are actually not promoting any of their merchandise in the windows. The windows are designed to generate seasonal spirit and goodwill. In smaller towns, store owners might create institutional displays to support a local high school football team or a local charitable fundraising effort.

Figure 9.2

Color Schemes

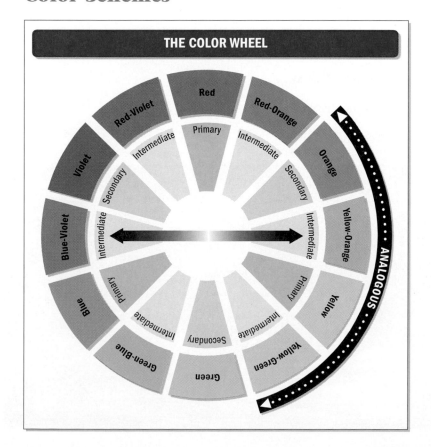

THE COLOR WHEEL

USING THE COLOR WHEEL
Designers use tools such as color wheels to help create a store's image. *What combination of colors is used in your favorite store?*

promotional display display designed to help sell merchandise

institutional display display designed to generate goodwill for the store

CONNECT

Describe an interesting display that you've seen in a store. Did you buy the merchandise displayed?

Interior Displays

Retailers use displays both outside and inside their stores. There are several styles of displays that are used to showcase merchandise in the store windows and inside the store. The two goals of these promotion displays are: to attract customers' attention and to encourage customers to buy the merchandise.

Retailers of all types use displays throughout their stores. The size of a store will usually determine who is responsible for creating and installing the store's displays. In small stores the owner and the sales associates probably create and install the displays. Large stores have people on staff who are experts in creating and installing displays. Those people are hired to do displays throughout the store and in the store windows.

The process for creating store displays involves the following steps:

1. Generate an idea or theme for the display.
2. Determine where the display will be placed in the store.
3. Meet with management to get approval for the idea or theme.
4. Determine which merchandise is most suitable for the display.
5. Install the display.
6. Maintain and dismantle the display.

Display Styles

Each display style has a purpose and advantages for the merchandise it showcases. There are several styles of displays that retailers use inside stores:

- Open display
- Closed display
- Room-setting display
- Point-of-sale display
- Store-decoration display

SHOWCASING MERCHANDISE Closed displays offer the advantage of security to retailers displaying expensive merchandise. *Do you think closed displays might also create more customer interest because merchandise cannot be touched but only viewed? Why?*

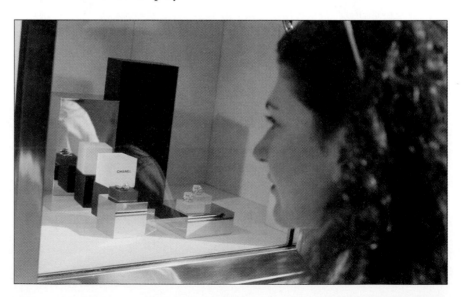

Electronic Fantasy Worlds

Fry's

At first glance, customers who enter Fry's Electronics store may think they have wandered onto a Hollywood movie set. Each of Fry's 22 stores—in California, Arizona, Texas, and Nevada—has its own unique look. A time warp away from gigabytes and motherboards, the store-design themes focus on the fantastic.

JUST IMAGINE

In southern California, San Marcos shoppers step into the lost civilization of Atlantis, complete with exotic fish and waterfalls. Fry's of Burbank plays host to space aliens who have crashed their saucer into the front entrance while on an intergalactic mission for a bargain. The marble floors and grand piano in northern California's Sunnyvale store echo the elegance of Silicon Valley. Fry's Houston store recreates the Texas oil industry with a field of gushing wells. The world's largest slot machine can be found in the Las Vegas store. But watch out for a giant snake, symbolic of the ancient Aztecs, slithering above the door of Fry's in Phoenix, Arizona.

SELECTION HEAVEN

Aside from the adventurous decoration, it's business as usual for Fry's customers. Low costs and a range of choices are found in aisle after aisle of the warehouse-sized stores.

Fry's Electronics first set up shop in 1985 in Sunnyvale, California, as one-stop shopping for hi-tech professionals. Although the computer department is still the "heart" of each store, today's 50,000 electronic items also include household appliances, audio and video wares, and a variety of games and toys.

With more stores and products in the works, Fry's plans to provide the latest technology in environments that stir the imagination. The company also hopes its stores are a place where everyday people, from computer enthusiasts to suburban parents, will feel equally at home.

1. If you were asked to think of a theme for an electronic store, what would it be?
2. If Fry's stores discontinued their spectacular store designs, do you think sales would be affected? Explain.

OPEN DISPLAY An open display features merchandise in a setting that allows the customer to touch and handle it. Shelves and racks hold the merchandise in open displays. The open shelves at Bath & Body Works stores hold the wide selection of bath products and lotions that the store sells. Open racks are often used to display belts. The open display allows customers to browse through the products while deciding which ones they want to buy.

CLOSED DISPLAY Display cases are used for closed displays. Display cases feature glass fronts and sides so customers can see the merchandise inside, but they can't touch it. Closed displays can hold merchandise that is either very valuable or very fragile. Fine jewelry is a good example of merchandise that is kept in closed display cases. Many men's stores place their most expensive, designer silk ties in closed-display cases to protect the merchandise from damage that comes from excessive handling by customers.

ALTERNATIVE STYLE

Bridget Odin
Store Display Designer
Home Works

What does your job entail?
"I create living-room displays at our stores. We also provide fabric choices in books so customers can customize their orders. I keep track of incoming styles and trends, and pay attention to customer requests to create complete sets of furniture and accessories that people can buy without needing to consult a designer. I work with a team and must be able to communicate visual ideas—and have a sense of humor under deadlines."

What do you like most about your job?
"Because we use in-store displays for self-service, my choices are important and influence customers. That's a lot of pressure, but it's very gratifying."

What kind of training did you have?
"I received a bachelor's degree in design and did internships during summer breaks."

What advice would you give students?
"Get the proper training at a design school or through a design major and do an internship at any retail store. Take photos of your work and keep a portfolio. Use your imagination about types of stores that need display work—and go for it!"

What is your key to your success?
"I love what I do. I feel fortunate to work in a creative field that provides a livelihood. I also continually research and stay current with design trends."

Why would communication skills be important for a designer?

Career Data:
Store-Display Designer

Education and Training
Degrees in design, marketing; classes in graphic arts and architecture

Skills and Abilities Creativity and eye for design, organizational skills, ability to work under pressure, and strong communication skills

Career Outlook Faster than average growth through 2010

Career Path A typical career path can begin on the sales floor or in an entry-level visual merchandising job, followed by promotion to manager and then director.

ROOM-SETTING DISPLAY Room-setting displays are assembled to allow customers to see how certain merchandise will actually look in their homes. Furniture stores use room settings to allow customers to visualize the furniture and accessories they sell. Home-improvement stores also use room settings to display their merchandise. A home-improvement store might set up a model kitchen to help sell cabinets, sinks, and flooring products. A room setting, complete with accessories, also encourages customers to purchase extra items. A furniture store that sets up a dining-room display will use a table and chairs and china cabinet. To make the room look complete, the store will add a rug, fill the china cabinet with dishes, and add a centerpiece accessory on the table. The customer can easily visualize the room setting in a home and may want to add a few of the accessories to his or her shopping list.

POINT-OF-SALE These displays are used primarily for impulse merchandise. Point-of-sale displays are near the cash register. This type of display is called point-of-sale because that is usually when the customer decides to buy the merchandise featured. Nordstrom's department stores use point-of-purchase displays at the cash registers in many of their clothing departments. For example, the displays may feature the Nordstrom Silk Wash. This product is for fine fabrics that are best laundered by hand. The price of Silk Wash is low, so it is easy for customers to add it to their total purchases.

STORE DECORATION Store decorations can promote a season or holiday and include items such as banners, signs, and props. For example, a store might use decorations such as pots of tulips and daffodils, and stuffed toy rabbits to celebrate the spring season. Many department stores also use banners within the store to promote sale events.

DISPLAY PROPS Retailers use **display props** to enhance a display. There are two types of display props. **Decorative props** enhance the merchandise that is being displayed. Adding flowers to a spring display will make the display more attractive and interesting. Creative display professionals use all sorts of props in unexpected ways to enhance the items on display and to attract customer attention. **Functional display props** hold the merchandise of a display. Mannequins are functional display props. Some store fixtures serve as other functional display props used to display merchandise. Several methods of presentation include:

1. Shelving—Merchandise is placed on shelves that are usually in wall systems.
2. Hanging—Clothing on hangers is placed on round racks or four-way racks, or on bars within wall systems.
3. Pegging—Merchandise is hung on peghooks usually in wall systems.
4. Folding—Merchandise (usually soft goods) is folded and placed on tables or shelves that line walls.
5. Stacking—Large merchandise is stacked on shelves, at the base of gondolas, or on flat platforms placed on the floor.
6. Dumping—Quantities of small merchandise is dumped in bins or baskets.

Case Study PART 2

A RETAIL "BYTE"
Continued from Part 1 on page 179

Addressing the fears of other computer dealers, Apple CEO Steve Jobs said, "Our strategy isn't to put our resellers out of business, but to work side by side with them. We think our stores will help resellers a lot by increasing exposure to the Mac."

The Apple Store shares its successful ideas with all dealers and stocks Apple Store-only goods. Its store-design features include: a "Genius Bar," where users can talk to a resident Apple expert, a theater with a 10-foot screen to show Apple demonstrations and developments, and home and office solutions and products. The products are placed in different "solution zones" on the selling floor. In flagship stores such as the one in New York City's Soho district, the zones are divided by striped glass and have maple-wood furniture. Building an identity, creating interest, and cultivating loyalty are essential strategies for store design, as well as for sales at the Apple Store.

ANALYZE AND WRITE
1. What were concerns from authorized Apple dealers?
2. Describe the design and purpose of the solution zones in the Apple stores.

QUESTION

What is the difference between functional and decorative props?

display props items used to enhance a display

decorative display props items used to enhance the merchandise that is being displayed

functional display props items used to hold the merchandise of a display

Merchandise to Display

Selecting the best merchandise to feature in a display requires good judgment and knowledge of which merchandise will be most attractive and pleasing to the store's customers. When retailers select items for a display, they look for merchandise that will sell well, looks good, and appeals to a wide range of customers. Retailers—particularly fashion retailers—want to display new merchandise as well as merchandise that is timely. For example, displaying timely merchandise means featuring patriotic merchandise shortly before July 4th or displaying swimsuits by the month of June.

Display Maintenance

Because the purpose of displays is to feature merchandise to encourage customers to buy, it is important that the store's displays be kept in the best condition possible. Displays should be checked daily to ensure that the merchandise is clean and that the entire display remains well arranged. Open displays require regular maintenance during store hours to make certain that the merchandise is sized and arranged correctly.

Not only should displays be well maintained, they should also be changed frequently. Customers should see something new and different each time they visit the store. Fresh, new displays help to keep the store an exciting and fun place in which to shop.

Maintaining and focusing on displays and all the other components of store design and visual merchandising will promote the store's image and its ultimate success.

Quick Check ✓

RESPOND to what you've read by answering these questions.

1. What are the two main purposes of store displays? _____

_____

_____

_____

2. What are two goals of a promotional display? _____

_____

_____

_____

3. What are the five styles of interior store displays? _____

_____

_____

_____

_____

marketingseries.glencoe.com

Worksheet 9.1

Store-Design Analysis

Go to your favorite mall and choose an interesting store to analyze. Describe each of the following elements that help create the store's image.

Name of store: _____

1. Front windows: _____

   _____

   _____

   _____

2. Front door: _____

   _____

   _____

   _____

3. Store sign: _____

   _____

   _____

   _____

4. Interior colors: _____

   _____

   _____

   _____

5. What kind of image does the store present? _____

   _____

   _____

   _____

   _____

6. What changes would you make to improve the store's image? ___

   _____

   _____

   _____

   _____

Worksheet 9.2

Displaying Good Taste

Types of Displays

Choose the best type of display from the list and a suggest a prop for each of the following merchandise items. Explain your choices.

- Open
- Closed
- Room setting
- Point-of-sale
- Store decoration

1. Men's ties: _____

_____

_____

_____

2. Skateboards: _____

_____

_____

_____

3. Engagement rings: _____

_____

_____

_____

4. Dishwashers: _____

_____

_____

_____

5. Cell phones: _____

_____

_____

_____

EXPLORING CAREERS IN VISUAL DESIGN

Trade magazines such as *VM + SD* post job openings in their print publications and on their Web sites. Use the Internet to find a store design and/or visual merchandising magazine to research career opportunities is this field and do these exercises. Then add this page to your career portfolio.

1. What is the name and URL of the trade publication you found? _____

_____

_____

_____

_____

2. List three job openings or career opportunities advertised. _____

_____

_____

_____

_____

3. Choose one of the three job openings to research further and write what you learn. _____

_____

_____

_____

_____

_____

4. What qualifications are necessary for the job? Would you be interested in pursuing this type of career further? Why?

_____

_____

_____

_____

_____

_____

CHAPTER SUMMARY

Section 9.1 Store Design

store image (p. 180)
fixtures (p. 183)
store layout (p. 183)
impulse purchases
    (p. 185)

- Store image can be described as the personality of the store. It affects how customers feel about the store and should reflect what is unique and special about the store.

- The function of store design is to make customers want to explore the store and to showcase the store's merchandise.

- Store layout is the arrangement of the store's merchandise, fixtures, and equipment. Its function is to present the store's merchandise to its best advantage and help sell merchandise.

Section 9.2 Visual Merchandising

visual merchandising
    (p. 186)
display (p. 186)
promotional display
    (p. 187)
institutional display
    (p. 187)
display props (p. 191)
decorative display props
    (p. 191)
functional display props
    (p. 191)

- Visual merchandising is the integrated look of the entire store.

- Visual merchandising is used in retailing to project the store's desired image.

- There are five styles of interior promotional displays. They are open display, closed display, room-setting display, point-of-sale display, and store-decoration display.

CHECKING CONCEPTS

1. **Explain** the importance of store image.
2. **Describe** how store design encourages customers to explore the store.
3. **Explain** the importance of store layout.
4. **Define** visual merchandising and explain how it is used in retailing.
5. **Describe** the styles of displays.
6. **Identify** the first three things a customer sees when he or she approaches a store.
7. **Describe** the steps for creating store displays.

Critical Thinking

8. **Compare** the two main purposes of displays.

CROSS-CURRICULUM SKILLS

Work-Based Learning

Thinking Skills—Seeing Things in the Mind's Eye

9. Think of a local retail business and imagine the store's window(s), front door, and sign. Explain how you would redesign these elements.

Interpersonal Skills—Serving Clients/Customers

10. Ms. Grant, a small-store owner, has one big table that she uses to check out customers, to check in orders, to eat lunch, and for gift-wrapping. Do you think this is good store layout? Why or why not?

School-Based Learning

Social Studies

11. In China, the colors black, white, and blue are associated with death, while red represents good luck, and yellow and pink represent happiness and prosperity. How would this affect displays in China?

Art

12. Imagine that you create displays for a local retail store. Create an institutional display for a holiday or charitable event. Use a cardboard box of any size to represent the store window.

Role Play: Employee of Grocery Store

SITUATION You are to assume the role of experienced employee of a large grocery store. Your store manager (judge) has asked you to recommend some products to display in the store to promote a picnic theme for the upcoming Memorial Day holiday. The store manager (judge) wants to include products from as many of the store's departments as possible.

ACTIVITY You are to recommend products from many departments and make recommendations about how they should be displayed to the store manager (judge).

EVALUATION You will be evaluated on how well you meet the following performance indicators:

- Plan/schedule displays and themes with management.
- Describe types of display arrangements.
- Create displays.
- Select and use display fixtures/forms.
- Present findings and recommendations.

Use the Internet to access the VisualStore Web site (sponsored by *VM+SD* magazine) and answer these questions.

- What does *VM+SD* stand for and what is its purpose?
- Go to the pull-down menu and click Industry News.
- Describe and explain one of the headlines.
- Name one job listed in the Help Wanted section of the Classified Ads.

➡For a link to the VisualStore Web site to do this activity, go to **marketingseries.glencoe.com**.

Chapter 10

Promotion and Advertising

Chapter Objectives

- Identify the types of promotion.
- Define promotional mix.
- Identify types of sales promotions.
- Explain the concept of publicity.
- Identify the categories of advertising.
- Explain the types of advertising.
- Identify the types of advertising media.

Be an active reader and use these reading strategies:

PREDICT what the section will be about.

CONNECT what you read with your life.

QUESTION as you read to make sure you understand the content.

RESPOND to what you've read.

X-TREME PROMOTION

Many retail products are promoted and advertised at special events and contests created for specific retail target markets. Sports events such as skateboard tournaments generate publicity for retail sponsors and product makers such as Hansen juices and DC Shoes.

Ken Block and Damon Way started the DC Shoe Company in San Diego in 1994. Going against the trend of edgy skateboarding styles, their skate shoes were made of high-tech materials and unique, fashion-conscious designs. They focused their sophisticated advertisements in skateboard magazines. They also promoted their shoes by calling on a team of world-class skaters, such as Damon's brother Danny Way, a champion skateboarder. He endorsed the skate shoe, and the company took off flying. With an expanded shoe line, they started making skateboard wear. The next logical step was to branch out to other sports. However, the skate-shop world is very specialized, and its target market is loyal to the sport. So what did DC Shoes do to continue growing while maintaining a loyal customer base?

ANALYZE AND WRITE

1. How has champion skateboarder Danny Way helped promote DC Shoes?
2. If you were promoting other sports products in connection with DC Shoes, what other sports would you choose to promote?

Case Study Part 2 on page 203

Retail Promotion

AS YOU READ...

YOU WILL LEARN

- To identify the types of promotion.
- To define promotional mix.
- To identify types of sales promotions.
- To explain the concept of publicity.

WHY IT'S IMPORTANT

Understanding the different types of promotion can help a retailer determine which one is best to use. Publicity is valuable and can enhance a store's image.

KEY TERMS

- promotion
- promotional mix
- merchandise promotions
- institutional promotions
- publicity
- public relations

PREDICT

Think of different ways that stores get publicity.

promotion any form of communication used by retailers to inform the public about their merchandise and services, or to enhance the image of the business

promotional mix the way that a retailer combines the four types of promotion

Expanding Store Image

Chapter 9 discussed the image that a retailer creates for a store. You learned how visual merchandising is a big part of creating the store's image. However, there are two additional elements that work with visual merchandising to create and enhance a store's image: promotion and advertising. All three elements—visual merchandising, promotion, and advertising—must work together to maintain and enhance a store's image.

What Is Promotion?

Promotion is part of the broad area of retail communication that takes place between retailers and their customers. **Promotion** is any form of communication used by retailers to inform the public about their business's merchandise and services, or to enhance the image of the business. There are four types of promotion:

- **Sales promotions**—techniques retailers use to encourage customers to come into a store

- **Publicity and public relations**—any unpaid mention of the business or activity that enhances the store's image

- **Advertising**—a paid message that a business sends to the public. (See Section 10.2.)

- **Personal selling**—individuals making contact with potential buyers to complete a sale; Chapter 11 examines this type of promotion.

The Promotional Mix

Retailers use these types of promotion to communicate with their customers. Every retailer combines the four types of promotion in different ways. One retailer might do a lot of advertising, while another might prefer to rely more heavily on sales promotion techniques. The way a retailer combines four types of promotion is called the **promotional mix**. Each retailer must determine the right combination of the types of promotion that best serves that business. All four parts of the promotional mix must work together to enhance the store's image.

Promotional Budget

Advertising and promotional activities cost money. To pay for those promotional activities, retailers set aside a portion of their business budgets for promotion. The promotional budget can be a percentage of the business's net sales (*net sales* is the amount that is left of gross sales after returns have been subtracted). That percentage is usually between 5 and 10 percent. So if there are more sales, there is more money available for promotion.

Promotional Activities

Promotions can take many forms. Creative retailers are always inventing new ways to get the message about their businesses and products to customers and to potential customers. Promotional activities can be grouped into broad categories—non-personal promotional activities and personal promotional activities.

Non-personal promotional activities do not directly involve store personnel. Advertising and public relations are forms of non-personal promotional activities. Store employees plan and execute the advertising and public relations efforts, but those employees do not come into direct contact with the customers; therefore, the activities are non-personal.

Personal promotional activities directly involve store personnel. Selling is a personal promotional activity because it directly involves a store employee interacting with a customer.

Merchandise promotions are promotions that involve the store's merchandise. Merchandise promotions help increase store sales or sales of a particular type of merchandise. For example, Macy's department store invites customers to visit the store for a free Lancôme gift with purchase. Potential customers may know about the store, but retailers use such promotions to get new and regular customers to come into the store to get a free gift. (see **Figure 10.1**).

MARKETING SERIES *Online*

Remember to check out this book's Web site for promotion and advertising information and more great resources at **marketingseries.glencoe.com**.

CONNECT

Name some free gifts you've received when buying certain products.

merchandise promotions
promotions that involve the store's merchandise

Figure 10.1

Customer Awareness

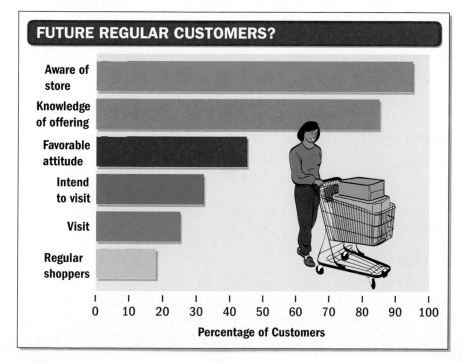

FUTURE REGULAR CUSTOMERS?

- Aware of store
- Knowledge of offering
- Favorable attitude
- Intend to visit
- Visit
- Regular shoppers

0 10 20 30 40 50 60 70 80 90 100

Percentage of Customers

FUTURE REGULAR CUSTOMERS? Retailers constantly work to raise peoples' awareness of their stores so that potential customers will become regular customers. *What do you think is the most effective method of promotion to attract customers?*

➤ **SPONSORING GOODWILL**
When customers see that a retail company is concerned with more than making a profit, they may be inclined to shop at that company's store. Giving back to the community can benefit everyone. *Can you think of charities sponsored by local businesses in your community?*

institutional promotions promotions designed to promote the image of a business or to build goodwill

TECH
NOTES

Electronic Shelf Labels
Permanent plastic labels may soon replace the paper price tags on store shelves. The new tags have liquid crystal displays similar to digital watches. Using electronic shelf labels (ESL) simplifies the pricing process and eliminates a lot of wasted time and paper. Equipped with radio frequency identification (RFID) tags, price tags can be updated for price changes remotely from a central computer.

➥Why has it taken so long for this technology to catch on in America? Answer this question after reading the information through **marketingseries.glencoe.com**.

Institutional promotions are promotions designed to promote the image of the business or to build goodwill for the business. Institutional promotions, such as event and parades, do not focus on selling merchandise. For example, Bloomingdale's department stores support the search for a cure for colon cancer. When Bloomingdale's sends out advertisements inviting customers to a fashion show and luncheon in support of colon cancer research, the store is not promoting any merchandise. This promotional activity demonstrates Bloomingdale's civic-minded attitude and builds goodwill while communicating that the store cares about its customers' health.

Sales Promotions

Retailers employ a variety of techniques when they decide to use sales promotions as one type of promotion in the promotional mix. Retailers use sales promotions to encourage customers to come into the store and to buy more merchandise. Retailers also use sales promotions to help introduce new products or services. There are a variety of sales promotion techniques:

- Contests

- Sales events

- Premiums

- Free samples

- E-mail

Contests

Retailers use contests to increase customer traffic. Customers may come to the store to enter a contest. If a retailer decides to select a contest winner by a drawing held in the store, the customer must be present to win. Customer traffic would increase again on the day of the drawing.

Some retailers hold contests to encourage customers to visit their Web sites. For example, a retailer might post a contest on the business's Web site. The contest might require customers to answer questions about the Web site, and then enter the responses electronically. The retailer holds a drawing from eligible entries received from the Web site. Winners are posted on the Web site, and the store awards contest winners store merchandise or store gift certificates. For example, a supermarket contest winner might win a Thanksgiving turkey. This type of contest can benefit a retailer who wants customers to explore the business's Web site.

Sales Events

Sales events usually fall into two categories—special sales and combination offers. Examples of *special sales* include a one-day shoe sale or a sale on spring flower bulbs during the fall planting season. The other type of sale or price reduction is the *combination offer*. The combination offer might be a "buy one, get one free" or "buy one, get one at half-price." For instance, a restaurant might offer a breakfast special. The special offer might be to purchase one breakfast at the regular price and get a second breakfast at half-price. This offer involves purchasing a combination of meals. Retailers use both of these types of sales events to increase overall sales or to increase sales of a particular kind of product.

Premiums

Premiums are small items that retailers give to customers. These premiums are available at a low cost or even free to the customers. Premiums include items that retailers give to customers when opening a new store or celebrating a special occasion. For example, a sporting-goods store might give customers free T-shirts to celebrate the grand opening. Of course, the store's name or logo would be imprinted on the promotional T-shirt.

Coupons are another well-known form of retail premiums. A *coupon* is a slip of paper that entitles a customer to a price reduction, or discount, on merchandise or services. There are coupons in the newspaper from grocery stores, drugstores, and even department stores. Another type of coupon is generated at the checkout stand of a store. A coupon is printed on the back of the customer receipt. The coupon encourages the customer to purchase a certain product again, or to try a different brand of the same product or the store's brand. For instance, your grocery receipt for one brand of peanut butter might have a coupon for 50 cents off a competing brand of peanut butter. Retailers also use coupons to help introduce new products. When a drugstore introduces

Case Study PART 2

X-TREME PROMOTION
Continued from Part 1 on page 199

Not wanting to risk losing loyal skater customers by expanding to other sports, Block and Way decided to stay focused on their skateboarding roots. They expanded but only into other extreme or active sports such as snowboarding, BMX, and surfing. Because many skateboarders may cross over and participate in these sports, DC's merchandise was compatible. The company used musicians and artists influenced by current advertising. They released limited-edition shoes with designs influenced by current bands, artists, and designers with whom skaters are familiar.

The company sponsors its endorsers such as Danny Way to keep the DC name in the minds of skateboard enthusiasts with exciting stunts covered by skateboard magazines. In fact, the world's biggest "air" was performed by Danny Way while he was wearing DC Shoes. DC also promotes its brand by selling to target markets where they live and shop—in malls or independent stores. These retailing strategies have kept DC's customers coming back and have attracted new customers, earning the company over $100 million annually.

ANALYZE AND WRITE

1. What types of promotion has DC Shoes used?

2. What other promotional methods would you suggest?

Selling Point

COMMUNITY GOODWILL
The first Macy's Thanksgiving Day Parade took place in 1924. It was organized by immigrant employees of the department store to show gratitude for their new American heritage.

QUESTION

What are some examples of free samples in specific types of stores?

publicity any unpaid mention of a retail business, its employees, or its merchandise in the media

public relations any activity produced to create a favorable image for a retail business

a new line of vitamins, the drugstore owner might decide to offer a discount coupon. The coupon encourages customers to try the new line of vitamins. The retailer might also offer a two-for-one introductory coupon. Retailers who want to increase sales and introduce new products or services often use coupons.

Free Samples

Customers appreciate free merchandise. That is why retailers offer free samples at stores. Retailers might also mail samples to customers. For example, a department store might mail samples of a new face cream or fragrance directly to customers' homes. Grocery stores might give away in-store samples of a new brand of pizza or egg rolls. Those samples are prepared in the store and given to customers to taste. Customers receive coupons with the sample. Retailers use free samples to encourage customers to try new products with hopes they will like them and buy them.

E-Mail

Many retailers make sales promotional offers to customers via e-mail. Retailers encourage customers to visit their business's Web sites. They make promotional offers to customers on the Web site. Retailers use those promotional efforts to encourage customers to visit the store or to shop online. Books-a-Million, a retail book store, periodically sends their Internet customers coupons for a discount when the customers visit a store during a time period. Retailers like e-mail promotions because they are inexpensive. Usually, customers can print out the e-coupons on their home printers. A retailer saves on the cost of printing the coupons and mailing when sending e-mail coupons.

Publicity

Publicity is any unpaid mention of a retail business, its employees, or its merchandise in the media. It is another type of promotion in the promotional mix. Publicity is a form of public relations. **Public relations** involve any activity produced to create a favorable image for a retail business. Publicity is a real advantage to retailers because it highlights activities sponsored by the retailer that benefit the community. Retailers use two forms of publicity—free publicity and special-activity publicity.

Free Publicity

Free publicity is exactly what its name implies. An activity that the store sponsors or a noteworthy product in the store can generate free publicity for the store. A small-town newspaper might publish an item about Joe's Dry Cleaners and its employee softball team winning a local competition. The mention of Joe's Dry Cleaners is free publicity for the business. That publicity costs the retailer nothing.

World Market

Everlasting Value

Composed of crystallized carbon, diamonds are the earth's hardest known substance. The first diamond on record dates back to India 3,000 years ago. Over the centuries, the diamond has been used as a talisman to protect against evil and as a medical aid. Today the diamond is one of the world's most popular gemstones. Diamonds are a symbol of love—associated with engagements, 75th wedding anniversaries, and April birthdays. "A diamond is forever," boasts one well-known advertisement.

Diamonds are found on every continent except Europe and Antarctica. Each year the world's diamond mines produce more than 100 million carats. (A carat is a unit of weight equaling 0.007 ounce.) The richest diamond mine in the world is located in Australia. It produces about one-third of the world's supply—35 to 40 million carats annually. The Australian deposit also supplies the rare and popular pink diamond.

Analyze the diamond industry's advertising slogan, "A diamond is forever." Do you think it is effective? Why?

AUSTRALIA

Special-Activity Publicity

Special-activity publicity is also free publicity because the store's special activity is published without charge. However, special-activity publicity does cost the retailer in other ways. For example, a fashion show for charity might feature the clothing and accessories sold by the retailer. The retailer must pay the salaries of the employees who select the clothing, write the commentary, and work at the fashion show. However, a newspaper article about the fashion show does not cost the retailer a dime because it is a newsworthy event, and it can also serve as free advertising for the store.

Math Check

MEGA-GEM
How much does the 3,107-carat Star of Africa diamond weigh in grams if one carat is .2 grams?

➡ For tips on finding the solution, go to **marketingseries.glencoe.com**.

Quick Check

RESPOND to what you've read by answering these questions.

1. What are the four types of promotion? _____

_____

2. What are five sales promotion techniques that retailers use? _____

_____

3. What are two types of publicity? _____

_____

 marketingseries.glencoe.com

Advertising

AS YOU READ ...

YOU WILL LEARN

- To identify the categories of advertising.
- To explain the types of advertising.
- To identify the types of advertising media.

WHY IT'S IMPORTANT

Understanding the categories of advertising helps to determine when and how to use each one.

KEY TERMS

- advertising
- product advertising
- institutional advertising
- retail advertising
- vendor advertising
- cooperative advertising
- media

PREDICT

Can you name two kinds of advertisements?

advertising paid message that a business sends to the public

product advertising paid message used by businesses to promote a product or group of products

institutional advertising paid message used to promote a business's image or to create goodwill for the business

The Importance of Advertising

You see advertising almost everywhere—in magazines, on taxicabs, on television, and on computer screens. It serves an important purpose for retailers and our economy. This section will examine advertising and its different forms, as well as how advertising helps retailers and their customers.

What Is Advertising?

Advertising is a paid message that a business sends to the public. Businesses use advertising for a variety of purposes. Advertisements can introduce a new or existing product or service, attract regular and new customers to a store, and promote the image of a retail business. Advertising is the third type of promotion used by retailers in the promotional mix.

Categories of Advertising

All types of advertising fall into two major categories—product advertising and institutional advertising. **Product advertising** is a paid message used by businesses to promote a product or group of products. Retailers use product advertising to:

- Help sell the products they are advertising.

- Introduce new products or services.

- Announce a sale on certain products.

- Encourage customers to visit the store.

For example, a grocery store would use product advertising to inform its customers that the store is carrying a new brand of frozen pizza.

Institutional advertising is a paid message used to promote the business's image or to create goodwill for the business. When retailers use institutional advertising, they are not calling attention to the products or services that the business offers for sale. Retailers use institutional advertising to highlight their business's involvement in community activities, or to thank customers for supporting a charitable fund-raising effort that the business supports. For example, Mazzarini's Grocery Store might run a newspaper ad congratulating the local high school championship football team. The ad is not promoting the grocery store products. The purpose of the ad is to create goodwill within the community by supporting the local team.

WRITING OUTSIDE THE BOX

Kimberley Freeman
Copywriter
Zag Studios

What does your job entail?
"I think of ideas for print, TV, and radio ads, and then write them. Copywriters start with a conception session and brainstorm ideas with an art director. The copywriter thinks of a headline, and the A.D. (art director) makes up a visual concept. Unless you are working at a huge, international agency, you usually get a variety of projects. You might work on chocolate one week and toothpaste the next. You might write a radio spot for Burger King one day and a magazine ad for a cruise ship the next week."

What kind of training did you have?
"After obtaining a bachelor's degree in psychology and English, I had two years of intensive 'ad school' at the Portfolio Center in Atlanta, Georgia. A New York agency saw my portfolio and hired me a few months before graduation."

What advice would you give students?
"Think 'outside the box.' It also helps to have a sense of humor and an open mind. The ability to write a fresh engaging style and the ability to work well with visual artists are important."

What is your key to success?
"In the client's eyes, success is more than a nice-looking ad. A good copywriter gets inside the target audience's head. Write for them, not at them."

Why do you think creativity and an open mind are important to create well-written ads?

Career Data: Copywriter

Education and Training Bachelor's degree in language, psychology, business, communications, English, or journalism

Skills and Abilities Creativity, good writing skills, and ability to work as a part of a team

Career Outlook Faster than average growth through 2010

Career Path Copywriters often begin in entry-level jobs at ad agencies, newspapers, or magazines.

Types of Advertising

In addition to the two categories of advertising, there are three types of advertising: retail advertising, vendor advertising, and cooperative advertising. Retailers use **retail advertising** which is advertising that retailers sponsor to promote their stores and products. For example, a sporting-goods retailer might run an ad to encourage customers to visit the store to stock up on tennis supplies.

Vendor advertising is advertising that manufacturers or suppliers sponsor to promote their products. Estée Lauder Cosmetics Company sponsors vendor ads in magazines to promote its fragrances and cosmetics products.

retail advertising advertising that retailers sponsor to promote their stores and products

vendor advertising advertising that manufacturers or suppliers sponsor to promote their products

Free Speech or False Speech?

Freedom of speech sometimes allows people to make false claims. However, when false claims are promoted through advertising, companies cannot hide behind the First Amendment of the U.S. Constitution. Many states, such as California, enforce their own state laws that deal with unfair trade practices and false advertising, and prohibit this type of advertising.

cooperative advertising advertising that features both the vendor's name and the local store where the vendor's product is available

media all of the methods used to get an advertising message to the public

CONNECT

Think of one of your favorite magazines. Do you think its advertising rates are high or low? Why?

Cooperative advertising is a combination of both retail and vendor advertising. Just as the name implies, cooperative advertising represents a combined effort of the vendor and the retailer. **Cooperative advertising** features both the vendor's name and the local store where the vendor's product is available. The vendor and the retailer share in the cost of the advertising. An example of cooperative advertising would be an advertisement for Coca-Cola that includes the name of the local grocery store where you could purchase Cokes. The ad might say that Coca-Cola is available at Smith's Grocery Store. Of course, Coca-Cola and Mazzarini's Grocery Store would share the cost of the advertisement in this case.

Types of Advertising Media

Retailers have a choice of media to carry their advertising messages to consumers. **Media** is all of the methods used to get an advertising messages to the public. There are four large categories of advertising media:

- Print media

- Broadcast media

- Online media

- Specialty media

Print Media

Print media includes advertising that uses printed material. Print media can include newspapers, magazines, direct mail, and billboards. Certain types of print media are more appropriate for particular retailers.

NEWSPAPERS Newspapers are a large segment of the print media category. Newspapers are published daily or weekly, and their advertising rates depend on the newspaper's readership, or number of people who read the newspaper each time it is published. Small, local, weekly papers have lower advertising rates than those of large daily papers. For example, the *Chicago Tribune* has a very large readership. Retailers of all types and sizes use newspaper advertising.

MAGAZINES Magazines are usually monthly or weekly publications. Magazines can have national, regional, or local distribution. Magazine advertising rates also depend on the size of the readership and whether the publication is a national, regional, or local magazine. Certain magazines appeal to readers with specific interests. For example, *Gourmet* magazine is designed for people who enjoy fine dining and preparing gourmet meals. Many of *Gourmet's* advertisers sell food-related products. A variety of other retailers advertise in the magazine because the publication has a large audience. Advertisers know those readers buy all types of products.

DIRECT MAIL Direct mail is any type of advertising that is mailed directly to customers. Direct mail can take the form of letters, catalogs,

Figure 10.2

Elements of Good Print Ads

ELEMENTS OF GOOD PRINT ADS	
Dominant Headline	Feature the main benefit being offered with the reason the consumer should act immediately. The benefit can be expanded in a sub-headline.
Dominant Design Element	Include a large picture or headline. Photos of real people attract more attention than do drawings. Action photos get reader's attention.
Simple Layout	The layout should lead the reader's eye from the headline to the illustration, and then to the text, price, and retailer's name and location. Complex decorations distract from the message.
Complete and Specific Information	Consumers look for information that will help them decide whether to visit the store. The ad should provide all the information needed, such as types of merchandise, brands, prices, sizes, and colors.
Distinct Visuals	To get consumers' attention, retailers should make their ads distinct from competitor ads. Distinctive art, layout, design, or typeface gets attention.
Store Name and Address	The store's name and location are the most important elements of a retail ad. Display this information clearly and prominently.

AD DESIGN Consumers see hundreds of different ads every week. Retailers must pay special attention to creating effective, well-designed advertisements to stand out in the crowd of competition. *Which information is most important in an advertisement?*

flyers, or coupons. Retailers who use direct mail generally use a mailing list that they have developed from their customer list or from a list of prospective customers, purchased from companies that create mailing lists.

If a retailer's customer database uses selective targeting to create a store's mailing list, direct marketing can be very effective. This type of media advertising provides personal contact with individual customers. Competing retailers are not as aware of these messages sent to consumers as they would be by viewing more public forms of advertising. A disadvantage of direct mailing is the expense to the retailer. If the database of customers is not current, or profile information has changed, then the advertisements, flyers, or catalogs may end up unread and discarded.

BILLBOARDS Billboards are outdoor signs that are placed in cities or near busy highways where many drivers can see them. Retailers who use billboards or other types of outdoor signage pay rental fees for the time and space they use.

Broadcast Media

Broadcast media consists of radio and television. Advertising rates for newspapers and magazines vary a great deal, as do the advertising rates for radio and television. The same rate-determining factors apply to

Hot Property

The Question of Denim

GUESS?, INC. The early 1980s were important years for the four Marciano brothers, immigrants who had just arrived from the south of France. In California they stumbled across the perfect name for their young company on a billboard promoting a new business with the single question, "Guess?" From there they built a fashion dynasty—and elevated denim to high fashion and advertising to fine art.

AD ART

The glory days of blue jeans had faded by the end of the 1970s. The Marcianos, however, had faith in the centuries-old fabric—and a plan. Combine European style with denim's Western tradition to create fashion that is timeless and chic. The brothers showcased their new designs on beautiful models posed against dramatic backdrops. The stunning photographs attracted customer attention, and the Guess? label became easily recognized on five continents. The "Guess? Girls" (supermodels such as Claudia Schiffer and Naomi Campbell) became pop icons of fashion. The artistic images used in the ads also caught the eye of the advertising industry. The Guess? promotional campaigns have received numerous awards, including the Clio—advertising's version of the Oscar®. The company's press books, or seasonal catalogs, have also been honored with a permanent display in the library collection of the Metropolitan Museum of Art.

Though jeans are a staple at Guess? stores, with sales from 6 million in 1982 to over 800 million in 2000, the clothing line has also expanded. Because of original promotion and advertising, the entire family can dress in Guess? Clothing—and Baby Guess?.

1. What do you think has the greater advertising value: Guess? fashion or art? Explain.
2. Guess? broke new ground in advertising with its artistic photography. What other companies today advertise their merchandise in the same way?

---

radio and television advertising. Costs depend on the time of day and the length of the advertisement. Late-night advertising time is generally less expensive than early-evening time, and so on.

TELEVISION Retailers can run TV commercials on national networks or on local television stations. TV commercial ads are called spots. Retailers typically promote sales or their store image through television commercials. They can also do product demonstrations. Production costs for television commercials can be expensive. In addition, the retailer buys airtime on television, which may be costly. However, television reaches a large audience, and ads can appear at any hour of the day. In fact, television stations charge lower prices for airtime at certain times, such as late at night.

RADIO The advantage of using radio advertising for retailers is that most radio-station audiences are specific target groups. A retailer can effectively tailor a message for that group. Also, radio ads are not as expensive to produce as are television ads. However, many listeners, or potential customers, may "tune out" the messages they hear on the radio and give limited attention to the ads. In addition, listeners cannot see the store image or products that are advertised on the radio.

Online Media

Online media advertising involves communication using the Internet. Retailers who advertise on the Internet place their ads on Web sites of other businesses or on home pages for Internet providers, such as AOL and Yahoo!. Those ads are viewed every time Internet users sign on to their accounts. This form of advertising is relatively new and is growing in use.

Specialty Media

The *specialty-media* method of advertising utilizes small, giveaway items upon which a retailer's message or business name is imprinted. Customers carry and use those items. When customers use those items, the business name or message may be seen by other customers or potential new customers. Hotels place pens and pads of paper near the telephones in their lobbies and sleeping rooms. Hotel patrons take those pens with them, and then they view the hotel name every time they use the pens in other locations.

QUESTION

What are some examples of specialty media?

STAR POWER For years, advertisements have featured celebrities to successfully promote retail businesses. *Would you buy products because they were pitched by a famous person? Why?*

Growing up, I got good at taking direction. "Say your line here." "Hit your mark there." And "Drink your milk." That's good advice for kids and adults. The calcium in milk helps bones grow till you're about 35 and helps keep them strong long after. So I still drink milk. Only now, I'm the one giving direction.

MILK
Where's your mustache?

Advertising Budget

Advertising can be very expensive. Most retailers must make careful choices about the media that is most appropriate to carry their messages to the public. Retailers budget for advertising in their promotional budgets. As we discussed earlier, the retail promotional budget is usually a percentage of the sales planned for a specific period.

Benefits of Advertising

Advertising offers benefits to the retailers who sponsor the advertising and to the customers who read or listen to it. Advertising informs customers about new products and services. It also helps those customers decide if the products and services being advertised are items that they might want or need. From the retailer's perspective, advertising helps to sell their products and services. Advertising also helps to attract customers into the retailers' businesses. Along with promotions, advertising is a key element that can enhance store image and contribute to the success of any retail business.

Quick Check ✓

RESPOND to what you've read by answering these questions.

1. What are the two major categories of advertising? _____

_____

_____

_____

_____

_____

2. What are the three types of advertising? _____

_____

_____

_____

_____

3. What are the four types of advertising media? _____

_____

_____

_____

_____

Name _____ Date _____

Worksheet 10.1

Promoting Good Business

Create a sales promotion campaign for a sporting-goods store or for a trendy clothing store. Describe each method you would use for sales promotion.

Name of Store _____

Type of Store _____

1. Coupons: _____

_____

_____

_____

2. Contests: _____

_____

_____

_____

3. Sales: _____

_____

_____

_____

4. Special events: _____

_____

_____

_____

5. In-store demonstrations: _____

_____

_____

_____

6. Free samples: _____

_____

_____

_____

Worksheet 10.2

Customer Communications

Write and design a print advertisement. You can use photos and text. Choose a popular store or imagine a favorite store. Refer to **Figure 10.2** for elements to include.

Name of Store _____

Type of Store _____

ORGANIZING PROMOTION AND ADVERTISING INFORMATION

1. Create a diagram or graphic organizer of the different types of promotional elements. Show the advantages and disadvantages of each.

2. Create a graphic organizer of the different types of advertising. Show the advantages and disadvantages of each.

Add this page to your career portfolio.

CHAPTER SUMMARY

Section 10.1 Retail Promotion

promotion (p. 200)
promotional mix (p. 200)
merchandise promotions
    (p. 201)
institutional promotions
    (p. 202)
publicity (p. 204)
public relations (p. 204)

- The types of promotion include sales promotions, publicity and public relations, advertising, and selling.

- The promotional mix is the different combinations of the types of promotion.

- The types of sales promotions include contests, sales events, premiums, free samples, and e-mail.

- The concept of publicity is any unpaid mention of a retail business, its employees, or merchandise in the media. The wise use of publicity can enhance a store's image.

Section 10.2 Advertising

advertising (p. 206)
product advertising
    (p. 206)
institutional advertising
    (p. 206)
retail advertising (p. 207)
vendor advertising
    (p. 207)
cooperative advertising
    (p. 208)
media (p. 208)

- The categories of advertising include product and institutional advertising.

- Advertising takes many forms. Knowledge of the types of advertising is valuable when planning the best type to use for a particular situation. Types include retail, vendor, and cooperative.

- Knowledge of the types of advertising media is necessary when determining the type of media that is best for a particular business or business situation. Types of advertising media include print, broadcast, online, and specialty.

CHECKING CONCEPTS

1. **Explain** the types of promotion.
2. **Define** the promotional mix.
3. **Identify** the components of promotional mix.
4. **Describe** sales promotional techniques.
5. **Explain** the concept of publicity.
6. **Describe** the categories of advertising.
7. **Explain** the types of advertising media.

Critical Thinking

8. **Discuss** why retail stores benefit from institutional promotions.

CROSS-CURRICULUM SKILLS

Work-Based Learning

Basic Skills—Speaking

9. You work for a retail marketing firm. Give a presentation of a promotional mix for a specialty clothing shop.

Basic Skills—Listening Skills/Writing

10. Interview an advertising salesperson from a newspaper, magazine, or radio or television station and find out about retail ads. Write a one-page report.

School-Based Learning

Language Arts

11. In groups of four, write and produce a 60-second commercial for a retail store. Use props and costumes. If available, use a video camera. Act out or show your taped commercial in class.

Math

12. Choose two nationally known, competing products, such as Pepsi and Coke, GM and Ford autos, or Apple and Dell computers. Contact the companies for summaries of their advertising budgets for one year. Compare the two budgets. Report your findings to the class.

Role Play: Bookstore Employee

SITUATION You are to assume the role of employee of a locally owned bookstore. The bookstore is located near the campus of a small university. The store owner (judge) is concerned about a national chain bookstore attracting students from the university. The owner (judge) has decided that sales promotion activities can help attract the university students.

(ACTIVITY) The store owner (judge) has asked for your recommendations about promotions the store could run to attract the university student business.

EVALUATION You will be evaluated on how well you meet the following performance indicators:

- Identify the elements of the promotional mix.
- Coordinate activities in the promotional mix.
- Explain the nature of a promotional plan.
- Explain the nature of positive customer/client relations.
- Present findings and recommendations.

The Clio is the award for advertisers, recognizing the best in television, print media, outdoor, radio, integrated media, innovative media, design, Internet, and student work.

- Access the Clio Awards Web site.
- Choose one press release, read it, and then write a summary.
- Read the summary to your classmates.

➡For a link to the Clio Award to answer these questions, go to **marketingseries.glencoe.com**.

Chapter 11

Selling

Chapter Objectives

- Identify characteristics of an effective retail sales associate.
- Describe tasks a retail sales associate must complete.
- Identify and discuss product information.
- Define customer buying motives and needs.
- Explain the steps of a sale.
- Explain how to overcome customer objections and identify suggestion-selling techniques.

POWER READ

Be an active reader and use these reading strategies:

PREDICT what the section will be about.

CONNECT what you read with your life.

QUESTION as you read to make sure you understand the content.

RESPOND to what you've read.

A CAR IS BORN

Why do you buy a sweater, a meal, or a car? Is it because of the price? The service? The brand? No matter what strengths a product may have, selling can determine if the customer buys or does not buy. Understanding how customers respond to different selling techniques can make or break a sale. Today many customers appreciate less haggling, as buyers of Saturn automobiles will agree.

The automobile Saturn was conceived in 1982 when General Motors Vice President Alex C. Mair and GM engineers Joe Joseph and Tom Ankeny brainstormed to find a new small-car project. It would compete with Japanese imports by emphasizing customer satisfaction and a team environment in its workforce. Dealers would have no-haggle sticker prices for customers, and workers would communicate and cooperate to make the best cars possible. After eight years of designing and testing, the first Saturn car rolled off the production line in 1990. The following year it went on to win the first of many honors, including *Popular Mechanics'* Design and Engineering Award, *Motor Week's* Driver's Choice Award, *Kiplinger's* Best in Class, and AAA's Best Car. Although Saturn auto dealers consistently rated high in customer satisfaction, brand loyalty toward the manufacturer was difficult to achieve—even with a case full of trophies. There were few returning customers. How did Saturn build a base of loyal customers?

ANALYZE AND WRITE

1. What are some reasons a consumer might avoid a new brand of automobile?
2. Why might Saturn have had difficulty in building up customer retention?

Case Study Part 2 on page 231

Preparing for the Sale

AS YOU READ ...

YOU WILL LEARN

- To identify characteristics of an effective retail sales associate.
- To describe tasks a retail sales associate must complete.
- To identify and discuss product information.
- To define customer buying motives and needs.

WHY IT'S IMPORTANT

Knowing about product knowledge, customer motivations, and how to be a good sales associate will prepare you for a career in the world of retailing.

KEY TERMS

- non-personal selling
- personal selling
- rational buying motive
- emotional buying motive
- product features
- product benefits

PREDICT

Is there a system to selling? What might it be?

non-personal selling the type of selling that does not involve interaction between people

Retail Sales

The objective of a retailer is to have what customers want when they want it. Once a retailer obtains the right merchandise at the right time, the merchandise must be sold to the customer. Retailing is all about selling. In this section, you will learn about selling and sales associates. You will look first at the characteristics of a good sales associate and then learn about the tasks a sales associate must perform on the job. Next the chapter will discuss product knowledge and how sales associates can acquire it and apply it during the selling process. The section concludes by examining customer buying motives and their impact on selling.

What Is Personal Selling?

You have learned about promotion and that personal selling is the fourth type of promotion in the promotional mix. Remember that the four types of promotion are sales promotion, publicity, advertising, and personal selling. Sales promotion, publicity, and advertising are known as non-personal selling. Those types of promotion reach customers and are forms of selling. **Non-personal selling** is the type of selling that does not involve interaction between people.

Personal selling is the type of selling that involves direct interaction between sales associates and customers. The interaction between the customer and sales associate leads to the sales associate determining the exact merchandise or service that will satisfy the customer's want or need, and the customer having a want or need satisfied.

The exchange between the customer and the sales associate is known as the *selling process*. Most personal selling takes place in retail stores. Personal selling also takes place when direct-sales associates make sales calls at customers' homes.

Characteristics of Sales Associates

Let's look at some of the characteristics of successful retail sales associates. Sales associates must have good *people skills*. They work with people all day, every day, so they should be able to interact and get along with all kinds of people. Sales associates must also want to help their customers by providing good customer service. In addition, sales associates need to have good personal habits. They should be well-groomed, and their work clothing should be neat and clean.

World Market

See Spot Speak

Have you ever wondered why your dog barks? Now you can find out, thanks to a clever new gizmo recently developed in Japan by Takara Co., Ltd., one of Japan's largest toy makers. Dog translators, or "Bow-Linguals," claim to promote communication between humans and our canine friends. Selling for about $120, the device interprets barks (or growls, yips, and whines). It works like this: A microphone, attached to your dog's collar, records barks and transmits them to a hand-held translator. The translator compares the sounds to a doggie database containing thousands of voiceprints from more than 50 pure and mixed breeds of dogs. When a match is made, the appropriate "emotion" pops up onscreen: *frustrated, happy, sad, on guard, assertive,* or *needy*. A relevant message, such as "Leave me alone" or "I'm ready to play," also appears onscreen.

Time magazine cited the dog translator as one of the "Coolest Inventions" of 2002. If you're a cat person, don't feel left out. Takara has developed a feline counterpart, "Meow-Lingual."

If you were a Bow-Lingual salesperson, what features would you highlight to a customer?

In addition to having these personal qualities and skills, sales associates should be willing and eager to learn. Sales associates must learn about the products and services they sell. They should familiarize themselves with store policies and follow those policies. Sales associates must also learn basic procedural skills. Those skills might include learning to open and close the store, how to operate the register, how to make change, and how to process bank or store charges. All of these skills are essential to the operation of the store and should be learned as quickly as possible.

The last important characteristic of successful sales associates involves ethical behavior. Ethical behavior means behaving with a sense of fairness and honesty to both customers and the retail employer.

personal selling the type of selling that involves direct interaction between sales associates and customers

The Sales Associate's Job

There are several tasks that are part of the sales associate's job. The tasks can be divided into two broad categories—selling tasks and non-selling tasks.

Selling Tasks

Selling tasks involve selling the merchandise or service the sales associate has been hired to sell or perform. Selling tasks include keeping the sales area neat and well-organized so customers can see the merchandise available. For example, in clothing stores, the tasks of keeping the fitting rooms neat and returning clothing to the sales area are big jobs that must be performed throughout the day. Sales associates must also handle merchandise returns.

CONNECT

Would you buy a TV from a salesperson who could not answer questions about the product? Why?

AT HOME WITH RETAILING

Steve Fritts
General Manager
Ethan Allen Home Interiors

What does your job entail?

"I oversee the entire retail operation—I'm responsible for administrative duties, selling, service, warehousing, training and development, and marketing. I make sure the store looks its best. I work with our visual merchandisers. As far as goals are concerned, I look at the sales results from house calls and presentations. I also look at the balance of product categories that are being presented. We'll consistently work eight- or nine-hour days—we're either selling or delivering. When we have slower sales, we're very busy delivering."

What kind of training did you have?

"I grew up in the business working in the business—then went through Ethan Allen training. It's osmosis as much as anything. I also majored in business."

What advice would you give students?

"Put the right people in the right places—utilize staff talents. Communication skills are important. For example, you can be a great designer, but if you cannot communicate or interact with people, it neutralizes your capabilities. If you can't speak well or listen well, your vision falls on deaf ears. Organizational skills are also important; this is a very detail-oriented industry, and being organized is very important."

What is your key to success?

"You have to have a passion for the product—you have to like it, or you can't sell it. Also, there's no substitute for knowing your business."

Why are communication skills so important in a sales position?

Career Data: General Manager

Education and Training
Associate's or bachelor's degrees in marketing, general business, and communication

Skills and Abilities
Communication skills, people skills, and organizational skills

Career Outlook Average growth through 2010

Career Path A sales career usually begins on the sales floor, with advancement related to sales results.

Another selling task involves reticketing returned merchandise and getting it ready to return to the sales area. If returned merchandise is defective in some way, then it should be handled according to store policy. Other selling-related tasks might include assisting customers with special orders and purchases of gift certificates or gift cards. Sales associates should also be able to answer customer questions and be able to direct customers to other merchandise in the store. That means knowing where to locate all store merchandise, even if that merchandise is outside the sales associate's department or area.

Non-Selling Tasks

Sales associates must also complete non-selling tasks. *Non-selling tasks* are sales tasks that are not directly related to working with a customer. One non-selling task might be helping to maintain the appearance and organization of the selling area. That means straightening stock and returning items to their places within the store or department. Sales associates make sure all colors, sizes, and styles of merchandise are in the sales area. If necessary, additional items should be brought to the sales area from the stock room. Sales associates should also note any items that are sold out and inform the manager. Sales associates also re-stock supplies at the cash register desk. That task includes replenishing the shopping bags and wrapping materials for merchandise.

Product Knowledge

If you are going to sell a piece of merchandise or a service, you should know as much as possible about it. Having *product knowledge* means being familiar with the merchandise or services being sold. Customers always have questions about the merchandise. A knowledgeable sales associate can provide the information that the customer needs in order to make an informed buying decision.

Where to Get Product Knowledge

Product knowledge can be acquired from a wide variety of sources. Sales associates who are eager to obtain information about the goods and services in their store can examine the products and learn by trying them or operating them. Sales associates can also learn about goods and services from their supervisors and other sales associates.

Knowing Your Niche
Retailers have long depended on Mickey, Barbie, and Superman to sell their products to kids. But selling requires knowing the customer's most current needs and wants too. Some parents resist the hype and pressure of branded merchandise targeted at their children. E-tailer Olive Kids caters to this niche of customers by offering logo-free bedding, toys, and accessories decorated with colorful, kid-friendly designs.

➡ Visit an Internet store and explain how it can also perform suggestion selling through **marketingseries.glencoe.com**.

◀ **YOU ARE WHAT YOU BUY**
Most countries require product information to be clearly labeled—especially on food, clothing, and household supplies. *Why might consumers need to know product information for these items?*

QUESTION

What are three sources of product information?

rational buying motive a motive that prompts customers to make a conscious decision based on a reasonable idea

emotional buying motive a motive determined by the way a product or service makes customers feel

THE PRODUCT ITSELF You can find product knowledge on labels or packaging attached to the merchandise. Labels, brochures, and packaging can provide directions, ingredients, components, and guarantee information. Reading that information can answer many questions and provide information about features and how the product operates.

THE PRODUCT'S MANUFACTURER Manufacturer representatives are another excellent source of information. Manufacturer representatives often receive special training about the products they sell and will gladly share that information with sales associates. This helps them to sell the products. Manufacturers may have Web sites that provide accessible information, they may have phone numbers to call for information about products.

TRADE PUBLICATIONS Trade publications are newspapers or magazines that specialize in information about particular businesses or industries. These publications often feature articles about trends, companies, as well as new products in their field of interest. For example, *Women's Wear Daily* is a well-known trade newspaper serving the women's clothing business. Retailers as well as consumers can also find out about product information and new trends by reading articles from trade publications.

Buying Motives

Do you know what might cause, or motivate, you to buy a certain brand of jeans over another brand? Customers choose to buy certain products for many reasons. Those reasons can be studied and analyzed to see what kinds of motives customers have for making purchases. The motives, or reasons, usually fall into two categories—rational buying motives and emotional buying motives. See **Figure 11.1** for a table that lists a few different buying motives.

Rational Buying Motives

A **rational buying motive** prompts customers to make a conscious decision based on a reasonable idea. For example, when you buy a flashlight, you might do so to have light when there is a power failure. You need the light provided by the flashlight to prevent falling or tripping on furniture. Your rational buying motive is that of safety. Another common rational buying motive is financial. For example, your new sweater must cost $50 because your clothing budget has only $50 left. You want the amount you pay for a product to fit your budget.

Emotional Buying Motives

An **emotional buying motive** is determined by the way a product or service makes you feel. Peer acceptance, power, and the pursuit of physical beauty are all emotional buying motives. Many customers do not necessarily recognize their motives as being emotional; they may prefer to think they have rational buying motives. For example, a special occasion is coming up. It might seem reasonable, or rational, to say, "I need a new outfit." But do you really need it? You might already have several things in your closet that you could wear. However, a new outfit might make you feel that you would look better, or it would make the special occasion seem more special. So, perhaps, the real buying motive in this case would be an emotional one.

Understanding Buying Motives

Of course, it is common to have a combination of both rational and emotional buying motives when making purchases. For example, you might buy a coat because you need protection from the winter weather. Self-protection is a rational motive. You may also buy a sleek ski jacket in the latest winter fashion color. Then you have the combination of the rational buying motive of self-protection with the emotional buying motive of beauty or peer acceptance. Understanding a customer's buying motive can help a sales associate determine which products to show a customer and which features to highlight to them.

Feature/Benefit Selling

Feature/benefit selling means using product knowledge to learn the features of a product, and then turning those features into concepts that the customer wants to buy. **Product features** are the physical aspects of a product. For example, if you were to purchase a television set, product features to consider would be the size of the screen, price, and whether the TV has a remote control.

product features the physical aspects of a product

Figure 11.1

Examples of Buying Motives

EXAMPLES OF BUYING MOTIVES	
Emotional Motives	**Rational Motives**
Power	Saves time
Love	Saves money
Peer acceptance	Makes life easier
Label recognition	Improves health
Prestige	Safe or improves safety
Nostalgia	Durable
Pride	Well-made
Pleasure	Fulfills a physical need such as hunger or protection from the elements
Aesthetic appeal, or beauty	

WHY DO YOU BUY? Customer buying motives can be a combination of both emotional and rational motives. *Do you think that buying recyclable goods would be an emotional or rational decision? Why?*

Product benefits are the advantages that a customer gets from the product features. For example, the large size of the TV screen, at 54 inches, might translate into the benefit of ease of viewing and pride of ownership. The feature of a remote control translates into the benefit of convenience. A customer wants to hear about those features. A sales associate selling that television can say, "Imagine how good the Sunday football game will look on that 54-inch screen." The customer can visualize himself or herself in front of the TV watching a favorite team. The physical feature becomes a benefit to the customer.

Why Prepare to Sell?

If you want to gain retail experience in the world of work, understanding the traits of a good sales associate will help you to develop those traits in yourself. Knowledge of these desirable traits will also help you when hiring and training sales associates. Knowing the tasks a retail sales associate must complete will help you in choosing a career in retailing.

Hot Property

Ben & Jerry's

Selling an Ice Cream Dream

Cherry Garcia, Chunky Monkey, Chubby Hubby, and One Sweet Whirled represent a line of more than 50 ice cream flavors that are fun to eat and fun to order. Ben & Jerry's Homemade, Inc., believes that selling ice cream—and frozen yogurt and sorbet—should be fun.

TAKING THE RIGHT STEPS
Found all around the world in stores and scoop shops, Ben & Jerry's ice cream made its debut in 1978 at a renovated gas station in Burlington, Vermont. The founders, childhood friends Ben Cohen and Jerry Greenfield, were off to a playful beginning selling ice cream. Initially, the company attracted its customers by projecting free movies against the gas station wall. Its one-year anniversary was Free Cone Day. In 1983, Ben & Jerry's built the largest ice cream sundae, weighing in at 102 pounds. In a 1986 cross-country marketing drive, they handed out free ice cream from the cowmobile, *Cow I*. Then *Cow II* followed in 1987 for another cross-country giveaway. There were free scoops for Wall Street in 1993, and so on. Ben & Jerry's sales soared, with one year showing a record-breaking increase of 143 percent.

BEYOND THE SALE
Along the way, the company also pitched social awareness. The Ben & Jerry's Foundation, established in 1985, funds community projects. Its goals include protecting rainforests, furthering education, providing for the homeless, and fostering children's rights. Ben & Jerry's ice cream dream has truly become "a joy to the soul and to the belly."

1. Consumers often suggest Ben & Jerry's flavors. How do you think this "sells" the ice cream?
2. Company employees get three free pints of ice cream every day. Do you think this also helps sell ice cream? Explain.

Acquiring product knowledge will help you gain information and the knowledge necessary to answer customer questions. Product information is very important when working in sales. Analyzing the product information will help you to determine specific information a particular customer is seeking. Understanding customer buying motives can help you know which sales techniques will be most effective for a particular customer. That knowledge can increase sales.

Quick Check ✓

RESPOND to what you've read by answering these questions.

1. What are two categories of sales associates' job tasks? _____

_____

_____

_____

_____

2. Why is it important for sales associates to have good product knowledge? _____

_____

_____

_____

_____

_____

_____

_____

_____

_____

_____

_____

3. What are the two types of customer buying motives? _____

_____

_____

_____

_____

Making the Sale

AS YOU READ ...

YOU WILL LEARN

- To explain the steps of a sale.
- To explain how to overcome customer objections and identify suggestion-selling techniques.

WHY IT'S IMPORTANT

Understanding the steps of a sale will help you to understand the selling process and to become a better sales associate.

KEY TERMS

- social greeting
- service greeting
- merchandise greeting
- objection
- suggestion selling

social greeting expression that acknowledges the customer's presence in the store or department

service greeting expression that offers assistance to the customer

merchandise greeting expression used when the sales associate mentions an item of merchandise

PREDICT

Should salespeople accept some objections to their products?

The Selling Process

In this section we will discuss the steps of a sale. Learning the steps of a sale will help you to understand how to better assist customers and how to sell. Selling is the most important skill for anyone who wants a career in retailing.

The Seven Steps of a Sale

In the selling process, a sales associate uses skills and knowledge to sell goods and services to customers. The selling process has seven steps: open the sale, determine customer needs, present the merchandise, overcome objections, close the sale, suggestion selling, and follow up after the sale. See **Figure 11.2** on page 230 to see these seven steps.

Step 1: Open the Sale

The opening of the sale is the first step the sales associate takes. This is the step where the sales associate establishes contact with the customer by greeting him or her. Just as you greet guests when they arrive at your home, you should greet customers as they enter the store or department. It is important to greet each customer in a friendly and sincere manner. There are three types of greetings, or expressions, to use when opening the sale— social greeting, service greeting, and merchandise greeting.

- The **social greeting** acknowledges the customer's presence in the store or department. A social greeting can be a simple "Hello" or "Good afternoon."

- The **service greeting** offers assistance to the customer. A sales associate may simply ask, "May I help you?"

- The **merchandise greeting** is used when the sales associate begins the dialogue with the customer by mentioning an item of merchandise. The mention of the merchandise can take the form of a statement or of a question, such as "These blouses have just arrived," or "Have you seen our new DVD players?" Both expressions are merchandise greetings.

Step 2: Determine Customer Needs

Once the sales associate has opened the sales process by greeting the customer, it is time to discover what the customer needs and wants. There are several methods that can help determine what the customer needs. Sometimes the customer will tell the sales associate what he or she

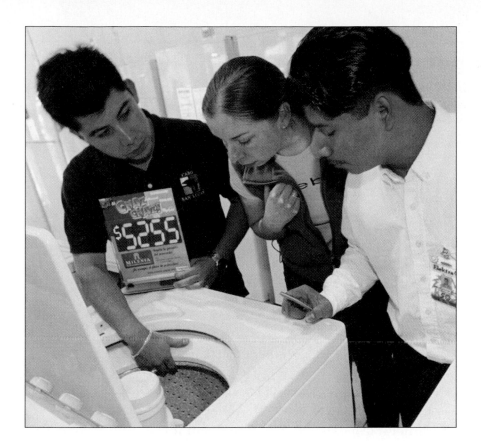

◀ **SHOW AND TELL** Actions speak louder than words. Demonstrating a product might be a better way to make a sale. *What special challenges might a salesperson have if he or she must physically demonstrate a product?*

wants. In most cases, however, this does not happen. The sales associate must learn to observe the customer and to ask questions.

By watching customer behavior, a sales associate is able to learn something about what that customer wants. When a customer looks at an item for a long time, that is generally a sign of interest. Another sign of interest is if the customer actually touches or holds the merchandise. Those observations are a starting place for determining customer needs.

Another way to determine customer needs is by asking questions. By asking open-ended questions, a sales associate can determine the customer's needs. *Open-ended questions* are questions that require more than a "yes" or "no" answer. If a customer is near the photo frame section in a store, the sales associate might ask what size frame the customer would like to see. The sales associate might then ask if the customer prefers metal or wood frames. Each answer helps the sales associate gain information to determine which photo frame will best suit the customer's needs.

Step 3: Present the Merchandise

When customer needs have been determined, the next step is to present the merchandise. When a sales associate presents merchandise, he or she shows the item to the customer. Presenting the merchandise also means involving as many of the customer's five senses as possible. The sales associate should also encourage the customer to try the product or service. For example, if you are presenting a CD player, play a CD so the customer can hear how good the sound quality is and see how easy the CD player is to operate. The sales associate also tells the customer about the merchandise in this step. This is the time to use feature selling or benefit selling. For example, show the customer that the CD

TECH NOTES

Coupons Go High Tech
Consumers in the United States use five billion coupons per year. The retailers who process these coupons make $500 million per year for their efforts. Most people find coupons in newspapers, magazines, or direct-mail packets. Some stores dispense coupons using electronic machines. Coupons can even be found online. At Supermarkets.com, shoppers can create a customized list of coupons. At the store, a clerk scans the barcode on the list, and the customer receives the discounts.

➥Read information and list three ways coupons benefit retailers through **marketingseries.glencoe.com.**

Figure 11.2

Seven Steps of Selling

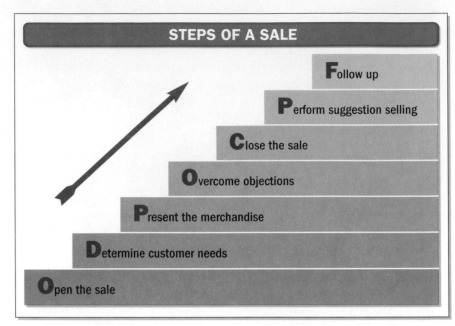

STEPS OF A SALE

Follow up

Perform suggestion selling

Close the sale

Overcome objections

Present the merchandise

Determine customer needs

Open the sale

CONNECT

Do you think that aggression is a good trait in a salesperson? Why?

Math Check

ADD IT UP

Each week, Tasca teaches karate to 31 students in a 90-minute class for $23 per person. She was also able to "sell" 11 students on taking weekly private lessons at $55 per lesson. How much does Tasca receive each week?

➡ For tips on finding the solution, go to **marketingseries.glencoe.com.**

objection question or concern that a customer has about merchandise being presented

player holds five CDs and how convenient it is to have favorite CDs ready to play. Demonstrate the CD player's durability by rapping it sharply. Show the merchandise in use and involve the customer by having him or her handle the merchandise.

Step 4: Overcome Objections

Customers may express an **objection**, or a question or a concern about the merchandise being presented by the sales associate. Customer objections should be acknowledged. It is important to remember that an objection is not a rejection of the merchandise. When a customer takes the time to voice an objection, this can be viewed as an expression of interest in the product and a desire for more information. For example, the customer looking at the CD player might say, "This CD player seems too lightweight to be durable." The sales associate should acknowledge the objection and again demonstrate the CD player's durability and point out that a warranty comes with it. A customer's objection should always be addressed to as soon as possible.

Sales associates can also anticipate objections. If the sales associate senses that a customer will raise an objection to durability, the sales associate can mention the product durability during the merchandise presentation. Sales associates should plan for objections. Customer objections are not obstacles to making a sale. Instead, objections are a way of giving the customer more product information or assurance about the product.

Step 5: Close the Sale

When the sales associate has answered the customer's objections and the customer has no more questions about the merchandise, it is time to close the sale. The close of the sale happens when the customer decides to make the purchase. It is the next step in the sales process. At that point the sales associate should ask the customer, "Shall I wrap this for you?" or "Would you like me to put this on your credit card?" When the customer responds affirmatively, the sale is closed. There are several variations for closing the sale, but the important point is that the customer decides to make the purchase.

Step 6: Perform Suggestion Selling

Suggestion selling is the selling of merchandise beyond the original merchandise. Suggestion selling is done after the customer agrees to purchase the original merchandise.

There are several ways that a sales associate can make suggestions after the close of the sale.

- *Suggest related items or services.* If the customer is purchasing a pair of pants, the sales associate might suggest a belt or shirt that accessorizes the pants. If a customer purchases a massage, a sales associate might suggest a facial.

- *Suggest a greater quantity of the item being purchased.* If a customer is purchasing a pair of socks, the sales associate could suggest that the customer purchase six pairs. That way, the customer will have plenty.

- *Suggest new merchandise or a new product.* When a customer purchases a haircut, the sales associate can suggest a new hair care product.

- *Inform the customer about any special sales in the store.* The customer will appreciate learning about possible bargains and might decide to take advantage of the opportunity.

Suggestion selling is a way to increase the amount of the original sale. It is also a way to help customers get something they might forget, something else they need, something they didn't know they needed, or just to help the customer take advantage of a bargain.

Step 7: Follow Up

The follow-up after the sale is the last step in the sales process. This step includes processing the sales transaction. The sales associate should process the transaction as quickly and efficiently as possible. Most customers do not like to wait. The merchandise should be wrapped neatly and with care so the merchandise does not get damaged in transit. Customers should be assured that they have made a good decision. For example, the sales associate can say, "You will enjoy your new CD player for many years." Finally, the sales associate can thank the customer and invite him or her to return.

Case Study — PART 2

A CAR IS BORN
Continued from Part 1 on page 219

Even with high customer-satisfaction ratings, Saturn struggled with achieving brand loyalty. So, to build a customer base, Saturn kept in touch with its car owners. In 1995, the company invited 38,000 enthusiasts to visit the factory. It also hired Saturn owners in many capacities. Many salespeople started off as owners. Likewise, Saturn specialists were sent to auto shows and other events to talk about the company and its cars. The promotion proved to be effective.

The vehicle's quality has been noted as well: Saturn is the only non-luxury car to consistently finish at the top or near the top of the J.D. Power and Associates Sales Satisfaction Index. Saturn is also the first American manufacturer to receive the honor of being the Best Overall Nameplate of vehicles marketed in Japan.

ANALYZE AND WRITE

1. Why would Saturn owners be effective representatives and salespeople?
2. Can you think of other businesses that utilize customers in marketing or sales?

---

suggestion selling the selling of merchandise beyond the original merchandise

QUESTION

What is one suggestion to make at the close of a sale?

Selling Point !

→ **THE UNHAPPY CUSTOMER**
An unsatisfied retail customer will tell nine people about his or her unpleasant experience.

Selling to Customers' Needs

Customers go to a store because they have a need for something. Understanding how to determine a customer's needs will help you find the right merchandise to satisfy those needs. Listening to customer objections and then responding with information that the customer wants and needs to know will help close the sale. Knowing how to handle objections can make the difference between a purchase and an unsatisfied customer. Then, once a sale is closed, a good sales associate can suggest related merchandise and services to extend the purchase. Being prepared for customers and knowing the seven steps of selling are key components of successful retailing.

Quick Check ✔

RESPOND to what you've read by answering these questions.

1. What are the seven steps of a sale? _____

_____

_____

_____

_____

_____

_____

2. What are three types of customer greetings? _____

_____

_____

_____

_____

_____

3. What are four ways a sales associate can use suggestion selling? ___

_____

_____

_____

_____

_____

_____

Worksheet 11.1

Suggestion Selling

The first column in this chart lists different products, or goods and services. Fill out the second column with an additional product you might suggest to a customer. In the last column, write how your suggestion might appeal to the customer with an emotional buying motive, a rational buying motive, or both kinds of buying motives.

Product	Suggestions	Motive (Rational/Emotional/Both)
New car		
Manicure		
Pair of blue jeans		
Rollerblades		
Dry cleaning		
Pet toy		
Yearly dental cleaning		
Bestselling book		
Sandwich in a restaurant		
Laptop computer		
DVD		

Worksheet 11.2

Handling Objections and Closing the Sale

A. Several customer objections are listed below. Write your response to each objection.

1. "I like this pair of pants, but they don't seem to fit very well."

_____

_____

_____

2. "These shoes are very stylish, but they seem on the expensive side."

_____

_____

_____

3. "I'm just looking."

_____

_____

_____

B. Some customer objections are clues for the sales associate to close the sale. Write how you would reply to each question below in order to close the sale.

4. "Do you offer any kind of guarantee on this?"

_____

_____

_____

5. "Would it take a long time for you to blow-dry my hair as well as cut it?"

_____

_____

_____

6. "I'm looking for a fishing pole for my uncle. Do you think he might like this one?"

_____

_____

_____

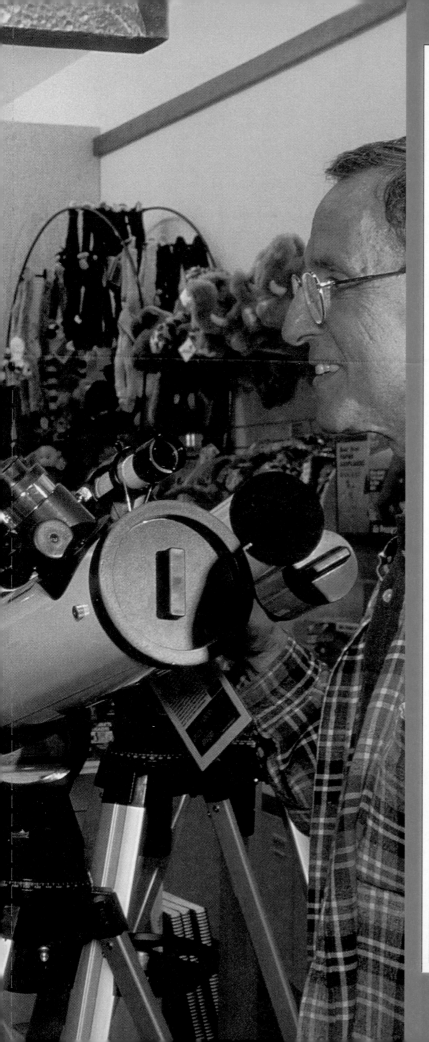

CLIMBING UP

Retailers must make choices about their customer-service policies. Will they demonstrate telescopes on the selling floor? Will they let customers handle the merchandise? Will they refund money for returned goods? Recreational Equipment, Inc. (REI), has developed a successful approach to retailing that includes unique customer services.

In 1938, it was not easy to find ice axes and other climbing gear. So Lloyd and Mary Anderson teamed up with 23 other mountain climbers to form REI to supply gear, clothing, and footwear for outdoor activities. Since then the Northwest-based cooperative has expanded its offerings to service hiking, camping, bicycling, paddling, winter sports, and other types of muscle-powered outdoor recreation. REI's 6,000 employees are among the happiest in the United States, and the company has been recognized by *Fortune* magazine as one of the 100 Best Companies to Work For in America. REI employees test every product sold, and they are allowed to borrow equipment for field testing. Customers can also become co-op members, or owners, for a lifetime fee of $15. They receive a portion of REI's profits, based on a percentage of their purchases, and vote for its board of directors. However, REI's climb to retail success has not been easy. Often it has catered to sports markets in their early stages. How did REI serve a market that was not established?

ANALYZE AND WRITE

1. Is it possible to sell products to a market too early? Explain.
2. How might allowing customers to become "co-owners" help a company?

Case Study Part 2 on page 251

The Customer's Role

AS YOU READ ...

YOU WILL LEARN

- To define customer service.
- To describe customer-service expectations.
- To explain word-of-mouth communication.

WHY IT'S IMPORTANT

Understanding how customer expectations affect the perception of customer service will help retailers provide appropriate levels of customer service.

KEY TERMS

- customer service
- customer survey
- word-of-mouth communication

PREDICT

List some expectations you have for retail customer service.

customer service the set of enhancements retailers offer customers to make shopping more convenient or rewarding

Understanding Customer Service

Customers are knowledgeable about their needs and wants. Today's customers are also sophisticated about their expectations as they shop. As a result, customer service is one of the major issues in retailing today. Retailers of all types care about customer service. They are concerned about the types of services they offer customers as well as the quality of customer service provided by the retailer's employees.

The manner in which retailers meet or exceed customer expectations has a big effect on a retailer's success. Retailers know this and are constantly striving to meet and *exceed* their customer's expectations. Retailers know that providing outstanding customer service will help them maintain a competitive edge. In this chapter you will learn about customer service from the perspectives of both the customer and the retail employee.

What Is Customer Service?

Customer service is the set of enhancements that retailers offer customers to make shopping more convenient or more rewarding. Types of customer services can include accepting credit cards and personal checks, delivery service, repair service, gift-wrapping, and placing special orders. **Figure 12.1** provides a comprehensive list of customer services.

All of those services are important for creating the right assortment of shopping services for the business's target customers. However, the store's employees must *deliver* those services properly. That is the quality of customer service. Delivery of customer service affects the customer's perception of the entire customer-service offering. It also affects the customer's level of satisfaction with his or her shopping experience.

Determining Customer Services

Retailers want to give their customers what they want. But how does a retailer know what the customers want? In other words, how does a retailer go about determining the right assortment of services to offer the business's customers? There are several methods the retailer can use to help determine that information.

Customers expect certain basic services. Most retailers offer those basic services, or customers will find it too difficult to shop at their stores. Basic services include accepting checks and credit cards, parking, and accepting purchase returns. Each retailer must determine what other services to offer. Some services may be particular to the type of

Figure 12.1

Customer Service Offerings

Acceptance of credit cards	Gift certificates
Acceptance of debit cards	Gift-wrapping services
Alterations of merchandise	Guarantees
Assembly of merchandise	Layaway
ATM terminals	Parking
Baby registry	Personal assistance
Bridal registry	Personal shoppers
Check cashing	Presentations on how to use merchandise
Child care	Repair services
Coat check	Restrooms
Complimentary refreshments	Return policies
Credit	Services for those with special needs
Delivery	Shopping carts
Demonstrations of merchandise	Special orders
Display of merchandise	Translations
Dressing rooms	Valet parking
Extended store hours	Warranties

SELLING ISN'T EVERYTHING
Customer service is about making the customers feel that all of their needs are met. *Which of these services have you used or encountered?*

business. For example, a book retailer may consider offering additional services such as merchandise delivery, child care, or a layaway plan. They might all sound like good services, but will the retailer's customer use those services?

There are a number of methods that retailers use to determine what their customers want. Some methods include using customer surveys, listening to customer comments, observing the competition, listening to store employees, and determining cost of services. Retailers use a mixture of some or all of these methods when making customer-service decisions.

Customer Surveys

A **customer survey** is a questionnaire designed to gain information from customers. In this case, the survey is designed to include questions about services customers feel would enhance their shopping experience or they would use. Customers are asked to respond to the questions. The customer responses provide the information the retailer needs to help make a decision about the services. See **Figure 12.2** on page 250 for an example of a questionnaire.

customer survey questionnaire designed to gain information from customers

Service With a Smile

Retailers who have extended their wares to the electronic channel can fall short in offering customer service. Even though convenience and low prices attract customers to Web site shopping, many online customers still expect the same personal attention that comes from good customer service. Nordstrom.com offers customers the same renowned customer service online as it does in its stores. Customers can ask online representatives questions about sizes, product features and availability—and expect a prompt, courteous response. The site also offers a Wish List, where customers can keep items they may want to buy in the future.

➡ Learn how to ask for and receive online customer service on a retail Web site through **marketingseries.glencoe.com.**

CONNECT
How would you respond to an angry customer?

Customer Comments

The customer can provide a lot of information if given the opportunity. Information from customer comments, including complaints and compliments, can help identify areas in which the store is doing well or may need improvement.

HANDLING CUSTOMER COMPLAINTS Dealing with customer complaints can be one of the most difficult parts of a retail job. Displeasure, anger, and other negative emotions often accompany complaints. However, when properly handled, customer complaints can provide the opportunity to transform an unhappy customer into a happy one. Some tips for dealing with customer complaints include:

- *Let the customer speak.* Let the customer tell his or her story.

- *Be empathetic.* Listen but do not make value judgments. Let the customer know you will do everything you can to help.

- *Apologize.* Be sure that your apology is sincere.

- *Take responsibility.* If you don't know how to deal with the complaint, find someone who can help.

- *Be positive.* Avoid negative language, such as "That's not my job" or "I don't know." Use positive or neutral statements, such as "Let me find someone who can help us with this."

- *Thank the customer for his or her comments.* Thanking the customer says that you appreciate knowing about a dissatisfaction or problem.

- *Research, identify, explain, and solve the problem.* Write down information related to the problem. Tell the customer what you are doing.

- *Follow up.* A phone call, e-mail, or letter will let the customer know that his or her concerns are not forgotten.

- *Log the incident and learn from the experience.* Keep a record of how the problem was handled so other employees will know how to deal with the situation in the future.

Observing the Competition

Retailers must be constantly watchful of the competition—especially when it comes to customer service. Remember that retailers are always looking for ways to stay ahead of the competition. Shopping the competition and observing their methods and customer-service offerings are good ways to stay informed. The methods the competition uses might give a retailer an idea that can lead to a competitive advantage. For example, one car-service center might offer a free car wash with oil change on Tuesdays. The competing car-service centers on the next block might not realize why they have a sudden drop in business on Tuesdays, if they are not watchful. To be competitive, they might offer a similar service, throw in a cup of coffee, or provide a three-day guarantee instead.

 marketingseries.glencoe.com

Fashionable Discounter

Stein Mart

Stein Mart describes itself as the finest upscale off-price specialty store in America. Although the stores offer low prices—about 25 percent to 60 percent less than other similar department stores—Stein Mart is not your average discount chain. There are no large plastic carts, no bright lights, and no wide aisles tracking through super-sized stores. Stein Mart customers shop the old-fashioned way. Each Stein Mart reflects "uptown" surroundings, provides friendly one-to-one customer service, and offers a stylish layout of quality items from housewares to fragrances to quality apparel for men, women, and children.

The major contributor to Stein Mart sales is ladies' wear. The Boutique, in particular, is a favorite of fashion-conscious customers. A Stein Mart hallmark, the Boutique features famous brands, designer names, and the Boutique ladies. Working only one day a week, the "ladies" are a liaison between the store and community, and they assist customers individually. They also keep their departments up to date with trendy items seen in current magazines, television shows, and movies.

Operating more than 260 stores in 29 states across the country, Stein Mart finds itself at home in a mixed, high-traffic neighborhood of high-end grocers, good bookstores, nice restaurants, and other well-known apparel shops. Stein Mart also takes its fashions on the road. One recent event, a fashion show for women in their in their 60s and 70s, demonstrates that the trendy styles can be worn—and modeled—at any age. "Fashion is not about age or size," said the show's Stein Mart commentator and fashion consultant, Miss Georgia of 1961, "It's an attitude."

1. When do you think customer service is most helpful?
2. Explain what you think this means: "The customer is always right."

Listening to Store Employees

Listening to store employees is another way to learn what customers want. Employees who have daily contact with customers acquire a great deal of firsthand information. Regular communication with store employees is a source of information that retailers should not forget. Store employees are the people who work with customers every day, and in some cases, may know them by sight or by name. Listening to employees provides the additional benefit of giving employees a sense of partnership in the process of planning customer services.

Cost of Services

Another factor to consider when planning customer services is the cost of those services. If certain services will increase operating expenses, then revenue from sales must increase to pay for those services. However, a retailer must also consider whether removing a service offering will negatively affect sales overall. Customers may be attracted to a retail store because of its services. Stores such as Nordstrom's and small specialty stores may have customers due to their excellent service.

MARKETING SERIES *Online*

Remember to check out this book's Web site for customer service information and more great resources at **marketingseries.glencoe.com**.

Mini-Mania

One of this decade's hottest cars, the Mini Cooper, was recently voted the "European Car of the Century"—the 20th century, that is—by a panel of 130 international judges. Designed in 1959 as an efficient, affordable car—an answer to Europe's fuel shortage—the Mini hit the streets of England in 1961. In one updated version or another, it has been on the road ever since. Dedicated to serving its customers, the British Motor Corporation built a car almost everyone can like. Sports-minded drivers appreciate the Mini's solid performance and smooth handling, commuters like its fuel efficiency, and parents appreciate its six air bags and stability. At only four feet wide and ten feet long, it's small enough to dart into tight places, but large enough to seat four adults. The newest models are some of the most technologically advanced cars of their size in the world. "The backlash of the SUV begins," crows one Mini distributor.

As a customer, what kind of service would you expect from a Mini dealer?

What Customers Expect

Customer-service perceptions have a lot to do with customers' expectations of how they should be treated when they visit a retail business. Customers expect to be treated fairly and honestly. They want to be treated with respect and want to feel they are valued guests.

The different types of customer services offered by competing retailers are generally quite similar. Customers learn to expect these services and will be disappointed if they are not there. If a competing retailer offers a new service or an existing service with a new twist, the competition will soon offer the same or a similar service. How can a retail business distinguish itself from a competitor?

The difference must come from the way the same services are delivered to the customer. That is where the retail employees and the customer treatment we just mentioned—friendly, fair, honest, respectful, and knowledgeable—makes the difference. For example, home delivery is a service customers expect from certain types of retailers. The customer's perception of the customer service is formed by the way the service is delivered by the employee. If the employee is sloppy in taking the address for the delivery, or if the employee is curt in asking for the order information, you can be sure the customer will feel like he or she has received poor customer service. If the employee is efficient, friendly, and businesslike while asking for the same information, the customer will feel assured about the order and feel like he or she has received good customer service.

Areas of Customer Service

Customer services can be categorized into two large areas: retailer dependability, and employee contact. This grouping of customer services categorizes the services that a retailer offers according to the function that a particular service offers.

RETAILER RELIABILITY SERVICES Retailer reliability services refer to the ability of the customer to depend on retailers to do what they say they will. In other words, does the retailer keep promises made to customers? Merchandise deliveries are a customer service that falls into this category. If you purchase a refrigerator, and the retailer promises to deliver it within a week of the purchase date, the delivery should take place as promised. If a retailer's delivery department promises to make a delivery between the hours of 9:00 A.M. and noon, the delivery should occur at that time. If the delivery is not made as promised, the customer becomes annoyed and sees the retailer as being unreliable. Other customer services that relate to a retailer's reliability are those dealing with service appointments and credit and billing issues.

EMPLOYEE CONTACT SERVICES Employee contact services refer to a customer's contact with store employees. Those services deal with how customers are treated when they shop at a retailer's business. Employee contact services involve the availability and accessibility of store employees to help customers locate merchandise or to be of assistance to the customer. Customer assistance can include the processing of sales, handling special orders, and checking back stock. This is a very important area of customer service. The sales associate is usually the only contact a customer has with store personnel. It is important that the employee-to-customer contact be a positive experience for the customer.

Store appearance also falls into the area of employee contact. The store's appearance is a direct reflection of the sales associates employed in the store. A messy, cluttered store or department sends a message to the customer that the employees do not care about the merchandise, and if this is so, they probably do not care about the customers. No retailer wants to send that message.

QUESTION

What are two areas of customer service?

 ALL ABOUT ATTITUDE
A good customer-service attitude can make the smallest service a reason for repeat business. *Do customers care if retailers keep their promises regarding customer service?*

Store Environment

The type of retail environment determines influence on the type of customer service expected by customers. Most people have very high expectations about the level of customer service from luxury retailers. In most cases, luxury retailers such as Tiffany's, Lexus, or the Ritz-Carlton hotel chain live up to those expectations. To maintain their reputation, they strive for excellence in all areas of the customer's retail experience. They offer customized details and promotions that are tuned to their prospective customers' expectations of high-quality service. However, even if the service is superior compared to most other retailers, if a luxury retailer fails to meet a customer's expectations, the customer will feel deprived of good customer service.

Word of Mouth

Advertising and creative promotional gimmicks are helpful. However, only a good shopping experience will keep a customer coming back to the store. If the service is great, a customer will have a good shopping experience without having to purchase anything. Why should great service matter? Because customers tell their friends, relatives, and work or school colleagues when they have experienced outstanding treatment. However, customers more frequently relate bad experiences. Customer conversations about their retail experiences are called **word-of-mouth communication**. Feedback from word-of-mouth communication has far-reaching effects. Positive word-of-mouth communication is a valuable asset. Negative word of mouth is damaging and difficult to overcome. Public consumer Web sites include forums where people rate retailers and comment on their experiences. Maintaining good customer service is more important than ever.

word-of-mouth communication customer conversations about their retail experiences

Quick Check ✓

RESPOND to what you've read by answering these questions.

1. What are four methods retailers use to determine customer preferences? _____

_____

_____

2. What are the two large areas of customer services? _____

_____

_____

3. Why is word-of-mouth communication so important? _____

_____

_____

_____

The Employee's Role

Representing the Business

Employees play the most important role in customer service. Retail employees provide most of the personal contact customers have with a retail business. Most of the time, the image the employee projects is the strongest impression of the business that the customer receives. The employee is the key player in the delivery of customer service. This section will discuss the different roles that employees and employers have in providing quality customer service.

Employees and Customer Service

The most important part of the sales associate's job is providing customer service. In Chapter 11, you learned about personal selling. You found out how effective personal selling helps to create a happy and loyal customer base. The way customers are treated during the selling process has an important effect on customer perceptions of the business. The follow-up after a sale serves to enhance the customer's positive perceptions of their retail experience.

Retail employees are often the only contact a customer has with a business. Retail employees are trained to handle the technical tasks of their job: how to process sales, use cash, and handle merchandise returns. However, many employees receive little training for providing customer service or management's expectations about customer service. Employees should be trained to handle all kinds of customer service situations, from dealing with an irate customer to handling special requests. Employees should also understand what customer service means in that particular retail establishment.

Factors Affecting Employees and Service

Factors other than employee training affect the level of customer service provided by employees. One of those factors is employee retention. **Employee retention** is a company's ability to keep workers employed for an extended period of time. Long-time employees feel comfortable with their environment and have a greater understanding of management's expectations than do new employees. The combination of comfort level and knowledge of expectations enables employees to provide a more consistent level of customer service. Long-term employees have probably remained at their places of employment because they are happy there. Happy employees pass their good feelings about their workplace on to their customers through their attitudes and actions. Customers also recognize long-time employees when they

AS YOU READ ...

YOU WILL LEARN
- To identify the employee's role in providing customer service.
- To explain the importance of employee empowerment and recognition.

WHY IT'S IMPORTANT
Understanding the employee's role in providing customer service is necessary to ensure its proper delivery. Empowering and recognizing employees encourages outstanding customer service.

KEY TERMS
- employee retention
- employee turnover
- low employee turnover
- high employee turnover
- empowerment

PREDICT

Name ways an employer could motivate employees to provide good customer service.

employee retention a company's ability to keep workers employed for an extended period of time

BUILDING RELATIONSHIPS

Paul Brzonkala
Vice President
Customer Focus Services

What does your job entail?
"As head of sales, I am responsible for developing revenue. I also act as the corporate controller. Because I manage the finances, I have the advantage of being able to craft my own deals. I can adjust the pricing model to meet the needs of each client by knowing what people, process, and technology components are required for each opportunity. My workload can vary greatly depending on what is happening. Each day I schedule some level of contact with my sales channels."

What kind of training did you have?
"I was asked to help build the IT (information technology) platform for a new call center for MCI. I eventually stayed to run the technology operations of what came to be MCI's outsourcing center. Over time, my roles and responsibilities increased. I joined Customer Focus, knowing that offshore business was where the next wave of opportunities would exist."

What skills are most important?
"Relationship building is extremely important. Business relationships are built on trust."

What is your key to success?
"Again, building relationships is the absolute key to success within a sales organization. Those relationships develop with communication and trust. Acting in our clients' best interests always brings credibility to our communications."

Give examples of relationship building in retail sales.

Career Data: Product Planner

Education and Training Bachelor's or master's degrees in operations, sales, or general business

Skills and Abilities Language skills, people skills, patience, and organizational skills

Career Outlook Average growth through 2010

Career Path Customer-service careers are varied. Many are entry level (at call centers), while others involve larger skill sets (e.g., technical support, dedicated support services.)

---

employee turnover the change in employment status at a company when employees leave their jobs

low employee turnover the change in employment status at a company when few employees leave their jobs

visit the store. That gives customers a feeling of continuity and stability about the business. They feel comfortable knowing that the employees are familiar with customer needs, preferences, and names.

EMPLOYEE TURNOVER Employee turnover is another factor that can affect customer service. **Employee turnover** is the term used for the change in employment status at a company when employees leave their jobs. **Low employee turnover** means that few employees leave their jobs and that the staff remains stable. Retail-service businesses know that customers prefer to see the same people working on their cars, giving them manicures, or performing dental work or physical therapy.

High employee turnover has the opposite effect. **High employee turnover** occurs when the staff changes frequently. There can be a variety of reasons for the high turnover rate, but high turnover affects customer service. New employees are less comfortable with their environment. They are not familiar with the placement of items of merchandise and supplies. There is a greater chance that new employees will provide a less consistent level of customer service. New employees are less knowledgeable about management's expectations. Customers who see new staff each time they enter a store may wonder why the staff changes frequently and lose confidence. The lack of personalized customer service may bother some customers.

COMPENSATION PACKAGES One way to ensure high employee retention is to offer employees a good *compensation package*. This is a series of benefits or incentives that an employer will offer to attract employees and keep them satisfied. Common benefits include health insurance, paid vacation, sick leave, maternity leave, bonuses, employee discounts, transportation vouchers, employee discounts, and stock options or partial ownership in the company.

Providing Customer Service

Management has an important role in helping employees provide quality customer service. Retail management must support the efforts of employees to provide excellent customer service. Management can do this through training and empowerment.

Managers should be responsible for setting goals for their employees. Many places of businesses have a *mission statement*, or a short paragraph that clearly states the purpose of the business and what the business hopes to achieve. Managers should make sure that their employees are aware of the mission statement and their roles.

Math Check

BONUS TIME

Livian has sold $2,320 worth of merchandise. How much will her commission be if she gets a 20 percent commission plus 5 percent on amounts over $1,000?

➥ For tips on finding the solution, go to **marketingseries.glencoe.com**.

high employee turnover the change in employment status at a company when the staff changes frequently

◄ **HOW CAN I HELP YOU TODAY? Customer service responsibilities can be very specific, but the underlying motive is the same—to give customers what they want.** *What special customer skills might an employee need in a city with a multicultural population?*

Figure 12.2

Customer Feedback Form

THE CUSTOMER'S VOICE
Many stores offer forms that customers can use to make complaints, give praise, or suggest improvements. *What other questions would you add to this form?*

What was the nature of your contact with us today?

- ○ Billing issue
- ○ Staff complaint or comment
- ○ Question
- ○ Service inquiry
- ○ Return or exchange
- ○ Other _____

Statements	Check as appropriate				
	Strongly Agree	Agree	Disagree	Strongly Disagree	No Comment or N/A
Staff was courteous and quick to answer questions.	○	○	○	○	○
Checkout/return process was timely and hassle-free.	○	○	○	○	○
Product selection was excellent.	○	○	○	○	○
Customer service selection was excellent.	○	○	○	○	○
Overall experience was positive.	○	○	○	○	○

Is there any staff member whom you would like to mention? List name.
_____
_____

Do you have any comments about any particular product or service?
_____
_____

Is there anything else we could have done to make your experience today more pleasurable?
_____
_____

Optional:
Name _____ Phone # _____

Street address _____

E-mail address _____ Date _____

CONNECT
Why might high turnover affect customer service?

Employee Empowerment

Empowerment means that employees are made part of the customer-service team. **Empowerment** is granting employees the responsibility for making decisions. Empowered employees do not have to tell customers that they have to check with the manager before they can fulfill customer needs. The employee can make the decision or obtain the correct information on the spot. Both employees and customers feel good about a situation when the employee can make that type of decision. However, management must make sure that employees are trained in customer service so that the service level throughout the store is uniform.

Employee empowerment is especially important when dealing with customer problems or complaints. All employees should be trained to listen carefully to the customer's problem or complaint, and then act quickly to resolve the problem.

Customer Feedback

Many retail establishments, both brick-and-mortar and online, offer customer feedback forms at the checkout counter or by request. Customers can make comments about different aspects of their retail experience. This is a way for managers to obtain specific information about complaints, praise, or concerns that customers have. See an example of a customer feedback form in **Figure 12.2**. Through feedback from customers, negative situations can be reversed, and customers may be retained.

Telephone Customer Service

Courteous, prompt customer service is vital on the telephone. Many catalog companies do not have a brick-and-mortar store for customers to visit, so the telephone contact is the only customer contact available to them. Because of this, outstanding telephone customer service is the lifeline of those businesses. This is also true for service retailers who rely on the telephone to make customer appointments or to take orders for food or other products. Since there is no live person in front of them, telephone customers may become impatient if they have to be transferred or must repeat account or product numbers. It is important to speak clearly and politely, and to be certain that the customer-service representative and the customer are communicating about the same thing. It is common for telephone customer-service representatives to repeat orders and customer inquiries so that there is no confusion about what was done or said.

Case Study — PART 2

CLIMBING UP
Continued from Part 1 on page 239

In order to serve its market that was not yet established, REI took pride in supporting sports. Since 1976, the retailer has donated more than $9 million to outdoor recreation groups and conservation clubs, such as Friends of the Boundary Waters Wilderness, the Colorado Mountain Club, and Leave No Trace. The cooperative has also taken steps to reduce its impact on the environment by using minimal packaging and recycling whenever possible. The store also encourages athletes. Indoor climbing walls are installed in REI stores so that customers can practice climbing and try out equipment. For more than 15 years, REI has served its customers by organizing domestic and international bicycling, trekking, kayaking, hiking, camping, and mountaineering trips.

ANALYZE AND WRITE

1. How does contributing money to organizations such as Friends of the Boundary Waters Wilderness help REI?
2. What are some other businesses that might be able to arrange themed trips?

QUESTION

What type of retailers benefits from good telephone customer service?

empowerment granting employees responsibility for making decisions

TECH NOTES

Who Was That Mystery Shopper?

From the moment mystery shoppers enter retail establishments, they are taking mental notes on every aspect of their experience. Retailers often hire companies that provide mystery-shopping services to evaluate their own customer service. Internet access has revolutionized the way mystery-shopping providers operate. Instead of filling out paper forms and mailing them off after completing an assignment, mystery shoppers receive and submit assignments online and via e-mail.

➡️ Write a short paragraph about what you think of this method of assessing employees after learning more about it through **marketingseries.glencoe.com**.

Internet Customer Service

Retailers who use the electronic channel to conduct their business also rely on excellence in customer service. Prompt customer service is especially important for e-tailers. Many Internet-access providers offer customer-service rating systems for online retailers. For example, the popular Web portal Yahoo! uses a system of stars to show excellence in customer service. An online retailer earning five stars from Yahoo! is able to display a caption that states, "Top Service. Yahoo! recommends this site for excellent customer service. The best of the best!" Any online retailer earning five stars will probably display that caption.

Employee Recognition

Employers must recognize employees who provide excellence in customer service. The employee's role in providing outstanding customer service should be rewarded. The reward does not have to be material. It can be something as simple as mentioning the employee and the outstanding service at a staff meeting. Some employers offer small rewards such as a gift certificate for ice cream or some other small incentive. Others may offer cash bonuses for innovative service. Recognition makes employees feel that they are contributing to the success of the business. In a way, employees are like customers: When they feel valued and appreciated, they usually remain loyal.

Because employees are often the main contact that a customer has with a retail establishment, employees must do their best to make sure that the customer impression is a positive one. Recognizing employees for doing an outstanding job will help motivate employees to continue to provide outstanding service to customers.

Quick Check ✔

RESPOND to what you've read by answering these questions.

1. What is the most important part of a sales associate's job? _____

_____

_____

2. Why is employee retention important in the delivery of outstanding customer service?

_____

_____

_____

3. What are the two ways management can help employees provide excellent customer service?

_____

_____

Name _____ Date _____

Worksheet 12.1

Store Environment

Visit two different retail stores—(1) one that appeals to you and (2) one that does not. Notice the appearance and environment of each store, and then answer the following questions about each store:

- What is the name and type of store?

- How is color used?

- Are the aisles open or cluttered?

- How is the merchandise displayed?

- What other details do you notice?

- Are sales associates helpful?

Store #1

_____

_____

_____

_____

_____

_____

_____

_____

_____

_____

Store #2

_____

_____

_____

_____

_____

_____

_____

_____

_____

_____

_____

Worksheet 12.2

Developing a Compensation Package

To keep good employees, employers need to offer employees a good compensation package. Contact three competing businesses in your community to learn about their compensation packages, including starting wages, benefits, vacation time, sick time, and any other benefits offered.

1. Store #1 Compensation Package:

_____

_____

_____

2. Store #2 Compensation Package:

_____

_____

_____

3. Store #3 Compensation Package:

_____

_____

_____

Compare and Contrast

4. Which store has the best compensation package? Why do you think it is the best?

_____

_____

5. Which store will most likely attract more good employees? Why? _____

_____

_____

_____

6. In which store would you like to work? Why? _____

_____

_____

_____

_____

_____

_____

Portfolio Works

RECOGNIZING EMPLOYEES

Imagine you manage an ice cream shop. Many of your employees are high school students who work weekends and after school.

1. List three things you can do to recognize employees who provide excellent customer service.

_____

_____

_____

_____

_____

2. List three things you can do to promote employee retention. _____

_____

_____

_____

_____

_____

3. List three things you can do to motivate employees to provide excellent customer service.

_____

_____

_____

_____

_____

4. List three things you can do to help employees feel empowered. _____

_____

_____

_____

_____

Add this page to your career portfolio.

CHAPTER SUMMARY

Section 12.1   The Customer's Role

customer service (p. 240)
customer survey (p. 241)
word-of-mouth
   communication
   (p. 246)

- The types and quality of customer services offered by a retail business can have an enormous effect on the success of the business. Customer service is the set of enhancements offered by retailers to customers that make shopping more convenient or rewarding.

- Customers have different customer-service expectations for different types of businesses. Understanding the role that customer expectations play in customers' perceptions of customer service will help store employees provide good customer service.

- Word-of-mouth communication involves customer conversations about their retail experiences. This type of communication can be either a valuable asset or a liability to overcome for a retailer.

Section 12.2   The Employee's Role

employee retention
   (p. 247)
employee turnover
   (p. 248)
low employee turnover
   (p. 248)
high employee turnover
   (p. 249)
empowerment (p. 251)

- Understanding the employee's role in providing customer service is necessary in order to ensure its proper delivery. Employees are the main contact that customers have with a retail establishment. They must make sure that the customer impression is a positive one.

- Empowering employees is an important step in the delivery of outstanding customer service. It is important for retailers to train and then trust the judgment of their employees to make on-the-spot decisions about customer service. Recognizing employees for doing an outstanding job will help motivate them to continue to provide outstanding customer service.

CHECKING CONCEPTS

1. **Define** customer service.
2. **Explain** positive customer/client relations.
3. **Explain** customer-service expectations.
4. **Discuss** the importance of word-of-mouth communication.
5. **Identify** the employee's role in customer service.
6. **Describe** management's role in customer relations.
7. **Explain** the concept of empowerment.

Critical Thinking

8. **Describe** what happens to a store if employees give poor customer service.

CROSS-CURRICULUM SKILLS

Work-Based Learning

Basic Skills—Listening Skills and Writing

9. Ask the manager of a store to recommend a long-time employee to interview. Ask the employee why he or she has stayed with the store. Write an article about your findings and share with the class.

Interpersonal Skills—Participating as a Team Member

10. Choose a retail store. Design a customer survey for the store and have your classmates fill out the survey. Write a report on the results.

School-Based Learning

Social Sciences

11. Ask permission from a retail store manager to spend several hours in the store. Observe how different employees interact with different customers. Give an oral report of your findings.

Arts

12. Design a poster that celebrates the good job by the employees of a retail store. Display the posters in class.

Role Play: Manager of a Supermarket Deli

SITUATION You are to assume the role of manager of the delicatessen department of a supermarket. The deli sells a variety of cold cuts and salads. The deli is very popular and busy during lunch hour. The supermarket and the deli pride themselves on outstanding customer service.

ACTIVITY You are to orient a new employee (judge) about customer service in the deli, particularly during the busiest hours.

EVALUATION You will be evaluated on how well you meet the following performance indicators:

- Demonstrate a customer-service mindset.
- Explain the nature of positive customer/client relations.
- Explain management's role in customer relations.
- Explain the concept of staff motivation.
- Orient new employees.

Use the Internet to access an online bookstore such as Barnes & Noble.

- Search for Empowering Employees.
- Click on the first book titled *Empowering Employees.*
- Scroll down to About the Book.
- Write a summary of the book from the About the Book section.

➡For a link to an online bookstore to begin this exercise, go to **marketingseries.glencoe.com**.

Chapter 13

Managing the Store

Chapter Objectives

- Identify important characteristics of store managers.
- Describe the store manager's role in merchandise management.
- Explain expense control.
- Explain the importance of managing store employees.
- Explain the importance of working with supervisors.
- Explain the importance of positive customer relations.

POWER READ

Be an active reader and use these reading strategies:

PREDICT what the section will be about.

CONNECT what you read with your life.

QUESTION as you read to make sure you understand the content.

RESPOND to what you've read.

EAT AT JOE'S

The same or different? Managing a deli-catessen with specialized meats and bakery goods—or managing a chain of specially priced grocery items imported from around the world? In many ways, managing both of these stores would be similar. However, pur-chasing a chain of food stores such as Trader Joe's and retaining its distinct character proved to be quite challenging.

In 1958, Joe Coulombe started a chain of convenience markets in Los Angeles. In 1967, Coulombe decided to change the stores' image, incorporating a seafaring theme. The managers were called *captains*, the assistant managers *first mates*, and everyone else *crew members*. All employees wore Hawaiian shirts and the walls were decorated with nets and planks. The stores were renamed "Trader Joe's" and offered hard-to-find, gourmet and healthy foods at low prices. Unique trail mixes, instant Indian food, French cheese, and organic cereals were some of the products sold under the Trader Joe's label. Although Trader Joe's stores are smaller than supermarkets and do not offer deli and bakery services, their unique mix of items and fair prices helped the prof-itable chain spread through California and gain a loyal following of customers in other states as well. In 1979, German businessmen Karl and Theo Albrecht bought the food chain from Coulombe. Were they be able to grow Trader Joe's business without it losing its edge?

ANALYZE AND WRITE

1. Why would a store like Trader Joe's not provide deli or bakery services?
2. How might Trader Joe's success be affected with new management?

Case Study Part 2 on page 265

The Store Manager's Role

AS YOU READ ...

YOU WILL LEARN

- To identify important characteristics of store managers.
- To describe the store manager's role in merchandise management.
- To explain expense control.

WHY IT'S IMPORTANT

Understanding the characteristics that are important in store managers is helpful in determining whether that is a job you would enjoy.

KEY TERMS

- multitasking
- delegate
- name brands
- private brands
- generic brands
- register till
- selling expenses

PREDICT

Name some of the most important duties performed by a store manager.

multitasking working on many tasks at the same time

delegate to put an employee in charge of a project to completion

What Does a Store Manager Do?

A retail store manager is in charge of the daily operations of a retail store—everything from making sure the doors open on time and managing finances to overseeing merchandise and the store's employees. The store manager's duties can be grouped into five large categories: merchandise management, store operations, expense control, personnel management, and customer relations.

Characteristics of a Store Manager

Managing a retail store involves completing a variety of tasks every day. A store manager may need to assist customers while training a new employee, restocking shelves, or retagging merchandise. A store manager must be well organized and able to work on a variety of tasks. Working on many tasks at the same time is called **multitasking**.

A successful store manager must also have good people skills. Store managers must like people and enjoy working with them—the store's employees as well as the store's customers and upper management personnel. To interact and get along with all these different people, a manager should have good listening skills and good communication skills.

The store manager also needs to be energetic and hardworking. There is a lot of work to be done in every retail store. Working long hours is often part of a retailing career. Most retail stores are open at least eight hours a day, and stores located in malls can be open ten hours a day or more. Some types of retail stores, such as supermarkets, are open even longer hours. Most stores are open seven days a week. A store manager is not expected to be at the store the entire time it is open, but the working hours can be extended. A store manager must also be able to delegate in order to get a lot of work accomplished. To **delegate** means putting an employee in charge of a project and then letting the employee complete that project.

Managing Merchandise

A store manager also handles all the tasks involved in getting the store's merchandise to the sales area and, ultimately, to the customer. Merchandise tasks include receiving merchandise into the store and ticketing the merchandise, if necessary. Merchandise tasks also include making decisions about where to place merchandise within the selling area as well as deciding what store fixtures to use for merchandise placement.

Receiving Merchandise

When new merchandise is received at a retail store, it becomes part of the store's inventory. If a merchandise-receiving procedure has not been established, then the store manager should develop one.

Receiving merchandise involves checking the merchandise received against the shipping invoice to ensure that all the merchandise is there and in good condition. However, establishing procedures for receiving merchandise can help reduce errors in the store's inventory figures. Receiving merchandise is a task that can be delegated to a responsible employee. Receiving procedures are usually not difficult to follow and can be easily taught to employees. Remember that the store manager is responsible for the store's inventory.

TICKETING AND RETICKETING MERCHANDISE Once merchandise has been properly received, the store manager must make sure that it is ticketed correctly. If the store is part of a large company, the merchandise might arrive with price tickets attached. When that is the case, the manager should be sure that the price and other ticket information are correct. If the store is a small one, the manager may need to ticket the arriving merchandise before placing it on the sales floor. Whatever the situation, it is important that all merchandise have correct price tickets.

It is sometimes necessary to reticket certain items of merchandise. Merchandise tickets sometimes get lost, removed, or damaged in the normal course of business. The manager or an employee must replace these tickets as soon as they are discovered missing.

MARKETING SERIES Online

Remember to check out this book's Web site for store management information and more great resources at **marketingseries.glencoe.com**.

WEARING MANY HATS **A retail store manager often handles more than one responsibility at a time.** *How do you think being organized could help a manager to multitask effectively?*

Hot Property

A Real Gem

Tiffany & Company

"Every so often, I walk in just to get a shot of elegance," says a longtime New Yorker. Tall doors, soft, plush carpet, a well-groomed staff, glittering window displays, and shiny glass showcases are trademarks of Tiffany & Company and their 220 stores and boutiques worldwide. Even the first Manhattan store on Broadway was advertised as a *fancy* goods shop in 1837.

THE STANDARD OF MANAGEMENT

Tiffany & Company was established as a symbol of elegance under the management of founder Charles L. Tiffany. His ideals set the standard for first-rate service, craftsmanship, and "classic products," including fine jewels. For almost two centuries, Tiffany has accepted only quality artisans and gems. Only 2 percent of gem-quality diamonds meet Tiffany standards. Creative designs have also become a Tiffany trademark, sought after by the public and found in museums everywhere. One Tiffany gem is particularly famous for its beauty and size. Purchased in 1878, the yellow Tiffany Diamond is among the world's largest at 128.54 carats. It is on permanent display at the Fifth Avenue shop in New York City.

NATIONAL TREASURES

Tiffany has also left its mark on American history. It created a presentational pitcher for Abraham Lincoln's presidential inauguration. During the Civil War, Tiffany manufactured metals, swords, and surgical tools for the Union Army. Later, the company designed a china service for President Lyndon Johnson's White House. Even the seven-pound, sterling-silver Super Bowl trophy was crafted by Tiffany. Then there is *Tiffany blue*, the special shade of blue that colors all Tiffany boxes, bags, and catalogs. It reminds customers that they have been in the company of royalty, presidents, and Hollywood legends.

1. Many stores sell expensive goods. What do you think makes a Tiffany store distinct?
2. Tiffany's Web site features tips on etiquette. How do you think this relates to the management of the stores?

CONNECT

Does the placement of a store's fixtures affect the way you shop and what you buy?

MERCHANDISING THE SELLING AREA Determining the placement of new merchandise on the selling floor is an important merchandise function. The manager should feature new merchandise so that customers will know the merchandise has arrived and that it is new. The store manager should also make sure that all the employees are aware of and educated about the new merchandise as well as know how to find it in the store.

Most retail stores use a variety of fixtures on which to display merchandise. Fixtures include all types of store furniture, including display cases, racks, and shelves. Different types of retail stores use different fixtures to hold their merchandise. Supermarkets, bookstores, and drugstores make extensive use of shelves. Clothing stores use straight racks to hang merchandise along walls, as well as rounders, which are freestanding circular racks.

Rounders can hold large quantities of merchandise, especially clothing on hangers. A *gondola* is another type of freestanding merchandise rack. Gondolas usually have shelves for holding merchandise and may display items such as sweaters.

Selecting the right type of fixture to hold merchandise is an important decision. Customers have to be able to see the merchandise. A manager should place and arrange merchandise so that it attracts the customers' attention and their interest. Regardless of whether merchandise is new or not, all merchandise should be arranged in a neat and tidy manner.

MERCHANDISE AND BRAND NAMES Many stores carry a combination of name brand, private brand, and generic brand merchandise. Name brands are sometimes known as *national brands*. **Name brands** are merchandise items that are designed and made by a specific manufacturer and sold under that manufacturer's name. For example, Polo-brand clothing is designed and made by the Polo Ralph Lauren Corporation. In your supermarket, Chips Ahoy cookies are created and produced by Nabisco, which is a brand owned by the Kraft Foods Corporation. Customers know name brands and expect a level of quality.

Private brands are merchandise items designed and made for the retailer selling them. They are sometimes called *store brands*. An example of a private brand is the Charter Club brand, which is made for and sold only at Macy's department store. Regular customers of a store come to know and depend on that particular store's private brands.

Generic brands are merchandise items that are sold without a brand name or private label. Many supermarkets carry generic brands, which appeal to cost-conscious customers because they are often cheaper than name brands. Recognizing these types of brands can be helpful when a store manager decides where to place merchandise in a store.

Working With Buyers

Store managers must also interact with the store's buyers. A buyer is the person who decides what merchandise a store will carry and how much it will carry, and he or she may negotiate a price with the supplier. Good communication between a store manager and buyer is important so that the buyer understands the preferences of a store's customers and considers those preferences when making buying decisions. Buyers want any information a store manager can provide so they can do a better job of providing merchandise that customers will buy.

Determining Markdowns

You learned about markdowns in relation to their effect on the price of merchandise in Chapter 7. It is important for a store manager to deal with markdowns efficiently. Large retailers determine items to be marked down and then send a list of these items to their individual stores. In a small store, the store manager may be the person who determines which merchandise needs to receive a price reduction. In either situation, it is important to correctly record the amount of the markdown and the number of items being marked down. That information is necessary for keeping accurate inventory records that list the value of the store's merchandise.

THE Dot Com SHOP

Online, Not in Line

While many dot-com stores closed their virtual doors in the 1990s, others, such as Varsity Books, survived and thrived. The e-tailer targeted the textbook market and scored by partnering with brick-and-mortar school bookstores. Varsity Books provides off-site store-management services, such as payroll, order tracking, inventory management, customer service, and storage. Students avoid long lines by ordering online from a book list customized for their schools.

➡ Examine an online bookstore and list the pros and cons of having an Internet company run a college bookstore through **marketingseries.glencoe.com**.

name brands merchandise items designed and made by a specific manufacturer, and sold under that manufacturer's name

private brands merchandise items that are designed and made for the retailer selling them

generic brands merchandise items that are sold without either a brand name or private label

Figure 13.1

Retail Manager's Responsibilities

Large Retail Store	Small Retail Store
Responsible for an entire store	Responsible for an entire store
Supervises several department supervisors	Supervises all workers
Interacts with buyer or with regional director	Acts as buyer
Handles customer inquiries and complaints	Handles customer inquiries and complaints
Reports to regional director regarding purchasing, budgeting, and accounting	Handles all purchasing, budgeting, and accounting
Reviews inventory and sales records	Has total responsibility for inventory and sales records

Selling Point !

HIGH COSTS
Labor costs comprise over 25 percent of sales and 50 percent of the operating costs in service department stores.

register till the drawer that holds the cash in the cash register

Store Operations

Another big part of the store manager's job is making sure that the store runs smoothly every day. To do this, the manager must take care of a number of tasks every day, such as opening and closing the store, and making bank deposits.

Opening the store each day sounds simple enough. However, there is more to opening the store than meets the eye. The store manager must be certain that the merchandise is neat and has been straightened from the previous day's business. All the store lights must be turned on. The **register till**, or drawer that holds the cash in the cash register, must have enough cash to start the business day. The register counter must be supplied with credit-card slips, pens, bags, and other supplies that the store requires. Then the store is ready to open for business. In addition, the manager must open the store each day at the time designated for opening. It is not acceptable to open the store later. If the store's opening time is set for 10:00 A.M., then the doors must be open by 10:00 A.M., and not 10:06 A.M.

The store manager may not always be at the store each day for opening. The manager can delegate that duty to the assistant manager or a trusted employee who has been trained to manage the store opening. Remember that when delegating this duty, the designated person will have the keys to the store. That is a big responsibility.

Closing the store involves many of the same responsibilities—but in reverse. At closing time each night, the manager must handle the cash and credit-card slips in accordance with store policy. Some stores deposit these at a bank each night; others keep them in the store safe.

Another responsibility of the store manager involves store maintenance. Store managers are not expected to clean the store themselves; they work with a maintenance person or crew. It is important for the store manager to be very specific about expectations for store maintenance. There should be no room for doubt about how and when the store is to be cleaned. The crew should vacuum or sweep the floors and empty the trash each day. Heavier cleaning, such as washing windows, should be scheduled at regular times. The store should look like opening day every day. The cleanliness of the store can enhance or damage the image of the store.

The size of the store usually determines how closely a manager works with cleaning crews, buyers, and others. In large chain stores, store managers may answer to a regional supervisor who coordinates with maintenance crews and buyers for the entire chain. **Figure 13.1** shows some of the different management responsibilities in a large store compared to a small store.

Expense Control

The expenses of operating a store can affect the price of the store's merchandise and the store's profit. A store manager must carefully examine store operating expenses and look for ways to keep them as low as possible. Operating expenses are the expenses (except merchandise expenses) involved in operating a store. Operating expenses include items such as rent and electricity. A store manager can control operating expenses by watching for waste and then stopping the waste. For example, the manager could make sure that the lights (except for security lights) are turned off at night. This can make a big difference in a store's electricity bill.

Managing Selling Expenses

The manager also manages and controls selling expenses. **Selling expenses** are the expenses associated with the store's sales associates. Selling expenses include sales associates' salaries and benefits. A store manager can carefully schedule the work times of sales associates so there are enough people to staff the store without having extra people on the schedule. The store manager must watch for customer shopping patterns. For example, a store located near office buildings will probably be busy during lunch hours and after work. Mid-afternoons may not be as busy because shoppers are back at their offices. A smart store manager would schedule more staff to work from 11:00 A.M. to 1:30 P.M. to cover the lunch hour, and then have fewer staff members working from 1:30 P.M. until the offices close. The manager might also schedule more people from 4:30 P.M. until 6:00 P.M. The savings from such planned scheduling can be huge.

Case Study — PART 2

EAT AT JOE'S
Continued from Part 1 on page 259

Because Trader Joe's was concentrated on the West Coast, the Albrecht brothers saw possibilities for growth. Under their direction, Trader Joe's expanded to over 200 stores across the country, including the Northwest, New England, and the Midwest. The store's formula has remained the same. Although the stores' aisles have become wider and the packaging simpler, the mix of organic, ethnic, exotic, healthy, and gourmet food has remained. Because the store sells its own lines of unique foods, tries out and discontinues foods constantly to eliminate dead stock, and handles its own packaging, marketing, and distribution, prices stay low. As a result, the chain earns about $1,000 per square foot of store space, twice the amount of typical supermarkets.

ANALYZE AND WRITE

1. Why did the Albrecht brothers see possibilities for growth at Trader Joe's?
2. What are some methods Trader Joe's uses to keep costs low? Would these methods work for a larger market?

selling expenses the expenses associated with the store's sales associates

QUESTION

Are selling expenses part of a store's operating expenses? Why?

ETHICAL PRACTICES

A New Chapter?

When faced with losses and debt, some retail businesses choose Chapter 11 bankruptcy over closing their doors permanently. Some companies fail despite this move that allows a store to get out of leases, renegotiate bills, and fend off vendors who are trying to collect debts. A store may also lay off staff members, even those who have built careers at a company. Some people believe this strategy is better than hanging the "going-out-of-business" sign in the window.

Managing Loss Expenses

The store manager must also work to control lost revenue and prevent shoplifting and employee pilferage. As discussed in Chapter 5, the store manager can educate sales associates about shoplifting and how to spot shoplifters with several guidelines:

- **Don't assume all shoplifters are poorly dressed.** Professional shoplifters try to blend in with regular customers to avoid suspicion.

- **Notice loiterers.** Less experienced shoplifters may stand around waiting for the right moment.

- **Notice groups.** Some shoplifters work in pairs or groups and distract employees as one of them steals.

- **Notice people with loose clothing.** Shoplifters may hide stolen merchandise under clothing or in large bags.

- **Notice eyes, hands, and body.** Shoplifters may watch employees more than the merchandise and move in an unusual manner as they hide items.

Keeping expenses under control is an important part of a store manager's job because having low expenses will keep merchandise prices reasonable and the customers happy.

Quick Check

RESPOND to what you've read by answering these questions.

1. What are the five large categories of a store manager's responsibilities? _____

_____

_____

_____

_____

2. Why is the ability to multi-task important to a store manager? _____

_____

_____

_____

_____

3. What are three areas in which a store manager can control expenses? _____

_____

_____

_____

Managing People

Managing Store Personnel

There is more to managing store personnel than planning employee work schedules. Managers are also responsible for hiring, training, supervising, and evaluating employees. These duties are among the most important of a store manager's responsibilities, because employees are the people who actually determine whether customers will enjoy shopping in a store and return to it.

Hiring Employees

Hiring employees involves finding suitable candidates for the positions that need to be filled. A manager usually advertises an open position in the local newspaper or online, and then reviews applications and chooses the most promising candidates to interview. During an interview, job candidates are told about the job and what will be expected of them. The store manager judges the ability of each candidate to perform those tasks and to fit in with the staff and the store image. After interviewing several candidates, the manager decides which person to hire.

Training Employees

The store manager must also assume the responsibility for training store employees. Employee training is always worth the time involved. New employees want to feel like they belong, and they want to do a good job. That will happen when employees know what to do and how to do it.

Training takes time, and sometimes that time is difficult to find. Store managers have much to do, but new-employee training is one of the most important tasks. Store managers must also engage in ongoing training of employees. When new products arrive or new services are added, store employees must train to know how to use the products and their features. Training does not stop after the initial training period—it is ongoing.

Supervising Employees

Supervising employees means ensuring employees do their jobs in a manner that is acceptable to the business. However, that is not all there is to employee supervision. A good store manager must motivate store personnel. **Motivation** is the act of encouraging employees to do their best at all times and making them feel appreciated. When store employees feel appreciated, their morale will be good. Employee **morale** is the attitude employees have regarding having a positive feeling or one of confidence and good spirits.

AS YOU READ . . .

YOU WILL LEARN
- To explain the importance of managing store employees.
- To explain the importance of working with supervisors.
- To explain the importance of positive customer relations.

WHY IT'S IMPORTANT

To be an effective store manager, you must be able to manage and motivate store personnel, deal effectively with supervisors, and create a positive atmosphere for customers.

KEY TERMS
- motivation
- morale
- teamwork

PREDICT

What are some store manager responsibilities regarding managing people?

motivation the act of encouraging employees to do their best at all times and making them feel appreciated

morale the attitude employees have regarding a positive feeling or one of confidence and good spirits teamwork a spirit of cooperation among employees as they work toward a common goal

A good store manager also works to build teamwork among the store personnel. We know that **teamwork** is a spirit of cooperation among employees as they work toward a common goal. Teamwork enables employees to work together so that all employees share in the feeling of accomplishment when storewide goals are met.

Evaluating Employees

Employee evaluation is the process of reviewing employees' performance of their duties and their general attitudes toward their jobs. Store managers and supervisors use employee evaluations to help determine pay

Profiles in Marketing

SELLING THE STORE

Dana Smith
Owner
The Stone Griffin

What does your job entail?
"My job involves pretty much everything in running a retail store. I only have part-time help, so I do everything: write book ads, do customer service, buy products, build the Web site, take digital photos for the Web site, take out the trash, clean, and on and on."

What skills are the most important?
"Wanting to sell. This is not as common as one would think. I have business neighbors who will not open until the posted hours, even when they are in the store and have a customer asking to come inside."

What kind of training did you have?
"The best training was on-the-job training with an open and inquiring mind."

What is your key to success?
"The most important thing to remember when running a retail store is that when customers walk in, the mission is to get them to buy—by offering a product they want. Many people get caught up with staging the store, cleaning the floors or whatever, forgetting that sales is what it is about. It's not *build it and they will come*—it's *see where they are and put stuff they want in their way*. I don't mean only location, but everything. If you put your product on racks, and they want to buy the racks, then sell the racks! Observe and think about what the customer does, how he or she reacts—and act accordingly."

How is flexibility important for managing a retail store?

Career Data: Store Manager/ Owner

Education and Training High school diploma, or associate's or bachelor's degrees in sales, advertising, marketing, or general business; on-the-job training

Skills and Abilities Creativity, communication skills, and confidence

Career Outlook Slower than average growth through 2010

Career Path An entry-level sales job can lead anywhere in the organization with appropriate skills.

increases, bonuses, and other forms of compensation. Store employees are usually evaluated on their contributions to a store's sales, customer relations, and merchandising efforts. Most companies evaluate employees' performances each year and set goals for the coming year.

Although every employee should have a formal evaluation each year, employee evaluation should be an ongoing process. Employees know when they are doing an exceptional job and should be praised. On the other hand, if an employee is not performing up to expectations, a manager can give a reminder in a nonthreatening manner to help get the employee back on the right track. Managers should inform their employees about what is required and expected before evaluations take place. **Figure 13.2** on page 270 shows a sample chart of some factors that a store manager could use to evaluate an employee.

Feedback from evaluations is very useful for improving employee skills. A manager can give more frequent formal evaluations for inexperienced employees if needed. However, these might be too time-consuming, and so the manager can also do informal evaluations to supplement the formal evaluation.

Working With Supervisors

In addition to working with the store's personnel, a store manager must also work with his or her supervisor. The store manager's supervisor in a large company is probably a regional or district manager who is in charge of several stores. In a small company, the store manager's supervisor might be the store's owner. In both situations, the store manager needs to practice many of the same traits a good store employee does. The store manager must be able to listen and really hear what the supervisor is saying, follow directions, and comply with store and company policy. Store managers must also be able to work as part of a team to achieve company-wide goals.

TECH
NOTES

**Bar Codes:
The Next Generation**

Radio frequency identification (RFID) is a new technology that can benefit retailers. An RFID tag can be attached to a product, enabling everyone to track the product as it moves. The tag contains a chip with information that can be picked up by a wireless-reader device, which relays data to a computer. The reader can also transmit information to the tag, such as date of purchase.

➡Read more about RFID and write a paragraph about how RFID will affect the retailing industry through **marketingseries.glencoe.com.**

GREAT LEADERS A good store manager can inspire employees to work together with team spirit. When everyone works together, they can all share accomplishments. *How do you think good morale promotes team spirit?*

CONNECT

Why should employee evaluation be an ongoing process?

marketingseries.glencoe.com

Figure 13.2

Evaluating Employees at a Clothing Store

FORMAL EVALUATION In most companies, supervisors meet with each employee once or twice a year to evaluate individual performance, based on specific factors, and to set goals for the coming year. *How would a formal evaluation be different from an ongoing evaluation conducted throughout the year?*

50% SALES/CUSTOMER RELATIONS

1. **Greeting**
   Approaches customers within 1–2 minutes with a smile and friendly manner. Uses open-ended questions.
2. **Product knowledge**
   Demonstrates knowledge of product, fit, shrinkage, and price, and can relay this information to the customer.
3. **Suggests additional merchandise**
   Approaches customers at fitting room and cash/wrap areas.
4. **Asks customers to buy and reinforces decisions**
   Lets customers know they've made a wise choice and thanks them.

25% OPERATIONS

1. **Store appearance**
   Demonstrates an eye for detail (color and finesse) in the areas of display, coordination of merchandise on tables, floor fixtures, and wall faceouts. Takes initiative in maintaining store presentation standards.
2. **Loss prevention**
   Actively follows all loss prevention procedures.
3. **Merchandise control and handling**
   Consistently achieves established requirements in price change activity, shipment processing, and inventory control.
4. **Cash/wrap procedure**
   Accurately and efficiently follows all register policies and cash/wrap procedures.

25% COMPLIANCE

1. **Dress code and appearance**
   Complies with dress code. Appears neat and well groomed. Projects current fashionable image.
2. **Flexibility**
   Able to switch from one assignment to another, open to schedule adjustments. Shows initiative, awareness of store priorities and needs.
3. **Working relations**
   Cooperates with other employees, willingly accepts direction and guidance from management. Communicates to management.

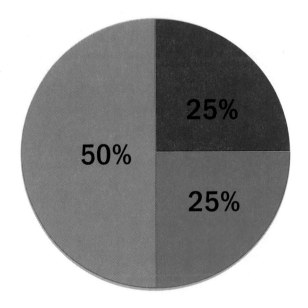

World Market

On the Road to Marrakech

At the crossroads of Europe and Africa, Morocco has been a center of buying and selling for centuries. Nowhere is the art of trade more apparent than in the marketplace of Marrakech. One of Morocco's largest and most famous markets, the Marrakech Market is a collection of endless stalls, or *souks*, tightly arranged along a maze of alleyways wide enough for pedestrians and the occasional donkey. Almost anything can be found here, such as the world's softest leather, handcrafted wicker items, aromatic perfumes and spices, orange juice, water sellers with dangling brass cups, flowing *caftans* for women and hooded *djellabas* for men. Even if you're feeling fine, the market's pharmacies with unusual remedies are worth the stop. If buying, be prepared to haggle with the shop managers. Some tips for bargaining include: Don't be the first to mention price, never seem too interested, and always bargain down. Like their ancestors, shopkeepers know how to sweeten any deal with hot tea and hospitality.

Do you think a store manager's responsibilities would be different in the Marrakech market than in an American store? Why?

Customer Relations

The last part of a store manager's job is customer relations. Good customer relations are crucial to the success of a store. Good customer relations mean making sure that customers are happy, enjoy shopping at the store, and want to continue shopping there. Most customer relations guidelines involve common sense and good manners:

QUESTION

What are three things a store manager must do when working with a supervisor?

- **Maintain a friendly store atmosphere.** Think of customers as guests and make them feel welcome. Let customers know you are happy that they are there.

- **Remember customers' names.** People love to be called by name. Customers are flattered when sales associates remember their names.

- **Remember customer preferences.** Take notes about items that a customer likes. When similar items arrive, contact the customer to inform him or her.

- **Offer top-notch service.** Encourage store employees to go that extra mile to make sure that customers are satisfied with their purchases.

- **Keep promises made to customers.** When a store employee promises a customer that he or she will place a special order or that alterations will be completed by a certain date, make sure that happens.

Math Check

MEASURING MARKDOWNS

Lois marks down all Halloween merchandise by 40 percent. How much would her shop take in if she sold 35 jack-o-lanterns originally priced at $9.95 and 50 ghosts originally priced at $14.95?

➡ For tips on finding the solution, go to **marketingseries.glencoe.com**.

RESOLVING PROBLEMS Sometimes customers may have legitimate complaints, or they may have too high expectations of service. If the retailer's level of service does not meet expectations, customer dissatisfaction can result. Retailers should always offer realistic customer-service claims in advertising campaigns to avoid a gap in expectations. When a customer has a complaint, a store employee or manager should allow the customer to communicate the problems without interruption. A manager or employee should also listen sympathetically so that the customer knows he or she is being heard and is important to the business. Finding a fair solution is the ultimate goal of dealing successfully with a customer complaint, because retailers want to keep their customers to coming back.

Creating positive customer relations is not difficult. Good customer relations are important and should never be overlooked. Store managers should always remind employees that the customer is most important. Doing so is just one task involved in personnel management as well as customer relations. By developing skills in those areas and in merchandise management and expense control, the store manager can contribute to the success of the retail business.

Quick Check

RESPOND to what you've read by answering these questions.

1. What are four parts of the store manager's job of managing store personnel? _____

_____

_____

2. List two skills needed to be a good manager. _____

_____

_____

_____

_____

_____

3. What are three things a store manager can do to help create good customer relations?

_____

_____

_____

_____

marketingseries.glencoe.com

Name _____ Date _____

Redesigning the Floor

Imagine that you manage a small retail store of your choice. The store owner has decided to redesign the layout of the store to make it more attractive and inviting to customers. Sketch out a plan for where to put the cash registers, dressing rooms, and certain kinds of racks to best use the store's space and appeal to customers. Use the space below to sketch your store. Then explain why your layout would be inviting to customers and effective for sales.

Name of store _____ **Type of store** _____

_____

_____

_____

_____

_____

Worksheet 13.2

Customer-Service Advantage

1. List three local stores where you like to shop and describe why you like to shop in them.

   _____

   _____

   _____

   _____

   _____

   _____

   _____

   _____

2. For each store, give one example of how the store offers good customer service.

   _____

   _____

   _____

   _____

   _____

   _____

   _____

   _____

   _____

   _____

3. For each store, give one example of something the store's manager could do to improve customer relations. _____

   _____

   _____

   _____

   _____

   _____

   _____

   _____

   _____

ASSESSING YOUR LISTENING SKILLS

Effective managers need good listening skills. This means being an active listener, or giving the speaker your complete attention. The simple assessment below will give you an idea of your active-listening skills. Read each statement. Then check **Yes** or **No** based on whether these statements relate to you.

		Yes	No
1.	My intention is to be an active and effective listener.	_____	_____
2.	I concentrate on the meaning and not on every word.	_____	_____
3.	I focus on the speaker and use eye contact.	_____	_____
4.	I am aware of emotions and nonverbal behavior.	_____	_____
5.	I withhold judgment until I hear the entire message.	_____	_____
6.	I am open to new information and ideas.	_____	_____
7.	I seek to understand the speaker's point of view.	_____	_____
8.	I do not interrupt, argue, or plan my response. I listen.	_____	_____
9.	I am mentally and physically alert and attentive.	_____	_____
10.	I paraphrase to clarify my understanding.	_____	_____

Total Yes responses: _____

Count your Yes responses. If you marked Yes to seven or more questions, you are well on your way to becoming an active and effective listener. If you did not, you have some work to do to improve those skills. Add this page to your career portfolio.

CHAPTER SUMMARY

Section 13.1 The Store Manager's Role

multitasking (p. 260)
delegate (p. 260)
name brands (p. 263)
private brands (p. 263)
generic brands (p. 263)
register till (p. 264)
selling expenses (p. 265)

- The characteristics of effective store managers include being well-organized, energetic, hard working, and able to multitask. They must have good people and listening skills, and be able to delegate.

- Store managers are responsible for merchandise management. They need to know how to facilitate the movement of merchandise from receiving, to sales floor, and to the customer.

- Expenses affect profit, so it is important for a store manager to control operating expenses, selling expenses, and loss expenses. Expense control keeps merchandise prices reasonable and customers happy.

Section 13.2 Managing People

motivation (p. 267)
morale (p. 267)
teamwork (p. 268)

- When managing store personnel, store managers plan employee work schedules and hire, train, supervise, and evaluate employees. These store-manager duties are important because employees help determine if customers will enjoy shopping in a store and return.

- The store manager needs to practice many of the same traits of a good store employee. This includes listening to and following the supervisor's directions, complying with store and company policies, and working as part of a team.

- Customer relations are also an important job of a store manager. Customer relations include all the components needed to promote happy customers who keeping coming back.

CHECKING CONCEPTS

1. **Identify** three characteristics of good store managers.
2. **Explain** one task the store manager performs in merchandise management.
3. **Name** the different types of brands that a retail store might carry.
4. **Define** operating expenses.
5. **Describe** one task associated with managing store personnel.
6. **Explain** the relationship between a store manager and his or her supervisor.
7. **Describe** good customer relations.

Critical Thinking

8. **Discuss** how the different duties of a store manager can be categorized.

CROSS-CURRICULUM SKILLS

Work-Based Learning

Basic Skills—Writing

9. You work for Pacific Sunwear. Your manager has asked you how to develop better customer relations. Write two paragraphs with your ideas.

Interpersonal Skills—Exercising Leadership

10. You are the manager of a Borders bookstore. List three ways you might control operating expenses.

School-Based Learning

History

11. For many years Woolworth stores were one of America's most popular shopping spots. Use the Internet or an encyclopedia to find out who started the Woolworth chain and why it was considered innovative.

Social Science

12. If you managed a store in a particular religious community, explain how your store might be affected.

 **CONNECTION**

Role Play: Assistant Manager of a Bakery

SITUATION You are to assume the role of assistant manager of a bakery located near a busy office park. Office workers stop by on their way to work to buy doughnuts, pastries, muffins, croissants, and bagels. The bakery also sells coffee. In the past the bakery has included packets of cream cheese and sugar in the bags with the items purchased. A new employee (judge) has been including large quantities of those condiments with the items he or she sells.

ACTIVITY You are to explain to the new employee (judge) the appropriate quantities to include with a purchase and why it is important not to waste the condiments.

EVALUATION You will be evaluated on how well you meet the following performance indicators:

• Explain the nature of overhead and operating costs.
• Explain the employee's role in expense control.
• Control the use of supplies.
• Identify factors affecting the business's profit.
• Conduct a training class/program.

 **INTERNET ACTIVITY**

Some retail store managers may work for U.S. companies located around the world. Use the Internet to access the McDonald's Web site and choose a country, and then find the following information.

• When did the first McDonald's open in your chosen country?
• What is the Unique Food featured?
• Where is the Unique Restaurant located?

➡For a link to McDonald's to do this exercise, go to **marketingseries.glencoe.com**.

TOYOTA'S SCION: DUDE, HERE'S YOUR CAR

Over a blustery Memorial Day weekend in San Francisco, a team of 20-something Toyota Motor Corporation reps in goatees and sunglasses set up shop near the intersection of Haight and Ashbury. With hip-hop blaring and banners heralding the new Scion brand, they encouraged passersby to test-drive new models. The willing got goodies like remote-control cars, clothing gift certificates, and music CDs. "It's an underground approach," said Una Hernandez, a 31-year old who took in the scene. "It probably raised my opinion about the car."

Toyota sure hopes so. In the most unorthodox new-car campaign in its 70-year history, the auto maker plans to roll out its Scion brand in the U.S. with a California launch on June 9. The event marks the company's first new nameplate since it introduced Lexus 14 years ago. Toyota is deploying a garage full of alternative marketing techniques. The goal: to win over young buyers, especially elusive 18- to 25-year olds. Says Brian Bolain, national manager of Scion sales and promotion: "Every generation wants to discover a brand and claim it as its own."

Still, it's far from clear if Toyota can replicate its success with Lexus. Generation Y is notoriously fickle. The Japanese auto maker is widely perceived by younger buyers as dowdy; its average driver in the U.S. is 46 years old. "In a few years, Toyota might become a Japanese Buick," says George C. Peterson, president of AutoPacific Inc., a consulting firm in Tustin, Calif.

To keep that from happening, Toyota needs to drive younger buyers into its showrooms. It has been laying the groundwork for Scion in California for more than a year. Guerrilla marketers have been putting up posters with slogans like "No Clone Zone" and "Ban Normality."

While the Scion is being sold as a whole new brand, it won't be getting dedicated dealerships. Instead, dealers are setting aside part of their showrooms for Scion. General manager Chris Ashworth figures he has spent $100,000 outfitting his Scion department with gray tile, a stereo system, and futuristic furniture. It will take him two years to earn back his investment. But if more traffic drives his way, that's fine with him.

By Christopher Palmeri in Los Angeles, with Ben Elgin in San Francisco and Kathleen Kerwin in New York

CREATIVE JOURNAL

In your journal, write your responses:

CRITICAL THINKING

1. Describe the promotion methods Toyota used for Scion. Why did Toyota use this type of promotion?

APPLICATION

2. If you were manager of an auto dealership, describe how you would design displays and store interiors to sell a Scion?

 Go to **businessweek.com** for current *BusinessWeek* Online articles.

UNIT LAB

The Virtuality Store

You've just entered the real world of retailing. The Virtuality Store offers the latest and most popular consumer goods and services. Acting as the owner, manager, or employee of this store, you will have the opportunity to work on different projects to promote the success of your business.

Get Creative—Plan the Visual Merchandising for a Store

SITUATION You are the manager of a bookstore/coffee bar called Read Along. The bookstore sells books, book-accessory items, and T-shirts and sweatshirts that feature humorous quips. The coffee shop sells a variety of coffees, latte, and coffee beverages, along with scones and biscotti. The owner of the business has lost the lease for the business, but a new location has been found. The new location is a long narrow space of 2,000 square feet. The owner has given you the task of creating the visual merchandising for Read Along. You are to include all aspects of visual merchandising.

ASSIGNMENT Complete these tasks:
- Plan the basic design of the store, including all the elements of visual merchandising you feel belong in your plan.
- Estimate the costs for the components of your plan.
- Create a final report.

TOOLS AND RESOURCES To complete the assignment, you will need to:
- Conduct research on the Internet, at the library, or by phone.
- Ask retailers about their experiences with effective visual merchandising.
- Have word-processing, spreadsheet, and presentation software.

RESEARCH Do your research:
- Determine the most important components of visual merchandising this type of store.

- Visit similar businesses and assess their visual merchandising.
- Get cost estimates for the fixtures, equipment, and other items to complete your visual-merchandising plan.

REPORT Prepare a written report using the following tools, if available:
- *Word-processing program*: Prepare a written report about your visual merchandising plan. List the fixtures, equipment, and other elements of your plan for the new store.
- *Spreadsheet program*: Prepare a chart comparing prices of the fixture and equipment options. Prepare a budget for your visual-merchandising plan.
- *Presentation program*: Prepare a ten-slide visual presentation with key elements of your visual-merchandising plan. Include key points, photos, other visuals (if applicable), and some text.

PRESENTATION AND EVALUATION You will present your report to your silent partner and the bank that may finance your plan. You will be evaluated on the basis of:
- Knowledge of visual merchandising and its components
- Continuity of presentation
- Voice quality
- Eye contact

■ PORTFOLIO
Add this report to your career portfolio.

UNIT 4

EXPLORING CAREERS IN RETAILING

"It's the constant and determined effort that breaks down resistance, sweeps away all obstacles.**"**

—Claude M. Bristol
Author

UNIT OVERVIEW

Retailing provides a wide variety of careers. The information you will learn in Unit 4 involves your future career. Making a decision about the job you choose is important since you will spend many hours a day at your job for most of your lifetime. This unit will give you information about retailing careers as well as the process of researching, finding, and getting a job.

Chapter 14 explores the different retail careers and opportunities, personal traits and skills helpful for a retail career, as well as sources of information. In Chapter 15, you will learn about planning for a retail career, looking for a job, and preparing a résumé. Chapter 16 will discuss the job application process, interviewing, and the experience of working at your new job in retailing.

■ UNIT LAB Preview

The Virtuality Store

Think about the many different jobs in the field of retailing. How do businesses fill all those positions?

Functions of Marketing

- Marketing-Information Management
- Financing
- Pricing
- Promotion
- Product/Service Management
- Distribution
- Selling

Foundations
- Professional Development
- Economics
- Business, Management, Entrepreneurship
- Communication, Interpersonal Skills

Academic Concepts • Technology

These foundations are highlighted in this unit:
- Professional Development
- Communication, Interpersonal Skills

Chapter 14

Preparing for Retail Careers

Section 14.1

Exploring Retail Careers

Section 14.2

Sources of Career Information

Chapter Objectives

- Describe career opportunities in retailing.
- Identify personal traits desirable for retailing.
- Identify career information to research.
- Explain career paths.
- Name sources of information about retail careers.
- Describe the ways to apply retail-career information.

POWER READ

Be an active reader and use these reading strategies:

PREDICT what the section will be about.

CONNECT what you read with your life.

QUESTION as you read to make sure you understand the content.

RESPOND to what you've read.

SHOE STORY

Many students begin their retail experiences in high school. They learn that retail success relies on finding the right merchandise for the right market. This student store sells items that student use—magnets, decals, pens, and pencils. Four young partners in New York City also discovered a specialized market and created a business around it.

In 1998, after noticing that Japanese collectors would pay hundreds of dollars for old Air Jordan athletic shoes, Rob Cristofaro, Arnaud Delcolle, Tony Aracabascio, and Tammy Brainard started Alife Rivington Club. Operating in New York City's Lower East Side, the four entrepreneurs began supplying the world's sneaker buyers with classic hard-to-find sneakers. They have sold woven Adidas shoes, distributed only in Asia, snakeskin Nike trainers, and even limited-edition models made for pro skateboarders. Alife has become a destination store for rap stars, actors, and local shoe connoisseurs, and has opened two unmarked New York locations (the stores have no signs). Other shoe manufacturers have realized that classic styles are hot and are selling similar styles in typical mall stores. How can Alife maintain customer interest in its shoes when larger, mainstream stores have begun to follow their lead?

ANALYZE AND WRITE

1. What inspired the business?
2. Name some other ordinary products that could be turned into limited-edition collectibles.

Case Study Part 2 on page 287

Exploring Retail Careers

YOU WILL LEARN

- To describe career opportunities in retailing.
- To identify personal traits desirable for retailing.

WHY IT'S IMPORTANT

Understanding the variety of retail careers will help you to match your skills, aptitudes, values, and lifestyle goals with a career.

KEY TERMS

- personal interests
- aptitude
- skill
- entrepreneurship
- trade associations
- central administration

PREDICT

Think of four job areas in the retail industry.

personal interests activities and pursuits that you enjoy most

aptitude a natural ability to do and learn something

skill the ability to do something

The World of Retailing Careers

There are so many career options in retailing that trying to decide on just one can be overwhelming. To make the decision less overwhelming, this chapter will first examine different career areas within retailing.

Chapter 1 discussed some of the major job areas in retailing. This chapter focuses on those areas of retailing as possible careers and discuss the wide variety of jobs available in each area. You will see that no matter what your interests are, there is a retail career that relates to your interests.

Personal Interests

You may spend a long time working in a career, so you should make sure that you enjoy what you do. The best way to find a career that you will enjoy is to consider your interests and aptitudes. Ask yourself: What are your best subjects in school? Do you like science or do you prefer history? Which extracurricular activities do you enjoy most? Would you rather play tennis or compete in a DECA event? Your choices reflect your personal interests. **Personal interests** involve activities and pursuits that you enjoy most.

Once you have determined your personal interests, you can begin to match them to jobs that require the same or similar interests, aptitudes, and skills. An **aptitude** is a natural ability to do and learn something. A **skill** is the ability to do something. For example, you may find that you understand math very easily. In that case, you have an aptitude for math. You might have studied piano for several years. Thus, you have learned musical skills through your piano lessons.

Careers in Retailing

Chapter 1 discussed retail career areas as classified by the National Retail Federation Foundation. Each retail career area is composed of a number of varied jobs. Not all of the areas include entry-level jobs; those jobs beyond store management and in corporate areas often require college education. However, as you look at the list of career areas, you will see plenty of opportunities for jobs at every level. You can begin your career in one area of retailing, and then change to another area later.

Marketing and Advertising

The marketing area of retailing includes all aspects of marketing, including visual merchandising. These jobs require analytical skills, creativity, and the ability to work with figures. There are also many jobs in this area for artists and designers. Entry-level jobs include display assistant and art department assistant. These jobs can lead to a position of head of advertising or head of marketing.

Store Operations

People in the store-operations career area work with the overall operation of stores, including the physical environment of a store. People who would enjoy this career are accurate, pay attention to detail, and can work at different tasks at the same time. Entry-level jobs in this area can lead to the position of head of store operations.

Loss Prevention

Loss prevention jobs deal with protecting a company's assets. Jobs in this area involve preventing merchandise theft and correcting paperwork discrepancies that affect inventories. These jobs require employees to have good observation skills and attention to detail. Entry-level jobs for this area include store security guard and can lead to the position of head of loss prevention.

Store Management

Store-management positions involve sales, staffing, and the daily running of the store. Store-management personnel must enjoy working with people and be able to motivate store employees. Store management is not an entry-level area. Store managers get their experience from having other jobs in retailing.

Finance

The area of finance deals with the accounting functions of the retail business. Entry-level jobs in finance include accounts-payable and accounts-receivable clerks. People working in this area can work up to the position of controller or chief financial officer (CFO). Finance positions require employees to pay attention to detail and have good math skills.

EXPERIENCE COUNTS
Getting a part-time job in retailing can give you real-world experience and help you to decide your career preferences. *Do you think role playing can substitute for on-the-job experience? Why?*

Hot Property

Portraits of the Artists

YA/YA, short for Young Aspirations/Young Artists, burst onto the scene in 1988. Jana Napoli, an artist living in New Orleans, noticed a group of inner-city high school kids hanging out on the street with nothing to do. Instead of anticipating trouble, Napoli saw budding artists. She put paint-brushes in their hands, placed them in a studio, and kick-started their creative juices. Soon young people, age 14 to 24, were channeling their energy into works of art. They were also sharpening their retail skills for the future.

In the beginning, the group could not afford canvases, so the YA/YAs painted thrift-shop furniture instead. Decades–old chairs and chests were transformed with hip images that reflected all aspects of life—love, anger, sadness, and hope.

Before long the unique art form caught the attention of the media. Heavyweights such as *Fortune* and *Rolling Stone* magazines, the *New York Times*, Oprah Winfrey, MTV, and the gang at *Sesame Street* spotlighted the young talent—and business boomed. YA/YA has created artwork for clients as varied as the United Nations, Burger King, and the 150-year-old Hammacher-Schlemmer catalog, which promises to feature only "the best, the only, and the unexpected."

YA/YA sells education as well as art. Although artists earn 50 to 80 percent from sales, they reinvest the rest of the money in program costs and college tuitions. The program also sells a philosophy that "given the right tools and a fertile environment, motivated people can do extraordinary things."

1. What do you think is the most positive aspect of YA/YA for the kids in the program?
2. In addition to artistic skills, what other work skills do you think YA/YAs learn?

Human Resources

Human resources jobs involve hiring and training employees, as well as handling employee benefits and employee relations. Human resources jobs require employees to have good people skills and good organizational skills. An entry-level job would be personnel department assistant. Employee-training jobs are not normally at the entry level because an employee trainer needs to have knowledge and experience in a business in order to teach that knowledge to others.

IT and E-Commerce

Jobs in this area of retailing deal with company Web sites and their development and maintenance. This career area also includes jobs that deal with data processing and information management. Jobs in information technology (IT) require employees to have excellent computer skills. There are many jobs available for Web designers. This type of position requires computer skills, creativity, as well as design skills. Entry-level jobs in IT and e-commerce retailing include Web-site maintenance and fulfillment clerks who process and fill online merchandise orders. Higher-level jobs include e-commerce director and Web-site manager, or head of informational systems and data processing. This career area is growing and will provide employment for years to come.

CONNECT

Do you think your personality would match well with a career in e-commerce? Why?

Sales and Sales-Related Careers

The most common job in the sales area is sales associate. Other sales-related jobs include cashier, stock clerk, and receiving clerk. These jobs are primarily entry level and are a good fit for people who enjoy working with other people and who are willing to learn. Sales and jobs related to sales are most often the stepping stones to many other positions in retailing. Working in this area of retailing gives employees a good sense of the duties for both store management and merchandise management.

Distribution Logistics and Supply-Chain Management

This career area deals with getting the merchandise to where it will be sold. It also includes jobs in the warehouse of a retail store. Qualifications for jobs in distribution logistics include attention to detail and good organizational skills. Some jobs also require employees to have good physical coordination and strength. Entry-level jobs in this area include traffic clerk, distribution clerk, and warehouse worker.

Merchandise Buying and Planning

The position of buyer is the main job in the area of merchandise buying and planning. There are many other jobs for people who plan merchandise purchases for stores and assist the buyer. These jobs require employees to pay good attention to detail and have good math skills. Jobs in this area are not entry level, because they require a buyer to have experience with and knowledge of customer preferences as well as prior experience with planning and handling merchandise in a retailing setting. Many people think of the job of buyer as a career position, particularly in the area of fashion retailing.

Entrepreneurship

Entrepreneurship is the process of owning and managing your own business. This is a career area with enormous potential for individuals who are willing to take risks and handle all the duties of running a retail business. If you have ever thought that you would like to own your own business, retailing offers many opportunities, from owning and running restaurants to clothing stores to specialty stores. It is important to acquire as much experience as possible in many aspects of running a retail business before starting your own. Experience greatly increases the chances of success for an entrepreneur.

Case Study · PART 2

SHOE STORY
Continued from Part 1 on page 283

Alife maintained customer interest in spite of larger stores copying their idea. The store kept growing its business by creating culture as well as selling it. Alife presented shows by artists such as Shepard Fairy and Ryan McGuinness, and commissioned exclusive, limited-edition shoes from Nike and Adidas. When these shoes are in stock, customers line up around the block to buy them. The store also has a policy of doing no advertising, no online sales, and refusing to reorder sold-out shoes. No reorders ensures that when customers buy special shoes, only a small number of other people will have them, making them more valuable. It's a tricky business to control supply to increase demand, but Alife has mastered it.

ANALYZE AND WRITE

1. Why would large shoe companies such as Nike or Adidas manufacture small runs of custom shoes for a store like Alife?
2. How does presenting art shows help Alife's shoe business?

---

entrepreneurship the process of owning and managing your own business

Selling Point ❗

LOW PRICES RULE
What's the biggest consumer complaint? Prices are too high!

trade associations
organizations made up of
individuals and businesses in
an industry that works to
promote that industry

central administration the
top-leadership branch of a
company

Retail-Industry Support

This career area encompasses **trade associations**, or organizations made up of individuals and businesses in an industry that work to promote that industry. The National Retail Federation is the umbrella trade association that serves all types of retailers. There are also smaller associations that assist specific types of retailers, such as restaurateurs and clothing retailers.

Trade associations employ lobbyists and people responsible for member education, industry promotion, and public relations. While most of these positions are mid- to high-level jobs, there are often entry-level positions for assistants to any of these positions. Most people who work for trade associations have previous experience in the fields represented by the trade associations.

Central Administration

The **central administration** is the top-leadership branch of a company. Jobs in this area include store-planning managers and executives, legal counsel, real estate brokers and managers, and company presidents. These jobs are not entry-level jobs; they require college education, years of experience, and proven managerial abilities. However, people in central administration may begin their careers anywhere in retail and work their way up. **Figure 14.1** illustrates several different career paths, or steps, leading from entry-level jobs to company president.

QUESTION

What is the difference between jobs in store operations and central administration?

Figure 14.1

Many Career Paths to One Destination

MULTIPLE OPTIONS If you have a lofty career goal in mind, it helps to remember that there are many ways to get there. *Can you think of other paths that would lead to a position of company president? Describe them.*

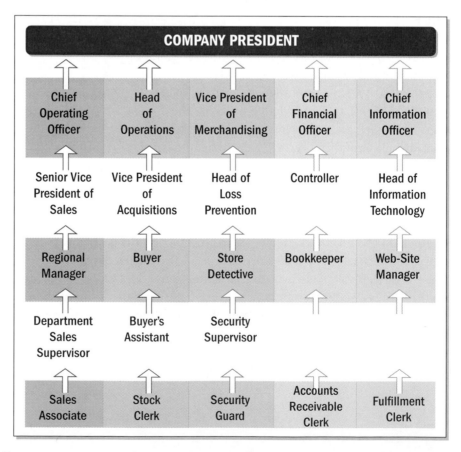

Traits Required for Retail Careers

Because there is a huge variety of jobs available in retailing, there are diverse characteristics and traits that can be useful for a retail career. However, remember that some traits are desirable for workers in all positions. One such trait is the ability to work with other people.

Retailing involves serving customer needs, so most people in retailing should enjoying working with people and should be able to get along with all types of people. Another valuable trait is responsibility. Employees are given the care of the business's customers, its merchandise, and its physical and electronic stores. People who want to enter retailing must be prepared to accept responsibility. Workers in retail must also be reliable and trustworthy. They must do what they say they will do, be where they are assigned, and do what is required of them.

Other traits that are desirable for retail employees also apply to employees in any job or career:

- Punctuality

- Honesty

- Loyalty

- Leadership potential

Quick Check ✓

RESPOND to what you've read by answering these questions.

1. Why is the career area of loss prevention important? _____

_____

_____

_____

_____

2. Which career area of retailing involves a company's overall leadership? _____

_____

_____

_____

_____

3. What are three desirable traits for employees in all career areas of retailing? _____

_____

_____

_____

_____

Sources of Career Information

AS YOU READ ...

YOU WILL LEARN

- To identify career information to research.
- To explain career paths.
- To name sources of information about retail careers.
- To describe the ways to apply retail-career information.

WHY IT'S IMPORTANT

To research careers and make wise career decisions, you should determine exactly what information you need and where you can find it.

KEY TERMS

- job forecast
- career path
- values
- lifestyle

PREDICT

What kind of information is important to know before choosing a career?

job forecast an estimate of the number of jobs that will be available for a career in the next five to ten years

career path the series of job experiences that you need to reach your career goal

Getting a Job in Retailing

Before you decide on a career in retailing, you should gather as much information as possible about the career areas that interest you. Career decisions have long-term effects on your life. Having more information will help you to make the best decisions.

Before You Begin

Before you begin gathering information about particular retail careers, decide what information you want to collect. For example, you might want to find out how much education the job requires beyond high school. Do you need a four-year college degree to get the job, or do you need a two-year associate degree? Are there any special training courses required?

You will also want to learn about the specific and general requirements of the job. Find the answers to these questions: How long is a typical workday? What is the salary range for people in the career that you are considering? What is the job forecast, for the career and job areas that interest you? The **job forecast**, or outlook, is an estimate of the number of jobs that will be available for a given career in the next five to ten years, and includes information about whether that career area is growing or declining.

You will also want to research the career path for the career areas that interest you. A **career path** is the series of job experiences that you need to reach your career goal. You can take the first steps on your career path while in high school. Many retail jobs require entry-level job experience, such as sales-associate experience that you can get while in school. Working in the retail field will also give you a good sense of whether retailing is the right career choice for you.

To keep all this information about different careers organized, you can create a job-search checklist. **Figure 14.2** shows a sample job-search checklist that you can copy and use to track information about different careers.

Where to Get Career Information

There are many sources of information about careers in retailing. Web sites offer general and retail-specific career information. You can also do research in your school library or the public library. However, people can be your best resources. Your school counselor, marketing teacher, or retailers all have information about retail careers.

Figure 14.2

Job-Search Checklist

Job	Education Required	Experience Required	Training Required	Normal Hours	Salary Range
1.					
2.					
3.					
4.					
5.					

KEEPING ORGANIZED Keeping a checklist can help you organize your career research. *In what other ways could a checklist help you in the process of choosing a career?*

The Internet

The Internet has a wealth of information available at your fingertips. Career Web sites such as Monster.com and CareerBuilder.com include extensive information about career strategies, industries, and specific companies. The U.S. Department of Labor's Web site is another good source of information about jobs. In particular, the *Occupational Outlook Handbook*, which is available online and in print form in the library, provides descriptions of thousands of jobs, as well as information about salary ranges and the outlook for the future.

The Web site for the U.S. Department of the Census provides forecasts about growth or decline for U.S. industries. You can find links to these and other valuable Web sites through the **marketingseries.glencoe.com** Web site.

Another source to access on the Internet is the Web site for the National Retail Federation and NRF Foundation which includes an excellent variety of career information specific to the retail industry, as well as links to many Web sites for retailers and colleges that offer retailing programs.

Libraries

Libraries are great sources for all types of information. Your school library probably has career information available. For example, your school or your public library may have the *Occupational Outlook Handbook*. Another resource you may find in the library is the *Career Guide to Industries*, which describes available jobs in a number of career areas.

TECH NOTES

Long-Distance Learning

Getting an education no longer requires you to always be in a classroom. Many colleges and universities offer distance-learning programs and online courses. Students can take courses through the Internet, completing work as their schedules allow. They can also interact with instructors and students through e-mail, online chat rooms, or virtual bulletin boards.

➥Is distance learning right for you? Answer this question after reading more information through **marketingseries.glencoe.com**.

CONNECT

What other Web site(s) might have job information?

More Than a Hobby

Collecting stamps is an all-American pastime and one of the world's most popular hobbies. If you are a philatelist (a stamp collector) you have probably heard of Liechtenstein, the postage-stamp nation. It is a tiny country in the European Alps that bears the name of its royal family.

Liechtenstein began to develop its stamp trade in 1912 as a way to increase revenue and show off the country at the same time. There has been only one problem in more than 90 years of trade: Stamps commemorating the 1980 Olympic Games in Moscow had to be destroyed when Liechtenstein and other nations chose to boycott the games for political reasons.

Today the government continues to issue new stamps every three months. Collectors quickly buy the visually beautiful stamps, many of which represent paintings found in the royal palace. Other stamps depict nature, history, sports, folklore—and humor.

What would you want to learn about a retail career in "philately" before working in a stamp store?

Math Check

CALCULATE JOB DECLINE

According to the U.S. Department of Labor, 148,000 people are employed as buyers—a job sector that is declining. If that career declines at a rate of two percent per year, how many buyers will be employed in three years? (Round up all fractions in your calculations.)

➡ For tips on finding the solution, go to **marketingseries.glencoe.com**.

School Counselor and Marketing Teacher

Your school counselor and marketing teacher are other great sources for career information. Counselors have access to many types of information about educational, training, and professional programs. Marketing teachers do a lot of research about careers related to marketing. They can discuss retail careers and help you contact businesses and associations that have information about specific careers.

Retail Professionals

To find out what it is really like to work in retail, speak to a retail professional directly. When you decide to contact a retailer, first, make an appointment for a time that is convenient for the retailer to meet or speak with you. Have your questions, arrive promptly, and be polite and respectful of the person's time. You might also ask if you could *shadow* the person for a day, which involves following the person while he or she works in order to see what he or she does in a real-world situation.

Trade Publications

Trade publications are magazines, newspapers, or newsletters that provide information targeted for a particular industry. Some trade publications are available online at the trade association's Web site or in libraries. Trade publications sometimes feature articles about careers in their industries and job listings. These publications are an excellent source for ongoing research and new information when you know which career area interests you the most.

ASSISTING CAREERS IN RETAILING

Sean Foreman
Human Resources Manager
The Home Depot, Inc.

What does your job entail?

"I'm in charge of all human resources operations for 39 stores in four Midwestern states. I spend my time counseling employees and giving advice. A big part of my job is devoted to management, staffing, and recruitment for those stores—and that takes some planning. Our industry is highly seasonal. We're weather-driven, so when the weather's good, we have a lot of business and the workload is doubled. In late fall and winter, that workload drops off substantially."

What are your most important skills?

"Human resources professionals need to know about more than just human resources. We need to understand every facet of the business. In doing so, we gain credibility. It's about being a businessperson."

What kind of training did you have?

"I have a bachelor's degree in human resources management. On-the-job training has been very important; I'm in my 17th year in retailing in the home-improvement industry."

What is your key to success?

"Providing leadership. When I look back on my day, my goal is to say: 'I have provided leadership.' My work is spread across four different states, so I've got to make sure I'm providing leadership at a high level."

Why would it be important for a human resources professional to understand all aspects of a specific retail business?

Career Data: Human Resources Manager

Education and Training Bachelor's or master's degree in human resources or business

Skills and Abilities Leadership abilities, confidence, language and people skills, and organizational skills

Career Outlook Average growth through 2010

Career Path Human resources professionals might begin on the sales floor and work up through store management; or they can begin at the humanresources level with an advanced degree.

Using the Information

Once you have gathered your career information, you have to make the information work for you. You can assemble the various bits of information into categories that will be useful to you.

Study the career information that you have and relate it to your personal goals. Broad personal goals include your values and the lifestyle you want to pursue. Your **values** are the factors that determine how you want to live your life. Personal values are the things in life that are

QUESTION

Name at least two sources of career information.

values the factors that determine how you want to live your life

MARKETING SERIES *Online*

Remember to check out this book's Web site for career information and more great resources at **marketingseries.glencoe.com.**

lifestyle the way you live your life and spend your time

important to you and the things in which you believe. Before you make any career decisions, examine how the career area fits into your value system. For example, if you value nature and want to protect the environment, you might consider a career with a company that sells environmentally friendly products.

Also examine career information in relation to the kind of lifestyle that you want. **Lifestyle** is the way you live your life and spend your time. Everybody wants to create a good life, but doing that means something different to each person. Lifestyle factors may include:

- Amount of time you spend at work

- Amount of leisure time you want

- Amount of money you make

- How you spend your money

The career that will enable you to live according to your personal values and to have the lifestyle that you want is the one that will help you attain happiness and will be the most rewarding for you.

Quick Check

RESPOND to what you've read by answering these questions.

1. What is one question you should answer when gathering career information? _____

_____

_____

2. Name one government publication that can provide useful career information. _____

_____

3. Regarding your personal goals, what are two factors to consider when making career decisions?

_____

Worksheet 14.1

Traits Required for Retail Careers

1. Make a list of your personal interests, aptitudes, and skills. Personal interests are the activities and pursuits that you enjoy most. An aptitude is your natural capability to do certain things. A skill is your capability to do certain things—things that you can learn to do and improve. For example, you may have an aptitude for math. That is a natural ability for you. You also may possess musical skills. Musical skills can be enhanced and improved through practice.

Personal interests:

_____

_____

_____

_____

_____

Aptitudes:

_____

_____

_____

_____

_____

Skills:

_____

_____

_____

_____

_____

2. Look at your personal interests, aptitudes, and skills. Then list five areas of retail that might be best for you. _____

_____

_____

_____

_____

_____

Worksheet 14.2

Stepping Up

1. Name an entry-level retail job that interests you.

_____

2. Fill in the career ladder starting at the bottom with that entry-level job, and then write the highest position you hope to achieve at the top.

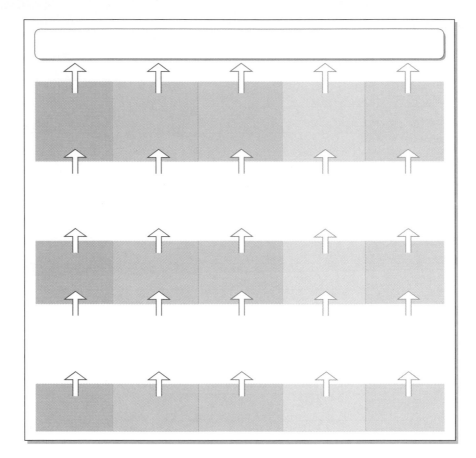

3. How many steps are on your career ladder? _____

_____

_____

_____

4. How long do you think it will take you to achieve your top goal? _____

_____

_____

_____

Portfolio Works

ORGANIZING CAREER INFORMATION

Design a graphic organizer, or chart that will help you organize information about any retail career that interests you. The categories should include:

- Education requirements
- Training requirement
- Length of work day
- Number of days to work each week

- Salary range
- Job forecast
- Career path
- Other information

Pick one job now and fill out your chart. Add this page to your career portfolio.

CHAPTER SUMMARY

Section 14.1 Exploring Retail Careers

personal interests
(p. 284)
aptitude (p. 284)
skill (p. 284)
entrepreneurship
(p. 287)
trade associations
(p. 288)
central administration
(p. 288)

- Career opportunities in retailing include career areas such as marketing and advertising, store operations, loss prevention, store management, finance, human resources, IT and e-commerce, sales and sales-related careers, distribution logistics and supply-chain management, merchandise buying and planning, entrepreneurship, retail industry support, and central administration. Awareness of career possibilities will help you match your skills, aptitudes, and personal interests with a job.

- Personal traits desirable for retailing include the ability to work with and get along with people, responsibility, reliability, trustworthiness, punctuality, honesty, loyalty, and leadership potential.

Section 14.2 Sources of Career Information

job forecast (p. 290)
career path (p. 290)
values (p. 293)
lifestyle (p. 294)

- Information to research about retail careers can include education requirements, special requirements, workday length, salary range, and the job forecast, or outlook on the number of jobs that will be available in the next five to ten years.

- A career path is the series of job experiences that you need to reach your career goal.

- Sources for career information include the Internet, your school counselor or marketing teacher, retail professionals, trade publications, and libraries, which carry publications such as the *Occupational Outlook Handbook*.

- Relate career-interest information to your personal goals to choose a career. Your personal goals include your values, or things in life that are important to you and your lifestyle.

CHECKING CONCEPTS

1. **Describe** career opportunities in retailing.
2. **Explain** how career paths function.
3. **Explain** the traits required for working in retailing.
4. **Identify** the kinds of career information you need to research.
5. **List** sources of career information.
6. **Explain** how to apply career information in your life.
7. **Define** personal values and list five of your own.

Critical Thinking

8. **Explain** why it is a good idea to get as much experience as possible with running a retail business before becoming an entrepreneur.

CROSS-CURRICULUM SKILLS

Work-Based Learning

Information—Organizing and Maintaining Information

9. Design a graphic organizer that will help you understand retail career areas. First list all the areas of retail careers, and then add key-word facts about each area of retail careers.

Interpersonal Skills—Serving Clients/Customers

10. Create a poster that illustrates the three traits that are desirable for all retail positions. Display your poster in class.

School-Based Learning

Computer Technology

11. Use the Internet to access a Web site that has information about retail careers. Read about two or three areas in retailing that you want to investigate as a possible career. Write a paragraph describing your findings and share it with your class.

Language Arts

12. Write a two-page journal entry that describes your personal values and lifestyle and how they relate to a retail career.

Role Play: High School Marketing Student

SITUATION You are to assume the role of a high school marketing student. As part of a classroom assignment, your class has been assigned the task of researching a career within the area of marketing. You have been assigned to research the retail industry.

ACTIVITY Your marketing teacher (judge) has asked to see a brief outline of the research material each class member has assembled. You are to meet with your marketing teacher (judge) for ten minutes.

EVALUATION You will be evaluated on how well you meet the following performance indicators:

- Describe career opportunities in retailing.
- Identify sources of career information.
- Explain employment opportunities in retailing.
- Explain types of retailers.
- Set personal goals.

Use the Internet to access the National Retail Federation's Web site.

- Click on Press Room in the left column.
- Click on any press release.
- Write a summary of the press release.
- Exchange summaries with another student.
- Ask the other student questions about the summary he or she wrote. Then have your partner ask you questions about your summary.

➡ For a link to the NRF to begin this exercise, go to **marketingseries.glencoe.com**.

Chapter 15

Starting Your Career

Chapter Objectives

- Explain how to make a career plan.
- Describe ways to prepare for a retail career.
- Apply job-search strategies.
- Identify information needed to prepare a résumé.
- Explain how to prepare a résumé.
- Identify references for a résumé.

POWER READ

Be an active reader and use these reading strategies:

PREDICT what the section will be about.

CONNECT what you read with your life.

QUESTION as you read to make sure you understand the content.

RESPOND to what you've read.

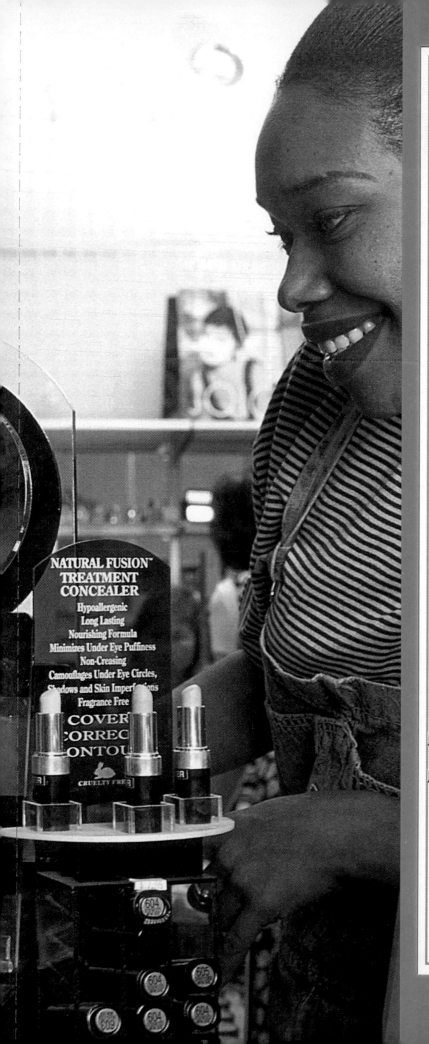

NONSTOP POP

A retailing career often begins with jobs in sales at large or small stores. A sales associate may work on the floor or behind the counter. There, sales associates learn how to meet the customer's needs and wants. As a child, John Nese became familiar with the family business from behind the counter. So, as an adult, he applied his experience and know-how to create something unique.

When John Nese took over Galco's Old World Market, he knew the family-owned Italian grocery store could not compete with supermarkets that had lower prices. So he decided to offer something that larger retailers could not—the greatest variety of sodas in the world.

In 1995, he began stocking hard-to-find soft drinks. Because plastic bottles or aluminum cans may affect the soda's flavor, Nese stocked glass bottles whenever possible and tried to find sodas that are sweetened with cane sugar and not corn syrup. He also changed the name of the store to Galco's Soda Pop Stop. Its shelves became home to Manhattan Special, Nehi orange, imported drinks from Australia and Europe, and more.

Eventually the shop offered more than 450 kinds of soda—and got attention from *Sunset* magazine, PBS, and the BBC. Galco's had found its niche, but how could it expand?

ANALYZE AND WRITE

1. What prompted Nese to change the type of products offered by Galco's?
2. If you were appling for a job at this store, what skill would you highlight?

Case Study Part 2 on page 313

Planning Your Retail Career

YOU WILL LEARN

- To explain how to make a career plan.
- To describe ways to prepare for a retail career.
- To apply job-search strategies.

WHY IT'S IMPORTANT

Creating a career plan can help you prepare for a retail career and can guide your job search.

KEY TERMS

- career plan
- career ladder
- career lattice
- body language
- networking
- employment agency

PREDICT

Why should you make a career plan now if you might change your mind about your career goals later?

career plan a written statement of career goals and the necessary steps to achieve them

career ladder the series of job steps you must take to achieve career goals

Make a Career Plan

You may be interested in several career areas in retailing, especially if they are compatible with your personal values and preferred lifestyle. Now what do you do? You begin to create a career plan. A **career plan** is a written statement of your career goals and the necessary steps to achieve them.

Compiling a career plan will help you determine which area of retailing most interests you. It will also help you decide which areas best suit your personal values and lifestyle needs. A career plan is also a tool to help you determine the educational requirements you need to satisfy and any special training you should complete.

Make a Realistic Career Plan

When you make a career plan for yourself, be realistic. Being realistic means making goals that you will be able to achieve. You may aspire to be the Chief Executive Officer (CEO) of Sears, but you may have a better chance of becoming a district or regional manager.

Remember that the management structure of most large corporations is shaped like a pyramid. There are fewer jobs higher in the corporate structure. There are many very capable people competing for those high-ranking corporate jobs. You can be one of them by preparing yourself with the necessary educational background and work experience. Remain focused on your career goals to reach them.

Make Specific Career Goals

As you make your career plan, be specific. A career goal that states, "I want to work in the supermarket area of retailing," is not specific. A career goal that states, "I want to gain supermarket job experience while in high school by getting a job as a produce clerk," is a specific career goal or objective.

It is important to recognize that a career plan is just a plan. Career plans are not meant to lock you into a specific career choice. Your career goals may change over time. As you gain more experience, you will experience many new things. You may find that you want to pursue a career in another area. So even though you need to make a career plan to guide your research and your goals, remain flexible and open to new experiences.

Career plans are tools to help you focus your thoughts about your future career and achieve your goals. If your career interests do change, you will have gained valuable experience in researching career and job information and in setting goals for yourself.

Retail Career Ladders and Lattices

Your ultimate career goal is probably a few years away, but you can begin with a first step. Your career planning should include how you will to get to your career goal. There are two tools that illustrate the steps toward achieving a career goal—career ladders and career lattices. They are two ways of looking at the same thing, which is the path to reach your career goals.

Most career paths follow a sequence of steps. The successful completion of the first step leads to the second step in what is called a career ladder. A **career ladder** is the series of job steps you must take to reach your career goal. A career ladder is a vertical look at career steps. See **Figure 15.1** for an example of a career ladder.

The other tool that illustrates the path toward a career goal is a **career lattice**, which is a combination of vertical and diagonal career steps that lead you to your career goal. This way of looking at a career path allows for more changing interests. A career lattice plan allows you to consider a greater variety of opportunities that can lead to the same career goal.

Retail Job Requirements

Before you look further into a career in retailing, you need to learn about the requirements of the specific job you want. When you examine the specific requirements for that job, look at some of the basic

career lattice a combination of vertical and diagonal career steps that lead to a career goal

---

Figure 15.1

Career Ladders

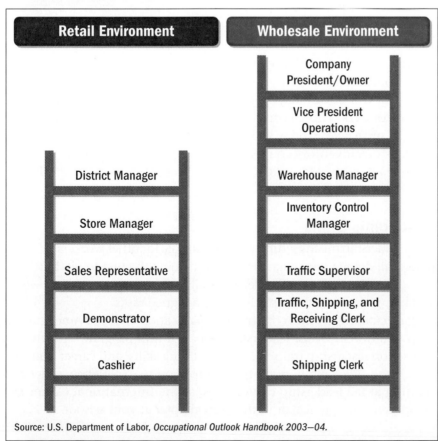

Retail Environment	Wholesale Environment
	Company President/Owner
	Vice President Operations
District Manager	Warehouse Manager
Store Manager	Inventory Control Manager
Sales Representative	Traffic Supervisor
Demonstrator	Traffic, Shipping, and Receiving Clerk
Cashier	Shipping Clerk

Source: U.S. Department of Labor, *Occupational Outlook Handbook 2003–04.*

STEP UP A career ladder suggests a straight career path from one job to another, each with more responsibility. A career lattice includes more horizontal movement and changes of interest. *Do you think most people's actual career paths resemble a ladder or a lattice? Explain.*

TECH NOTES

Retail Internships

There are many opportunities for students to gain experience in retailing. Some retailers post information about paid internship programs on their company Web sites. These programs are offered during the summer months when students have more time to focus on work. Some companies even provide applicants with online résumé builders and other Web-based tools.

➡Explore retail internship opportunities and then create a résumé based on your career goals through **marketingseries.glencoe.com**.

body language the gestures and facial expressions that people use to communicate nonverbally

skills you need to succeed at any job: communication skills, skills in working with people, basic math skills, leadership skills, and teamwork skills. If you feel that you are not skilled in some of these areas, do not get discouraged. All of these job skills can be learned and improved with a little time and effort.

Communication Skills

Having communication skills means that you are able to speak to people and communicate your ideas to them. These skills involve speech and writing. The ability to write reports in a clear and logical manner is a big part of communication on the job.

Communication also means the ability to listen and understand what people are really saying. Pay attention to a person's words and to his or her body language. **Body language** is the gestures and facial expressions that people use to communicate nonverbally. When you have good communication skills, you understand what people are trying to say, and you are able to make yourself understood.

People Skills

The ability to work with people is another basic employment skill. Also known as *people skills*, working well with people simply means being pleasant, friendly, and professional in your personal relations with your fellow employees, supervisors, and customers. Being friendly does not mean that you have to become best friends with everyone; it means being pleasant and accepting other people for who they are. Courtesy, consideration for others, honesty, and a sense of fairness contribute to having good people skills.

Basic Math Skills

Having basic math skills means having the ability to accurately perform basic computations—addition, subtraction, multiplication, and division. You will most likely begin your retail career as a sales associate, cashier, or clerk. Those positions require the ability to add a sales check and calculate taxes. You will also need to help with inventory counts at a retail store. Inventory counts require keeping accurate written records of these amounts. Math skills are vitally important to successfully perform these tasks.

Leadership Skills

Basic leadership means setting a good example for other workers by being punctual, doing your assigned work, and being the first to pitch in with a group work assignment. Leadership skills include using your time wisely and being efficient at completing your assigned tasks.

Participating in DECA (Distributive Education Clubs of America) can help you develop your leadership skills. DECA's program of activities focuses on leadership training, team-building skills, and career training. DECA also offers many opportunities for you to experience leadership training at fall leadership conferences, at the International Career Development Conference, or in the local chapter at your school.

Teamwork Skills

Teamwork means working as part of a group to achieve a shared goal. Many businesses put a heavy emphasis on teamwork skills because many tasks require a team of employees to complete them. Each employee contributes his or her share of the tasks to produce a result that is greater than each employee would be able to produce by working alone.

Preparing for Your Retail Career

What are two things you can do in high school and after you graduate to prepare yourself for a career in retailing? You can get a good education and build work experience.

Education

Most jobs in today's economy require a high school diploma. Some retail jobs require formal education beyond high school. You should complete as much education as possible. The highest-level management or executive position requires a four-year college degree and often an advanced degree such as a master's degree in business administration. For other high- and mid-level management positions, a four-year college degree may not be required but is usually preferred.

Whether you decide on a four-year college degree, a two-year degree from a community college, or job-related training at a technical school, focus your course work on furthering your career goals. For example, math classes will help you improve your math and analytical skills. English classes will help you develop communication and critical-thinking skills. Extracurricular activities, such as sports or marching band, can help develop leadership and teamwork skills.

RETAILING AND DECA Marketing classes and participation in DECA provide good preparation for a career in retailing. DECA's competitive events offer students an opportunity to compete with other students from around the nation and the world in career-specific competitive events. Several events focus on skills required in the field of retailing. You can choose one of DECA's team competitive events related to retailing and practice your team-building skills while you prepare for an event that will teach you about a segment of the retail industry. DECA membership also provides you with membership in a professional student organization, which will be a valuable listing on your résumé.

NRF ACCREDITATION The National Retail Federation's Skill Standards Accreditation provides another opportunity to prepare for a retailing career. By passing a test that measures the skills required to be

 SPECIAL TEAMS Many retailers make an effort to employ workers with special needs. *How would leadership and teamwork skills help you work effectively with fellow employees who have special needs?*

Math Check

COMPARING PAYCHECKS

Jonas has been working at a toy store and earns $8 per hour. During the school year, he worked 20 hours a week. Now that school has ended, he will work 35 hours per week. How much more money will Jonas earn each week over the summer than he did each week during the school year?

➡ For tips on finding the solution, go to **marketingseries.glencoe.com**.

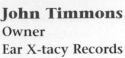

OPEN FOR MUSIC

John Timmons
Owner
Ear X-tacy Records

What does your job entail?

"I oversee the entire day-to-day operation of my store. I manage the employees, make sure the store is properly stocked with music, help our customers—and best of all, listen to music."

What kind of training did you have?

"I wasn't planning on owning a record store. After graduating from high school, I got a job in a local record store. There, I learned how to handle customer service; how to order and buy from the distributors; how to schedule and deal with employees; and how to keep inventory and other financial records. I worked my way up to assistant manager, and then store manager—but the training for my job never stops. I have been in the business for 27 years, and I still learn about it every day."

What advice would you give students?

"In any retail business, people skills are most important. Being able to listen to your customers, and being able to talk to them in a polite and informed manner are very important skills."

What is your key to success?

"Service and selection. Anyone who is a music fan can find what they want at our store. We have the most extensive selection of music available in our city, and we make a point to hire only enthusiastic employees who are not only knowledgeable about music, but friendly and helpful as well."

Why do you think people skills might be more important than knowledge of music in a record store?

Career Data:
Store Owner

Education and Training
Associate's, bachelor's, or master's degree in business; on-the-job experience

Skills and Abilities Excellent communication skills, strong organizational skills, and creativity

Career Outlook Average growth through 2010

Career Path Entry-level positions provide experience. Real-world skills are crucial for advancement.

CONNECT

What kind of work experience do you have—paid or unpaid?

a professional sales associate and customer-service provider, you can become certified as a professional sales associate.

Work Experience

Work experience of any type is helpful when applying for jobs. For example, if your only work experience is babysitting, you can demonstrate that you are reliable and able to accept responsibility. Summer jobs or jobs unrelated to retailing can also provide experience and develop basic employment skills.

Pieces of History

In 1961, one of the 20th century's most notorious symbols of political division was built. It was called the Berlin Wall. Snaking 30 miles through the capital city of Berlin, the massive concrete barrier separated communist East Berlin from the non-communist West Berlin. With the end of communism in Eastern Europe in 1989, the Berlin Wall came down. Thousands of Berliners took part in dismantling it.

Some people carried away only small mementos of the wall. Others saw a retailing opportunity and hauled pieces away by the pound. A thriving new market developed. Entrepreneurs sold bits and pieces of the Berlin Wall as tourist souvenirs in the forms of key rings, doorstops, paperweights, pendants, and bookends. One savvy Berliner made his fortune selling tiny fragments affixed to postcards. Though only small sections of the wall survive today as memorials, remnants of the wall are found all around the world. However, most of the wall was crushed and used to build roads.

How did some people create career opportunities from the fall of the Berlin Wall?

Sources for Retail Jobs

Now that you are ready to start looking for a job in retailing, where do you begin your job search? There are several sources you can use to find your first retail job:

- Networking

- Employment agencies

- Employment ads

- Internet job listings

Networking

Networking involves contacting people you know to get information or advice on job leads. You can contact family members and family friends to ask for help in looking for a retail job. You might have a family member who works for a retailer or a friend may know someone in the retail business. Many jobs are found through networking.

Another good networking resource is your marketing teacher. Your marketing teacher may know of specific jobs or may be familiar with employers in your area whom you might contact.

If you have been employed in the past, your former employer can be another networking resource for you. Even if your former employer is not in a retailing business, he or she may know someone who is in that field.

> **QUESTION**
>
> What do you think is the best source for jobs—ads, agencies, networking, or Web sites? Why?

networking contacting people you know who can assist with your job hunt

ETHICAL PRACTICES

Stay-at-Home Scams

Home businesses can be convenient for stay-at-home parents who need extra income, but they can also turn out to be scams. A company in Florida advertised that for a small investment, anyone could start a greeting card company. The Florida company promised to provide a "locator" who would set up guaranteed sales. It turned out there was no "locator," and after people sent their money, the company disappeared. Many people have lost money on stay-at-home business scams. Before starting your own business, be sure to do your research.

employment agency a business that specializes in helping people find jobs

Employment Agencies

An **employment agency** is a business that specializes in helping people find jobs. Employers who need workers send a job description of the open position to the employment agency. The agency then matches the requirements of the job to the qualifications of job seekers who are registered with the agency. The agency then sends the best candidates to the employer for interviews.

There are two types of employment agencies: public and private. Public employment agencies are sponsored by states or the federal government and do not charge fees to the employer or to the job applicant. They are financed by tax dollars. Private employment agencies usually charge a fee to the employer for their services. If you decide to use a private employment agency, be sure to ask about fees before you sign any agreements.

Employment Ads

The classified advertising section in a newspaper is the traditional job source where employers post ads for jobs they need to. The classified ads of your local newspaper list the jobs that are available in your community. You can also find out the qualifications for those jobs and the wages offered. In many cities, the Sunday paper has the most job listings. However, not every available job is listed in the classified ads. In fact, many jobs are never advertised. They are filled through networking or by people who apply directly to a company.

The Internet

The Internet is a good place to find job openings. Many companies post job listings on their Web sites or on job Web sites such as Monster.com and CareerBuilder.com. On these sites, you can search by job title, keyword such as "retail," location, or even salary.

There are many resources that a determined and resourceful person can use to find employment. It just takes some time and effort.

Quick Check ✓

RESPOND to what you've read by answering these questions.

1. What are two things to keep in mind when making a career plan? _____

_____

_____

2. What are five basic skill requirements of most jobs? _____

_____

_____

3. What are four sources you can use to find a job in retailing? _____

_____

Preparing Your Résumé

Elements of a Résumé

When you have decided which retail jobs interest you, it is time to prepare to apply for a job. Before applying for any job, you need to prepare a résumé. A **résumé** is a document that provides a summary of your work experience, your education, your skills, and your interests and activities. A résumé is a brief summary that introduces you on paper. It should be one page in length, unless you have extensive work experience. You want to provide potential employers with information—but not so much that they will not take the time to read it.

Contact Information

The first thing on your résumé should be your *contact information*: your name, address, telephone number, and e-mail address. That information will enable a potential employer to contact you.

Objective

You should inform a prospective employer about the type of position you are seeking. To do this, include a simple *job objective* statement, which is a statement that briefly describes the type of job you are seeking. For example, "Job Objective: To obtain an entry-level position in the area of clothing retailing." Keep your objective brief at no more than two sentences.

Skills

Many people include a section on their résumé for *skills*. This listing is especially important if you have little job experience. List your special skills that directly apply to the position you seek. For example, you may list the computer software programs that you know how to use, your typing speed, or your knowledge of inventory systems. This section is not always required but may help distinguish you from other candidates. **Figure 15.2** on page 311 shows a sample of a *skills résumé* for someone with little work experience who is applying for a retail position.

Experience

The next section on your résumé should describe your *work experience*. For each job you've had, list your job title, the company you worked for, and your duties. If you are still in high school, no one expects you to have had many jobs. However, do include all jobs you've held, even those that do not directly apply to retailing, such as pet-sitting. Employers

YOU WILL LEARN

- To identify information needed to prepare a résumé.
- To explain how to prepare a résumé.
- To identify references for a résumé.

WHY IT'S IMPORTANT

A résumé is your first, and perhaps only, chance to make a good impression on a potential employer. A good résumé will help you get a job.

KEY TERMS

- résumé
- references
- cover letter

PREDICT

What information do you think you should include in a résumé?

résumé a document that provides a summary of information about a person's education, work experience, activities, and interests

CONNECT

What can you put in the experience section if you have never had a job?

may research your past experience, and you should be honest. You can also include any volunteer work that you have done.

Be brief but specific so that an employer gets a good idea of what you have done in your past jobs and how much responsibility you have handled. If you regularly baby-sit for a local family, describe it in detail. For example, "Regularly care for two children, ages 2 and 5. Prepared meals, planned activities, made sure the children were in bed on time." Complete sentences are not necessary for the descriptions.

List your jobs in reverse time order, with the most recent job first, and state the dates you worked. If you had a summer job, you might write, "June to September 2003." If you still work at that job, write, "June 2003 to present." If you have a reasonable amount of work experience, this section will be the focal point of your résumé. A résumé with this focus is a *chronological résumé.*

Education

In the *education* section, include information about your education. List the name of your high school and the years you have attended. You may want to list marketing classes or special seminars you have taken that relate to the job for which you are applying. This section of your résumé may be very brief.

Activities and Honors

In the last section of your résumé, the *activities and honors* section, list school clubs, teams, or organizations to which you belong, and how long you have belonged to them. List the organizations in which you hold leadership positions first, and note the leadership position you hold. Include any honors you have received and add a note of explanation if necessary. If you've received an award from the local Rotary Club or from another community organization, note the reason you received the award. Keep your description very brief.

FIRST IMPRESSIONS
Your résumé is the first chance you have to make a good impression on an employer. *Do you think it would be important to include work experience on your résumé if you were answering a job ad that said, "No experience required"? Explain.*

Figure 15.2

Sample Skills Résumé

HIGH SCHOOL EXPERIENCE A skills résumé is suitable for a job hunter without much experience. It highlights skills, abilities, and experience. *What skills have you learned in school that might qualify you for a specific job? Explain.*

Name
Address
Phone number

Job Objective   To obtain an entry-level position in the area of clothing retailing.

SKILLS

Computer Skills
- Proven ability to learn new software systems quickly
- Trained teachers and staff in computer and word-processing skills

Communication Skills
- Excellent communication with customers, teachers, staff, and parents
- Created a newsletter for parents and staff
- Drafted effective business correspondence

Hardworking
- Worked outside of school since age 16
- Worked 20 hours a week

Organizational Skills
- Demonstrated ability to organize office information system
- Accurate and detailed bookkeeping inventory
- Organized fundraiser for American Cancer Society

WORK EXPERIENCE

2004–2005   Salesperson
                 Johnson's Men's Store, Amber, Ohio
                 - Assisted customers, answered phones
                 - Assisted manager with the installation of a new computer
                   inventory system

2002   Intern Salesperson
                 X-Sports Shack, Amber, Ohio
                 - Assisted customers, answered phones
                 - Installed software package to improve efficiency of cashier

EDUCATION

2005   Freshman, Ohio State University
                 Major: Business
2004   High School Diploma, Jackson Tate High School
                 Amber, Ohio

AWARDS AND ACTIVITIES

2004   President, Marketing Club
2002   Outstanding Business Student Award

Keeping Current

You need to constantly update your résumé because the information on the résumé changes as you gain experience, learn new skills, advance in school, earn awards, and join new organizations. Review your résumé often and make any revisions as they are needed. Doing so will save you time because you are updating while the information is fresh in your mind. A current résumé is a crucial tool in your job-search efforts.

References

references people who know you and who can answer questions about your work habits and character

In addition to a résumé, prepare a list of references. **References** are people who know you and who can answer questions about your work habits and character. Employers may ask for three references.

The references you provide should be people who know you well or who have worked with you and can talk about your good qualities, such as work skills, responsibility, leadership abilities, promptness, and trustworthiness. You may want to ask current or former employers, teachers, your school counselor, or a family friend to be a reference. Before you include anyone on your reference list, be sure to ask for that person's permission.

Hot Property

Copies and More

kinko's

Kinko's might have been called "Paul's." Instead, Paul Orfalea named his new copy business for his most distinct feature—curly red hair. In 1970, the start of his career was as distinctive as his hair.

Orfalea is living proof of an old saying: "Small opportunities are often the beginning of great enterprises." As a student at the University of Southern California, Orfalea noticed that the school copy machine charged 10 cents a page. So he rented a former hamburger stand and one copy machine, and charged customers half the price—5 cents a page. The copy stand became so popular that the copier was rolled out onto the sidewalk to make room for customers.

DUPLICATING SUCCESS

Kinko's opened more stores off campus and became a blessing for small businesses without corporate budgets and for those working out of their homes—more than 40 million Americans in 2000. As consumer needs grew, so did Kinko's services. Today customers still make copies at Kinko's—16 billion annually—but they also purchase custom-designed posters, personalized stationery, computer rentals, e-mail service, fax service, and even teleconferencing.

With more than 1,200 locations across four continents, Kinko's has become a "great enterprise" and a leader in the communications field. Besides that, Kinko's has created a pop-culture phenomenon that has been featured in TV sitcoms, such as *Seinfeld*, and in comedy skits on late-night comedy shows, including *Late Night With David Letterman*.

1. What do you think is the most important skill that is required of employees at Kinko's?
2. What do you think was the most important aspect of starting Kinko's: funding, marketing, or its product? Explain.

On a separate sheet of paper, type "References" at the top, then type each person's name, address, phone number, and e-mail address. For current or former employers, teachers, or counselors, you should list the person's title and the company or school.

Generally, employers do not ask for references until an interview. It is acceptable to write "References available upon request," at the bottom of your résumé. However, have the list prepared before you apply for a job. If an employer immediately asks you for an interview, you will be ready.

More About Networking

The people who are included in the references section of your résumé are part of your own personal network, the web of people you know from all areas of your life. The people may not all be managers or company presidents, but they can be sources of information when you are looking for job openings. You probably already have a network of people from a variety of sources:

- **Supporters** Think of the people who support you on a daily basis. Write down the names of all the people in your life who help you get things done. They may be student assistants, administrative assistants, advisors, classmates, friends, family, or support staff.

- **Professionals** Consider the professionals in fields who have expertise and whom you respect. If you are a student, these professionals may be counselors, professors, teachers, administrators, and support staff. If you are a salesperson, they might be hotel workers, suppliers, or office staff.

- **Promoters** Other contacts may be people who have already helped you with a previous job. They help encourage and promote your career. They give you advice and can help you look at your career direction. If you are a student, these promoters might be club or academic advisors, instructors, coaches, and counselors. If you work at a store, these people may be co-workers, customers, and clients.

- **Role Models** Which successful people who work in your career area could serve as your role models? Even if you don't know them, they can provide inspiration and an example that you would like to follow. These people may be instructors, professors, community leaders, authors, and experts in their professions.

- **Mentors** You may know people who are not only promoters, but who also provide you with opportunities and guidance. Mentors can be role models, or they can be professionals outside your career area who take an interest in your career.

Case Study PART 2

NONSTOP POP
Continued from Part 1 on page 301

Galco's Soda Pop Stop was established as a small store, but its owner John Nese wanted to expand. So the store began distributing hard-to-find sodas to other southern California stores, giving retailers as well as consumers access to 450 types of soda. Any store or restaurant can find the information on the Web site, which also handles retail mail-order sales.

Nese sees the expansion of the family business as a smart financial move. It is also a way to compete with Coke and Pepsi who use up all the shelf space that could be available for the hard-to-find sodas. By reviving the popularity of lesser known drinks, he fights one of the biggest misconceptions about Galco's—that it is simply a soda museum. Actually, it is a thriving store that is converting its soda drinkers to its cause.

ANALYZE AND WRITE
1. What are some obstacles to the growth of Soda Pop Stop?
2. What other kind of business could be developed from the Galco's Soda Pop Stop?

QUESTION

Why should your résumé and cover letter be error-free?

cover letter a brief letter that provides a short introduction about the sender and states why that person is a strong candidate for the job

GETTING ORGANIZED Keep your networking system organized so you can refer to it when needed. Here are a few tips:

- List names of contacts in a notebook or on your computer and update it often.

- If you meet a new contact, ask for a business card or write down the information on a note card. If appropriate, get the person's home phone number or e-mail address.

- Jot down information about this person on the back of the card. Include interests, current projects, or possible opportunities. Keep the cards in a file.

- Set up worksheets that list all your contacts on one or two pages. This allows you to view your entire network.

Cover Letter

When you send your résumé to apply for a job, always include a **cover letter**. A cover letter is a brief letter that provides a short introduction. It tells why you believe you are a strong candidate for the job and explains how you match the job description. The cover letter should be short—no more than one page—and may include information that is not on your résumé. For example, if you are applying for a sales position at a fishing store, it may help to note on your cover letter that you have fished since you were a child.

Always close your cover letter by thanking the person for his or her time and invite him or her to call you. Be sure to proofread your letter. Include your name, address, phone number, and e-mail address on your cover letter as well as on your résumé.

A Good Start

By creating a career plan, learning job-search strategies, and preparing a good résumé, you will be prepared to find the right job opportunities and be on your way to a successful retail career.

Quick Check ✓

RESPOND to what you've read by answering these questions.

1. What types of information should be included on your résumé? _____

_____

2. Why is it important to list offices and memberships on your résumé? _____

_____

3. What are three types of references you can include on your résumé? _____

_____

Worksheet 15.1

Writing a Career Plan

1. Write a statement of your career goals. Make your statement clear and specific. Be realistic in your career goals.

_____

_____

_____

_____

_____

_____

_____

_____

_____

_____

_____

2. Write the steps you need to take in order to accomplish your career goals. Be sure to include education and any skills you may need to acquire.

_____

_____

_____

_____

_____

_____

_____

_____

_____

_____

_____

_____

Worksheet 15.2

Work-Experience Review

1. Perhaps the most important section of your résumé is the "Work Experience" section. To prepare this section, first list all your work experience, including babysitting, mowing lawns, pet-sitting, and volunteering.

_____

_____

_____

_____

_____

2. For each job, list everything you do. You can shorten the list later, but for now, list every single thing you do at that job. After you have listed the job duties, prioritize them, putting a number "1" next to the duty that is most important to your employer, number "2" next to the next-most important duty, and so on.

_____

_____

_____

_____

_____

_____

_____

_____

_____

3. Compile this information into résumé format, listing the most important job duties first.

_____

_____

_____

_____

_____

_____

_____

_____

_____

YOUR TIME-MANAGEMENT SKILLS

Employers like to know that their employees can use their time efficiently and effectively. Look at the time-management factors below and indicate how you would demonstrate them to potential employers. Then add this page to your career portfolio.

Factors	Demonstration
Dependability	
Efficiency	
Effectiveness	
Responsibility	
Positive Attitude	
Persistence	
Ability to plan and set goals and priorities	
Visionary	
Ability to follow through	
High Energy	
Ability to handle stress	
Ability to focus	
Respect for others' time	
Ability to overcome procrastination	
Reputation as a doer and a self-starter	

CHAPTER SUMMARY

Section 15.1　Planning Your Retail Career

career plan (p. 302)
career ladder (p. 302)
career lattice (p. 303)
networking (p. 307)
employment agency
　(p. 308)

- A career plan is a written statement of your career goals and the necessary steps to achieve them. When making career plans you should be realistic and specific.

- To prepare for a retail career, you should complete high school and any formal education beyond high school that is needed for a particular career goal. Acquiring work experience is also helpful.

- To look for a job in retailing, you can use networking, employment agencies, employment ads, and the Internet.

Section 15.2　Preparing Your Résumé

résumé (p. 309)
references (p. 312)
cover letter (p. 314)

- A résumé is a document that provides a summary of personal information, including your work experience, your education, and your interests and activities.

- You should begin your résumé with personal information and the position you are seeking. Include sections on work experience and education followed by any offices or memberships in school clubs or positions on teams. The last section lists references.

- References are people who know you and can answer questions about your work habits and your character. They may be former employers, teachers, and family friends.

CHECKING CONCEPTS

1. **Define** a career plan.
2. **Describe** ways to make career plans.
3. **Identify** steps you can take to prepare for a retail career.
4. **Explain** four job-search strategies.
5. **Identify** information to assemble when preparing a résumé.
6. **Explain** how to prepare a résumé.
7. **Describe** the different types of references you can use on your résumé.

Critical Thinking

8. **Explain** the importance of making a career plan realistic and specific.

CROSS-CURRICULUM SKILLS

Work-Based Learning

Technology—Selecting Technology

9. Explain two ways a computer can help you with a job search.

Basic Skills—Speaking

10. Imagine that a family member's friend works as a manager in a store where you would like to work. Write what you would say if you called this person to ask about applying for a job at the store.

School-Based Learning

Math

11. If the annual salary for a job is listed as $43,500, what is the monthly pay before taxes are taken out? What is the weekly pay before taxes?

Language Arts

12. Use a dictionary to find the history of the word *résumé*. Share in class.

Role Play: High School Marketing Student

SITUATION You are to assume the role of a high school marketing student. You are a senior, and this is your second year in marketing. Your marketing class has been asked by another teacher in the school to help teach a sophomore class about the importance of preparing a résumé before applying for a job. Your marketing teacher (judge) has assigned class members to prepare a lesson about résumés.

(ACTIVITY) You are to plan your assignment about résumé preparation and explain the various sections of a résumé.

EVALUATION You will be evaluated on how well you meet the following performance indicators:

- Prepare a résumé.
- Assess personal interests and skills needed for success in business.
- Conduct training class/program.
- Follow directions.
- Prepare simple written reports.

Use the Internet to access Monster.com and answer these questions.

- Click on Get Career Advice and list the six different headings shown.
- Go back to the Home Page and click on Search Jobs.
- Choose a location and a job category that interests you and write down the information that Monster.com gives you.

➡️For a link to Monster.com, go to **marketingseries.glencoe.com**.

Chapter 16

Getting a Job in Retailing

Section 16.1

Job Application Process

Section 16.2

Starting Your Retailing Job

Chapter Objectives

- Explain how to complete a job application form.
- Describe how to interview for a job.
- Write a follow-up letter after a job interview.
- Explain the importance of punctuality on the job.
- Explain the importance of accepting responsibility.
- Describe how to foster positive working relationships.

POWER READ

Be an active reader and use these reading strategies:

PREDICT what the section will be about.

CONNECT what you read with your life.

QUESTION as you read to make sure you understand the content.

RESPOND to what you've read.

CONSCIOUS RETAILING

In 1990, while large music chains were putting smaller stores out of business, the first Amoeba Music store opened in Berkeley, California. Amoeba Music offered independent and international music in addition to popular hits. The shop supported the local music community by hosting free concerts by local and touring musicians, publishing guides to new music, and releasing compilation CDs featuring up-and-coming artists. It hired music experts who could educate and answer questions for customers. Amoeba also set aside a portion of its profits for the Rainforest Action Network, showing concern for the earth as well as the arts.

Amoeba's vast selection of rock, reggae, soul, jazz, country, classical, international, and every other genre of music has made it a destination store for locals and visitors. However, changes in the music business, such as online sales and mail ordering, offer new challenges. Can an old-fashioned record and CD store survive retail evolution?

ANALYZE AND WRITE

1. What type of interview questions do you think the manager of a record store would ask a prospective employee?
2. What special skills or qualities do you think a record-store employee should have?

Case Study Part 2 on page 331

Job Application Process

AS YOU READ ...

YOU WILL LEARN

- To explain how to complete a job application form.
- To describe how to interview for a job.
- How to write a follow-up letter after a job interview.

WHY IT'S IMPORTANT

To get the job you want, you have to be prepared to fill out a job application and complete a job interview. Preparation will help you be more confident and more likely to get the job.

KEY TERMS

- job application form
- interviewer
- follow-up letter

PREDICT

What steps do you think you will need to complete the job-application process?

Before You Apply

Chapters 14 and 15 focused on where to find job openings in retailing and how to create your résumé. However, before you apply for a job, there is something else you should do—research the company that is offering the job. You will learn more about the job by researching what the company does, how big it is, where its headquarters are located, and what kind of customers it attracts.

You may not always be able to research the company. Companies may advertise job openings without stating the company name. However, when you do know the name of the company, it is a good idea to do some research before you send your résumé.

How to Research a Company

You can begin your research by listing the company's retail businesses in your community and the types of employment they provide. Then visit one of the company's stores. Notice the types of products they sell and the kinds of customers they attract. Talk to the people who work there about whether they like working for that company. Ask people you know about the business and get information online or at the library.

Many retail companies, large and small, have their own Web sites. Visit the company's Web site and learn as much as you can. Many companies post a mission statement that describes the company's goals. The Web site will give you a sense of whether the company is casual or conservative, as well as suggest the type of people who work there. Take notes so that you will remember the information you find.

Learning about a business before you apply for employment will help you learn what you can expect from the company, how much opportunity there is for advancement in the company, and perhaps the pay you could expect to earn. You may also be able to determine whether the company's values match your own. Moreover, researching the company will help you formulate questions to ask during a job interview.

Applying for the Job

You are now ready to begin applying for your job in retailing. Begin with your cover letter. Write your cover letter specifically for the job. If the company requests specific experience or skills, explain why you have the experience and skills they seek in an employee. Be sure to include any information the company requests.

Some companies will ask that you apply in person. If you do, make sure your clothes are clean and you are well-groomed. Bring your résumé.

When you interview, you will probably be asked to fill out a job application form. The **job application form** is a document that asks for your contact information, work experience, education, activities, and references. Although the form asks for much of the same information that is on a résumé, the company still requires that the information be on this form.

Read the application before you begin to write in answers. Fill out the job application with a blue or black pen. Other colors look unprofessional. Print clearly and neatly, making sure that every answer is legible. Complete all questions that apply. If a question does not apply to you, write "N/A," which is short for "not applicable," in the space provided.

Use your full name, not your nickname. Complete all the work experience and education questions. Having a copy of your résumé will make it easy to provide the information, because you can just copy it onto the application form. Attach a copy of your résumé to the application form.

If you have questions about the application form or any of the questions on it, ask the person who gave you the application to explain. Read the application again once you have completed the form. Double-check to see if you have answered all the questions and that the application form is neat and legible.

job application form a document that asks for an applicant's contact information, work experience, education, activities, and references

Hot Property

Making a Better Pretzel

Legend has it that in 610 A.D., an Italian monk rolled leftover dough into a shape that resembled the arms of a student in prayer. The first pretzel, called *pretiolas* (Latin for "small rewards"), was invented. Much later, in 1989, a young woman tried to make a better pretzel, and a retail empire called Auntie Anne's was born.

Anne Beiler started her career by selling her hand-rolled pretzels from a farmer's market stand in Downingtown, Pennsylvania. They became such a hit that the stand's other selections—pizza and ice cream—were eliminated. Soon a second pretzel stand opened. Within a year the first Auntie Anne's was franchised. The rest is history.

The pretzel's popularity spread quickly by word of mouth—and aroma. Hand-rolled in front of customers, the golden-brown pretzels are sold in 11 varieties, including original, maple crumb, cinnamon sugar, garlic, and parmesan herb.

RISING PROFITS FOR EVERYONE

By 2003, people in more than 750 locations all over the world enjoyed the soft pretzel with the 30-minute freshness guarantee. Anne Beiler found her calling as head of a corporate staff numbering 100 and franchises employing over 8,000 people.

Although *Entrepreneur* magazine ranks Auntie Anne's in the top 100 fastest growing franchises, healthy profits mean different things to different companies. Success has enabled Anne and her husband Jonas to serve the community. In 1992, they opened the Family Resource and Counseling Center, which has helped more than 10,000 families.

1. First-time Auntie Anne's retailers are allowed to buy only one franchise at a time. What could be the reasons?
2. Suggest ways that a prospective franchise buyer or employee might research this company.

CONNECT

How can you emphazise your qualities to an interviewer?

Before the Interview

One of the best things you can do to prepare for a job interview is to get a good night's sleep the night before your interview appointment. You will be well rested and that will help you be more alert. A job interview is your chance to impress a prospective employer and show that you have the skills, personality, and values that the employer seeks. Interviews can be stressful, but if you prepare beforehand, you will feel more comfortable and confident.

What to Wear

Another way to prepare is to decide ahead of time what you will wear to the interview. Remember that you want to make a good impression during the interview. The clothing you decide to wear will depend upon the type of company where you are applying. Visit the business beforehand to see what the employees are wearing. Then pick an outfit that is just a bit more formal than what the employees usually wear. It is always a good idea to dress a little more conservatively than you normally would. Wear something that makes you feel comfortable.

Regardless of what you decide to wear to your interview, make sure your clothes are clean and pressed. Your shoes should also be clean and polished. The same goes for your personal grooming—your hair should be clean and combed, and be sure your nails are clean and trimmed. Check your appearance in a full-length mirror before you leave home. Remember that you want to make a good first impression to get the job.

BUSINESS DRESS? The clothes you choose for your interview should give the impression that you are serious about getting the job—but also that you understand the type of store and its customers. *What do you think you should wear to a job interview at a skateboard shop? Explain.*

Anticipate Questions

A job interview is also the interviewer's opportunity to meet and get to know you. The **interviewer** is the company representative who assesses your qualifications for the job by talking to you and asking questions. Many interviewers start by saying, "Tell me about yourself." This is your chance to spend a minute describing your background, experience, and skills. **Figure 16.1** lists several standard interview questions. Practice answering these questions before you go to an interview. You might even ask a friend or family member to role-play an interviewer to help you rehearse. Rehearsing will help you sound more relaxed and confident during the actual interview.

The interviewer will probably also ask you questions about items on your résumé. Prepare for those questions by reviewing the information on your résumé and planning explanations of everything on it. You might be asked about your participation in activities through your marketing class or DECA chapter. The interviewer might also ask about teams in which you participate or other school and civic activities you have listed on your résumé.

Pre-Employment Testing

Sometimes you will be asked to take some form of pre-employment test before the job interview. The test might be a brief grammar, math, spelling, or typing test, depending on the job. Pre-employment tests are designed to demonstrate that you are capable of completing the basic tasks required of the job. Once you complete the pre-employment testing, you are ready for the next step—the job interview.

TECH NOTES

Job Hunting Online

A wide selection of online resources awaits job seekers interested in a retail career. Many Web sites have job listings for current openings. Some offer additional features, such as tips on résumé writing and interviewing. These online tools allow job seekers to discover job opportunities locally and nationally.

➡️ Find and list two retail positions in your city or town that interest you through **marketingseries.glencoe.com**.

interviewer the company representative who assesses a job candidate's qualifications for the job by talking and asking questions

---

Figure 16.1

Interview Questions

1. Tell me about yourself.
2. Why do you want to work here?
3. What do you know about this company?
4. What are your goals?
5. Why did you choose this career?
6. What motivates you to go the extra mile on a project or job?
7. What was your most memorable classroom experience?
8. What are your strengths and weaknesses?
9. What has been your most significant achievement?
10. How would your last boss and classmates describe you?
11. Why should we hire you?

GOOD PREPARATION These questions give you a chance to emphasize your strengths and your job skills. You can use them to rehearse for a job interview. *Do you think it is fair for an interviewer to ask you about your weaknesses? Explain.*

Selling Fine Silver

People have used silver for thousands of years. In fact, it is one of the oldest metals known to humans.

In the 16th century, Spanish adventurers discovered Mexican silver mines in the town of Taxco. In the late 1920s, an American architect set up Taxco's first silver shop. The venture paid off, and soon his apprentices and associates began to open their own small shops. For almost 75 years, Taxco has employed and promoted the skills of thousands of artisans. Today the region is the silver capital of the world and has six working mines. The small hillside city is home to 300 silversmiths.

If you're looking for real silver (92 percent pure) and fine workmanship, then stop in Taxco. With silver shops on every street, tourists can find almost anything—from ornate jewelry and tiny silver boxes to baby rattles. If you cannot find an item, the silversmiths can always make it.

What interview questions might a silver-shop owner ask when interviewing a prospective salesperson for a job?

Prepare to Communicate

According to communication experts, only ten percent of our communication is represented by what we say, 30 percent by our sounds, and 60 percent by our body language. Many Web sites offer interview-preparation resources for people looking for jobs. If you prepare for an interview, you will you feel more relaxed and confident.

➡ View a job-interview preparation site and list three ways to prepare through **marketingseries.glencoe.com**.

During the Job Interview

Many people become nervous at the thought of a job interview even if they have prepared beforehand. There are some things that you can do during the job interview to help you feel self-confident and relaxed. Be sure to arrive on time, and do not bring friends with you.

Introductions

When the interview begins, either the person who took your application will introduce you to the interviewer, or you will introduce yourself. If the interviewer offers a hand, shake hands firmly but not too firmly. Look the interviewer in the eye while saying hello and giving your name. Remember to smile with confidence.

Answering Questions

Once introductions are complete, the interviewer will offer you a seat. Sit up straight and avoid leaning back in the chair. If you lean slightly forward, your body language will show that you are interested.

The interviewer will probably begin the interview by telling you about the job and asking you questions. Listen closely. Answer each question clearly and enunciate so the interviewer can understand you. When you have anticipated some of the questions and practiced your answers, you can answer with confidence. You may be asked a question for which you have no answer. If that happens, then simply say that you are not sure of the answer or that you need to think about the question.

Asking Questions

As the interview ends, the interviewer may give you an opportunity to ask your own questions. This is your chance to show that you have researched the company and that you are really interested in the job. The interviewer will expect you to have questions. You may want to ask about the company's mission, how many employees it has, what opportunities are available for professional growth and promotion, or what type of employee the company hopes to find. This is also the time to ask about the job itself if the interviewer has not provided information about hours you would be working.

Ending the Interview

The interview will come to a close when the interviewer has asked the questions needed to form an opinion about your abilities and qualifications—and after answering any questions you have asked.

Before you leave, remember to thank the interviewer for the opportunity to interview for the position and for the time spent with you.

Follow-Up

After you leave, mentally review the interview. Try to determine which parts of the interview demonstrated your strong points and which needed improvement.

Write a **follow-up letter** after your interview. The letter should briefly thank the interviewer and should restate your interest and qualifications for the job. Send your letter on the same day that your interview takes place or on the day after.

QUESTION

What are things you should do when introduced to an interviewer?

follow-up letter a brief letter to thank an interviewer and to restate the job candidate's interest and qualifications

---

Quick Check

RESPOND to what you've read by answering these questions.

1. What are three things you should remember when completing a job application form?

_____

_____

_____

2. What is the purpose of pre-employment testing? _____

_____

_____

_____

3. What are the two purposes of a follow-up letter after a job interview? _____

_____

_____

_____

Starting Your Retailing Job

AS YOU READ ...

YOU WILL LEARN

- To explain the importance of punctuality on the job.
- To explain the importance of accepting responsibility.
- To describe how to foster positive working relationships.

WHY IT'S IMPORTANT

Getting the job is just the beginning. Knowing what your employer expects will help you succeed at your job.

KEY TERMS

- punctuality
- responsibility
- initiative

PREDICT

What qualities do you think employers value in employees?

punctuality the practice of arriving at work on time and staying there until scheduled to leave

responsibility completing the tasks assigned to you and being trustworthy

Doing Your Job

Your first job in retailing is the beginning of your career. You want your employer to be happy with the job you do. You should also be happy with your job. There are many things you can do to get off to a good start in your new job and point your career in the right direction.

A Good Start

To make your new job a good experience for you and for your employer, use the following strategies: Be punctual. Always arrive on time. Be a responsible employee and complete all your assignments and tasks. Show initiative. Understand the value of positive working relationships. Learn to handle and gain from mistakes. These are just a few things that will make you a successful employee. **Figure 16.2** lists the top 10 qualities that employers seek in their employees.

Punctuality

Punctuality means arriving at work on time and staying there until you are scheduled to leave. Employers make schedules for their employees. Schedules ensure that there is adequate coverage for a sales associate position on the selling floor and that there is enough staff to perform other tasks required during a particular time period. Employers rely on their employees to be punctual so their schedules will work.

When employees are late for work, they force other employees to cover for them and do more work. When employees leave early, they might leave tasks undone or incomplete. Lack of punctuality is a major concern for employers and one that can lead to dismissal, or being fired. You want to make sure that you allow yourself plenty of time to get to work and to your assigned area. If you are assigned to work at 9 A.M., then be in your assigned job area at that time—not any later.

Responsibility

Responsibility means completing the tasks assigned to you and being trustworthy. As a responsible employee at your job, you do the work assigned—and you avoid talking on the phone or chatting often with your friends.

Retail jobs may involve taking financial responsibility for the store. If you are a sales associate, you have access to the cash drawer, credit slips, and even customers' credit-card numbers. You may also receive a special discount on anything you buy in the store. Being responsible means not abusing this information and these privileges. Of course, you should never take money from the register or use a customer's credit-card number, and you should also not give your friends your employee discount without your supervisor's approval.

Initiative

The best employees are those who show **initiative**, which means doing things that need to be done without being asked. You can show initiative by straightening up the store when you are not helping customers. Initiative does not mean taking over someone else's responsibility without being asked. For example, if you see that a light bulb has burned out in the dressing rooms, but replacing bulbs is not part of your regular job, first tell your supervisor and ask how you should proceed.

When you take initiative, you also show that you are interested in learning more tasks and taking on more responsibilities. Employers appreciate workers who are willing to learn and do what needs to be done without being asked.

Positive Working Relationships

You will be working with other people at your job, including other employees and your supervisor. It is important to be polite and friendly with your coworkers. You all must work together to keep the store running and the customers happy. When everyone is pleasant and cooperative, it makes the time at work more enjoyable and more productive.

You must also work with your supervisor. It is important to listen to directions given by your supervisor and to complete the tasks you are assigned. Going out of your way to complete all your tasks, even if it means staying a few extra minutes, shows your supervisor that you are conscientious and someone to consider for future promotions.

ETHICAL PRACTICES

Taking Responsibility

In 1996, it was discovered that some clothes sold under the Kathy Lee Gifford label were made by Honduran children who were paid 31 cents an hour. Gifford denied knowing about the child labor, but she apologized—and also fought back. After donating $1 million to the Association to Benefit Children, her company began to regulate the factories. Gifford and other celebrity endorsers pressured clothing manufacturers to watch labor practices.

initiative doing things that need to be done without being asked

---

Figure 16.2

Top 10 Employee Skills and Qualities

1. Communication skills (verbal and written)
2. Honesty/integrity
3. Teamwork skills (working well with others)
4. Interpersonal skills (relating well to others)
5. Motivation/initiative
6. Strong work ethic
7. Analytical skills
8. Flexibility/adaptability
9. Computer skills
10. Organizational skills

Source: *Job Outlook 2003*, National Association of Colleges and Employers

BASIC JOB SKILLS In every industry, employers seek these skills in employees. *Why do you think analytical skills are important?*

What would you do if you noticed that another employee was not fulfilling his or her responsibilities?

Learning From Mistakes

It takes a few weeks for new employees to learn all the procedures and responsibilities of a new job. During that time it is natural to make a few mistakes. When you make a mistake, acknowledge it. Your supervisor will be able to teach you the correct way to handle the same situation in the future. Listen carefully to his or her directions so you can learn from the mistake and not repeat it.

If you have any questions about procedures or the way a situation should be handled, ask your supervisor. It is better to ask for clarification than to make a mistake. In a short time, you will know the procedures and be comfortable in your new job.

Profiles in Marketing

YOUR FUTURE IN RETAILING

Robin Ryan
Career Coach and Author
What to Do With the Rest of Your Life

What are the most important things to remember when starting a career?

"Pursue a position that will allow you to get training from a boss who will mentor you. The money doesn't matter as much as the opportunity to learn. Sometimes a smaller organization can give you the experience that a big organization can't provide. In a smaller retail store, you can move up faster. Also remember that customer-service skills matter most. While you're still in high school, get a job in retail at Starbucks, Gap, or any store that interests you. You'll have experience to put on your résumé."

What are the biggest mistakes people make when looking for a first job?

"Number one—looking only on the Internet. Number two—having a terrible résumé. Number three—expecting to start out at the top. It doesn't work that way. You start out on the floor and work your way up."

What are the most important things to put on a résumé?

"I recommend a one-page résumé that includes actions and results. Stress customer-service skills, retail experience, and sales experience—even if it's selling Girl Scout cookies. Include any place where you've worked with others. You might have done that at school by working on a committee. All of your experiences are important."

What kind of unpaid experience would be important for getting an entry-level job in retailing?

Career Data: Entry-Level Sales Associate

Education and Training High school diploma, bachelor's or master's degrees in business or marketing for advancement

Skills and Abilities Communication skills and customer-service skills

Career Outlook Average growth through 2010

Career Path Entry-level sales associates begin by working on the floor of a retail store and gain experience in all aspects of selling. Promotions can lead to all levels of the retail business.

Understanding Performance Reviews

Employers regularly give employees evaluations on how well they are performing their jobs. Performance review systems are different at each company, but they can often help you improve your skills. Many businesses use a standard form, and supervisors usually conduct performance reviews yearly. Sometimes you can request a review and avoid waiting for your next formal evaluation to get feedback on your performance.

Prepare for your appraisal so you can get the most out it. Try to be accurate, pleasant, and as helpful as possible. You can respond to any comments or suggestions from your employer and discuss the findings. Performance reviews give you a chance to communicate and better understand what your employer expects of you.

Successful Living

As you begin your new job, you will be having new experiences and learning new things. Retail work can require a lot of energy. For example, working on a sales floor can be physically demanding. Staying balanced and healthy during this period and beyond will help you form positive work habits and make your life more enjoyable. By practicing a few simple strategies, you will be able to stay focused on success in any workplace environment:

- **Be organized.** The night before you have to be at work, arrange your clothes and any items needed for your job. Get up early to prepare.

- **Get enough rest.** Go to bed at the same time every night. Get enough sleep so that you can feel energized, focused, and enthusiastic when you awaken.

- **Eat healthy foods.** Eat a balanced diet of foods rich in vitamins and fiber, such as whole grains, vegetables, fruits, low-fat milk, and protein.

- **Exercise regularly.** Exercise can actually increase your energy. Try getting up a little earlier to do 15 minutes of exercise. Walk at lunchtime or break time, or go to a gym regularly.

- **Pursue your own interests.** Take time to do things you enjoy, such as hobbies, sports, reading, spending time with friends, or writing.

- **Think positively.** Get in the habit of viewing yourself as a competent, positive, and professional person. Visualize your day before you begin each day. See yourself handling problems in a calm, positive, and creative matter.

Math Check

LIVING WAGES

Larissa is applying for two entry-level retail jobs. One pays $9.50 an hour for 35 hours a week. The other pays $8.50 an hour for 40 hours a week. Which job would give Larissa more income each week?

➡ For tips on finding the solution, go to **marketingseries.glencoe.com**.

QUESTION

Why is it important to get along with co-workers?

Lifelong Success

As you begin your retailing career, you can apply positive habits. By demonstrating your skills, good characteristics, and high standards of ethics, you will experience success on the job and throughout your entire life.

Quick Check

RESPOND to what you've read by answering these questions.

1. What are four things you can do to get a good start at a new job? _____

_____

2. Why is punctuality important at work? _____

_____

3. What does it mean to show initiative? _____

_____

Worksheet 16.1

A Good Job Interview

Make a list of positive qualities and negative qualities you think you would display in a job interview. Study the negative qualities. What do you need to do to change them?

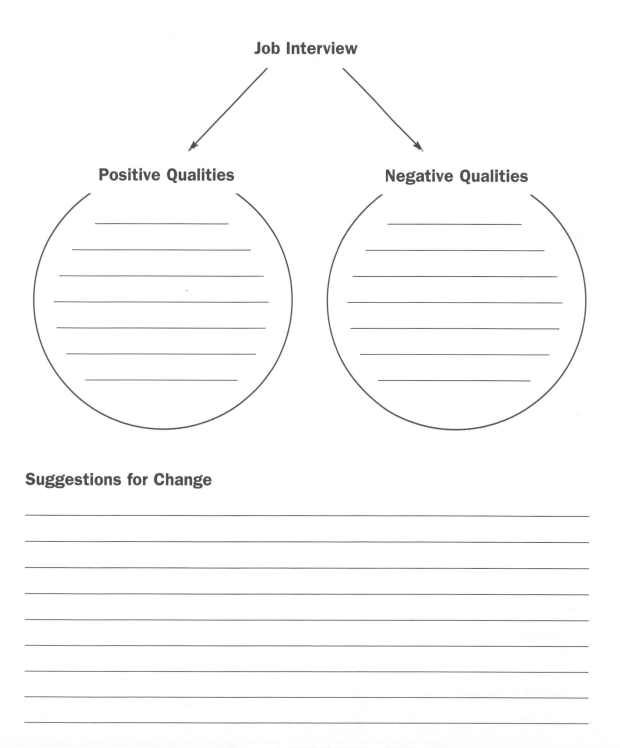

Job Interview

Positive Qualities

Negative Qualities

Suggestions for Change

_____

_____

_____

_____

_____

_____

_____

_____

_____

Name _____ Date _____

Worksheet 16.2

Your Qualities and Skills

The table below shows the qualities and skills that employers seek in employees.
For each quality or skill, write something that you can do to demonstrate that quality at school and at work.

Quality/Skill	Demonstration	
	At School	At Work
Communication skills (verbal and written)	_____	_____
Honesty/integrity	_____	_____
Teamwork skills (works well with others)	_____	_____
Interpersonal skills (relates well to others)	_____	_____
Motivation/initiative	_____	_____
Strong work ethic	_____	_____
Analytical skills	_____	_____
Flexibility/adaptability	_____	_____
Computer skills	_____	_____
Organizational skills	_____	_____

Portfolio Works

PREPARING FOR A JOB INTERVIEW

You have a job interview scheduled for next week. Make a five-day list of what you need to do to prepare for the interview. Include any skills you need to practice, what you plan to wear, and what you need to do to prepare your wardrobe. Also make a list of what you need to take with you to the interview. Be sure to include your résumé and references. Then add this page to your career portfolio.

Day #5

_____

_____

Day #4

_____

_____

Day #3

_____

_____

Day #2

_____

_____

Day of interview

_____

_____

_____

_____

Items to take to the interview

_____

_____

_____

_____

CHAPTER SUMMARY

Section 16.1 Job Application Process

job application form
(p. 323)
interviewer (p. 325)
follow-up letter (p. 327)

- Completing a job application is an important step in the job application process. Care and attention to the application form by printing legibly and neatly and answering all questions will help you get to the interview stage of the process.

- Knowing what to do before you interview for a job can help give you confidence. When you are confident, you are able to provide good answers to the questions you are asked.

- A follow-up letter after a job interview will make the interviewer aware that you care about the job. The follow-up letter will serve to thank the interviewer for the time spent during the interview and will allow you to again express your interest in the job.

Section 16.2 Starting Your Retailing Job

punctuality (p. 328)
responsibility (p. 328)
initiative (p. 329)

- Employers rely on their employees to be on time. Employers plan employee schedules to provide employees to help customers during those hours. When employees are late or leave early, other employees may have to cover for them.

- Being responsible at work is important. It means that you will complete the tasks assigned to you.

- Positive working relationships contribute to a pleasant work environment. Employees who are able to work as a team accomplish more work and foster positive relationships. Customers prefer to shop in a store that projects a positive work environment.

CHECKING CONCEPTS

1. **Explain** how to complete a job application form.
2. **Identify** ways to prepare for pre-employment testing.
3. **Describe** two questions asked by interviewers.
4. **Describe** the reasons for a follow-up letter after a job interview.
5. **Explain** the importance of punctuality on the job.
6. **Explain** the importance of accepting responsibility.
7. **Describe** why positive working relationships are important.

Critical Thinking

8. **Explain** why you think employers want a job applicant to write "N/A" as an answer to questions that do not apply to the applicant.

CROSS-CURRICULUM SKILLS

Work-Based Learning

Interpersonal Skills—Participating as a Team Member

9. Form teams of five or six students. Make a list of companies your team will contact to obtain job applications. Obtain job applications from the companies on your team's list. Compare the applications and discuss your findings with other teams.

Personal Qualities—Self-Management

10. Make a list of questions you would like to ask a job interviewer. Exchange your list with another student. Compare the two lists.

School-Based Learning

Arts

11. Create a poster that illustrates the five things needed to get a good start on a new job. Display the poster in the classroom and explain it to the class.

Language Arts

12. Write a short story about an employee who lacks responsibility. Read your story aloud in class.

 **CONNECTION**

Role Play: Store Employee

SITUATION You are to assume the role of employee of a home-furnishings store in your local community. A new employee (judge) has just been hired. This is the new employee's first job. The new employee (judge) knows that you have been employed by this store for two years.

ACTIVITY The new employee (judge) has asked for your advice about how to make a good start on his or her new job. You are to explain how to get the job started in a positive manner to the new employee (judge).

EVALUATION You will be evaluated on how well you meet the following performance indicators:

- Orient new employees.
- Explain the concept of staff motivation.
- Assess employee morale.
- Give directions for completing job tasks.
- Foster positive working relationships.

 **INTERNET ACTIVITY**

Use the Internet to learn about employment opportunities with a major department store such as Macy's or Kohl's.

- Click on Jobs, Career, or Employment.
- Choose a job that sounds interesting to you.
- Write a summary of the job and job requirements.

➡️For a link to Internet maps to begin this exercise, go to **marketingseries.glencoe.com**.

BusinessWeek News

TAPS FOR MUSIC RETAILERS?

In late April Madonna gave a rare in-store concert before 400 fans to plug her new *American Life* album. Outside the event, which took place at Tower Records in New York's Greenwich Village, another 2,000-plus fans thronged. But the splashy appearance obscured a harsh backstage truth: Tower Records is in such deep trouble that its parent MTS, Inc., has put the company on the block.

Tower is not the only music retailer singing the blues these days. Declining CD sales, the hit from online downloads, and growing competition from the likes of Amazon.com, as well as discounters such as Wal-Mart and Target are pushing specialty music retailers to the wall. Best Buy has put its Musicland unit up for sale, Wherehouse Entertainment has filed for bankruptcy, and Britain's HMV has closed two of its nine U.S. stores. The continuing drumbeat of bad news has some predicting that the traditional music store will soon go the way of the eight-track player.

In the mid-1990s, two seismic shifts shook the industry: Big discounters started pushing CDs far more aggressively, and a slew of music stores popped up on the Web. Tower, Sam Goody, and others launched e-tail operations of their own. But they were no match for Amazon.com or for eBay. None of the record stores has been able to use the Web to boost total revenues.

Discounters such as Wal-Mart Stores, Inc., and category killers such as Circuit City Stores, Inc., stock cut-price CDs. The strategy clearly works: Today 42 percent of the recorded music sold in America comes from the discounters and category killers.

Another problem is consumers' growing appetite for grabbing music online. Downloading, legal or otherwise, has already hit CD sales hard: Since 1999, annual retail music sales have slid 15 percent, to $8.9 billion in 2002.

Stores will have to move with the times if they have any chance of survival. For example, the London-based Virgin Megastore chain plans to test an in-store service that charges customers to download songs to portable music players. "Who knows?" says Glen Ward, CEO of Virgin North America, "Maybe they'll come back and get the album." Who knows, indeed?

By Louise Lee, with Kerry Capell

CREATIVE JOURNAL

In your journal, write your responses:

CRITICAL THINKING

1. If you were starting a career in music sales, where would you apply for a job and why?

APPLICATION

2. If you were an employee at a retail record store, what suggestions would you make to increase sales?

 Go to **businessweek.com** for current *BusinessWeek* Online articles.

UNIT LAB

The Virtuality Store

You've just entered the real world of retailing. The Virtuality Store offers the latest and most popular consumer goods and services. Acting as the owner, manager, or employee of this store, you will have the opportunity to work on different projects to promote the success of your business.

Staff Your Store—Recruit New Employees

SITUATION You are an employee of the Alliance Appliance Company. You work in the human resources department. Alliance is a large retailer of home appliances. The merchandise ranges from major appliances—refrigerators, stoves, and dishwashers, to small appliances—handmixers, food processors, and electric can openers. Business is booming and Alliance is growing. Alliance Appliances needs employees of all types. The business is in need of employees ranging from employees to work on the loading dock, sales associates, service repair technicians, and office personnel. Create a plan for recruiting employees for the company and present it to the company owner. Include recruiting employees for positions with Alliance Appliances.

ASSIGNMENT Complete these tasks:
- Plan your employee recruitment plan using various media.
- Estimate the costs of your employee recruitment plan.
- Create career ladders for the different types of positions mentioned above.
- Create a final report.

TOOLS AND RESOURCES To complete the assignment, you will need to:
- Conduct research about the jobs and career positions, and the benefits of employment available at Alliance appliances. Use the library, the Internet, and the telephone.
- Ask other retail business owners about their employee recruitment plans.
- Have word-processing, spreadsheet, and presentation software.

RESEARCH Do your research:
- Find the best media to spread the word about your employment needs.
- Study recruitment plans of other businesses and determine which are most effective.
- Visit the NRF Foundation Web site and research retail career ladders.
- Get cost estimates for creating and implementing your recruitment plan.

REPORT Prepare a written report using the following tools, if available:
- *Word-processing program*: Prepare a written report that includes an outline of your employee recruitment plan, the media selected, and the number of employees you think you plan should attract.
- *Spreadsheet program*: Prepare a budget chart for your recruitment plan. Prepare a chart of the career ladders you determine
- *Presentation program*: Prepare a ten-slide visual presentation with key points, some visuals, and a little text.

PRESENTATION AND EVALUATION You will present your report to your silent partner and the bank that may finance your plan. You will be evaluated on the basis of:
- Knowledge of retail careers and career recruitment
- Continuity of presentation
- Voice quality
- Eye contact

PORTFOLIO
Add this report to your career portfolio.

Appendix

MATH SKILLS BUILDER

WRITING NUMBERS AS WORDS AND ROUNDING NUMBERS

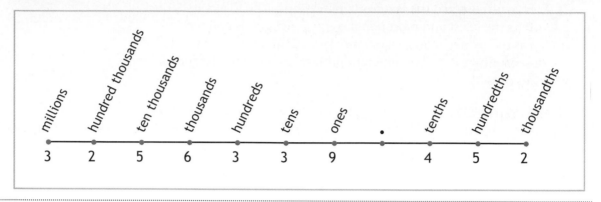

The place-value chart shows the value of each digit in the number 3,256,339.452. The place-value chart can help you write numbers.

EXAMPLE

482
  8.557
$39.45

SOLUTION

four hundred eighty-two
eight and five hundred fifty-seven thousandths
thirty-nine and forty-five hundredths dollars
or thirty-nine and $^{45}/_{100}$ dollars

Place value is also used in rounding numbers. If the digit to the right of the place value you want to round is 5 or more, round up by adding 1 to the number in the place value. Then change all the digits to the right of the place value to zeros. If the number is 4 or less, round down by changing all the numbers to the right of the place value to zeros.

EXAMPLE

Round 4765 to the nearest hundred.

SOLUTION

4765   **A.** Find the digit in the hundred place. It is 7.

4765   **B.** Is the digit to the right 5 or more? Yes.

4800   **C.** Add 1 to the hundreds place. Change the digits to the right to zeros.

EXAMPLE

Round 0.843 to the nearest tenth.

SOLUTION

0.843   **A.** Find the digit in the tenth place. It is 8.

0.843   **B.** Is the digit to the right 5 or more? No.

0.8   **C.** Do not change the tenths digit. Drop the digits to the right.

WRITING NUMBERS AS WORDS AND ROUNDING NUMBERS

Dollar and cents amounts are often rounded to the nearest cent, or the hundredths place.

EXAMPLE $26.7443   **SOLUTION** $26.74
$683.1582 $683.16

PROBLEMS

Write as numbers.
1. three thousand four hundred ninety-nine
2. one hundred eleven and $^{32}/_{100}$ dollars
3. two hundred six and eighty-eight thousandths

Write in word form.
4. 572
5. 2.897
6. $325.10

Round to the nearest place value shown.

7. ten thousand	327,975		11. one	28.91
8. thousand	816,777		12. tenth	86.379
9. hundred	26,312		13. hundredth	5.5787
10. ten	6336			

Round 23,793,611 to the place value shown.
14. millions
15. ten millions
16. thousands
17. hundreds
18. ten thousands
19. hundred thousands

Round to the nearest place value shown.

20. cent	$87.2671		23. ten dollars	$5,982
21. ten cents	$213.432		24. hundred dollars	$12,785
22. one dollar	$671.98			

APPLICATIONS

25. As an accountant for the advertising agency of Phillips & Phillips, Marcia Strasser writes many checks. Write each check amount in words.
    a. $27.83
    b. $121. 77
    c. $569.14
    d. $8,721. 65

26. Juan Sanchez, an inventory clerk for a lumber yard, often rounds inventory figures for easier handling. Round the number from the inventory list to the nearest ten.
    a. grade 1 oak   519 ft.
    b. grade 2 oak   795 ft.
    c. grade 1 pine   323 ft.
    d. grade 2 pine   477 ft.

Appendix

ADDING AND SUBTRACTING DECIMALS

When adding decimals, write the addition problem in vertical form. Be sure to line up the decimal points. When adding amounts with different numbers of decimal places, write zeros in the empty decimal places.

EXAMPLE $15.27 + 16.39 + 36.19$

SOLUTION
```
  15.27
  16.39
+ 36.19
-------
  67.85
```

EXAMPLE $58.2 + 3.97 + 8 + 123.796$

SOLUTION
```
   58.2          58.200
   3.97           3.970
   8.             8.000
+123.796       +123.796
              ----------
               193.966
```

When subtracting decimals, write the subtraction problem in vertical form. Be sure to line up the decimal points. When subtracting amounts with different numbers of decimal places, write zeros in the empty decimal places.

EXAMPLE $78.63 - 42.41$

SOLUTION
```
  78.63
- 42.41
-------
  36.22
```

EXAMPLE $149.9 - 28.37$

SOLUTION
```
  149.9          149.90
 -28.37          -28.37
 ------          ------
                 121.53
```

Adding and subtracting amounts of money is just like adding and subtracting decimals. The decimal point separates the dollars and cents. Remember to put a dollar sign in the total.

EXAMPLE $74.99 + 8.76

SOLUTION
```
 $74.99
 + 8.76
 ------
 $ 83.75
```

EXAMPLE $750 - 43.29

SOLUTION
```
 $750.00
  -43.29
 -------
 $706.71
```

PROBLEMS

1.
```
  19.87
  32.24
+ 27.55
```

2.
```
  4.377
  6.829
+ 2.707
```

3.
```
   8.3
  12.78
+322.437
```

4.
```
  46.65
   3.5
+125.397
```

5.
```
 $ 2.77
  35.96
+ 10.37
```

6. $22.19 + 47.75 + 13.88 + 19.85$
7. $0.78 + 9.82 + 36.242 + 37.4$
8. $6.7 + 27.81 + 653.47 + 5.5$
9. $54.32 + 0.37 + 2.5 + 0.797$
10. $\$6.22 + \$53.19 + \$.33 + \$7.85$
11. $\$4.78 + \$12.50 + \$22 + \$17.10$

12.
```
  3.75
 -2.18
```

13.
```
  376.55
 - 27.42
```

14.
```
  468.47
 -233.55
```

15.
```
  367.05
 -219.87
```

16.
```
 $363.27
  -79.14
```

ADDING AND SUBTRACTING DECIMALS

17. $547.7 - 127.6$
18. $76.99 - 3.87$
19. $695.13 - 428.1$
20. $3076 - 2205.50$
21. $\$300 - \$5.75$
22. $\$445.19 - \$175.76$

APPLICATIONS Complete the sales receipts by finding the subtotals and the totals.

23.

Date 6/1/--	Auth. No. 86430	Identification	Clerk DL	Reg./Dept.	☑ Take ❑ Send
Qty	Class	Description	Price	Amount	
1		dress		11	98
1		jacket		85	99
2		hosiery	12.99 ea	25	98

a. Freight charges will be included with your invoice at the time of shipping. You will be billed the published rates from UPS, US Postal Service.

	Subtotal	?	
CUSTOMER SIGNATURE X _Shelley Turner_	Tax	13	30

b. Sales Slip | Total | ? |

24.

Date 3/14/--	Auth. No. 42	Identification	Clerk JR	Reg./Dept.	☑ Take ❑ Send
Qty	Class	Description	Price	Amount	
1		couch		599	95
1 pr		draperies		279	88

a. Freight charges will be included with your invoice at the time of shipping. You will be billed the published rates from UPS, US Postal Service.

	Subtotal	?	
CUSTOMER SIGNATURE X _Betty Clark_	Tax	57	19

b. Sales Slip | Total | ? |

Complete the bank deposit slips by finding the subtotals and the total deposits.

25.

		DOLLARS	CENTS
CASH	CURRENCY	72	00
	COINS		
CHECKS	LIST SEPARATELY 95-76	413	12
	98-11	25	00
	95-13	211	10
a.	SUBTOTAL	?	
↺	LESS CASH RECEIVED	50	00
b.	TOTAL DEPOSIT	?	

a.
b.

26.

		DOLLARS	CENTS
CASH	CURRENCY	23	00
	COINS	7	44
CHECKS	LIST SEPARATELY 85-76	175	66
	88-11	23	33
		12	87
a.	SUBTOTAL	?	
↺	LESS CASH RECEIVED	75	00
b.	TOTAL DEPOSIT	?	

a.
b.

27.

		DOLLARS	CENTS
CASH	CURRENCY		
	COINS	4	75
CHECKS	LIST SEPARATELY 57-12	25	95
	57-10	38	11
a.	SUBTOTAL	?	
↺	LESS CASH RECEIVED	25	00
b.	TOTAL DEPOSIT	?	

a.
b.

28. You are a cashier at a coffee shop. Compute the correct change for each of the following orders.

	Customer's Order	Customer Gives You	Change
a.	$8.76	$10.00	
b.	$12.94	$15.00	
c.	$9.30	$10.50	
d.	$16.11	$20.00	
e.	$5.57	$5.75	
f.	$22.02	$25.00	
g.	$7.12	$7.15	
h.	$3.33	$5.00	
i.	$28.04	$30.04	
j.	$6.12	$10.25	

Appendix

MULTIPLYING AND DIVIDING DECIMALS

When multiplying decimals, multiply as if the decimal numbers were whole numbers. Then count the total number of decimal places in the factors. This number will be the number of decimal places in the product.

EXAMPLE

$$
\begin{array}{r}
18.7 \leftarrow \text{factor} \\
\times\, 0.34 \leftarrow \text{factor} \\
\hline
748 \\
561 \\
\hline
6358 \leftarrow \text{product}
\end{array}
$$

SOLUTION

$$
\begin{array}{r}
18.7 \leftarrow 1 \text{ decimal place} \\
\times\, 0.34 \leftarrow +2 \text{ decimal places} \\
\hline
748 \\
561 \\
\hline
6.358 \leftarrow 3 \text{ decimal places}
\end{array}
$$

If the product does not have enough digits to place the decimal in the correct position, you will need to write zeros. Start at the right of the product in counting the decimal places and write zeros at the left.

EXAMPLE

$$
\begin{array}{r}
0.63 \\
\times\, 0.05 \\
\hline
315
\end{array}
$$

SOLUTION

$$
\begin{array}{r}
0.63 \leftarrow 2 \text{ decimal places} \\
\times\, 0.05 \leftarrow +2 \text{ decimal places} \\
\hline
0.0315 \leftarrow 4 \text{ decimal places}
\end{array}
$$

When multiplying amounts of money, round the answer to the nearest cent. Remember to put a dollar sign in the answer.

EXAMPLE

$$
\begin{array}{r}
\$2.25 \\
\times\, 1.5 \\
\hline
3.375
\end{array}
$$

SOLUTION

$$
\begin{array}{r}
\$\,2.25 \leftarrow 2 \text{ places} \\
\times\, 1.5 \leftarrow +1 \text{ place} \\
\hline
\$3.375 \leftarrow 3 \text{ places}
\end{array}
$$

$\$2.25 \times 1.5 = \$3.375$
$= \$3.38$
rounded to the nearest cent

When multiplying by 10, 100, or 1000, count the number of zeros. Then move the decimal point to the right the same number of spaces.

EXAMPLE

8.32×100

SOLUTION

$8.32 \times 100 = 8.32 = 832$ 100 has 2 zeros; move decimal 2 places.

PROBLEMS

1. $\begin{array}{r} 18.3 \\ \times\, 2.5 \\ \hline \end{array}$
2. $\begin{array}{r} 27.5 \\ \times\, 8.2 \\ \hline \end{array}$
3. $\begin{array}{r} 56.8 \\ \times\, 0.33 \\ \hline \end{array}$
4. $\begin{array}{r} 88.1 \\ \times\, 0.23 \\ \hline \end{array}$

5. $\begin{array}{r} 0.57 \\ \times\, 0.14 \\ \hline \end{array}$
6. $\begin{array}{r} 0.88 \\ \times\, 0.07 \\ \hline \end{array}$
7. $\begin{array}{r} 0.93 \\ \times\, 0.04 \\ \hline \end{array}$
8. $\begin{array}{r} 0.323 \\ \times\, 0.005 \\ \hline \end{array}$

9. $\$17.85 \times 15.5 = \$276.675 =$
10. $\$25.24 \times 6.3 = \$159.012 =$
11. $\$18.15 \times 6.5 = \$117.975 =$
12. $\$14.98 \times 8.7 = \$130.326 =$

13. $33.8 \times 10 =$
14. $55.399 \times 100 =$
15. $0.518 \times 1000 =$
16. $532.788 \times 10,000 =$

MULTIPLYING AND DIVIDING DECIMALS

APPLICATION

17. Below are partial payroll records for Fanciful Flowers. Complete the records by calculating gross earnings (hourly rate x hours worked), Social Security tax (gross earnings × 0.062), Medicare tax (gross earnings × 0.0145), federal income tax (gross earnings × 0.15), and state income tax (gross earnings × 0.045). Round each deduction to the nearest cent. Find the total deductions and subtract from gross earnings to find the net pay.

	Employee	Hourly Rate	Number of Hours	Gross Earnings	Social Security Tax	Medicare Tax	Federal Inc. Tax	State Inc. Tax	Total Deductions	Net Pay
a.	M. Smith	$8.25	24	**198.00**	12.28	2.87	29.70	8.91	53.76	144.24
b.	R. Nash	$9.15	33	**301.95**	18.72	4.38	45.29	13.59	81.98	219.97
c.	C. Young	$7.75	15	**116.25**	7.21	1.69	17.44	5.23	31.57	84.68
d.	D. Cha	$9.15	30	**274.50**	17.02	3.98	41.18	12.35	74.53	199.97

When dividing decimals, if there is a decimal point in the divisor, you must move it to the right to make the divisor a whole number. Move the decimal point in the dividend to the right the same number of places you moved the decimal point in the divisor. Then divide as with whole numbers.

$$\text{divisor} \rightarrow 6\overline{)840} \leftarrow \text{dividend} \qquad 140 \leftarrow \text{quotient}$$

EXAMPLE

$$3.44\overline{)15.5488}$$

SOLUTION

$$3.44\overline{)15.5488}$$

$$
\begin{array}{r}
4.52 \\
344\overline{)1554.88} \\
-1376 \\
\hline
1788 \\
-1720 \\
\hline
688 \\
-688 \\
\hline
\end{array}
$$

Add zeros to the right of the decimal point in the dividend if needed.

EXAMPLE

$$0.42\overline{)0.147}$$

SOLUTION

$$0.42\overline{)0.147}$$

$$
\begin{array}{r}
0.35 \\
42\overline{)14.70} \quad \text{zero added}\\
-126 \\
\hline
210 \\
-210 \\
\hline
\end{array}
$$

When the dividend is an amount of money, remember to place the dollar sign in the quotient and round the answer to the nearest cent.

EXAMPLE

$$48\overline{)\$95.12}$$

SOLUTION

$$
\begin{array}{r}
\$1.981 \\
48\overline{)\$95.120}
\end{array}
$$

$$95.12 \div 48 = \$1.98 \text{ rounded to the nearest cent.}$$

MULTIPLYING AND DIVIDING DECIMALS

When dividing by 10, 100, or 1000, count the number of zeros in 10, 100, or 1000 and move the decimal point to the left the same number of places.

EXAMPLE

$$15,213.7 \div 1000$$

SOLUTION

$$15,213.7 \div 1000 = 15213.7$$
$$= 15.2137$$

1000 has 3 zeros; move decimal 3 places

PROBLEMS

Round to the nearest hundredth or the nearest cent.

18. $2.7\,\overline{)11.61}$

19. $1.3\,\overline{)7.67}$

20. $6.2\,\overline{)44.02}$

21. $0.3\,\overline{)1.62}$

22. $.05\,\overline{)1.47}$

23. $.04\,\overline{)28.4}$

24. $8.3\,\overline{)46.99}$

25. $3.4\,\overline{)178.3}$

26. $88\,\overline{)\$356.68}$

27. $45\,\overline{)\$42.79}$

28. $15\,\overline{)\$87.32}$

29. $14.1\,\overline{)7.823}$

APPLICATIONS

30. Your family is looking into buying a late model, used car. Calculate (to the nearest tenth) the gas mileage for the following types of cars.

	Type of Vehicle	Miles	Gallons of Fuel	Miles per Gallon
a.	Subcompact	631	17.8	
b.	4-door sedan	471.4	16.6	
c.	Minivan	405.1	18.2	
d.	Compact	512.2	15.7	
e.	SUV	298.1	23.2	

FINDING A PERCENTAGE

Finding a percentage means finding a percent of a number. To find a percent of a number, you change the percent to a decimal, then multiply it by the number.

EXAMPLE 30% of 90 is what number?

SOLUTION $30\% \times 90 = n$ — In mathematics, *of* means "times" and *is* means "equals."
— Let n stand for the unknown number.

$0.30 \times 90 = n$ Change the percent to a decimal.

$27 = n$ Multiply.

$30\% \text{ of } 90 = 27$ Write the answer.

EXAMPLE The delivery charge is 8% of the selling price of $145.00. Find the delivery charge.

EXAMPLE The student had 95% correct out of 80 questions. How many answers were correct?

SOLUTION
$8\% \times \$145.00 = n$
$0.08 \times \$145.00 = n$
$\$11.60 = n$
$8\% \times \$145.00 = \$11.60$ delivery charge

SOLUTION
$95\% \times 80 = n$
$0.95 \times 80 = n$
$76 = n$
$95\% \times 80 = 76$ correct

PROBLEMS

Find the percentage.

1. 25% of 60
2. 45% of 80
3. 40% of 30
4. 33% of 112

5. 58% of 420
6. 50% of 422
7. 3% of 100
8. 2% of 247

9. 110% of 65
10. 7% of 785
11. 1% of 819
12. 4% of 19.5

13. 185% of 95
14. 200% of 720
15. 135% of 860
16. 120% of 3.35

17. 4.5% of 50
18. 1.25% of 300
19. 33.3% of 80
20. 67.2% of 365

Round the answer to the nearest cent.

21. 7% of $35.78
22. 6.5% of $80
23. 10% of $93.20
24. 5.5% of $135

25. 4.25% of $65.00
26. 2.75% of $115
27. 125% of $98
28. 7.5% of $150

29. 0.3% of $450
30. 0.15% of $125
31. 8.2% of $19.89
32. 5.25% of $110.15

Appendix

APPLICATIONS

33. The following items appeared in a sales flyer for a major department store. Calculate the amount saved from the regular price as well as the sale price for each item. Round to the nearest cent.

		Amount Saved	Sale Price
a.	Save 25% on juniors knit shirts. Reg. $18.		
b.	Save 30% on women's dresses. Reg. $69.99		
c.	Save 20% on men's shoes. Reg. $135.		
d.	Save 25% on all nursery cribs. Reg. $119.99		
e.	Save 25% on all boxed jewelry sets. Reg. $19.99		
f.	Save 30% on family athletic shoes. Reg. $59.99		

34. Student Sean Hu received these test scores. How many answers were correct on each test?

	Subject	Test Score	Number of Items	Correct Answers
a.	Math	90%	80	
b.	English	70%	90	
c.	Science	80%	110	
d.	Spanish	90%	50	
e.	Government	85%	100	

35. Sales taxes are found by multiplying the tax rate times the selling price of the item. The total purchase price is the selling price plus the sales tax. Find the sales tax and total purchase price for each selling price. Round to the nearest cent.

	Selling Price	Tax Rate	Sales Tax	Total Purchase Price
a.	$14.78	4%		
b.	$22.50	5%		
c.	$3.88	6%		
d.	$95.85	6.5%		
e.	$212.00	7.25%		
f.	$85.06	8.25%		
g.	$199.99	7.455%		

Appendix

UNITS OF MEASURE

Here are abbreviations and conversions for units of measure in the customary measurement system.

Length	Volume	Weight
12 inches (in) = 1 foot (ft)	2 cups (c) = 1 pint (pt)	16 ounces (oz) = 1 pound (lb)
3 ft = 1 yard (yd)	2 pt = 1 quart (qt)	2000 lb = 1 ton (t)
5280 ft = 1 mile (mi)	4 qt = 1 gallon (gal)	

Here are symbols and conversions for units of measure in the metric system.

Length	Volume
1000 millimeters (mm) = 1 meter (m)	1000 milliliters (mL) = 1 liter (L)
100 centimeters (cm) = 1 m	**Mass**
1000 m = 1 kilometer (km)	1000 grams (g) = 1 kilogram (kg)

To convert from one unit of measure to another, use the conversions lists above.

When converting to a smaller unit, multiply.

EXAMPLE

SOLUTION

Convert 5 feet to inches.

Use 12 in = 1 ft

5 ft: $5 \times 12 = 60$

5 ft = 60 in

Convert 4 meters to centimeters.

Use 100 cm = 1 m

4 m: $4 \times 100 = 400$

4 m = 400 cm

When converting to a larger unit, divide.

EXAMPLE

SOLUTION

Convert 6 pints to quarts.

Use 2 pt = 1 qt

6 pt: $6 \div 2 = 3$

6 pt = 3 qt

Convert 6500 grams to kilograms.

Use 1000 g = 1 kg

6500 g: $6500 \div 1000 = 6.5$

6500 g = 6.5 kg

PROBLEMS

Make the following conversions.

1. 12 yd to feet
2. 8 gal to quarts
3. 9 lb to ounces
4. 2 ft to inches
5. 3 lb to ounces
6. 5 L to milliliters
7. 2.4 km to meters
8. 24 pt to cups
9. 3.6 kg to grams
10. 99 in to yards
11. 15 qt to gallons
12. 66 oz to pounds
13. 18 qt to gallons
14. 24 oz to pounds
15. 7000 g to kilograms
16. 60 cm to meters
17. 2200 mL to liters
18. 350 cm to meters
19. 29 kg to grams
20. 17.3 L to milliliters
21. 522 g to kilograms
22. 10.122 mL to liters
23. 72 cm to millimeters
24. 432.2 cm to meters
25. 1 yd 7 in to inches
26. 5 ft 7 in to inches
27. 3 qt 1 pt to pints
28. 6 lb 9 oz to ounces
29. 4 gal 1 qt to quarts
30. 3 yd 1 ft 5 in to inches
31. 5 gal 3 qt 1 pt to pints
32. 3 m 57 cm 29 mm to millimeters

advertising paid message that a business sends to the public

aptitude a natural ability to do and learn something

basic stock list list used for items a store should always have in stock

body language the gestures and facial expressions that people use to communicate nonverbally

career ladder the series of job steps you must take to achieve your career goals

career lattice a combination of vertical/diagonal career steps that lead to a career goal

career path the series of job experiences that you need to reach your career goal

career plan a written statement of career goals and the necessary steps to achieve them

catalog retailer vendor who sells merchandise through printed or electronic catalogs

central administration the top-leadership branch of a company

central business district an exterior shopping area that has developed without much planning

centralized buying a type of buying in which all buying for a chain is completed from one location

chain stores stores that have at least two locations and are owned by one company or person

channel of distribution path merchandise takes from where it is made to the final consumer

competitive advantage an intangible factor that makes one retail store more desirable to customers than its competitors

convenience merchandise merchandise that is purchased by customers without much planning or thought

convenience store a small retail outlet that sells convenience foods as well as staples and household items at higher prices

cooperative advertising advertising that features both the vendor's name and the local store where the vendor's product is available

corporation a form of business for which a charter is granted by the state in which the business will be established. The corporation sells stock to investors who become the owners of the corporation.

cost of goods sold the price a retailer pays for the merchandise that is for sale

cover letter a brief letter that provides a short introduction about the sender and states why that person is a strong candidate for the job

customer service the set of enhancements retailers offer to make shopping more convenient or rewarding

customer survey questionnaire designed to gain information from customers

dating terms terms that deal with the date when the bill for merchandise has to be paid

decentralized buying buying decisions made at the local store level

decorative display props items used to enhance the merchandise being displayed

delegate to put an employee in charge of a project to completion

demographics statistics that describe a population in terms of personal characteristics

department store a retailer that separates merchandise into different departments, or sections

direct channel path that leads directly from manufacturer to consumer

direct mail mail delivered to your home to sell merchandise

direct selling a method of retailing in which a company representative or salesperson calls at the customer's home to sell the company's products or services

discount department store a department store that sells merchandise at low prices

display a presentation of merchandise to attract customers so they will examine the merchandise

display props items used to enhance a display

E

ease of access ability of customers to get in and out of a business site easily

emotional buying motive a motive determined by the way a product or service makes customers feel

employee retention a company's ability to keep workers employed for an extended period of time

employee turnover the change in employment status at a company when employees leave their jobs

employment agency a business that specializes in helping people find jobs

empowerment granting employees responsibility for making decisions

entrepreneur person who takes the risk of opening a new business, often acting as the manager and operator of the business

entrepreneurship the process of owning and managing your own business

e-tailing the selling of goods or services to the customer by means of the Internet

F

fashion merchandise merchandise that sells well for several seasons but not as long as staple merchandise

financial services retailer a retailer who provides personal financial services

fixtures permanent or moveable store furnishings that are used to hold or display merchandise

FOB free on board, or the ownership of merchandise in transit determines if freight charges are free

follow-up letter a brief letter to thank an interviewer and to restate the job candidate's interest and qualifications

food retailer a retailer that sells food and related goods

franchise agreement or contract between the franchisor and franchisee to sell a company's goods or services at a designated location

franchisee person or persons who pay a fee to a company to operate a business under the franchisor's trade name

franchisor a business that leases its trade name and operating system to another person, or franchisee

freestanding location a store that is not attached to other retail stores

functional display props items used to hold the merchandise of a display

G

general-merchandise retailer a retailer that sells a large variety of merchandise

generic brands merchandise items that are sold without either a brand name or private label

geographics information about where customers live

goods tangible items that are made, manufactured, or grown

H

high employee turnover the change in employment status at a company when the staff changes frequently

hospitality and lodging services retail services that provide you with a place to live in comfort for one or several days

I

impulse purchases items that are inexpensive and that customers buy without much thought

independent store a store that is owned privately, having one location

indirect channel path that follows more than one step

infomercial a long TV commercial advertising merchandise that can be bought by mail order, telephone, online, or in a store

initiative doing things that need to be done without being asked

institutional advertising paid message used to promote a business's image or to create goodwill for the business

institutional display display designed to generate goodwill for the store

institutional promotions promotions designed to promote the image of a business or to build goodwill

interest expenses expenses paid to finance loans a business obtains

interviewer the company representative who assesses a job candidate's qualifications for the job by talking and asking questions

inventory control managing inventory levels to ensure enough merchandise to meet sales goals without having too much inventory on hand

inventory merchandise retailers have for sale

invoice a bill for merchandise

job application form a document that asks for an applicant's contact information

job forecast an estimate of the number of jobs that will be available for a career in the next five to ten years

junior department store a smaller version of a department store that does not carry as many merchandise lines

kiosk a freestanding, small shopping space usually located in a mall

lease a rental agreement between a landlord and a renter for property

lifestyle the way you live your life and spend your time

low employee turnover the change in employment status at a company when few employees leave their jobs

maintenance and repair-service retailer a retailer who provides services that require special training and/or special equipment

mall shopping area that is usually enclosed and has customer parking near the mall building

manufacturer business that makes or produces a good for sale

markdown reduction in the original selling price of merchandise or services

market segmentation a way of analyzing a market by specific characteristics in order to create a target market

market share one retailer's part of total sales of merchandise and services in the retailer's selling area

markup difference between the cost price of merchandise or services and selling price

media all of the methods used to get an advertising message to the public

merchandise assortment the number of items within a merchandise line

merchandise greeting expression used when the sales associate mentions an item of merchandise

merchandise life cycles customer-acceptance levels and buying levels of an item of merchandise

merchandise plan a basic budgeting tool that assists the retailer or buyer in meeting departmental or classification goals

merchandise promotions promotions that involve the store's merchandise

merchandise variety the product or merchandise lines that a retailer carries

model stock list list used for fashion merchandise

morale the attitude employees have regarding a positive feeling or one of confidence and good spirits

motivation the act of encouraging employees to do their best at all times and making them feel appreciated

multichannel retailing the use of more than one method for reaching customers

multitasking working on many tasks at the same time

NAICS North American Industry Classification System, a system used to categorize industries in North America, developed by the United States, Canada, and Mexico

namebrands merchandise items designed and made by a specific manufacturer, and sold under that manufacturer's name

networking contacting people you know who can assist with your job hunt

never-out list list used for the most popular merchandise that should always be in stock

non-personal selling the type of selling that does not involve interaction between people

non-store retailing a form of retailing that takes place in areas other than fixed-location store

objection question or concern that a customer has about merchandise being presented

off-price retailer a retailer who buys merchandise directly from the manufacturer and sellsit at low prices

open-to-buy amount of money available to purchase merchandise after other purchases have been subtracted

operating expenses everyday expenses such as rent, office supplies, telephone, salaries, and utilities

outlet store a manufacturer-owned store, also called a factory store, that sells overproduced or returned merchandise at low prices

partnership an agreement between two or more persons to go into business together

personal interests activities and pursuits that you enjoy most

personal selling the type of selling that involves direct interaction between sales associates and customers

personal services services you use to enhance physical or emotional well-being

price amount of money a retailer asks a customer to pay for merchandise or a service

private brands merchandise items that are designed and made for the retailer selling them

producer channel manufacturer also owns its retail stores; product goes from manufacturer to retail store to consumer

product advertising paid message used by businesses to promote a product or group of products

product benefits the advantages that a customer derives from the product features

product features the physical aspects of a product

product mix the types of merchandise that a retailer offers for sale

products goods and services that have monetary value

profit the money left after expenses are deducted from sales

promotion any form of communication used by retailers to inform the public about their merchandise and services, or to enhance the image of a business

promotional display display designed to help sell merchandise

promotional mix the way that a retailer combines the four types of promotion

psychographics studies of consumer lifestyles as reflected in attitudes, interests, and opinions

public relations any activity produced to create a favorable image for a retail business

publicity any unpaid mention of a retail business, its employees, or its merchandise in the media

punctuality the practice of arriving at work on time and staying there until scheduled to leave

purchase order order form that lists the style numbers of the merchandise being purchased, the amount, the delivery date, and terms of purchase

quantity discounts discounts offered for large purchases

rational buying motive a motive that prompts customers to make a conscious decision based on a reasonable idea

recreation and tourism services a category of the retailing industry that provides leisure activities

references people who know you and who can answer questions about your work habits and character

register till the drawer that holds the cash in the cash register

rental services services that provide a way to use goods without having to purchase anything

responsibility completing the tasks assigned to you and being trustworthy

résumé a document that provides a summary of information about a person's education, work experience, activities, and interests

retail advertising advertising retailers sponsor to promote their stores and products

retail customer purchaser of goods and services from retailers

retail mix the combination of decisions retailers make to create and operate a store

retailing the selling of products to the customer

return on investment percentage figure representing the return (or profit) on the cost of merchandise or services plus the expenses necessary to sell them

risk a situation or occurrence that can lead to financial loss for a business

risk management handling business risks in a way that minimizes negative impact on the business

sales associates retail employees who sell merchandise and products to customers

seasonal merchandise merchandise that sells well at certain times of the year

selling expenses the expenses associated with the store's sales associates

service greeting expression that offers assistance to the customer

service retailer a retailer who sells something that is intangible or does not last very long

services intangible things that people do for us that make us feel better or enhance our lives

services mix the number and kinds of services offered by a retail establishment

shipping terms terms that deal with how the merchandise will get from manufacturer to the store, who pays for shipping, and when ownership changes hands

shopping center a group of retail stores and service businesses operated as one business by one owner

single proprietorship a business that is owned by one person

skill the ability to do something

social greeting expression that acknowledges the customer's presence in the store or department

specialty store a store that sells a limited type of merchandise

staple merchandise merchandise that sells well over a long period of time

stock turnover the number of times the average inventory is sold during a time period, usually a year

store image the personality of the store, made up of many parts that work together to create a store's image

store layout the arrangement of the store's merchandise, fixtures, and equipment

store-based retailer a retailer that operates and conducts business from a fixed location

street vendors vendors who make their products available from sidewalk locations.

strip center a group of stores that features a parking lot in front and is not an enclosed shopping area

suggestion selling the selling of merchandise beyond the original merchandise

supercenter a combination of a large discount department store and a discount supermarket

supermarket a self-service department store that sells mostly food and other retail merchandise

target market the specific group of people on whom a retailer focuses merchandising and service decisions

target-market profile a description of the target-market customers

teamwork a spirit of cooperation among employees as they work toward a common goal

telephone selling a method of retailing in which a company representative phones a customer's home and makes a sales presentation

trade area geographic area from which a store draws most of its customers and sales

trade associations organizations made up of individuals and businesses in an industry that works to promote that industry

traffic the number of people who pass a retail location during a given period of time

TV shopping channels channels that feature hosts who sell merchandise by describing merchandise as shown on the television screen

values the factors that determine how you want to live your life

variety store a small retail outlet that sells a variety of low-priced merchandise

vending machine a machine that sells merchandise by inserting coins or bills into the machine, pressing a button, and receiving the item being purchased

vendor company from which a buyer purchases merchandise

vendor advertising advertising that manufacturers or suppliers sponsor to promote their products

visibility ability of the site to be easily seen by customers

visual merchandising the integrated look of the entire store

want slip a form used to inform a buyer of a specific request from a customer for merchandise that the store or department does not have in stock or does not carry

warehouse club a large store that offers volume discount prices and minimal variety, presentation, and service

wholesaler one who buys large quantities of a product and then resells it in smaller quantities to retailers

word-of-mouth communication customer conversations about their retail experiences

Index

Index

Index

Index

Index

Credits

Bill Aron/PhotoEdit **238–239**; Paul Barton/CORBIS **xii/TM6**, **90**; Dave Bartruff/CORBIS **26–27**; B.Bird/Zefa/Masterfile **8**; Bernard Boutrit/Woodfin Camp/PictureQuest **54**; Tim Boyle/Getty Images **178–179**; David Butow/CORBIS SABA **188**; Carpix **278**; Ron Chapple/Getty Images **138**, **TM16**; Martin Child/SuperStock **40**; Bob Daemmrich/Stock Boston,Inc./PictureQuest **114–115**; Keith Dannemiller/CORBIS SABA **229**;DECA **xvii**, **294**; Lon C.Diehl/PhotoEdit **305**; Robert Frerck/Getty Images **134–135**; Farrell Grehan/CORBIS **144**(l); Jeff Greenberg/PhotoEdit **TM38**, **124**; Jeff Greenberg/PhotoEdit/PictureQuest **103**; John Henley/CORBIS **48–49**; Noel Hendrikson/Masterfile **324**; Catherine Karnow/CORBIS **154–155**; Christina Kennedy/PhotoEdit **245**; Bob Krist/CORBIS **TM27**(l), **338**; Dan Lamont/CORBIS **74**; John Lamb/Getty Images **222**; Robert Landau/CORBIS **160**; Robert Landau/CORBIS **39**; Roger Allyn Lee/SuperStock **TM27**(r), **70–71**; Chris McElcheran/Masterfile **119**; Louis K. Meisel Gallery/CORBIS **82**; John and Lisa Merrill/CORBIS **268**; Raoul Minsart/Masterfile **99**; Antonio Mo/Taxi/Getty Images **53**; Michael Newman/PhotoEdit **198–199**, **211**, **269**, **293**, **300–301**, **310**; Pavlovsky/Corbis Sygma **19**; Jose Luis Pelaez, Inc./CORBIS **118**; H&S Produktion/CORBIS **i/TM1**(cl); Royalty-free/Photodisc/Getty Images **144**(r), **223**; Royalty-free **TM13**; Royalty-free/CORBIS **60**, **280–281**, **330**; Royalty-free/Digital Vision/Getty Images **190**; Royalty-free/Photodisc/Getty **i/TM1**(b), **xiii/TM7**, **4–5**, **144**(r), **146**, **223**; Royalty-free/PictureQuest **i/TM1**(cr), Royalty-free/Wonderfile/Masterfile **174**; Royalty-free/Wonderfile/Masterfile **94–95**; Rachel Royse/CORBIS **306**; Jeffery Allan Salter/Corbis Saba **282–283**; Chuck Savage/CORBIS **x**, **32**, **285**, **320–321**, **332**; Alan Schein Photography/CORBIS **92–93**; Clayton Sharrard/PhotoEdit **157**; S. Shipman/Getty Images **261**;Rhoda Sidney/PhotoEdit/PictureQuest **10**; Ariel Skelley/CORBIS **100**; Joseph Sohm; ChromoSohm Inc./CORBIS **176–177**; Dave Starrett/Masterfile **248**; Park Street/PhotoEdit **TM27**(bc), **158**; LWA-Dann Tardif/CORBIS **249**; Steve Vidler/Superstock **xi/TM5**, **2–3**; LWA-Stephen Welstead/CORBIS **218–219**; David Young-Wolff/PhotoEdit **202**; Paul Wright/Masterfile **207**; Michael S. Yamashita/CORBIS **182**; Gary Yeowell/Getty Images **258–259**.